Southern Living

...ual Recipes

Oxmoor House®

CLASSIC HOPPIN' JOHN
(PAGE 39)

CHOCOLATE MAYONNAISE
CAKE (PAGE 37)

CLOCKWISE FROM TOP LEFT:

- SAVANNAH RED RICE (PAGE 31)
- COUNTRY CAPTAIN CHICKEN (PAGE 33)
- HARRY YOUNG'S BURGOO (PAGE 25)
- CAPITOL HILL BEAN SOUP (PAGE 32)

SMOKY WHITE BEAN SOUP
(PAGE 40)
HERBED SHRIMP-AND-RICE
SALAD (PAGE 40)
ALMOND-CHICKEN WRAP
(PAGE 40)

LEMON-ORANGE POUND CAKE (PAGE 54)

CLOCKWISE FROM TOP LEFT:

• COLD LEMON SOUFFLÉS WITH WINE SAUCE (PAGE 55)

• FLORIDA ORANGE GROVE PIE (PAGE 53)

• SHAKER LEMON PIE (PAGE 55)

• GRAND MARNIER CAKES (PAGE 56)

CLOCKWISE FROM TOP LEFT:

- TERIYAKI SALMON BOWLS WITH CRISPY BRUSSELS SPROUTS (PAGE 49)
- TURKEY WITH SHALLOT-MUSTARD SAUCE AND ROASTED POTATOES (PAGE 46)
- SHRIMP, SAUSAGE, AND BLACK BEAN PASTA (PAGE 51)
- CARAMELIZED ONION, SPINACH, AND PORK STRATA (PAGE 48)

KENTUCKY HOT BROWN CASSEROLE (PAGE 46)

BUTTERMILK BISCUITS
WITH HAM, (PAGE 69)

SPARKLING CITRUS PUNCH (PAGE 71)

CLOCKWISE FROM TOP LEFT:

- PORK CHOPS WITH TOMATO-BACON GRAVY (PAGE 75)
- FRESH SALMON CAKES WITH BUTTERMILK DRESSING (PAGE 77)
- CREAMY FETA-AND-HERB DIP (PAGE 76)
- DAY-AFTER-SAINT PATRICK'S DAY SOUP (PAGE 79)

CHICKEN NIÇOISE SALAD
(PAGE 88)

STRAWBERRY-LEMON CRÊPE CAKE (PAGE 85)

STRAWBERRY-MANGO
SEMIFREDDO (PAGE 86)

STRAWBERRY-RHUBARB PRETZEL PIE (PAGE 84)

Our Year at Southern Living®

Dear Friends,

For half century, issue after issue, the recipes in *Southern Living* have been selected to inspire readers to cook and to explore the flavors of the South through the region's iconic dishes and contemporary trends. Our editors research the region's culinary history, stay abreast of new ingredients, identify great restaurants, and highlight the many Southern cooks who are making a mark on today's food scene to select the stories and recipes worth sharing. Our Test Kitchen pros tinker with flavors, hone techniques, and test and retest recipes to perfect each and every one we publish so that you can cook with confidence. Rest assured, if you find a recipe in the pages of *Southern Living*, you know it is worth cooking and sharing . . . pinning or posting.

Our enduringly popular What Can I Bring? column banishes doubts about coming up with the perfect nibble or covered dish to take to any gathering. Monthly food features offer inspiration for cooking bumper crops, holiday entertaining, or updating classics with new flavors and ingredients. The *SL* Cooking School pros share their tested and perfected tips for streamlining prep, mastering methods, and upgrading your pantry. And in Save Room you will find decadent endings to any meal sure to satisfy your sweet tooth. As always, we include an exclusive bonus section. This year "Our Best Breakfast & Brunch" collection will help you kickstart every morning with a dose of deliciousness.

We know you will enjoy having this year of *Southern Living* recipes at your fingertips.

Dig in, y'all!

Katherine Cobbs

Katherine Cobbs
Executive Editor

Contents

17 Our Year at *Southern Living*
20 Top-Rated Recipes

23 January

24 Old Family Favorites
34 QUICK FIX: Weeknights Done Light
37 SAVE ROOM: The Southern Secret to Chocolate Cake
38 SOUTHERN CLASSIC: New Year, Same Hoppin' Tradition
40 *SL* COOKING SCHOOL

43 February

44 The Beauty of Slow Cooking
52 A League of Their Own
57 QUICK FIX: Super Bowls
60 SOUTHERN CLASSIC: The Mystery of Hummingbird Cake
63 WHAT CAN I BRING?: Game Day Potatoes
64 SAVE ROOM: The King of Cakes
65 *SL* COOKING SCHOOL

67 March

68 A Beautiful Easter Brunch
72 QUICK FIX: Bacon Makes Everything Better
76 WHAT CAN I BRING?: Vegging Out
77 HEALTHY IN A HURRY: Wild about Salmon
78 DINNER IN AMERICA: Pot Roast, Please
79 ONE AND DONE: Luck of the Leftovers
80 *SL* COOKING SCHOOL

81 April

82 Strawberry Sidekicks
88 QUICK FIX: Chicken Salad Gets a Makeover
91 ONE AND DONE: The French Onion Casserole
92 HEALTHY IN A HURRY: One-Pot Primavera
93 SAVE ROOM: Sweet Tarts
94 *SL* COOKING SCHOOL

95 May

96 Gotta Love Crab
102 QUICK FIX: Next-Level Kebabs
106 ONE AND DONE: Modern Mediterranean
107 WHAT CAN I BRING?: Pick a Pepper
108 HEALTHY IN A HURRY: The Spice is Right
109 SAVE ROOM: Thyme for Pie
110 *SL* COOKING SCHOOL

111 June

112 Forgotten Fruit Desserts
118 The Soul of a Chef
121 QUICK FIX: You Say Tomato
124 DINNER IN AMERICA: Lasagna Gets a New Look
125 HEALTHY IN A HURRY: Salad for Supper
126 WHAT CAN I BRING?: Let Them Eat Shrimp
127 SAVE ROOM: Twice as Nice
128 *SL* COOKING SCHOOL

129 July

130 All-American Desserts
135 Fried and True
142 QUICK FIX: Pick a Side
144 SOUTHERN CLASSIC: Stirring Up Controversy
146 HEALTHY IN A HURRY: Summer Scallops
147 WHAT CAN I BRING?: Ready to Roll
148 *SL* COOKING SCHOOL

149 August

150 Soiree in the Swamp
156 QUICK FIX: No-Cook Summer Suppers
159 ONE AND DONE: Sizzling Skillet Steak
160 WHAT CAN I BRING?: Tasty Tomato Bites
193 SAVE ROOM: Just Chill
194 SOUTHERN CLASSIC: Summer Succotash
196 HEALTHY IN A HURRY: Pizza Night Alfresco
198 *SL* COOKING SCHOOL

199 September

200 The Southern Living Tailgating Playbook
206 FALL BAKING: Bake Another Batch
210 BACK-TO-SCHOOL SPECIAL: Snack Attack
212 DINNER IN AMERICA: Easier Enchiladas

213 October

214 The Savory Side of Pumpkin
219 Fall Layers
228 QUICK FIX: More Cheese, Please
232 WHAT CAN I BRING?: Muffin Pan Pies
233 COMFORT FOOD: Low-and-Slow Pork Supper
234 *SL* COOKING SCHOOL

235 November

236 Thanksgiving at the Farm
240 Friendsgiving at Joy's
246 Let's Talk (Smoking) Turkey
248 It's Called Dressing, Not Stuffing
250 Pass the Gravy
252 Respect the Relish Tray
253 Here Come the Casseroles
258 Old Faithfuls
262 "Look What Aunt Lisa Brought!"
266 THE LEFTOVERS: Make the Best Sandwich of the Year
267 THE LEFTOVERS: Chili for a Crowd
268 *SL* COOKING SCHOOL

269 December

270 Simply Spectacular
289 Merry Christmas, Sugar!
294 Gingerbread Takes the Cake
302 Peace of Cake

321 Bonus: Our Best Breakfast & Brunch

349 Metric Equivalents

350 Indexes

350 Recipe Title Index
354 Month-by-Month Index
358 General Recipe Index

367 Favorite Recipes Journal

Mini Mushroom-and-Goat Cheese Pot Pies, page 232

Top-Rated Recipes

We cook, we taste, we refine, we rate, and at the end of each year, our Test Kitchen shares the highest-rated recipes from each issue exclusively with *Southern Living Annual Recipes* readers.

JANUARY

- Chocolate Mayonnaise Cake (page 37) Mayonnaise, our not-so-secret ingredient, makes this dreamy chocolate cake ultra-moist. Coffee adds an extra depth of flavor.
- Pecan Crunch Tart (page 42) Fear phyllo dough no more: This simple and oh-so-delicious twist on classic pecan pie is easier than it looks.
- Classic Hoppin' John (page 39) The classic combination of thick-cut bacon, black-eyed peas, and Carolina Gold rice rings in the New Year in true Southern style.
- Farro Bowl with Curry-Roasted Sweet Potatoes and Brussels Sprouts (page 36) Wholesome but satisfying, these bowls are brimming with spiced, roasted vegetables and filling farro for an easy meal you can feel good about.
- Old-Fashioned Chicken and Dumplings (page 26) Mrs. Morton Smith submitted this well-loved recipe in 1983 and we haven't stopped cooking it since. Buttermilk yields extra fluffy dumplings and rolling the dumplings on a well-floured surface helps thicken the broth.

FEBRUARY

- Braised Lamb Shanks with Parmesan-Chive Grits (page 45) Slow-cooking yields especially tender lamb shanks that are sublime when served over cheesy, creamy Parmesan-Chive Grits.
- Cuban Black Bean-and-Yellow Rice Bowls (page 57) The MVP of busy weeknights, our favorite super bowls come together quickly and are topped with tangy radish slices, creamy avocado, and roasted plantains.
- Florida Orange Grove Pie (page 53) Light and fluffy piles of citrus cream tucked into a meringue shell create an impressive ending to any dinner.
- Lemon-Orange Pound Cake (page 54) Refreshingly simple, this pound cake is drizzled with both sweet vanilla and zesty lemon-orange icing.

MARCH

- Home-Style Slow-Cooker Pot Roast (page 78) Step up your Sunday supper game with the help of your slow cooker. This comforting meal cooks all day for maximum flavor and minimal hands-on time.
- Creamy Rice with Scallops (page 73) Smoky bacon and tender scallops, plus a generous dose of sweet yellow corn, create an indulgent, risotto-like dish that you'll want to make again and again.
- Coconut-Carrot Cake with Coconut Buttercream (page 71) Why choose when you could have the best of both carrot cake and coconut cake? Coconut buttercream, a dusting of toasted flaked coconut, and carrot curls top off this impressive sweet treat.
- Pork Chops with Tomato-Bacon Gravy (page 75) This date-night-worthy meal, served with fresh green beans and a memorable Tomato-Bacon Gravy, comes together in under an hour.
- Creamy Feta-and-Herb Dip (page 76) We love serving crudités and pita chips with this tangy, creamy, and delightfully addictive dip.

APRIL

- Mini Coconut-Key Lime Pies (page 93) We put the lime and the coconut in these petite pies and created a party-worthy treat.
- Strawberry-Banana Pudding Icebox Cake (page 87) This iconic Southern dessert, perfect for the dog days of summer, sets in the fridge so that you can avoid turning on the oven.
- Pasta Primavera with Shrimp (page 92) Snap peas, Broccolini, and shrimp are what one-pot meal dreams are made of. Chopped red bell pepper and spinach add even more fresh flavor.
- French Onion Soup Casserole (page 91) There aren't many ways to improve the classic rich and cheesy soup, but this casserole, chock-full of caramelized Vidalia onions, is definitely one of them.

MAY

- Thyme-Scented Blueberry Pie (page 109) Just a touch of fresh thyme transforms a simple blueberry pie. Top each fragrant slice with a scoop of vanilla ice cream.
- Crab Pie (page 98) This flavorful twist on quiche, stuffed with crabmeat, sautéed spinach, and cream cheese, is a fun addition to your next brunch spread.
- Best-Ever Crab Cakes with Green Tomato Slaw (page 101) Best-ever? You bet. One taste of our favorite crunchy crab cakes topped with green tomato-studded slaw, and we think you'll agree.
- Queso-Filled Mini Peppers (page 107) Serve platters of these stuffed mini peppers at your next gathering and get ready to share the recipe with grateful guests.
- Crab-and-Bacon Linguine (page 97) White wine, bacon, and cream, oh my! The star of the show is a pound of fresh jumbo crabmeat that brings all the rich flavors together.

JUNE

- Peach-Bourbon Upside-Down Bundt Cake (page 127) The decidedly Southern combination of caramelized peaches and bourbon, baked in a Bundt pan, makes this the perfect cake to bring to a potluck or serve after Sunday supper.
- Berry Sonker with Dip (page 115) What's a sonker, you say? This beloved dessert, from Surry County, North Carolina, is baked in a large, deep pan and topped with a creamy vanilla sauce called "dip." Our version features a winning combination of blueberries, blackberries, and raspberries.
- Blueberry-Lemon Crunch Bars (page 115) Grab a fork and a glass of milk: These old-fashioned bars, freshened up with a buttery, pecan-laced crust and zesty blueberry filling, make the perfect after-school or just-because snack.
- Strawberry Kuchen (page 117) Juicy strawberries and sliced almonds top our version of the classic German cake. You'll be pleasantly surprised how easy it is to make.
- Pasta with Shrimp and Tomato Cream Sauce (page 122) It is very, very hard not to have seconds of this easy yet decadent pasta. Cherry tomatoes and fresh tarragon offset the heavy cream and plump shrimp provide seaside flavor wherever your kitchen may be.

JULY

- Basic Pimiento Cheese (page 144) The pâté of the South is equally at home smeared between two thick slices of white bread or perched atop a fancy cracker at a cocktail party. We show you how to dress up our favorite spread, including options for Chipotle Pimiento Cheese and zesty Horseradish Pimiento Cheese.
- Fried Delacata Catfish (page 138) Bathing the catfish in whole milk or buttermilk helps neutralize any fishy odors and well-seasoned breading ensures a spicy and herbal bite.
- Cheddar-Caramelized Onion Bread (page 140) Toasted caraway seeds add an unexpected flavor to this comforting bread that's rich with sweet caramelized onions and pockets of melted Cheddar.
- Whipped Sweet Potato Butter (page 141) Serve this sweet and salty concoction with chunks of Cheddar-Caramelized Onion Bread (page 140).
- Fourth of July Confetti Roulade (page 133) Celebrate America's birthday in style with generous slices of this festive roulade topped with a fresh lemon frosting and red, white and blue sprinkles.
- Red Velvet Ice-Cream Cake (page 132) Our secret ingredient? A teaspoon of unflavored gelatin helps stabilize the whipped cream frosting so it stays in place, even on a hot Southern summer afternoon.

AUGUST

- Seared Hanger Steak with Braised Greens and Grapes (page 154) Featuring earthy collard greens, red grapes, and a jolt of flavor from Swamp Pop Noble Cane Cola (or Dr Pepper, if you're in a pinch), this flavorful steak is a fun nod to its Cajun roots.
- Blackberry Trifles with Pecan Feuilletage and Mascarpone-Cane Syrup Mousse (page 155) If you fall in love with the feuilletage as much as we did, make another batch and serve on its own for an easy, crowd-friendly dessert or crumbled over ice cream for a party of one.
- Grilled Steak with Blistered Beans and Peppers (page 159) This sizzling steak is a welcome break from your usual grill go-to. The entire meal comes together in your cast-iron skillet.
- Best-Ever Succotash (page 195) Packed with produce, succotash is the ideal solution to a late-summer garden bounty. We forgo the heavy cream in favor of butter, which adds rich flavor without dulling the dish.
- No-Bake Peanut Butter-Fudge Ice-Cream Pie (page 193) Fudge-drizzled slices of this rich pie are perfect during warmer seasons but we recommend indulging year-round. After all, the classic combination of peanut butter and chocolate never goes out of style.

SEPTEMBER

- Skillet Enchiladas Suizas (page 212) Serve this family-friendly favorite straight out of the skillet. Everyone can pick their own toppings, such as crumbled Cotija cheese, pickled red onions, and thinly sliced radishes.
- Warm Cheese-and-Spicy Pecan Dip (page 204) The classic flavor of gloriously gooey cheese dip gets a spicy upgrade, thanks to the addition of crunchy, cayenne-spiced pecans. Serve with rounds of toasted baguette slices for premium dipping.
- Pumpkin Spice-Chocolate Marble Loaves (page 209) Anything but basic, this pumpkin spice-inspired quick bread features a swirl of rich chocolate. Our recipe makes two loaves so you can share one with a lucky neighbor. Or, divide the batter into eight mini loaf pans for optimum holiday gifting.
- Cranberry-Apple Tartlets (page 208) Refrigerated pie crust makes life a little easier and helps these cheery tarts come together quickly.
- Toasted Oatmeal Cookies (page 209) These aren't your traditional oatmeal cookies. Toasting the oatmeal takes only 20 minutes, but it imparts a unique flavor that we highly recommend. Butterscotch chips and toasted pecans finish the flavor profile.
- Brown Butter-Maple-Pecan Blondies (page 209) Nutty brown butter transforms any baked good, and the humble blondie is no exception. If your family prefers walnuts, simply substitute them for the pecans called for here.

OCTOBER

- Pumpkin-and-Winter Squash Gratin (page 216) Each bite of potato, squash, and pumpkin includes gooey Gruyère cheese and herbed breadcrumbs. Try serving this savory casserole alongside your traditional Thanksgiving spread.
- Slow-Cooker Chicken Stew with Pumpkin and Wild Rice (page 216) Hearty and perfect for cozy fall nights, this savory stew delivers all-day simmered flavor in less than 4 hours.
- Apple Stack Cake (page 226) You might be tempted to dive right in, but apple stack cakes taste best after sitting for a few days to "ripen" so the layers and filling blend together. It's worth the wait!
- Blackberry Jam Cake (page 226) From the cinnamon-scented layers to creamy caramel frosting, this impressive dessert is inspired by Kentucky's jam cake tradition.
- Lemon-and-Chocolate Doberge Cake (page 227) New Orleans has a delicious answer to the common conundrum: lemon or chocolate? Thanks to this impressive half-and-half, you don't have to choose. How sweet is that?
- Mini Mushroom-and-Goat Cheese Pot Pies (page 232) Refrigerated pie crusts are a smart shortcut for these bite-size appetizers. Stuffed with a creamy herb-and-mushroom mixture, they are sure to be a crowd-pleaser.
- Pumpkin Beer-Cheese Soup (page 215) Pumpkin's savory side shines in this comforting soup. Sprinkle each bowl with crispy croutons and smoky bacon for a satisfying crunch.

NOVEMBER

- Stacy and Joyce's Cornbread Dressing (page 239) From-scratch chicken broth and the boxed convenience of corn muffin mix collide in this divine dressing.
- French Onion Puff Pastry Bites (page 243) The perfect welcoming nibble to woo your holiday guests right at the front door.
- Pumpkin Layer Cake with Caramel-Cream Cheese Frosting (page 245) Tailor made for Turkey Day, the classic flavors of pumpkin pie shine in this moist layer cake.
- Oxbow Bakery Pecan Pie (page 259) Flaky crusts and sublime fillings have made Becky Wolfe's pies big in Texas and beyond.
- Corn Pudding (page 256) This rich and flavorful make-ahead and bake-later recipe takes day-of pressure off the Thanksgiving chef.
- Pumpkin Spice Magic Cake (page 263) Inspired by a Mexican dessert called "chocoflan," this decadent cake gets its distinctive sweetness from cajeta, a Mexican caramel sauce.
- Mini Turkey Pot Pies with Dressing Tops (page 244) These savory skillet pies will have you wishing Thanksgiving leftovers were always around.

DECEMBER

- Gingerbread-and-Pear Upside-Down Cake (page 301) Warm spices of clove, allspice, and cardamom lend an exotic note to this caramelized skillet cake.
- Best White Cake (page 303) Whether you dress it up or keep it simple, this luscious layer cake will make knees buckle.
- Ginger-Pecan Bourbon Balls (page 291) Show your affection with this boozy confection that marries the holiday season's favorite cookie with Southern favorites—bourbon and pecans.
- Buttermilk-Pecan Pralines (page 291) Steeped in history, the South's favorite candy is rich, buttery, and downright irresistable.
- Make-Ahead Croissant Breakfast Casserole (page 286) One bite of this hearty one-dish breakfast may have your loved ones asking for seconds rather than opening presents.
- Pork Crown Roast (page 287) Elegant and impressive, the piece de resistance of the holiday table is a guaranteed crowd-pleaser.
- Savory Sweet Potato Casserole (page 287) The holiday meal isn't complete without the South's favorite spud whipped and baked in wondrous waves and topped with a sweet, nutty topping—marshmallows not included.

January

24 **Old Family Favorites** These prized reader recipes pulled from our archives are worth adding to your recipe box

34 QUICK FIX **Weeknights Done Light** We've got winter comfort food that's both hearty and healthy

37 SAVE ROOM **The Southern Secret to Chocolate Cake** A refrigerator door staple is the key to moist cake

38 SOUTHERN CLASSIC **New Year, Same Hoppin' Tradition** The ABCs of making the Lowcountry, good-luck field pea classic

40 *SL* COOKING SCHOOL **New Year's Resolutions** From lunchbox inspiration and perfectly cooked fish fillets to working with phyllo, our kitchen pros have got you covered

Old Family Favorites

Exploring the *Southern Living* recipe archives is like paging through a cherished photo album. Each dish sparks a story, a laugh, or a "What were we thinking?" snicker. While some of our tastes have changed since the magazine started more than 50 years ago (we were once big fans of molded tuna rings), there are hundreds of other timeless recipes. Many of these gems deserve a second look, including these nine reader recipes that we hand-picked from our archives. Some of the dishes, such as Savannah Red Rice, may have already earned a permanent spot in your recipe box. Others, like Country Captain Chicken or Capitol Hill Bean Soup, might be unfamiliar. We hope these "lost classics" bring back heartwarming recollections of meals past or help you make delicious new memories.

"IF IT WALKED, CRAWLED, OR FLEW, it goes in burgoo." That old adage once applied to this stew that hails from Kentucky, originally made with an assortment of game and livestock cooked in giant cauldrons known as burgoo kettles. It's a classic Southern stew, made in huge quantities over a smoldering fire, stirred by cooks using boat oars long enough to reach the bottoms of the pots. They would prepare enough burgoo to feed an entire community, often selling it at fund-raisers or doling it out to attendees at political rallies and stump speeches. These days, burgoos are still meant to be shared, but they have been scaled back to feed large families instead of small towns. Most recipes, such as this one, still call for a variety of meats and a long list of vegetables—but only those found easily at a local grocery store.

HARRY YOUNG'S BURGOO

This hearty stew freezes well, which is a good thing because it feeds a large crowd and you may have leftovers. It tastes even better the next day when the flavors have had time to marry.

ACTIVE 45 MIN. - TOTAL 5 HOURS
SERVES 25

- **1 (2- to 2 ½-lb.) bone-in pork loin roast**
- **1 (3 ½-lb.) whole chicken**
- **3 qt. water**
- **4 lb. 80/20 ground beef**
- **6 cups frozen whole kernel corn (about 2 lb.)**
- **5 cups frozen purple hull peas (about 1 ¾ lb.)**
- **5 cups frozen lima beans (about 1 ¾ lb.)**
- **3 cups chopped cabbage (about 16 oz.)**
- **3 cups diced russet potato (about 16 oz.)**
- **3 cups chopped yellow onion (about 12 oz.)**
- **1 (32-oz.) bottle tomato or vegetable juice (such as V8)**
- **1 (28-oz.) can crushed tomatoes, undrained and chopped**
- **2 cups frozen cut okra (about 10 oz.)**
- **3 cups diced carrots (about 1 lb.)**
- **1 ½ cups chopped green bell pepper (about 6 oz.)**
- **¾ cup chopped celery (about 3 stalks)**
- **¼ cup chopped fresh flat-leaf parsley**
- **1 Tbsp. crushed red pepper**
- **1 Tbsp. kosher salt**
- **1 Tbsp. celery salt**
- **1 ½ tsp. black pepper**

1. Combine pork, chicken, and water in a large Dutch oven; bring to a boil over medium-high. Cover and reduce heat to medium-low. Simmer 2 hours. Remove meat, reserving cooking liquid in Dutch oven. Let meat cool about 15 minutes. Remove and discard bone from pork; shred pork. Shred chicken, discarding skin and bones. Refrigerate shredded chicken and pork in airtight containers until ready to add to recipe in Step 2.

2. Brown one-third of ground beef in a large skillet over medium-high, stirring to crumble, until no longer pink, 6 to 7 minutes; drain. Transfer beef to a large bowl. Repeat procedure twice with remaining ground beef. Stir ground beef, corn, peas, lima beans, cabbage, potato, yellow onion, tomato juice, tomatoes, okra, carrots, green bell pepper, celery, parsley, red pepper, kosher salt, celery salt, and black pepper into reserved cooking liquid in Dutch oven. Bring to a boil over high. Reduce heat to medium-low, and simmer, stirring often, 2 hours, adding in shredded pork and chicken during last 15 minutes.

—Harry M. Young, Jr.
Herndon, KY, January 1987

THE MOST FAMOUS CHICKEN DISH in the South is probably fried chicken, but a good case can also be made for chicken and dumplings. Fried chicken celebrates the poultry in abundance, when everyone can get a piece or two. Chicken and dumplings makes the most of chicken in scarcity, when a single bird must feed a multitude. Although it gets top billing, the meat itself isn't the star of the meal. The dumplings hold sway, and people are particular about how they're made. Some like small strips of pastry dropped into the bubbling pot, either free-form and puffy or rolled thin and cut like noodles. Others prefer soft drop-biscuit dumplings that float atop the stew. No matter the style, this dish combines essential, resourceful Southern cuisine and the comfort of home cooking, all in one bowl.

OLD-FASHIONED CHICKEN AND DUMPLINGS

Mrs. Morton Smith experimented for years with different methods of making the perfect chicken and dumplings. When she submitted this recipe, she told us that buttermilk was the secret to dumplings with a light texture. She also kneaded them on a well-floured surface because the extra flour thickens the broth.

ACTIVE 30 MIN. - TOTAL 1 HOUR, 50 MIN.
SERVES 6

- 1 (2 ½- to 3-lb.) whole chicken
- 2 celery stalks, roughly chopped (about 1 cup)
- 2 medium carrots, roughly chopped (about 1 cup)
- 2 qt. water
- 2 ½ tsp. kosher salt
- ½ tsp. black pepper
- 2 cups all-purpose flour, plus more for work surface
- ½ tsp. baking soda
- 3 Tbsp. vegetable shortening
- ¾ cup whole buttermilk
- Chopped fresh chives

1. Place chicken, celery, and carrots in a Dutch oven; add water and 2 teaspoons of the salt. Bring to a boil over high; cover, reduce heat to medium-low, and simmer until tender, about 1 hour. Remove chicken from broth, and let stand until cool enough to handle, about 15 minutes. Remove and discard skin and bone from chicken, and cut meat into bite-size pieces. Bring broth to a boil over high; stir in pepper.

2. Meanwhile, combine flour, baking soda, and remaining ½ teaspoon salt in a large bowl; cut in shortening with a pastry blender (or use your fingers) until mixture resembles coarse meal. Add buttermilk, stirring with a fork until dry ingredients are moistened. Turn dough out onto a well-floured surface, and knead lightly 4 or 5 times.

3. Pat dough to ½-inch thickness. Pinch off dough in 1 ½-inch pieces, and drop into boiling broth. Reduce heat to medium-low, and cook, stirring occasionally, until desired consistency is reached, about 8 to 10 minutes. Stir in chicken. Garnish servings with chives.

—Mrs. Morton Smith
Homewood, AL, October 1983

REUNION PEA CASSEROLE

Refrigerated crescent roll dough gives this comforting casserole a golden, buttery crust with minimal effort. Add coleslaw or salad on the side, and you'll have an easy, homey supper that will feed the whole family—and then some.

ACTIVE 35 MIN. - TOTAL 1 HOUR, 35 MIN.
SERVES 12

- **1 lb. mild Italian sausage, casings removed**
- **2 (16-oz.) cans black-eyed peas, drained**
- **1 (4-oz.) can chopped green chiles, drained**
- **1 tsp. garlic powder**
- **¼ tsp. ground cumin**
- **¼ tsp. dried oregano**
- **½ tsp. black pepper**
- **½ tsp. kosher salt**
- **2 Tbsp. unsalted butter**
- **2 cups sliced yellow squash (about 10 oz.)**
- **2 cups sliced zucchini (about 10 oz.)**
- **1 cup chopped yellow onion (about 1 small onion)**
- **4 large eggs, well beaten**
- **8 oz. mozzarella cheese, shredded (about 2 cups)**
- **8 oz. Cheddar cheese, shredded (about 2 cups)**
- **2 (8-oz.) cans refrigerated crescent rolls**

1. Preheat oven to 350°F. Cook sausage in a large skillet over medium, stirring to crumble, until browned, about 8 minutes. Drain sausage well, setting skillet aside. Transfer sausage to a large bowl, and stir in peas, chiles, garlic powder, cumin, oregano, pepper, and salt.
2. Melt butter in reserved skillet over medium, and add squash, zucchini, and onion. Cook, stirring occasionally, until softened, about 8 to 10 minutes; drain well. Cool 5 minutes. Stir together eggs and cheeses in a separate bowl; fold in squash mixture.
3. Separate crescent roll dough into 2 long rectangles; pinch dough seams together. Place dough in a lightly greased 13- x 9-inch baking dish; press dough on bottom and up sides to form crust, using a knife to cut away excess dough. Bake in preheated oven until crust begins to set, about 10 minutes.
4. Remove from oven, and layer sausage-pea mixture over crust; top with squash mixture. Return to oven, and bake until casserole is set, 25 to 30 minutes. Let stand 15 minutes before serving.

—Joyce Carroll
Athens, TX, January 1987

THIS WELCOMING, OVER-THE-TOP CASSEROLE was designed to satisfy and delight a crowd, perhaps at a big family reunion or church supper. The sausage-and-cheese filling is a bit rich, but it sure is tasty. The recipe calls for black-eyed peas, the mainstay Southern legume. Over the years, black-eyed peas have become the most common and familiar type of field pea—you can always find cans of them on grocery store shelves. However, there are often other delicious choices on the same shelf or in the freezer case, such as purple hull or crowder peas. In the summer, look for less common peas with wonderful names like Whippoorwill, Lady Cream, and Pinkeye at your local farmers' market. Feel free to substitute any of them in this recipe. Like all good casseroles, this one is forgiving and accommodating.

BEEF STEW IS THE BENEVOLENT KING of all stews. Familiar yet never tiresome, chunks of tender beef and potatoes in rich brown gravy will always bring comfort and joy to our tables. Little things are what elevate a good stew to become a great one. Taking time to sear the beef is integral to flavor in both the meat and the gravy, as is letting it simmer low and slow until the beef is spoon-tender. Busy cooks might be tempted to purchase packages of so-called stew meat at the market, but it pays to follow this recipe and take a few minutes to cut up an economical chuck roast. Stew meat is a mixture of scraps left over when a butcher trims a range of cuts to go in the meat case, and these random pieces won't cook the same way or finish at the same time. The uniformity of a well-marbled chuck roast yields consistent results and the best flavor.

BEEF STEW

Originally, this recipe called for the stew to be cooked in a wok, which was trendy at the time. We prefer using a Dutch oven because it provides a large, flat surface to properly brown the meat.

ACTIVE 35 MIN. - TOTAL 4 HOURS, 15 MIN.
SERVES 8

- **3 Tbsp. all-purpose flour**
- **2 ½ tsp. kosher salt**
- **½ tsp. black pepper**
- **2 lb. boneless chuck roast, cut into 1-inch cubes**
- **⅓ cup vegetable oil**
- **4 cups sliced yellow onion (about 2 medium onions)**
- **1 (12-oz.) can pale beer (such as Yuengling Traditional Lager)**
- **1 Tbsp. soy sauce**
- **1 Tbsp. Worcestershire sauce**
- **1 Tbsp. steak sauce (such as A.1. Original Sauce)**
- **1 garlic clove, crushed**
- **2 bay leaves**
- **½ tsp. dried thyme**
- **2 lb. russet potatoes, peeled and cut into 1 ½-inch pieces (about 4 medium potatoes)**
- **3 medium carrots, peeled and cut diagonally into 1-inch pieces**
- **1 (10-oz.) pkg. frozen English peas**
- **2 Tbsp. chopped fresh flat-leaf parsley (optional)**

1. Combine flour, salt, and pepper in a shallow bowl; dredge beef in flour mixture. Heat half of oil in a Dutch oven over medium-high; add half of beef, and cook until browned all over, about 5 to 6 minutes. Transfer to a bowl. Repeat procedure with remaining oil and beef.
2. Add onion to Dutch oven, and cook until softened, about 6 minutes. Stir in beer, soy sauce, Worcestershire sauce, steak sauce, garlic, bay leaves, and thyme; bring to a boil. Add beef; cover and reduce heat to medium-low. Simmer until beef is tender, 2 ½ to 3 hours.
3. Stir in potatoes and carrots; cover and simmer until potatoes and carrots are tender, about 30 minutes. Stir in peas; cook an additional 2 minutes. Discard bay leaves. Top each serving with chopped parsley, if desired.

—M. DeMello
Hollywood, FL, February 1986

JAMBALAYA IS A LOUISIANA SPECIALTY of rice, meat, and vegetables, but those words—although accurate—don't capture its magic as a crowd-pleasing one-pot feast. Dishes with deep and diverse roots in a community rarely have specific or verifiable stories of their origins, but *The Dictionary of American Food and Drink* reports that jambalaya was born late one night when a hungry traveler arrived at a New Orleans inn long after dinner had been served. According to the story, the inn's cook, a man named Jean, was asked to *"balayez"* or "sweep something together" to feed the guest. The words "Jean balayez" later became jambalaya. This recipe (which is made with smoked turkey, ham, and sausage) comes from Covington, Louisiana, the parish seat of St. Tammany Parish, north of Lake Pontchartrain.

JAMBALAYA DE COVINGTON

This recipe from a Louisiana kitchen is made with a caramel-colored roux. When preparing it, stir the oil-and-flour mixture constantly as it cooks and do not let it overbrown.

ACTIVE 30 MIN. - TOTAL 1 HOUR, 55 MIN.
SERVES 8

- **1 lb. smoked turkey necks**
- **5 cups water**
- **1 1/2 cups uncooked long-grain rice**
- **1/2 lb. andouille or other smoked link sausage**
- **1/4 cup vegetable oil**
- **1/4 cup all-purpose flour**
- **1 medium bunch scallions**
- **1 cup chopped yellow onion (about 4 oz.)**
- **1 cup chopped celery (about 4 stalks)**
- **1/2 chopped green bell pepper (from 1 bell pepper)**
- **1 Tbsp. finely chopped fresh flat-leaf parsley or celery leaves**
- **1 Tbsp. finely chopped garlic (about 4 cloves)**
- **1/2 cup tomato sauce**
- **1 tsp. garlic salt**
- **1/2 tsp. black pepper**
- **1/2 tsp. paprika**
- **1/2 tsp. dried thyme**
- **1/4 tsp. cayenne pepper**
- **1 1/3 cups diced smoked ham (about 1/2 lb.)**

1. Preheat oven to 350°F. Place turkey necks in a large saucepan; add water, and bring to a boil over high. Cover, reduce heat to medium-low, and simmer about 1 hour. Drain, reserving 4 cups cooking liquid. Remove and reserve meat from turkey necks, discarding bones.
2. Bring 3 cups reserved cooking liquid to a boil in a medium saucepan over high. Add rice; cover and bring to a boil. Reduce heat to medium-low, and cook until rice is tender, about 18 minutes. Remove from heat, and let stand, covered, 5 minutes.
3. Place sausage on a rimmed baking sheet; bake in preheated oven 20 minutes. Chop sausage.
4. Combine oil and flour in a large Dutch oven; cook over medium, stirring constantly, until roux is the color of caramel, 6 to 8 minutes. Slice scallions, separating green and white parts. Reserve sliced green parts of scallions. Add sliced white parts of scallions (about 3 tablespoons), chopped yellow onion, celery, bell pepper, parsley, garlic, and tomato sauce to the roux.
5. Cook, stirring often, until vegetables are tender, about 15 minutes. Add remaining 1 cup cooking liquid; bring to a boil. Add garlic salt, black pepper, paprika, thyme, and cayenne, stirring well. Add turkey, sausage, and ham, stirring well. Remove from heat. Serve over rice, and sprinkle each serving with reserved sliced green parts of scallions.

—Joanne Champagne
Covington, LA, October 1987

PECANS AND PORK, two iconic ingredients in Southern cooking, come together in this ingenious main dish. What makes this recipe feel both classic and contemporary is the delicious sauce made from beer—and not just any beer, but Abita beer, from a legendary Louisiana brewery. Abita was founded in 1986, years before the local craft-brewing craze took off across the South. This pork chop recipe came from chef Horst Pfeifer of Bella Luna restaurant in New Orleans' French Quarter. He grew up in a small Bavarian farm town, so cooking with beer is second nature for him. Although Bella Luna was one of many culinary casualties of Hurricane Katrina in 2005, Pfeifer now owns Middendorf's Restaurant, an 84-year-old institution in Akers, Louisiana.

PECAN-BREADED PORK CHOPS WITH BEER SAUCE

Louisiana chef Horst Pfeifer combined dry mustard, celery salt, and pecans to create a memorable breading for pork chops. Serve them with your favorite vegetable and some crusty bread on the side for mopping up the rich, gravy-like sauce.

ACTIVE 20 MIN. - TOTAL 35 MIN.
SERVES 4

- **2 (1-oz.) white bread slices**
- **1 tsp. dry mustard**
- **1 tsp. celery salt**
- **1/4 tsp. black pepper**
- **1 cup pecan pieces**
- **3/4 cup all-purpose flour**
- **2 large eggs, lightly beaten**
- **1/4 cup whole milk**
- **4 (3/4-inch-thick) bone-in pork loin chops**
- **1/4 cup butter**
- **Beer Sauce (recipe follows)**

1. Preheat oven to 350°F. Combine bread, dry mustard, celery salt, and pepper in a mini food processor; process until finely chopped. Add pecan pieces, 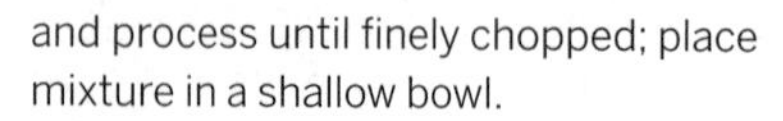and process until finely chopped; place mixture in a shallow bowl.
2. Place flour in a second shallow bowl. Stir together eggs and milk in a third shallow bowl. Dredge pork chops in flour, shaking off excess. Dip chops in egg mixture and then in pecan mixture, coating all sides and shaking off excess.
3. Melt 2 tablespoons of the butter in a large nonstick skillet over medium-high; add 2 chops, and cook until browned, about 2 minutes on each side. Transfer chops to a rimmed baking sheet. Repeat with remaining 2 tablespoons butter and 2 chops.
4. Bake in preheated oven until a thermometer inserted into chops registers 145°F, 10 to 15 minutes. Serve immediately with Beer Sauce.

BEER SAUCE

ACTIVE 10 MIN. - TOTAL 20 MIN.
MAKES ABOUT 1 CUP

- **1 Tbsp. vegetable oil**
- **1/2 cup chopped yellow onion (about 1/2 medium onion)**
- **1 1/2 tsp. caraway seeds**
- **1 garlic clove, minced**
- **1 cup dark beer (such as Abita Turbodog)**
- **1/2 cup condensed beef consommé, undiluted**
- **1/4 tsp. black pepper**
- **1 1/2 Tbsp. cornstarch**
- **1 1/2 Tbsp. water**

1. Heat oil in a small saucepan over medium; add onion, caraway seeds, and garlic. Cook, stirring often, until tender, about 4 minutes.
2. Stir in beer, beef consommé, and pepper. Bring mixture to a boil, stirring occasionally; reduce heat to medium-low, and simmer until reduced to 1 cup, about 10 minutes.
3. Stir together cornstarch and water in a small bowl until smooth; add to beer mixture.
4. Cook over medium, stirring constantly, until mixture boils and begins to thicken. Boil, stirring constantly, until thickened and glossy, 1 minute.

—Horst Pfeifer
New Orleans, LA, October 1995

THE SOUTH IS KNOWN for its rice-based dishes, but only one has been labeled as the defining dish of the Georgia coast. Savannah Red Rice is essentially a pilaf (also known as pilau, perloo, perlou, and so forth), in which long-grain rice simmers in a seasoned broth until tender. It's simple, but when this dish is well made, the bright, acidic tomatoes and smoky bacon give it a complex flavor. The rice on top will be fluffy and separate while the grains on the bottom develop a crisp crust. The secret to getting this magical mix of textures is to resist the temptation to lift the lid and stir the ingredients during cooking. To avoid that mistake, follow this recipe, which has you bake the rice in the low, even heat of the oven instead. Leaving it covered for a few minutes before serving improves the textures as well.

SAVANNAH RED RICE

This savory, slightly spicy baked rice recipe can stand on its own as a main dish or work as a hearty side served along with chicken, shrimp, or pork.

ACTIVE 25 MIN. - TOTAL 1 HOUR, 10 MIN.
SERVES 6

- **5 bacon slices**
- **2 cups chopped yellow onion (about 1 large onion)**
- **½ cup chopped celery (about 3 stalks)**
- **½ cup chopped green bell pepper (from 1 small bell pepper)**
- **1 cup uncooked long-grain rice**
- **1 (16-oz.) can chopped whole tomatoes, undrained**
- **¾ cup chicken broth**
- **½ tsp. kosher salt**
- **½ tsp. black pepper**
- **½ tsp. cayenne pepper**
- **¼ tsp. hot pepper sauce**

1. Preheat oven to 350°F. Cook bacon in a medium skillet over medium until crisp, about 8 minutes; transfer bacon to a plate lined with paper towels, reserving drippings in skillet. Crumble bacon.
2. Add yellow onion, celery, and bell pepper to reserved drippings in skillet; increase heat to medium-high. Cook, stirring often, until vegetables are tender, 5 to 6 minutes.
3. Stir in rice, tomatoes, chicken broth, salt, black pepper, cayenne pepper, and hot pepper sauce. Spoon into a lightly greased 2-quart baking dish. Cover with aluminum foil, and bake in preheated oven until rice is tender, 40 to 45 minutes. Top with crumbled bacon.

–Millie Givens
Savannah, GA, November 1989

HEARTY BEAN SOUP has been on the menu in the Senate's restaurant every day since at least 1903. You could say it's a rare unanimous mandate. According to one story, the tradition was started by a congressman from Idaho who contended the soup should always include mashed potatoes, presumably Idaho potatoes. Another story attributes the soup request to a senator from Minnesota who simply loved the stuff, despite no obvious ingredient connection to his home state. Senate Bean Soup (the more common name for this dish) is so iconic that it has its own recipe page on the Senate website, one version with spuds and one without. It's easy to see why it's so popular. The soup is inexpensive, easy to prepare, and although it needs to simmer for a couple hours, requires little attention beyond an occasional stir.

CAPITOL HILL BEAN SOUP

If you don't have time to soak the dried beans for 8 hours or overnight, try this quick-soak method. Put the beans in a large pot, add water to 2 inches above the beans, and bring to a boil. Cover, remove from heat, and let stand 1 hour. Drain the beans, and then cook according to the recipe.

ACTIVE 20 MIN. - TOTAL 10 HOURS, 25 MIN., INCLUDING 8 HOURS SOAKING

SERVES 12

- **1 lb. dried white navy beans, sorted of debris and rinsed**
- **1 (about 1-lb.) ham bone or uncured ham hock**
- **2 ½ qt. water**
- **1 large russet potato (about 8 oz.)**
- **3 cups chopped celery (about 6 stalks)**
- **3 cups chopped yellow onion (about 3 medium onions)**
- **1 garlic clove, minced**
- **3 tsp. kosher salt**
- **¾ tsp. black pepper**
- **¼ cup chopped fresh flat-leaf parsley**

1. Place beans in a Dutch oven; add water to cover, and soak 8 hours or overnight. Drain beans. Add ham bone and water. Cover and bring to a boil over high; reduce heat to medium-low, and simmer 1 hour.

2. Rinse potato; pierce with a fork, and wrap potato in a paper towel. Microwave on HIGH until tender, about 4 to 5 minutes; peel and mash potato. Stir potato, celery, onion, garlic, salt, and pepper into bean mixture; simmer over medium-low until beans are tender, about 1 hour. Remove ham bone from Dutch oven, and let stand until cool enough to handle, about 20 minutes. Remove and discard bone and fat; dice meat, and stir into bean mixture. Top each serving with chopped parsley.

—Lois Wilson
Ackerly, TX, October 1980

THIS GORGEOUS CHICKEN DISH is one of those regional classics that many natives either grew up eating all the time or have never heard of before—but no one should miss out. It originated in the Lowcountry, that sunny area around Charleston and Savannah known for deep ports, salt marshes, and excellent cuisine. Country Captain Chicken has been a staple of Junior League cookbooks in the Southeast since at least the 1950s and is found in various forms in cookbooks from as far back as the 19th century. Chicken pieces are browned in butter or bacon fat and then braised in tomato sauce redolent with aromatic spices such as curry powder, nutmeg, and plenty of pepper. Lowcountry cooking often makes brilliant use of the spices that arrived aboard ships that sailed into the local harbors, perhaps with a country captain at the helm.

COUNTRY CAPTAIN CHICKEN

This recipe was originally prepared with drumsticks, but we prefer using chicken thighs. The key to creating a depth of flavor in this dish is to use high-quality curry powder. It should be so fresh that opening the jar perfumes the kitchen.

ACTIVE 1 HOUR - TOTAL 1 HOUR, 30 MIN.
SERVES 6

- **3/4 cup all-purpose flour**
- **1/2 tsp. paprika**
- **1/4 tsp. cayenne pepper**
- **2 tsp. kosher salt**
- **12 bone-in, skin-on chicken thighs**
- **2 Tbsp. vegetable oil**
- **1/4 cup butter**
- **1/2 cup chopped fresh flat-leaf parsley, plus more for garnish**
- **2 cups chopped yellow onion (about 2 medium onions)**
- **3 cups chopped green pepper (about 3 medium peppers)**
- **2 garlic cloves, minced (about 2 tsp.)**
- **1 1/2 Tbsp. curry powder**
- **1 tsp. black pepper**
- **1/2 tsp. ground nutmeg**
- **2 (14.5-oz.) cans chopped tomatoes, undrained**
- **1/2 cup raisins**
- **6 cups hot cooked rice**
- **Toasted slivered almonds**

1. Combine flour, paprika, cayenne, and 1 teaspoon of the salt in a large ziplock plastic freezer bag. Place chicken thighs, a few at a time, in bag of flour mixture, shaking to coat. When all chicken thighs are coated, discard flour mixture.

2. Heat oil and 2 tablespoons of the butter in a large Dutch oven over medium, stirring until melted. Add 4 to 5 chicken thighs, skin side down, and cook until well browned and crisp on 1 side, 6 to 7 minutes. Turn and cook until browned on other side, about 2 minutes. Transfer thighs to a plate, reserving drippings in Dutch oven. Repeat twice with remaining thighs.

3. Add chopped parsley, onions, bell peppers, garlic, curry powder, black pepper, nutmeg, and remaining 2 tablespoons butter and 1 teaspoon salt to reserved drippings in Dutch oven; cook over medium, stirring often, until onion is tender. Stir in tomatoes and raisins.

4. Bring mixture to a boil over medium-high; reduce heat to medium-low, and return chicken to Dutch oven. Cover and simmer 15 minutes; uncover and cook until a thermometer inserted into chicken thighs registers 165°F, about 15 minutes. Serve chicken and sauce over rice. Garnish with almonds and reserved chopped parsley.

—Julie Zadeck
Shreveport, LA, October 1994

Weeknights Done Light

Resolutions? Bring 'em on. Try these fast, fresh, good-for-you winter dinners

Sweet-and-Spicy Sheet Pan Chicken with Cauliflower and Carrots

Seedless grapes are the secret ingredient in this dish. They melt and caramelize while roasting, adding a subtle hint of sweetness to the sauce.

ACTIVE 30 MIN. - TOTAL 1 HOUR, 20 MIN.
SERVES 4

- **1½ Tbsp. honey**
- **1½ tsp. smoked paprika**
- **¾ tsp. cayenne pepper**
- **½ tsp. black pepper**
- **4 Tbsp. olive oil**
- **2 tsp. kosher salt**
- **4 (10-oz.) bone-in, skin-on chicken breasts**
- **1 medium (2-lb.) head cauliflower, cut into 1-inch florets**
- **6 medium carrots, peeled and cut into 2-inch pieces**
- **1 medium-size red onion, cut into ½-inch wedges**
- **2 cups red seedless grapes**
- **2 lemons, quartered**
- **1 Tbsp. fresh lemon juice (from 1 lemon)**
- **1 Tbsp. cornstarch**
- **1¾ cups chicken stock**
- **3 Tbsp. unsalted butter**
- **¼ cup chopped fresh flat-leaf parsley**
- **1 cup uncooked couscous**
- **¼ cup toasted almond slices**

1. Preheat oven to 475°F. Whisk together first 4 ingredients, 3 tablespoons of the oil, and 1¾ teaspoons of the salt in a large bowl. Add chicken, cauliflower, carrots, red onion, grapes, and lemon wedges; toss to coat. Spread mixture on a large rimmed baking sheet in a single layer. Place chicken pieces on top, skin side up. Roast in preheated oven until vegetables are tender and a thermometer inserted in center of chicken registers 165°F, 35 to 40 minutes.
2. Transfer vegetables and chicken to a platter; tent with aluminum foil. Scrape any juices and browned bits from baking sheet into a small saucepan over high. Whisk in lemon juice, cornstarch, and ¼ cup of the stock. Bring to a boil, whisking constantly, until thickened, 2 minutes. Remove from heat; add butter and 2 tablespoons of the parsley. Whisk until butter melts.
3. Bring remaining 1½ cups stock, 1 tablespoon oil, and ¼ teaspoon salt to a boil in a medium saucepan over medium-high. Add couscous; stir and cover. Remove from heat; let stand 5 minutes. Fluff couscous with a fork. Divide couscous, chicken, and vegetables among 4 serving plates. Top with sauce, almonds, and remaining 2 tablespoons parsley.

Molasses-Soy Glazed Salmon and Vegetables

This tangy glaze is a great match for salmon, but it also pairs well with chicken and shrimp. Avoid thin fish fillets; they will cook before the vegetables are finished.

ACTIVE 15 MIN. - TOTAL 35 MIN.
SERVES 4

- **⅓ cup soy sauce**
- **¼ cup molasses**
- **1 Tbsp. freshly grated ginger**
- **1 Tbsp. rice vinegar**
- **2 tsp. minced garlic (about 2 garlic cloves)**
- **1 bunch scallions (about 5 oz.)**
- **6 oz. sugar snap peas (about 1½ cups), trimmed**
- **2 medium-size yellow bell peppers, cut into ½-inch-thick wedges**
- **2 Tbsp. olive oil**
- **4 (6-oz.) skin-on salmon fillets**
- **¾ tsp. kosher salt**
- **½ tsp. black pepper**
- **2 (8.8-oz.) pkg. precooked microwavable brown rice**
- **4 tsp. toasted sesame seeds**
- **4 lime wedges (optional)**

1. Preheat oven to 400°F. Combine soy sauce, molasses, ginger, vinegar, and garlic in a small saucepan over medium. Cook, stirring often, until mixture simmers and reduces to about ½ cup, about 2 minutes. Remove from heat.
2. Thinly slice green parts of scallions; reserve. Cut white parts of scallions into 1-inch pieces, and place on a large rimmed baking sheet. Add sugar snap peas and bell peppers. Drizzle vegetables with oil, and toss to coat. Spread in an even layer.
3. Place salmon fillets, skin side down, nestled in vegetable mixture; spoon about 1 tablespoon molasses mixture over each fillet. Reserve remaining molasses mixture. Sprinkle salmon and vegetables evenly with salt and pepper. Place in preheated oven, and bake until vegetables are tender and lightly browned, salmon is cooked to medium, and glaze is golden, 16 to 18 minutes.
4. Prepare rice according to package directions; divide evenly among serving plates. Place salmon and vegetables on plates; sprinkle with scallion slices and sesame seeds. Serve with remaining molasses mixture and, if desired, lime wedges.

Molasses-Soy Glazed Salmon and Vegetables

Sausage and Kale Pesto Pizza

Instead of the usual tomato sauce, this tasty deep-dish pizza is topped with a vibrant green pesto made with fresh basil and kale. Don't skip preheating the cast-iron skillet, which helps create a nice crisp crust.

ACTIVE 35 MIN. - TOTAL 50 MIN.
SERVES 4

- **1 lb. fresh whole-wheat prepared pizza dough**
- **8 oz. sweet Italian sausage, casings removed**
- **6 Tbsp. extra-virgin olive oil,**
- **1 large sweet onion, thinly sliced (about 4 cups)**
- **¾ tsp. kosher salt**
- **1 cup chopped curly kale leaves (about 1¼ oz.)**
- **½ cup loosely packed fresh basil leaves**
- **1¼ oz. Parmesan cheese, shredded (about ½ cup)**
- **2 garlic cloves**
- **1 Tbsp. plain yellow cornmeal**
- **1 (6-oz.) container fresh mozzarella cheese, torn**
- **3 oz. feta cheese, crumbled (about ¾ cup)**
- **¼ tsp. crushed red pepper**

1. Let pizza dough stand at room temperature 30 minutes.
2. Preheat oven to 500°F with an oven rack in center of oven. Meanwhile, cook sausage in a large nonstick skillet over medium-high until no longer pink, 6 to 8 minutes, breaking it into small pieces. Transfer to a plate lined with paper towels. Without wiping skillet, add 2 tablespoons of the oil to drippings in skillet. Add sliced onions and ½ teaspoon of the salt; cook over medium, stirring often, until onions are golden brown and tender, about 10 minutes. Remove from heat.
3. Combine kale, basil, Parmesan, garlic, 2 tablespoons of the oil, and remaining ¼ teaspoon salt in a food processor. Process until smooth, stopping to scrape down sides, about 30 seconds.
4. Heat a 12-inch cast-iron skillet over medium for 2 minutes. Add 1 tablespoon of the oil to skillet; swirl to coat. Sprinkle skillet with cornmeal. Stretch or roll dough into a 14-inch circle, and carefully place in hot skillet, pressing onto bottom and up sides. Increase heat to medium-high; cook until dough begins to bubble, 2 to 3 minutes. Working quickly, spread kale pesto over bottom of crust; top with sausage, onions, mozzarella, and feta. Sprinkle with crushed red pepper. Brush exposed crust edges with remaining 1 tablespoon oil. Place skillet in preheated oven on middle rack, and bake until cheeses are melted and crust is golden brown, 12 to 15 minutes.

Farro Bowl with Curry-Roasted Sweet Potatoes and Brussels Sprouts

The farro can be prepared up to two days in advance. Store it covered in the refrigerator, and then reheat before serving.

ACTIVE 15 MIN. - TOTAL 40 MIN.
SERVES 4

- **1 lb. Brussels sprouts, trimmed and halved**
- **12 oz. sweet potatoes, peeled and cut into ¾-inch cubes (about 3 cups)**
- **2 large shallots, peeled and sliced ¼ inch thick (about 1 cup)**
- **3 Tbsp. butter, melted**
- **1 Tbsp. curry powder**
- **1 Tbsp. minced garlic (about 3 garlic cloves)**
- **½ tsp. black pepper**
- **1 tsp. kosher salt**
- **4 cups plus 1 Tbsp. water**
- **1½ cups uncooked pearled farro, rinsed**
- **½ cup plain whole-milk yogurt**
- **1 Tbsp. fresh lemon juice (from 1 lemon)**
- **¾ cup toasted pecan halves**

1. Preheat oven to 425°F. Combine Brussels sprouts, sweet potatoes, shallots, butter, curry powder, garlic, pepper, and ½ teaspoon of the salt in a large bowl; toss to coat. Spread vegetable mixture in a single layer on a large rimmed baking sheet. Bake in preheated oven until vegetables are tender and lightly browned, 20 to 25 minutes.
2. While vegetables roast, bring 4 cups of the water and remaining ½ teaspoon salt to a boil in a medium saucepan over high. Add farro, and cook according to package directions; drain.
3. Stir together yogurt, lemon juice, and remaining 1 tablespoon water in a bowl. To serve, spoon hot cooked farro into 4 wide, shallow bowls. Divide vegetable mixture evenly among bowls; sprinkle each with pecans, and serve with yogurt mixture for topping.

Ziti with Mushroom, Fennel, and Tomato Ragu

While any pasta shape will work with this hearty vegetarian dish, we prefer penne or ziti; these noodles help capture every last bite of the chunky sauce.

ACTIVE 40 MIN. - TOTAL 1 HOUR, 10 MIN.
SERVES 6

- **5 Tbsp. extra-virgin olive oil**
- **1 (8-oz.) pkg. cremini mushrooms, trimmed and quartered**
- **1 (8-oz.) pkg. button mushrooms, trimmed and quartered**
- **3 medium portobello mushroom caps, gills scraped, coarsely chopped**
- **1 small fennel bulb, trimmed and finely chopped (about 2 cups)**
- **1 small sweet onion, vertically sliced (about 2 cups)**
- **1 Tbsp. minced garlic (about 3 garlic cloves)**
- **1½ tsp. kosher salt**
- **½ tsp. black pepper**
- **2 Tbsp. tomato paste**
- **½ cup dry red wine**
- **1 (28-oz.) can crushed San Marzano plum tomatoes**
- **1 (15-oz.) can fire-roasted diced tomatoes, drained**
- **1 (2- x 3-inch) Parmesan cheese rind**
- **1 lb. uncooked ziti or penne pasta**
- **½ cup panko (Japanese-style breadcrumbs)**
- **2 oz. Parmesan cheese, finely grated with a Microplane grater (about 1¼ cups)**
- **6 Tbsp. chopped mixed fresh herbs (such as basil, parsley, and sage), divided**

1. Heat 4 tablespoons of the olive oil in a large Dutch oven over medium-high. Add mushrooms, and cook, stirring occasionally, until moisture has evaporated and mushrooms are golden brown, about 10 minutes. Add fennel, onion, garlic, salt, and pepper; cook, stirring often, until vegetables are almost tender, about 6 minutes.
2. Add tomato paste, and cook, stirring constantly, 1 minute. Add wine, and cook, stirring to release browned bits from bottom of Dutch oven, 1 to 2 minutes. Add crushed tomatoes, diced tomatoes, and Parmesan rind; bring to a boil. Reduce heat to medium, and cook, stirring occasionally, until sauce thickens, about 20 minutes.
3. Meanwhile, cook pasta according to package directions; drain and keep warm.
4. Heat remaining 1 tablespoon oil in a small skillet over medium-high. Add panko, and cook, stirring often, until golden and toasted. Transfer to a bowl, and cool completely, about 10 minutes. Stir in grated Parmesan and 2 tablespoons of the mixed herbs.
5. Remove and discard Parmesan rind. Stir remaining ¼ cup mixed herbs into sauce. Divide ziti among serving bowls; top with sauce, and sprinkle with toasted panko.

MAYONNAISE IS THE KEY TO ULTRA-MOIST CHOCOLATE CAKE.

The Southern Secret to Chocolate Cake

A surprising ingredient makes this classic dessert a forever favorite

Chocolate Mayonnaise Cake

The deep flavor of this dessert, which is enhanced with coffee, contrasts nicely with the light and fluffy buttercream.

ACTIVE 25 MIN. - TOTAL 2 HOURS, 10 MIN.
SERVES 10

- **1½ cups hot strong brewed coffee**
- **1 cup unsweetened cocoa**
- **3 cups all-purpose flour**
- **2 tsp. baking soda**
- **½ tsp. baking powder**
- **½ tsp. plus ¼ tsp. salt**
- **2½ cups granulated sugar**
- **4 large eggs**
- **1 cup mayonnaise (such as Duke's)**
- **2 tsp. vanilla extract**
- **1¼ cups bittersweet chocolate chips**
- **2 Tbsp. light corn syrup**
- **3–4 Tbsp. heavy cream**
- **¾ cup unsalted butter, softened**
- **4 cups powdered sugar**

1. Whisk together hot coffee and cocoa in a bowl. Let stand until room temperature, about 20 minutes. Preheat oven to 350°F. Grease and flour 3 (9-inch) round cake pans.

2. Whisk together flour, baking soda, baking powder, and ½ teaspoon of the salt in a bowl. Combine granulated sugar and eggs in a large bowl. Beat with an electric mixer on medium-low speed until light and fluffy, about 4 minutes. Beat in mayonnaise and 1½ teaspoons of the vanilla on low speed. Alternately add flour mixture and coffee mixture to egg mixture in 5 additions, beginning and ending with flour mixture. Divide batter evenly among prepared pans. Bake in preheated oven until a wooden pick inserted in center comes out with a few moist crumbs, 22 to 25 minutes.

3. Cool cake layers in pans on a wire rack 20 minutes. Remove cake layers from pans; cool completely on rack, about 30 minutes.

4. Place chocolate chips, light corn syrup, and 3 tablespoons of the heavy cream in a microwavable bowl. Microwave on HIGH until smooth, about 1 minute, stirring every 15 seconds. Let stand until room temperature, 10 minutes.

5. Combine butter, remaining ¼ teaspoon salt, 2 cups of the powdered sugar, and remaining ½ teaspoon vanilla in bowl of a heavy-duty stand mixer; beat on low speed until smooth. Beat in chocolate mixture on low speed until smooth. Beat in remaining 2 cups powdered sugar and, if needed, remaining 1 tablespoon cream, 1 teaspoon at a time, until spreadable consistency is reached.

6. Place 1 cake layer on a serving plate. Spread ½ cup frosting over top. Top with second layer; spread ½ cup frosting over top. Top with third layer. Spread remaining frosting over sides and top of cake.

New Year, Same Hoppin' Tradition

Ring in 2018 with a generous helping of this Southern staple

EVEN BEFORE the Christmas decorations are stowed away or the resolutions take effect, Southerners welcome the New Year with a bowl of hoppin' John, the iconic Lowcountry dish consisting of field peas (typically black-eyed or red peas) and rice. Folklore says that eating field peas, especially with a side of greens, brings good fortune in the year ahead–the peas symbolize coins, while leafy greens represent dollar bills.

Long before it was a holiday tradition, hoppin' John was a humble everyday meal. Like many treasured Southern recipes, its roots can be traced back to West Africa, where rice and cowpeas were grown and eaten. Some food experts believe that West African slaves who were brought to the Lowcountry paired the two ingredients to make a nourishing dish that also reminded them of home. Early recipes were nothing fancy. The one for "Hopping John" (the "g" fell off many years later) in *The Carolina Housewife,* which was originally published in 1847 by Sarah Rutledge, calls for "one pound of bacon, one pint of red peas, one pint of rice" all thrown together in the same pot.

The creative cooks in our Test Kitchen have developed dozens of new interpretations of the recipe over the years, including Hoppin' John Soup with Cornbread Croutons and "Big Easy" Gumbo served with a scoop of hoppin' John on top. That last one, however, was not well received by gumbo and black-eyed pea purists alike.

This January, we're going back to basics by focusing on technique and ingredients. Even if you aren't the superstitious type, hoppin' John is a filling and comforting meal that hits the spot on a cold winter day. It's a simple pleasure after a month of holiday indulgences.

THE ABC'S OF HOPPIN' JOHN

PORK
Thick-cut bacon adds the right amount of smokiness; a ham hock can overpower the dish.

PEAS
Fresh or frozen black-eyed peas hold up best after a lengthy simmer. Lowcountry cooks prefer using Sea Island red peas.

RICE
Carolina Gold, an heirloom long-grain type, has a sweet, mild flavor and a toothsome texture.

Classic Hoppin' John

ACTIVE 25 MIN. - TOTAL 1 HOUR, 30 MIN.
SERVES 6

- **6 thick-cut bacon slices, chopped**
- **4 celery stalks, sliced (about 1½ cups)**
- **1 medium-size yellow onion, chopped (about 1½ cups)**
- **1 small green bell pepper, finely chopped (about 1 cup)**
- **3 garlic cloves, chopped (about 1 Tbsp.)**
- **1 tsp. chopped fresh thyme**
- **½ tsp. black pepper**
- **¼ tsp. cayenne pepper**
- **1½ tsp. kosher salt**
- **8 cups lower-sodium chicken broth**
- **4 cups fresh or frozen black-eyed peas**
- **2 Tbsp. olive oil**
- **1½ cups uncooked Carolina Gold rice**
- **Fresh scallions, sliced**

1. Cook bacon in a Dutch oven over medium-high, stirring occasionally, until starting to crisp, about 10 minutes. Add celery, onion, bell pepper, garlic, thyme, black pepper, cayenne, and 1 teaspoon of the salt. Cook, stirring occasionally, until onion is tender, about 8 minutes. Add broth and black-eyed peas, and bring to a boil over medium-high. Reduce heat to medium-low, and simmer until peas are tender, about 40 minutes. Drain pea mixture, reserving cooking liquid. Return pea mixture and 1 cup of the cooking liquid to Dutch oven. Cover to keep warm; set aside.

2. Heat oil in a medium saucepan over medium-high. Add rice and cook, stirring often, until fragrant and lightly toasted, 3 to 4 minutes. Stir in 3 cups of the reserved cooking liquid and remaining ½ teaspoon salt. Bring to a boil, and reduce heat to medium-low; cover and cook until rice is tender, 15 to 18 minutes. Fluff rice with a fork, and gently stir into pea mixture in Dutch oven. Stir in remaining cooking liquid, ¼ cup at a time, until desired consistency is reached. Sprinkle servings with sliced fresh scallions.

COOKING (SL) SCHOOL

TIPS AND TRICKS FROM THE SOUTH'S MOST TRUSTED KITCHEN

NEW YEAR'S RESOLUTIONS

Pam Lolley
Test Kitchen Professional

RESOLUTION #1

Pack a Better Brown-Bag Lunch

"You can whip up one of these filling weekday lunches the night before or make it in the morning prior to heading out. All three of these recipes will travel well and be delicious meals you'll look forward to eating."

Smoky White Bean Soup

Almond-Chicken Wrap

Herbed Shrimp-and-Rice Salad

Smoky White Bean Soup

ACTIVE 15 MIN. - TOTAL 25 MIN.
SERVES 2

Cook 1 chopped bacon slice in a saucepan over medium until crispy, about 6 minutes. Remove bacon; drain on paper towels, reserving drippings in skillet. Cook ½ cup chopped yellow onion, ¼ cup chopped celery, 1 minced garlic clove, and 1 tsp. chopped fresh thyme in reserved drippings in saucepan, 3 minutes. Stir in 1½ cups chicken broth; 1 (15-oz.) can cannellini beans, drained and rinsed; 1 seeded and chopped plum tomato; 1 bay leaf; and ¼ tsp. each kosher salt and black pepper. Bring to a boil over medium-high; reduce heat to medium-low, and simmer, stirring occasionally, 8 minutes. Serve hot.

Almond-Chicken Wrap

ACTIVE 10 MIN. - TOTAL 10 MIN.
SERVES 1

Stir together 1 Tbsp. spicy brown mustard and ½ tsp. honey. Spread mixture on 1 whole-grain flatbread wrap. Top with 1½ cups fresh baby spinach, 1 Tbsp. thinly sliced red onion, 1 Tbsp. chopped lightly salted smoked almonds, 1 sandwich-cut bread-and-butter pickle, and 3 oz. chopped cooked chicken. Roll up; serve.

Herbed Shrimp-and-Rice Salad

ACTIVE 15 MIN. - TOTAL 15 MIN.
SERVES 2

Cook 1 (8.5-oz.) pkg. precooked microwavable basmati rice according to package directions; spoon into a medium bowl. Add ½ lb. peeled and deveined cooked shrimp and 3 Tbsp. each chopped red bell pepper, yellow bell pepper, and scallions. Stir in 1 Tbsp. each chopped fresh parsley and dill and ¼ cup bottled lemon vinaigrette salad dressing. Serve over 2 cups salad greens; top with 2 Tbsp. crumbled feta cheese.

RESOLUTION #2

Cook Flawless Fish Fillets

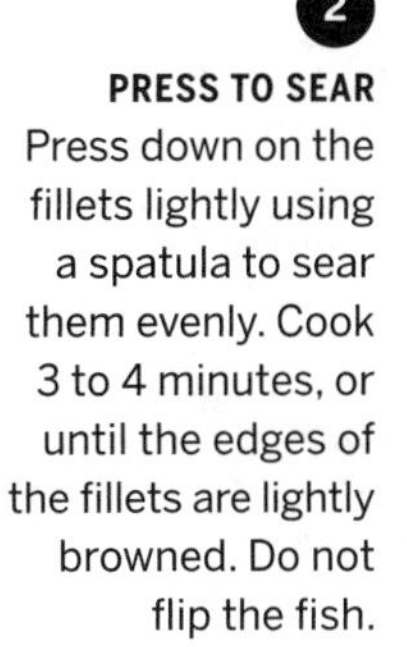

Robby Melvin
Test Kitchen Director

"Nearly any type of fish can be pan-seared, but this technique works best with firm fillets that are at least 1½ inches thick, such as grouper, halibut, red snapper, or salmon. Serve them along with a favorite side dish, and you've got a healthy and easy dinner."

1

START WITH A HOT SKILLET
Preheat the oven to 425°F. Pat the fish dry on both sides; season with salt and pepper. Heat 2 Tbsp. olive oil in an ovenproof skillet over medium heat. Once the oil is hot, carefully place the fillets in the pan.

2

PRESS TO SEAR
Press down on the fillets lightly using a spatula to sear them evenly. Cook 3 to 4 minutes, or until the edges of the fillets are lightly browned. Do not flip the fish.

3

FINISH IN THE OVEN
Transfer the skillet to the preheated oven, and cook until the fillets are done, 4 to 5 minutes. Serve immediately, seared side up.

RESOLUTION #3

Conquer Your Fear of Phyllo Dough

Deb Wise
Test Kitchen Professional

"Delicate, tissue-thin phyllo dough is a great way to add crunch to both sweet and savory recipes, but it can tear and dry out easily. Next time, remember these three simple, handy tips for working with this notoriously finicky ingredient."

1. PLAN AHEAD
Defrost unopened packages of phyllo dough overnight in the refrigerator. Chilled dough is easier to work with than room-temp dough.

2. GO QUICKLY
Phyllo dries out fast, so work as quickly as possible. Keep the dough covered with plastic wrap and a damp (not wet) towel during assembly.

3. USE A LIGHT HAND
Brush or spray the layers of dough lightly with oil or melted butter. This will help create crisper layers with better texture and separation.

Layers of phyllo make this tart crust flaky, buttery, and perfectly crunchy.

Pecan Crunch Tart

ACTIVE 25 MIN. - TOTAL 1 HOUR

SERVES 8

- **10 (14- x 9-inch) frozen phyllo pastry sheets (from 1 [1-lb.] pkg.), thawed (such as Athens)**
- **½ cup unsalted butter**
- **½ cup light corn syrup**
- **⅓ cup packed dark brown sugar**
- **¼ cup heavy cream**
- **1 tsp. vanilla extract**
- **⅛ tsp. baking soda**
- **¼ tsp. salt**
- **2 cups chopped toasted pecans**
- **Whipped cream**

1. Preheat oven to 375°F. Place phyllo on a work surface; cover with plastic wrap and a damp towel to prevent from drying out. Lightly coat a 9-inch tart pan with removable bottom with cooking spray. Microwave ¼ cup of the butter in a small microwavable bowl on HIGH until butter melts, about 20 seconds. Brush 1 phyllo sheet lightly but completely with melted butter, and place, buttered side up, in prepared tart pan, pressing pastry into edges of pan. Brush another phyllo sheet with butter in the same way, and press pastry into pan, buttered side up, at a 45° angle to the first sheet. Repeat procedure with remaining 8 phyllo sheets, covering the bottom and sides of pan with a uniformly thick layer of phyllo. Trim overhanging pastry, leaving ½ inch of phyllo over the edges of the pan. Fold overhanging phyllo to inside, and press to adhere.

2. Microwave remaining ¼ cup butter in a small microwavable bowl on HIGH until butter melts, about 20 seconds. Combine melted butter, light corn syrup, dark brown sugar, heavy cream, vanilla extract, baking soda, and salt in a bowl, stirring well. Stir in chopped toasted pecans. Pour mixture evenly into prepared pan. Bake in preheated oven until browned and bubbly, 20 to 25 minutes. Cool in pan on a wire rack 15 minutes. Remove from pan, and place on a serving plate. Serve tart warm or at room temperature with whipped cream.

February

44 **The Beauty of Slow Cooking** A bit of prep and hours of hands-off cooking yield sublime dinners—no stove required.

52 **A League of Their Own** The best citrus desserts from the cookbooks of the South's Junior Leagues

57 QUICK FIX **Super Bowls** We've got one-dish dinners sure to tempt everyone in the house

60 SOUTHERN CLASSIC **The Mystery of Hummingbird Cake** The lure and lore of our most famous cake

63 WHAT CAN I BRING? **Game Day Potatoes** Flavorful one-bite 'tater skins are so good they may just replace the wings at your next Super Bowl party

64 SAVE ROOM **The King of Cakes** A new spin on a the classic Mardis Gras cake

65 *SL* COOKING SCHOOL **Slow-Cooker Edition** Notable tips, hacks, and prep instructions for making the most of your slow cooker, plus a guide to selecting the perfect model too

CARBONARA WITH BRAISED LAMB
page 45

THE BEAUTY OF SLOW COOKING

Relaxed winter nights call for satisfying no-fuss suppers. Pick your protein of choice, toss in fresh ingredients, and let the slow cooker do the rest

START WITH...

LAMB SHANKS

Lengthy slow-cooking yields drop-off-the-bone tenderness in every bite. The secret to restaurant-quality results is to select shanks of roughly the same size that have been trimmed of excess fat and the tendons along the bone. Save the braising liquid–it makes an incredible sauce.

ACTIVE 30 MIN. - TOTAL 6 HOURS, 30 MIN.
SERVES 4

- 2 Tbsp. olive oil
- 4 lamb shanks (about 11 oz. each), trimmed
- 2 ½ tsp. kosher salt
- 1 tsp. black pepper
- 2 medium-size yellow onions (about 1 lb.), cut into 1-inch wedges
- 2 large carrots, cut into 2-inch pieces
- 3 garlic cloves, smashed
- ½ cup dry red wine
- 1 cup crushed tomatoes
- ¼ cup chicken broth
- 1 tsp. ground cumin

1. Heat oil in a large skillet over medium-high. Sprinkle lamb with salt and pepper. Cook until browned, 3 minutes per side. Remove from skillet. Add onions, carrots, and garlic; cook, stirring occasionally, until slightly softened, 4 minutes. Add red wine; cook, until mostly evaporated, 3 minutes. Transfer to a 6-quart slow cooker. Stir in tomatoes, broth, and cumin. Nestle lamb into tomato mixture. Cover; cook on LOW until very tender, 6 hours.

2. Transfer lamb to a plate. Pour cooking mixture through a wire-mesh strainer into a bowl; discard solids. Reserve strained liquid.

Braised Lamb Shanks with Parmesan-Chive Grits

ACTIVE 20 MIN. - TOTAL 40 MIN. - **SERVES 4**

Bring 2 cups reserved strained cooking liquid to a simmer in a saucepan over medium. Whisk together 1 Tbsp. each cornstarch and water. Whisk cornstarch mixture into cooking liquid; cook until thickened and reduced by half, about 12 minutes. Set sauce aside; keep warm. Whisk 1 cup uncooked stone-ground yellow grits into 4 cups boiling water in a medium saucepan; cook, whisking, until smooth, about 45 seconds. Return to a boil; cover and reduce heat to medium-low. Cook until tender, 20 minutes. Whisk in 2 ½ oz. finely shredded Parmigiano-Reggiano cheese, ¼ cup chopped fresh chives, 2 Tbsp. unsalted butter, and 2 ½ tsp. kosher salt. Divide grits among 4 bowls. Top each with a Lamb Shank, some sauce, and chopped fresh chives.

Shepherd's Pie

ACTIVE 20 MIN. - TOTAL 35 MIN. - **SERVES 6**

Heat 2 Tbsp. olive oil in a 10-inch cast-iron skillet over medium-high. Add 1 ½ cups each chopped yellow onion and carrots; cook until tender, about 10 minutes. Add 2 Tbsp. tomato paste, 1 Tbsp. chopped rosemary, 2 tsp. each chopped garlic and fresh thyme, 1 ½ tsp. kosher salt, and ¾ tsp. black pepper. Cook until fragrant, about 2 minutes. Add ½ cup dry red wine; cook until completely evaporated, about 2 minutes. Sprinkle with 3 Tbsp. all-purpose flour; cook 1 minute. Gradually add 1 ½ cups beef stock, stirring until completely incorporated. Cook until thickened, 6 to 7 minutes. Stir in 12 oz. shredded Lamb Shank meat and 1 cup thawed frozen green peas. Remove from heat. Stir ¼ cup heavy cream into 1 prepared and warm 24-oz. pkg. mashed potatoes. Spread potatoes over lamb mixture, covering surface completely. Broil on HIGH 6 inches from heat until lightly browned, 4 to 6 minutes. Garnish with chopped fresh flat-leaf parsley.

Carbonara with Braised Lamb

ACTIVE 25 MIN. - TOTAL 30 MIN. - **SERVES 4**

Heat 1 Tbsp. olive oil in a skillet over medium, and cook 4 oz. finely diced pancetta until browned, about 3 minutes. Add 4 sliced garlic cloves and ¼ tsp. crushed red pepper; cook until just starting to brown, 1 to 2 minutes. Whisk together 3 large egg yolks, 1 large egg, 1 ½ oz. each finely shredded pecorino Romano cheese and Parmesan cheese, and ½ tsp. black pepper in a large bowl. Cook 12 oz. bucatini pasta in salted water according to package directions. Drain; reserving 3 Tbsp. pasta water. Add hot pasta and reserved pasta water to bowl with egg mixture. Toss until cheese is melted and yolks are thickened. Stir in pancetta mixture. Transfer pasta to a serving platter. Top with 8 oz. shredded Lamb Shank meat. Garnish with ½ oz. finely shredded pecorino Romano cheese and torn fresh flat-leaf parsley leaves.

START WITH...

TURKEY BREAST

Unlike roasting, slow-cooking locks in moisture, creating juicy and flavorful meat. Keep the skin on (it will be removed later) to seal in the herbed butter rub.

ACTIVE 10 MIN. - TOTAL 5 HOURS, 10 MIN.
SERVES 8

- ½ cup unsalted butter, softened
- 1 Tbsp. chopped fresh thyme
- 2 tsp. finely chopped garlic (from 2 garlic cloves)
- 2 tsp. chopped fresh rosemary
- 2 tsp. chopped fresh sage
- 1 tsp. lemon zest (from 1 lemon)
- 1 Tbsp. kosher salt
- 1½ tsp. black pepper
- 1 (6- lb.) bone-in, skin-on whole turkey breast
- ½ cup chicken broth

Stir together butter, thyme, garlic, rosemary, sage, lemon zest, 2 teaspoons of the salt, and 1 teaspoon of the pepper in a medium bowl until well incorporated. Rub butter mixture under turkey skin. Sprinkle outside of turkey with remaining 1 teaspoon salt and ½ teaspoon pepper. Pour chicken broth in bottom of a 6-quart slow cooker; add turkey, skin side up. Cover and cook on LOW until a thermometer inserted into thickest portion registers 165°F, 4½ to 5 hours. Remove turkey; remove skin from turkey, and reserve for later use.

Turkey with Shallot-Mustard Sauce and Roasted Potatoes

ACTIVE 25 MIN. - TOTAL 45 MIN. - **SERVES 4**

Toss 1 lb. halved multicolored fingerling potatoes with 2 Tbsp. olive oil, 2 tsp. chopped garlic, ¾ tsp. kosher salt, and ½ tsp. black pepper on a rimmed baking sheet. Bake at 375°F until tender, about 25 minutes. Cook reserved skin from Turkey Breast in 1 Tbsp. olive oil in a skillet over medium until it is browned and fat has rendered, about 5 minutes. Remove and discard turkey skin, reserving drippings in skillet. Add ⅓ cup minced shallots. Cook until shallots are tender, about 2 minutes. Add ¼ cup dry white wine; cook until reduced by half, about 2 minutes. Add ¾ cup chicken broth; ¼ tsp. kosher salt; and 1 tsp. each coarse-grain mustard, Dijon mustard, and chopped thyme. Simmer 2 minutes. Remove skillet from heat; stir in 2 Tbsp. unsalted butter until melted. Serve sauce over sliced Turkey Breast and potatoes.

Kentucky Hot Brown Casserole

ACTIVE 30 MIN. - TOTAL 1 HOUR, 30 MIN.
SERVES 6

Cook 12 oz. chopped bacon in a large skillet over medium until crisp, about 12 minutes; remove bacon. Reserve bacon drippings. Toss together 16 oz. cubed thick-cut white bread slices (such as Texas toast), ½ cup melted unsalted butter, 1 tsp. kosher salt, and ½ tsp. black pepper on a baking sheet. Bake at 375°F until toasted, about 16 minutes. Whisk together 6 large eggs, 2 cups whole milk, 1½ tsp. kosher salt, and ½ tsp. each black pepper and dry mustard in a large bowl. Add 2 oz. finely shredded Parmesan cheese, 10 oz. chopped Turkey Breast, ½ cup bacon, 3 Tbsp. bacon drippings, and bread cubes. Pour mixture into a lightly greased 11- x 7-inch baking dish. Bake at 375°F until golden brown and set, about 45 minutes, shielding with foil during last 10 minutes to prevent excess browning, if needed. Whisk together 2 Tbsp. each unsalted butter and all-purpose flour in a small saucepan over medium until smooth, about 1 minute. Gradually whisk in 1 cup whole milk; cook until thickened and mixture just begins to bubble, about 4 minutes. Remove from heat; whisk in 4 oz. finely shredded Parmesan cheese, ½ tsp. black pepper, and ¼ tsp. kosher salt. Spoon sauce over casserole. Top with 1 cup diced fresh tomatoes, 2 Tbsp. chopped fresh flat-leaf parsley, and remaining ¼ cup bacon.

Wedge Salad with Turkey and Blue Cheese-Buttermilk Dressing

ACTIVE 15 MIN. - TOTAL 15 MIN. - **SERVES 4**

Whisk together ½ cup whole buttermilk, 1 grated garlic clove, 3 Tbsp. each mayonnaise and sour cream, 2 Tbsp. each finely chopped fresh chives and flat-leaf parsley, 1½ oz. crumbled blue cheese, 1¼ tsp. kosher salt, ½ tsp. black pepper, and ¼ tsp. paprika in a medium bowl. Divide 1 large quartered iceberg lettuce head among 4 plates. Spoon dressing evenly over lettuce. Top evenly with 10 oz. chopped Turkey Breast, 1 cup chopped fresh tomato, ¼ cup crumbled blue cheese, and 2 Tbsp. each finely diced red onion and chopped fresh chives.

START WITH...

CHICKEN

A long, low cook time makes the meat ultra tender, and a few minutes under the broiler crisps the skin.

ACTIVE 15 MIN. - TOTAL 3 HOURS, 50 MIN. - **SERVES 4**

2	Tbsp. olive oil
1	Tbsp. kosher salt
1½	tsp. paprika
1½	tsp. chopped fresh thyme
1	tsp. black pepper
¼	tsp. cayenne pepper
1	(4½-lb.) whole chicken
1	lemon, halved
4	garlic cloves
4	small yellow onions (about 1 lb.), quartered
2	large carrots, cut into 2-inch pieces
2	celery stalks, cut into 2-inch pieces
¼	cup water

1. Combine first 6 ingredients. Rub mixture on outside and under skin of chicken. Stuff cavity with lemon, garlic, and 4 onion quarters.

2. Place 2 inverted shallow ramekins in a 6-quart slow cooker. Place carrots, celery, and remaining onion quarters around ramekins; add water. Place chicken, breast side up, on ramekins. Cover; cook on HIGH until a thermometer inserted into the breast registers 165°F, 3½ hours. Transfer chicken to a cutting board; let rest 15 minutes.

3. Preheat broiler to HIGH with oven rack 6 inches from heat. Remove ramekins. Pour stock mixture through a wire-mesh strainer into a bowl; discard solids. Reserve stock for later use. Cut chicken into 6 pieces. Place, skin side up, on a rimmed baking sheet. Broil until skin is golden and crispy, 4 to 6 minutes.

Skillet Chicken Pot Pie with Leeks and Mushrooms

ACTIVE 35 MIN. - TOTAL 1 HOUR, 10 MIN. - **SERVES 6**

Heat 2 Tbsp. unsalted butter in a 10-inch cast-iron skillet over medium. Cook 1½ cups each peeled and diced russet potatoes and chopped leeks and ½ cup chopped carrots until slightly softened, about 8 minutes. Add 8 oz. sliced cremini mushrooms, 2 tsp. each kosher salt and chopped garlic, and ¾ tsp. black pepper. Cook until potatoes and mushrooms are tender, about 8 minutes, adding water, 1 Tbsp. at a time, if vegetables stick to skillet. Stir in 12 oz. shredded, skinless Chicken and 1 cup frozen, thawed green peas; remove from heat. Melt 6 Tbsp. unsalted butter in a saucepan over medium, and whisk in 2½ Tbsp. all-purpose flour; cook, whisking constantly, 1 minute. Gradually whisk in 1½ cups reserved strained stock (or chicken broth); cook until thickened, about 6 minutes. Add ¼ cup heavy cream and 1 Tbsp. hot sauce. Stir cream mixture into chicken mixture. Place a thawed 10-inch square puff pastry sheet over filling, letting corners drape over edge of skillet. Brush lightly with egg wash, and cut 3 or 4 slits in top of pastry sheet. Bake at 400°F until golden and bubbly, 20 to 22 minutes. Let stand 15 minutes.

Spicy Red Curry with Chicken

ACTIVE 20 MIN. - TOTAL 35 MIN. - **SERVES 4**

Heat 1 Tbsp. canola oil in a saucepan over medium-low; cook ¼ cup chopped shallot, 1 Tbsp. finely chopped lemongrass, 1½ tsp. grated fresh ginger, and 1 tsp. chopped garlic until fragrant, 3 minutes. Add ¼ cup jarred red curry paste; cook 1 minute. Add 1½ cups reserved strained stock (or chicken broth), 1 (14-oz.) can coconut cream, and ½ of a thinly sliced red Fresno chile. Simmer, uncovered, until thickened, 15 minutes. Add 1 Tbsp. fresh lime juice and 2 tsp. fish sauce. Divide 3 cups cooked jasmine rice, 12 oz. sliced Chicken, and curry mixture among 4 bowls. Top with sliced red Fresno chile, basil leaves, and lime wedges.

Chicken Biscuit Sandwiches

ACTIVE 15 MIN. - TOTAL 15 MIN. - **SERVES 4**

Whisk together ¼ cup mayonnaise; 1½ Tbsp. apple cider vinegar; ½ tsp. black pepper; and ¼ tsp. each hot sauce, Worcestershire sauce, kosher salt, garlic powder, and granulated sugar in a large bowl. Add 12 oz. shredded, skinless Chicken; toss to coat. Combine 1 cup shredded red cabbage, 2 Tbsp. chopped scallions, 2 tsp. olive oil, and ¼ tsp. kosher salt. Top bottom halves of 8 split, toasted 2-inch buttermilk biscuits evenly with chicken mixture and red cabbage mixture. Top each with 3 sweet-hot pickle slices; cover with biscuit tops.

START WITH...

PORK CHOPS

The key to slow-cooked pork is choosing the right cut (shoulder blade chops) and brining it.

ACTIVE 25 MIN. - TOTAL 5 HOURS, 55 MIN.
SERVES 4

- 4 cups warm water
- 1/3 cup granulated sugar
- 2 tsp. mustard seeds
- 1 bay leaf
- 1/3 cup plus 1 1/2 tsp. kosher salt
- 2 (1-inch-thick) bone-in pork shoulder blade chops (about 3 1/4 lb. total)
- 3/4 tsp. black pepper
- 2 Tbsp. canola oil
- 2 medium-size yellow onions (about 1 lb.), sliced (about 4 cups)
- 1/2 cup apple cider
- 1/4 cup chicken broth
- 1 Tbsp. coarse-grain mustard

1. Combine first 4 ingredients and 1/3 cup of the salt in a large bowl; whisk until salt and sugar dissolve. Add pork chops, submerging completely; cover and chill 1 1/2 hours. Remove from brine; discard brine. Pat dry, and sprinkle with pepper and remaining 1 1/2 teaspoons salt.

2. Heat oil in a large skillet over medium-high. Cook pork chops until browned, 3 to 4 minutes per side. Remove from skillet. Add onions; cook, stirring occasionally, until softened, about 6 minutes. Add apple cider. Cook until reduced slightly, 2 minutes. Transfer onion mixture to a 6-quart slow cooker; stir in broth and mustard. Place pork chops on top of onion mixture. Cover; cook on LOW until pork is tender, 4 hours.

Caramelized Onion, Spinach, and Pork Strata

ACTIVE 20 MIN. - TOTAL 1 HOUR, 40 MIN.
SERVES 6

Toss 10 oz. (1-inch) French bread cubes with 3 Tbsp. olive oil, 1 tsp. kosher salt, and 1/2 tsp. black pepper. Bake at 375°F until lightly toasted, about 10 minutes. Heat 1 Tbsp. olive oil in a large nonstick skillet over medium-low. Add 4 cups chopped sweet onion and 1/2 tsp. kosher salt. Cook until deeply browned, about 30 minutes. Add 3 oz. chopped baby spinach; cook until wilted, about 1 1/2 minutes. Cool 15 minutes. Whisk together 6 large eggs, 2 cups whole milk, 2 tsp. kosher salt, and 1/2 tsp. each black pepper and dry mustard in a large bowl. Add 10 oz. chopped Pork Chops, 3 oz. shredded Swiss cheese, bread cubes, and onion mixture to egg mixture; stir to combine. Pour into a lightly greased 11- x 7-inch baking dish. Place on a rimmed baking sheet. Sprinkle with 3 oz. shredded Swiss cheese. Bake at 375°F until golden brown and set, about 45 minutes, shielding with foil during last 10 minutes to prevent excess browning, if needed.

Pork-and-Shaved Vegetable Salad

ACTIVE 35 MIN. - TOTAL 35 MIN. - **SERVES 4**

Combine 6 cups torn Lacinato kale, 2 cups shaved multicolored carrots, 1 cup shaved peeled parsnips, and 1 small peeled and thinly sliced golden beet in a large bowl. Cook 8 oz. chopped thick-cut bacon in a large skillet over medium until crisp, about 10 minutes. Remove bacon using a slotted spoon; drain on paper towels, and transfer to bowl with kale mixture. Reserve drippings in a bowl; wipe skillet clean. Cook 12 oz. sliced Pork Chops in 1 Tbsp. drippings over medium-high until browned, about 1 1/2 minutes per side. Remove and set aside. Reduce heat to medium-low. Add 1/4 cup drippings to skillet (adding olive oil, if needed). Add 1/2 cup thinly sliced shallot, 1/2 tsp. kosher salt, and 1/4 tsp. black pepper; cook until tender, about 3 minutes. Remove from heat; whisk in 1/4 cup sherry vinegar and 1 Tbsp. honey. Pour dressing over kale mixture; toss gently to coat. Top with pork and 1/2 cup candied pecans.

Sliced Pork Chops with Brown Butter-Golden Raisin Relish

ACTIVE 15 MIN. - TOTAL 40 MIN. - **SERVES 4**

Toss 1 lb. peeled sweet potatoes cut into wedges with 2 Tbsp. olive oil, 1 tsp. kosher salt, and 1/2 tsp. black pepper. Bake at 450°F until tender, about 25 minutes. Cook 1/3 cup unsalted butter in a small skillet over medium until foam subsides and butter is golden brown, about 4 minutes. Immediately transfer butter to a medium bowl. Add 1/2 cup golden raisins, 2 Tbsp. sherry vinegar, and 3/4 tsp. granulated sugar; stir to dissolve sugar. Let stand 10 minutes. Stir in 1/2 cup each chopped fresh flat-leaf parsley and Castelvetrano olives and 2 Tbsp. olive oil. Divide 3 cups cooked couscous among 4 plates; top with sliced Pork Chops and relish, and serve with sweet potatoes.

START WITH...

SALMON

Slow-cooking makes for a tender, not-one-bit-dry fillet. Use a fattier variety of salmon like king (Chinook) or Atlantic. Ask the fishmonger for the thickest piece. The parchment paper lining lets you poach and remove the whole fillet. An aromatic lemongrass blend flavors the salmon while elevating it for even cooking.

ACTIVE 15 MIN. - TOTAL 2 HOURS, 15 MIN.
SERVES 6

- **4** lemongrass stalks, bruised and cut into 4-inch pieces
- **1** fennel bulb (about 14 oz.), sliced
- **4** scallions, halved crosswise
- **⅓** cup water
- **⅓** cup dry white wine
- **1** (2-lb.) center-cut, skin-on salmon fillet
- **1** tsp. kosher salt
- **½** tsp. black pepper

1. Fold a 30- x 18-inch piece of parchment paper in half lengthwise; fold in half again crosswise (short end to short end) to create a 4-layer-thick piece. Place folded parchment in bottom of a 6-quart slow cooker, letting ends extend partially up sides.

2. Place half of lemongrass, fennel, and scallions in an even layer on parchment in slow cooker. Add water and wine. Sprinkle salmon with salt and pepper; place on lemongrass mixture. Top salmon with remaining lemongrass, scallions, and fennel. Cover and cook on HIGH just until salmon flakes easily with a fork, 1 to 2 hours. Using parchment paper liner as handles, lift salmon from slow cooker, allowing liquid to drain off. Discard mixture in slow cooker.

Salmon Bagel Sandwiches

ACTIVE 15 MIN. - TOTAL 15 MIN. - **SERVES 4**

Combine 4 oz. softened cream cheese, 3 Tbsp. each sliced fresh chives and finely chopped radishes, 2 tsp. chopped fresh dill, ½ tsp. lemon zest, and 1½ tsp. fresh lemon juice. Spread mixture on bottom halves of 4 split bagels with seeds, garlic, and onion (such as everything bagels). Divide 1 cup arugula, 8 oz. flaked Salmon, and ½ cup each thinly sliced red onion and English cucumber among bagel bottoms; cover with tops.

Teriyaki Salmon Bowls with Crispy Brussels Sprouts

ACTIVE 20 MIN. - TOTAL 30 MIN. - **SERVES 4**

Toss 12 oz. quartered Brussels sprouts with 1 Tbsp. olive oil, 1 tsp. kosher salt, and ½ tsp. black pepper on a rimmed baking sheet. Bake at 425°F until tender and starting to crisp, 20 to 25 minutes. Heat 1 Tbsp. olive oil in a skillet over medium-high, and cook 6 oz. sliced shiitake mushroom caps and ½ tsp. kosher salt until tender, 3 to 4 minutes. Add mushrooms to baking sheet with Brussels sprouts; wipe skillet clean. Cook ½ cup pineapple juice, 2 Tbsp. soy sauce, 1 Tbsp. brown sugar, and 1 tsp. cornstarch in skillet over medium, whisking constantly, until thickened, about 3 minutes. Brush ¼ cup sauce on about 1¼ lb. cooked Salmon; sprinkle with 1 tsp. sesame seeds. Place Salmon on baking sheet with mushrooms and Brussels sprouts; broil on HIGH 6 inches from heat until glaze has thickened, about 2 minutes. Divide 3 cups cooked brown rice among 4 bowls. Top evenly with Salmon, Brussels sprouts, mushrooms, and 1 cup matchstick carrots. Drizzle with remaining sauce; serve with lime wedges.

Citrus-Salmon Salad

ACTIVE 15 MIN. - TOTAL 15 MIN. - **SERVES 4**

Combine ¼ cup each white wine vinegar and thinly sliced shallots; let stand 5 minutes. Whisk in ⅓ cup extra-virgin olive oil, 2 Tbsp. fresh orange juice, 1 tsp. each honey and Dijon mustard, ½ tsp. each orange zest and kosher salt, and ¼ tsp. black pepper. Divide 6 oz. torn butter lettuce, 2 cups sliced Belgian endive, 1½ cups orange segments, 1 chopped ripe avocado, and 8 oz. flaked Salmon among 4 plates. Drizzle with dressing, and sprinkle with ¼ cup sliced toasted almonds.

START WITH...

BLACK BEANS

Soaking dried beans can make them mushy and bland. Instead, slow-cook them in broth kicked up with smoky bacon and sautéed aromatics.

ACTIVE 15 MIN. - TOTAL 6 HOURS, 15 MIN.
SERVES 6

- 1 lb. dried black beans
- 1 ½ tsp. canola oil
- 1 yellow onion, chopped (about 1 ¾ cups)
- 1 red bell pepper, chopped (about 1 cup)
- 3 thick-cut bacon slices, chopped (optional)
- 3 garlic cloves, chopped (about 1 Tbsp.)
- 1 jalapeño chile, halved lengthwise
- 6 cups lower-sodium chicken broth or vegetable broth
- 1 ½ tsp. kosher salt
- 1 tsp. light brown sugar
- 1 tsp. ground cumin
- ½ tsp. black pepper
- ½ tsp. chopped fresh oregano

1. Rinse and sort beans. Heat oil in a large skillet over medium-high. Add onion, bell pepper, and, if desired, bacon. Cook, stirring occasionally, until onions are tender, about 8 minutes. Add garlic, and cook, stirring often, until fragrant, about 30 seconds.
2. Transfer onion mixture to a 6-quart slow cooker; add beans, jalapeño chile, chicken broth, salt, brown sugar, cumin, pepper, and chopped oregano. Cover and cook on LOW until beans are tender, about 6 hours.

Black Bean Tostadas with Mango-Avocado Salsa

ACTIVE 10 MIN. - TOTAL 40 MIN. - **SERVES 4**

Boil ½ cup apple cider vinegar; ¼ cup water; and 2 tsp. each granulated sugar and kosher salt in a small saucepan over medium-high until sugar and salt dissolve, 3 to 5 minutes. Pour vinegar mixture over 1 cup thinly sliced red onion in a medium bowl; cover and chill at least 30 minutes. Toss together ½ cup each jicama matchsticks, chopped mango, and chopped ripe avocado; 2 Tbsp. each finely diced jalapeño chile and fresh cilantro; 1 Tbsp. fresh lime juice; 1 tsp. olive oil; and ½ tsp. kosher salt in a medium bowl. Lightly mash 2 cups drained Black Beans, 1 Tbsp. minced chipotle pepper in adobo sauce, and ¼ tsp. kosher salt; spread mixture on 4 corn tostada shells. Top with mango mixture and ¼ cup pickled red onions. Sprinkle tostadas with ¼ cup crumbled queso fresco (fresh Mexican cheese) and 1 Tbsp. chopped fresh cilantro.

Black Bean Burgers with Comeback Sauce

ACTIVE 25 MIN. - TOTAL 1 HOUR, 25 MIN. - **SERVES 4**

Stir together ¾ cup mayonnaise; 3 Tbsp. sweet chili sauce; ¾ tsp. smoked paprika; and 1 Tbsp. each ketchup, hot sauce, and Worcestershire sauce. Process 1 ½ cups drained Black Beans and ¼ cup mayonnaise mixture in a food processor until smooth, about 10 seconds. Stir together pureed bean mixture, 2 cups drained Black Beans, 1 large beaten egg, 1 ½ cups panko (Japanese-style breadcrumbs), 2 Tbsp. grated yellow onion, and 1 tsp. kosher salt in a large bowl. Cover and chill mixture 30 minutes. Form bean mixture into 4 (8 oz.) patties; chill 30 minutes. Heat 2 Tbsp. olive oil in a large cast-iron skillet over medium-high, and cook patties until they're heated through and a crust forms, about 4 minutes per side. Top each patty with 1 Muenster cheese slice; cook until melted. Divide remaining mayonnaise mixture evenly among 4 toasted brioche buns; add 1 patty, 1 butter lettuce leaf, and 2 tomato slices to each bun.

Shrimp, Sausage, and Black Bean Pasta

ACTIVE 25 MIN. - TOTAL 25 MIN. - **SERVES 6**

Heat 1 Tbsp. canola oil in a large skillet over medium-high, and cook 8 oz. diced andouille sausage until browned, about 4 minutes. Using a slotted spoon, transfer sausage to a plate. Add 1 Tbsp. canola oil, 1 lb. peeled and deveined large raw shrimp, and 1 tsp. Cajun seasoning to skillet. Cook until shrimp are opaque, 1 to 2 minutes per side. Remove shrimp to plate with sausage. Cook 12 oz. casarecce pasta in salted water according to package directions; drain. Meanwhile, add 1 Tbsp. canola oil; 2 tsp. chopped garlic, ¾ tsp. kosher salt; and 1 cup each chopped yellow onion and red bell pepper to skillet, and cook until tender, about 6 minutes. Remove from heat. Add sausage, shrimp, 1½ cups drained and rinsed Black Beans, hot cooked pasta, 4 Tbsp. unsalted butter, and 2 Tbsp. fresh lemon juice. Toss until butter is melted and pasta is evenly coated, about 3 minutes. Garnish with ¼ cup sliced scallions.

Florida Orange Grove Pie, page 53

A League of Their Own

Five incredible desserts that celebrate two beloved things in the South: citrus season and Junior League cookbooks

Junior Leagues are fixtures of the Southern social and civic scene, throwing great parties and orchestrating some of the most formidable fund-raising endeavors in the country. For at least 50 years, one of the most effective methods of raising money was through the creation of a cookbook that cataloged and celebrated the food of a community.

Compared to a simple black-and-white, comb-bound paperback from a small-town volunteer fire department, a Junior League cookbook looks more like a bookstore best seller. With fetching hardback covers, tested recipes, edited text, and color photographs, some of these publications are as much at home on a coffee table as they are on a kitchen counter.

Junior League cookbooks, especially the vintage volumes, memorialize a sense of time and place. The best ones enshrine these women and the worlds they lived in. If a cookbook hails from your hometown, it's a part of that community's history. If it has your mother's name in it, it's a family heirloom.

Of course, the recipes are usually fabulous, because what league member would deign to share a bland or boring dish? We combed through iconic Junior League cookbooks and chose five desserts that showcase this year's fresh crop of winter citrus. Like all of the other recipes featured in the pages of this magazine, they had to pass muster in our own Test Kitchen. Not surprisingly, each one earned rave reviews, although we couldn't resist adding a few of our own twists here and there.

A classic Junior League cookbook does plenty of good in ways beyond what we usually consider community service. It fills the gaps in our recollections and renditions of cherished dishes on our family tables, rekindling old culinary flames and reminding us to pass along our treasured food memories.

Florida Orange Grove Pie

The Gasparilla Cookbook

TAMPA, FLORIDA

This is a great old-timey angel pie with a crust made of baked meringue instead of pastry. In a state where orange groves still cover miles of farmland, of course a cook would turn to citrus to pile atop the crisp candy-like crust. Originally published in 1961, *The Gasparilla Cookbook* exhibits the melding of Spanish, Italian, Greek, Cuban, and Southern influences on the recipes of the region. It appears in the McIlhenny Hall of Fame for community cookbooks that sell more than 100,000 copies.

Florida Orange Grove Pie

ACTIVE 30 MIN. - TOTAL 4 HOURS, 30 MIN.

SERVES 6 TO 8

- **4 large egg whites**
- **1/4 tsp. cream of tartar**
- **1 1/2 cups granulated sugar**
- **5 Tbsp. finely chopped walnuts**
- **5 large egg yolks**
- **2 Tbsp. fresh lemon juice (from 1 lemon)**
- **1/8 tsp. salt**
- **3 Tbsp. orange zest (from 1 large orange)**
- **2 cups heavy cream**
- **2 Tbsp. powdered sugar**
- **1 (20-oz.) jar refrigerated mandarin orange segments (such as Del Monte), drained**

1. Preheat oven to 275°F. Beat egg whites with an electric mixer on medium speed until foamy, about 1 minute; beat in cream of tartar. Increase speed to high, and beat until medium peaks form, about 2 minutes. Add 1 cup of the granulated sugar, 1 tablespoon at a time, beating well after each addition. Beat on high speed until stiff peaks form, about 2 to 3 minutes.

2. Spread meringue on bottom and up sides of a 9-inch glass or ceramic pie plate coated with cooking spray. Sprinkle chopped walnuts over edge of meringue, lightly pressing to adhere. Bake in preheated oven until lightly browned, about 1 hour. Cool completely on a wire rack, about 30 minutes.

3. Whisk together egg yolks, lemon juice, salt, 2 1/2 tablespoons of the zest, and remaining 1/2 cup granulated sugar in the top of a double boiler. Cook over simmering water, stirring constantly, until mixture thickens, about 8 to 10 minutes. Place top of double boiler in a bowl of ice water, and let stand, stirring occasionally, until completely chilled, about 20 minutes. Transfer mixture to a medium bowl.

4. Beat cream and powdered sugar with electric mixer on high speed until medium peaks form, about 3 to 4 minutes.

5. Stir 1/2 cup of the whipped cream into egg-citrus mixture. Gently fold 1 cup of the whipped cream into egg-citrus mixture. Gently fold 1 cup of the mandarin orange segments into mixture. Transfer to prepared meringue pie shell, smoothing top. Mound remaining whipped cream on top of pie, making a well in the center. Arrange remaining orange segments on top center of pie. Sprinkle with remaining 1/2 tablespoon orange zest. Chill 2 to 3 hours before serving.

Lemon-Orange Pound Cake

Stop and Smell the Rosemary

HOUSTON, TEXAS

Stop and Smell the Rosemary was a sea change in community cookbooks, even among Junior League versions, raising the bar for self-published titles across the nation. Since it first appeared in 1996, it has received numerous awards and accolades for being one of the best community cookbooks in the country. It includes a recipe for Lemon-Orange Pound Cake, which is sublime in its simplicity, but we decided to fancy it up a bit with a Bundt pan and two contrasting icings.

Lemon-Orange Pound Cake

ACTIVE 25 MIN. - TOTAL 2 HOURS, 20 MIN.
SERVES 10 TO 12

CAKE
- **2 cups granulated sugar**
- **½ cup unsalted butter, softened, plus more for greasing pan**
- **½ cup vegetable shortening**
- **6 large eggs**
- **3 cups all-purpose flour, plus more for pan**
- **1½ tsp. baking powder**
- **½ tsp. salt**
- **½ tsp. baking soda**
- **1 cup whole buttermilk**
- **1 tsp. vanilla extract**
- **1 tsp. lemon extract**

VANILLA ICING
- **2 cups powdered sugar**
- **3 Tbsp. whole milk**
- **¼ tsp. vanilla extract**

LEMON-ORANGE ICING
- **2 cups powdered sugar**
- **1 Tbsp. fresh lemon juice**
- **1 Tbsp. fresh orange juice**
- **1 drop of yellow food coloring gel**

ADDITIONAL INGREDIENTS
- **Thin lemon or orange slices (optional)**

1. Prepare the Cake: Preheat oven to 350°F. Grease and flour a 12-cup Bundt pan.

2. Beat sugar, butter, and shortening in a large bowl with an electric mixer on medium speed until light and fluffy, 5 to 6 minutes. Add eggs, 1 at a time, beating well after each addition.

3. Whisk together flour, baking powder, salt, and baking soda in a bowl. Alternately add flour mixture and buttermilk to butter mixture in 5 additions, beginning and ending with flour mixture, beating until blended after each addition. Beat in vanilla and lemon extracts. Transfer batter to prepared pan; smooth top. Bake in preheated oven until a wooden pick inserted in the center comes out clean, 45 to 50 minutes. Cool in pan on a wire rack 10 minutes; remove from pan, and cool completely on rack, 30 to 40 minutes.

4. Prepare the Vanilla Icing: Whisk together powdered sugar, milk, and vanilla in a bowl until smooth. Drizzle icing over Cake, letting it drip down sides. Refrigerate 10 minutes to allow icing to set.

5. Prepare the Lemon-Orange Icing: Whisk together powdered sugar, fresh lemon and orange juices, and yellow food coloring gel in a bowl until smooth. Drizzle Lemon-Orange Icing over Vanilla Icing, letting it drip down sides. Let stand until set, about 20 minutes. Garnish with thin lemon or orange slices, if desired.

Shaker Lemon Pie

Mountain Measures

CHARLESTON, WEST VIRGINIA

This old-fashioned pie is made with thinly sliced whole lemons–peels and all. The recipe originated in Shaker communities in areas where the South meets New England and the Midwest. Shaker cooks considered lemons an important part of a healthy diet, even though they were expensive and hard to come by, so they devised this pie to make use of every bit of the fruit. The Charleston, West Virginia, Junior League included this Shaker Lemon Pie in its 1974 *Mountain Measures* cookbook, and it's been a favorite of bakers ever since.

Shaker Lemon Pie

ACTIVE 15 MIN. - TOTAL 4 HOURS, 55 MIN.
SERVES 6 TO 8

- **2 lemons (about 9 oz. each), sliced paper thin (rind and all)**
- **2 cups granulated sugar**
- **4 large eggs, lightly beaten**
- **1 (14.1-oz.) pkg. refrigerated piecrusts (such as Pillsbury)**
- **Vanilla ice cream (optional)**

1. Combine lemon slices and sugar in a shallow bowl; let stand until lemon slices are juicy, 4 hours or overnight. Remove any seeds that float to the surface.
2. Preheat oven to 450°F. Stir eggs into lemon mixture thoroughly.
3. Line a 9-inch pie plate with 1 piecrust. Pour lemon mixture into shell. Cover with top crust, and crimp edges. Cut decorative steam vents in top crust.
4. Bake at 450°F for 15 minutes. Without removing pie from oven, reduce temperature to 350°F. Bake until a knife inserted in center comes out clean, about 25 minutes. Cover piecrust edges with aluminum foil, if becoming too brown. Serve pie warm or at room temperature. Top slices with vanilla ice cream, if desired.

Cold Lemon Soufflés with Wine Sauce

A Sterling Collection

MEMPHIS, TENNESSEE

Soufflés have always been an expression of elegant entertaining, but this one is chilled and held in place with a bit of gelatin, which means the hostess doesn't have to rush the quivering creation to the table before it collapses. *A Sterling Collection* is a compilation of favorite recipes gleaned from a number of cookbooks produced by the Memphis chapter. This soufflé also appeared in an anthology of best Junior League recipes in the country, so it's a keeper for sure.

Cold Lemon Soufflés with Wine Sauce

ACTIVE 55 MIN. - TOTAL 3 HOURS, 15 MIN.
SERVES 8

SOUFFLÉS

- **1 (¼-oz.) envelope unflavored gelatin**
- **¼ cup cold water**
- **5 large eggs, separated**
- **2 tsp. lemon zest plus ¾ cup fresh juice (from about 5 lemons)**
- **1½ cups granulated sugar**
- **1 cup heavy cream**

WINE SAUCE

- **½ cup granulated sugar**
- **1 Tbsp. cornstarch**
- **½ cup water**
- **1 tsp. lemon zest plus 3 Tbsp. fresh juice (from 1 lemon) and more zest for topping (optional)**
- **2 Tbsp. salted butter**
- **½ cup dry white wine**

1. Prepare the Soufflés: Sprinkle gelatin over cold water in a small bowl. Let stand 5 minutes.
2. Combine egg yolks, lemon zest, lemon juice, and ¾ cup of the sugar in top of a double boiler over boiling water. Cook, stirring constantly, until lemon mixture is slightly thickened, 8 to 10 minutes. Remove pan from heat, and stir in gelatin until completely combined and smooth. Transfer mixture to a large bowl. Place bowl in an ice bath, and

let stand, stirring occasionally until mixture has cooled, about 15 minutes. Thoroughly clean top of double boiler.
3. Combine egg whites and remaining ¾ cup granulated sugar in top of double boiler over simmering water; cook, stirring constantly, until sugar dissolves and mixture is hot, 4 to 5 minutes. Transfer into a medium bowl, and beat with an electric mixer on high speed until medium peaks form, 7 to 8 minutes.
4. Beat cream with electric mixer on high speed until medium peaks form, 3 to 4 minutes.
5. Gently fold egg white mixture into yolk mixture. Gently fold whipped cream into egg mixture. Divide Soufflé mixture evenly among 8 (8-ounce) ramekins or dessert glasses. Cover and chill 2 hours or overnight.
6. Prepare the Wine Sauce: Whisk together sugar and cornstarch in a small saucepan. Stir in water, lemon zest, and lemon juice until smooth. Bring to a boil over medium-high; reduce heat to medium, and cook until thickened, about 3 minutes. Remove from heat, and stir in salted butter until melted and combined; stir in dry white wine. Cover and chill until ready to serve. Drizzle Wine Sauce over Soufflés, and sprinkle with lemon zest, if desired.

Grand Marnier Cakes

Tea-Time at the Masters

AUGUSTA, GEORGIA

Layer cakes might be the cover girls, but a pound cake holds sway in our kitchens. This recipe reflects the Southern practice of adding a bit of liqueur or other spirits to a cake to ensure it stays moist and delicious. Many cookbook collectors swear by this beloved book that debuted in 1977, suggesting that an Augusta tee time is prestigious but an Augusta teatime is priceless. While the original recipe called for the cake to be baked in a tube pan, we opted for mini Bundt pans for a tea party-worthy presentation.

Grand Marnier Cakes

ACTIVE 25 MIN. - TOTAL 1 HOUR
SERVES 12

CAKES
- 2 ½ cups all-purpose flour, plus more for pan
- 1 ½ tsp. baking powder
- 1 tsp. baking soda
- ¼ tsp. salt
- 1 ¼ cups granulated sugar
- 1 cup salted butter, plus more for pan
- 3 large eggs
- 1 cup sour cream
- 2 Tbsp. orange zest (from 1 large orange)
- ½ cup finely chopped roasted blanched almonds

GLAZE
- ½ cup granulated sugar
- ½ cup orange liqueur (such as Grand Marnier)
- ¼ cup fresh orange juice (from 1 large orange)

ADDITIONAL INGREDIENTS
- 1 cup heavy cream
- 1 Tbsp. powdered sugar
- Orange segments, such as blood orange, navel, or mandarin (optional)

1. Prepare the Cakes: Preheat oven to 325°F. Grease and flour 12 mini Bundt pans.

2. Whisk together flour, baking powder, baking soda, and salt in a bowl.
3. Beat sugar and butter with an electric mixer on medium speed until light and fluffy, 4 to 5 minutes. Add eggs, 1 at a time, beating well after each addition.
4. Add flour mixture and sour cream to sugar mixture in 5 additions, beginning and ending with flour mixture. Add orange zest and almonds, and beat on medium speed until combined.
5. Divide batter evenly among prepared Bundt pans, and smooth tops. Bake in preheated oven until a wooden pick inserted in center comes out clean, 16 to 18 minutes. Let stand in pans on a wire rack 10 minutes; remove from pans to wire rack.
6. Prepare the Glaze: Combine sugar, orange liqueur, and orange juice in a small saucepan; bring to a boil over medium, stirring constantly until sugar dissolves. Brush hot Glaze over warm Cakes.
7. Beat heavy cream and powdered sugar with electric mixer on high speed until medium peaks form, about 3 to 4 minutes. Top each of the glazed Cakes with a dollop of whipped cream, and garnish with orange segments, if desired.

Super Bowls

Our game plan for beating the weeknight rush? Whip up wholesome, hearty dinners that will please everyone around the table

Cuban Black Bean-and-Yellow Rice Bowls

Brighten up dinnertime with this colorful, customizable meal. Start with bowls filled with rice, black beans, and plantains, and then let everyone add their favorite toppings.

ACTIVE 15 MIN. - TOTAL 50 MIN.

SERVES 4

- **2 ripe plantains, peeled and diagonally sliced ½ inch thick (about 1 lb.)**
- **2 Tbsp. olive oil**
- **1 tsp. kosher salt**
- **1 (10-oz.) pkg. yellow rice**
- **1 small jalapeño chile, seeded and finely chopped (about 1 Tbsp.)**
- **1¼ cups chopped red onion (from 1 onion)**
- **2 (16-oz.) cans seasoned black beans, drained (do not rinse)**
- **¼ cup water**
- **1 tsp. ground cumin**
- **4 radishes (about 3 oz.), chopped**
- **1 ripe avocado, diced**
- **¼ cup chopped fresh cilantro**
- **1 lime, quartered**

1. Preheat oven to 400°F. Line a baking sheet with parchment paper. Place plantain slices in a single layer on parchment; drizzle with 1 tablespoon of the oil, and sprinkle with ½ teaspoon of the salt. Roast in preheated oven until lightly browned and very tender, 16 to 18 minutes. Set aside.

2. Prepare rice according to package directions.

3. While rice and plantains cook, heat remaining 1 tablespoon oil in a saucepan over medium. Add jalapeño and 1 cup of the red onion; cook, stirring often, until tender, about 3 minutes. Stir in black beans, water, cumin, and remaining ½ teaspoon salt; cook until liquid is slightly reduced, 5 to 6 minutes.

4. Divide cooked rice evenly among 4 bowls. Top each with beans, roasted plantains, chopped radishes, and diced avocado. Sprinkle with chopped cilantro and remaining ¼ cup red onion. Serve with lime wedges.

Soba Noodle-and-Shrimp Bowls

Buckwheat flour gives soba noodles an earthy, nutty flavor that is a great match for shrimp. Rinse the noodles when you drain them to remove any excess starch, which can cause them to stick together. Before seasoning the shrimp, pat them dry with paper towels to help them form a nice crust in the skillet.

ACTIVE 25 MIN. - TOTAL 35 MIN.
SERVES 4

- **1 (8-oz.) pkg. soba noodles**
- **3 Tbsp. rice vinegar**
- **3 Tbsp. sesame oil**
- **3 Tbsp. soy sauce**
- **2 Tbsp. light brown sugar**
- **1 Tbsp. Sriracha chili sauce**
- **1½ lb. large peeled and deveined raw shrimp**
- **½ tsp. kosher salt**
- **½ tsp. black pepper**
- **½ tsp. garlic powder**
- **2 Tbsp. canola oil**
- **1½ cups matchstick carrots**
- **1½ cups snow peas (about 4 oz.)**
- **½ cup thinly sliced red onion (from 1 small onion)**
- **Chopped fresh cilantro (optional)**

1. Cook noodles according to package directions; drain and chill until ready to serve. Whisk together rice vinegar, sesame oil, soy sauce, brown sugar, and Sriracha in a bowl; set aside.
2. Pat shrimp dry with paper towels; sprinkle evenly with salt, pepper, and garlic powder. Heat 1 tablespoon of the oil in a large skillet over medium-high. Add shrimp; cook, stirring often, until slightly crispy and cooked through, 3 to 4 minutes. Transfer shrimp to a plate, and cover with aluminum foil to keep warm.
3. Wipe skillet clean, and add remaining 1 tablespoon oil. Add carrots, snow peas, and red onion; cook over medium-high, stirring often, until vegetables are tender-crisp, 4 to 5 minutes. Remove from heat, and toss with 3 tablespoons of the vinegar mixture.
4. Toss chilled noodles with ¼ cup of the vinegar mixture; divide evenly among 4 bowls. Top each with vegetable mixture and shrimp. Sprinkle with cilantro, if desired, and serve with the remaining vinegar mixture.

Couscous Pilaf with Roasted Carrots, Chicken, and Feta

Flavored with golden raisins, toasted almonds, and an ingeniously simple lemon-brown butter sauce, this fluffy couscous is delicious on its own, but roasted carrots and chicken turn it into a memorable one-bowl meal.

ACTIVE 20 MIN. - TOTAL 1 HOUR, 5 MIN.
SERVES 4

- **4 large carrots, peeled and diagonally sliced ¼ inch thick (about 12 oz.)**
- **1 Tbsp. olive oil**
- **¼ tsp. black pepper**
- **1 tsp. kosher salt**
- **½ cup butter**
- **2 tsp. lemon zest, plus ¼ cup fresh juice (from 1 large lemon)**
- **1½ cups water**
- **1 cup uncooked couscous**
- **½ cup golden raisins**
- **⅓ cup chopped fresh flat-leaf parsley, plus more for garnish**
- **¼ cup sliced toasted almonds**
- **2 cups shredded rotisserie chicken, warmed (about 12 oz., from 1 chicken)**
- **2 oz. feta cheese, crumbled (about ½ cup)**

1. Preheat oven to 450°F. Combine carrots, oil, pepper, and ½ teaspoon of the salt on a large rimmed baking sheet. Toss to coat; spread in an even layer. Bake in preheated oven until tender, 16 to 18 minutes, stirring once. Remove from oven.
2. While carrots roast, melt butter in a small saucepan over medium-high. Cook until milk solids turn golden brown and have a nutty fragrance, swirling pan occasionally as mixture bubbles, about 5 minutes. Transfer to a bowl; let stand 1 minute. Stir in lemon juice; set aside.
3. Bring water and remaining ½ teaspoon salt to a boil in a medium saucepan over high. Stir in couscous. Cover and remove from heat; let stand 5 minutes. Fluff with a fork; stir in raisins, parsley, almonds, and 5 tablespoons of the browned butter mixture.
4. Combine carrots, chicken, and 2 tablespoons of the browned butter mixture in a bowl; toss to coat. Divide couscous pilaf evenly among 4 bowls; top with chicken-carrot mixture. Sprinkle with cheese; drizzle with remaining 1 tablespoon browned butter mixture. Top with lemon zest and parsley.

Pork-and-Farro Bowl with Warm Brussels Sprouts-Fennel Salad

We paired a warm vegetable salad with whole-grain farro and pork tenderloin for a healthy meal that's still hearty. Fresh tarragon in the vinaigrette brings out the anise notes in the fennel, but you can substitute fresh thyme or rosemary if you prefer a milder flavor.

ACTIVE 30 MIN. - TOTAL 55 MIN.
SERVES 4

- 2 Tbsp. apple cider vinegar
- 2 tsp. chopped fresh tarragon
- 1 tsp. Dijon mustard
- 1 tsp. honey
- 6 Tbsp. olive oil
- 1 ¼ tsp. kosher salt
- ¾ tsp. black pepper
- 1 (1-lb.) pork tenderloin
- 1 cup quick-cooking farro
- 12 oz. Brussels sprouts, thinly sliced (about 4 cups)
- 1 fennel bulb (about 6 oz.), thinly sliced (about 2 ½ cups), fronds torn and reserved for garnish
- 2 Tbsp. thinly sliced shallot (from 1 medium shallot)
- 1 medium Fuji apple, chopped

1. Whisk together vinegar, tarragon, mustard, honey, 4 tablespoons of the oil, ½ teaspoon of the salt, and ¼ teaspoon of the pepper in a small bowl.
2. Preheat oven to 400°F. Heat a cast-iron skillet over medium-high. Sprinkle ½ teaspoon of the salt and remaining ½ teaspoon pepper on all sides of the pork. Add 1 tablespoon of the oil to skillet; swirl to coat. Place pork in skillet, and cook, turning to brown on all sides, 3 to 4 minutes. Transfer to a rimmed baking sheet; place in preheated oven. Cook until a thermometer inserted in thickest portion registers 145°F, 10 to 15 minutes. Transfer to a cutting board; let rest 10 minutes.
3. Meanwhile, prepare farro according to package directions. Drain; stir together farro and 2 tablespoons of the vinaigrette.
4. Heat remaining 1 tablespoon oil in cast-iron skillet over medium-high. Add Brussels sprouts, fennel, shallots, and remaining ¼ teaspoon salt; cook, stirring, until wilted, 5 to 6 minutes. Add 2 tablespoons of the vinaigrette; toss to coat.
5. Slice pork. Divide farro, Brussels sprouts mixture, and pork evenly among 4 bowls. Top with apple; drizzle with remaining vinaigrette. Garnish with fennel fronds.

Skirt Steak and Cauliflower Rice with Red Pepper Sauce

No longer just a trend, cauliflower "rice" crumbles can be found in many grocery stores. They make a tasty (and low-carb) substitute for grains.

ACTIVE 30 MIN. - TOTAL 40 MIN.
SERVES 4

- ¾ cup sliced roasted red bell pepper
- 2 Tbsp. chopped shallot
- 1 Tbsp. seeded, chopped red Fresno chile (from 1 chile)
- 1 tsp. minced garlic
- ½ tsp. paprika
- 1 Tbsp. plus 1 tsp. red wine vinegar
- 6 Tbsp. plus 1 tsp. olive oil
- 2 ½ tsp. kosher salt
- 1 lb. skirt steak
- ½ tsp. black pepper
- 2 scallions
- 2 (1-lb.) pkg. riced cauliflower or 7 cups crumbles from 1 (2 ½-lb.) head cauliflower
- ¼ cup chopped fresh flat-leaf parsley
- 2 cups arugula (about 2 oz.)

1. Combine roasted bell pepper, shallot, chile, garlic, paprika, 1 tablespoon of the vinegar, 2 tablespoons of the oil, and ½ teaspoon of the salt in a food processor. Process until smooth, stopping to scrape down sides of the bowl, if needed.
2. Pat steak dry; sprinkle both sides with pepper and 1 teaspoon of the salt. Heat 1 tablespoon of the oil in a large cast-iron skillet over high. Add steak to skillet; cook to desired degree of doneness, 4 to 5 minutes per side for medium. Transfer to a cutting board; let rest 10 minutes.
3. Meanwhile, chop scallions, keeping white and green parts separate. Wipe skillet clean. Heat 3 tablespoons of the oil in skillet over high. Add white scallion parts; cook, stirring often, until slightly softened, 2 minutes. Add riced cauliflower and remaining 1 teaspoon salt; cook, stirring often, until cauliflower is tender, about 5 minutes. Remove from heat; stir in parsley.
4. Whisk together remaining 1 teaspoon each of oil and vinegar in a bowl. Add arugula; toss to coat. Cut steak across the grain into thin slices.
5. Divide cauliflower rice evenly among 4 bowls; top with steak, arugula, and sauce. Sprinkle with green scallion parts.

The Mystery of Hummingbird Cake

Forty years later, we have yet to untangle the story behind our most popular three-layer dessert

IT'S HARD TO TELL the story of Southern food sometimes. Our recipe boxes are littered with half-truths, sort-of-remembered details, and threats of "I'd tell you, but I'd have to kill you." Red velvet cake isn't Southern–it started as Waldorf Astoria cake. The backstory: Someone got charged a mint for the hotel's recipe and then shared it for revenge. It's the forerunner to the notorious Neiman Marcus cookie recipe, which isn't from the Dallas-based department store either. Notice a pattern here?

This leads us to the Hummingbird Cake, which was first submitted to *Southern Living* in 1978 by Mrs. L.H. Wiggins of Greensboro, North Carolina, and has become the magazine's most popular recipe since. Indisputably, it is a beautiful cake: three layers flavored with canned pineapple and bananas and topped with Cream Cheese Frosting. The oil-and-egg batter is simply stirred together, skipping the creaming business and creating a moist cake that keeps well. And who can resist that name?

Dig deeper, though, and the story doesn't hum smoothly. Only a little is known about Mrs. Wiggins: She was a widow from Virginia who evidently worked as a housemother at The University of North Carolina at Greensboro, and she died in 1995 at the age of 81. But we don't really know much more beyond that. Carl Wilson of the *Greensboro News & Record* recalls the paper running a story in 2014 asking for anyone who knew her, but they didn't get a single reply. He says, "The mystery of Mrs. L.H. Wiggins still remains."

Then there's the cake itself. Mrs. Wiggins may have been the first to create a layered version, but she wasn't the first to make the cake. It started as a tube cake with no icing. Simple spiced cakes with canned pineapple and bananas popped up in community cookbooks throughout the early Twentieth Century, when these once-exotic fruits became more commonplace in grocery stores. The recipes usually sported names like A Cake that Lasts (most likely because it stayed moist and kept well) or Bird of Paradise Cake.

Helen Moore, the former food editor of *The Charlotte Observer*, ran a version of the dessert on September 7, 1969, noting, "I came across a recipe called Doctor Bird Cake." She also explained that the doctorbird is a nickname given to the swallow-tailed hummingbird, Jamaica's national bird. The cake was baked in an 8-inch tube pan, and it included undrained, canned crushed pineapple; diced bananas; and no frosting.

In 1980, Moore repeated the recipe, this time explaining that it came in a letter from a Jamaican airline, apparently part of a press packet promoting island trips. In this version, though, the tube pan had grown to 10 inches, the bananas were mashed instead of sliced, the batter included 2 cups of chopped nuts, and the cake now had a rich cream cheese frosting.

Here we are, 40 years later but no closer to the truth. Was the cake's origin really Jamaican, or was it a convenient recipe that sounded somewhat tropical? Mrs. Wiggins flitted into our lives and moved on quickly, just like hummingbirds in the summertime. She left us with a nice cake, though. That's plenty to remember her by.

Hummingbird Cake

ACTIVE 20 MIN. - TOTAL 2 HOURS

SERVES 12

CAKE LAYERS

- **3 cups all-purpose flour, plus more for pans**
- **2 cups granulated sugar**
- **1 tsp. salt**
- **1 tsp. baking soda**
- **1 tsp. ground cinnamon**
- **3 large eggs, beaten**
- **1½ cups vegetable oil**
- **1½ tsp. vanilla extract**
- **1 (8-oz.) can crushed pineapple in juice, undrained**
- **2 cups chopped ripe bananas (about 6 bananas)**
- **1 cup chopped toasted pecans**
- **Vegetable shortening**

CREAM CHEESE FROSTING

- **2 (8-oz.) pkg. cream cheese, softened**
- **1 cup salted butter or margarine, softened**
- **2 (16-oz.) pkg. powdered sugar**
- **2 tsp. vanilla extract**

ADDITIONAL INGREDIENT

- **¾ cup toasted pecan halves**

1. Prepare the Cake Layers: Preheat oven to 350°F. Whisk together flour, sugar, salt, baking soda, and cinnamon in a large bowl; add eggs and oil, stirring just until dry ingredients are moistened. Stir in vanilla, pineapple, bananas, and toasted pecans.

2. Divide batter evenly among 3 well-greased (with shortening) and floured 9-inch round cake pans.

3. Bake in preheated oven until a wooden pick inserted in center comes out clean, 25 to 30 minutes. Cool in pans on wire racks 10 minutes. Remove from pans to wire racks, and cool completely, about 1 hour.

4. Prepare the Cream Cheese Frosting: Beat cream cheese and butter with an electric mixer on medium-low speed until smooth. Gradually add powdered sugar, beating at low speed until blended after each addition. Stir in vanilla. Increase speed to medium-high, and beat until fluffy, 1 to 2 minutes.

5. Assemble cake: Place 1 Cake Layer on a serving platter; spread top with 1 cup of the frosting. Top with second layer, and spread with 1 cup frosting. Top with third layer, and spread remaining frosting over top and sides of cake. Arrange pecan halves on top of cake.

For a fancy finish, gently press ½ cup chopped toasted pecans around the sides of the frosted layer cake.

Our classic cake recipe makes two dozen cupcakes. Top them with sparkling pineapple wedges.

INGREDIENTS FOR SUCCESS

VEGETABLE OIL
This cake gets its moist, quick-bread-like texture from vegetable oil instead of butter.

CANNED PINEAPPLE
Do not drain the juice; it adds flavor to the cake batter and keeps it moist.

BANANAS
Pick out a ripe but not overripe bunch (look for brown flecks on the skin).

PECANS
Toast the nuts for the most flavor.

Hummingbird Cupcakes

ACTIVE 20 MIN. - TOTAL 1 HOUR, 10 MIN.

MAKES 24 CUPCAKES

Prepare batter for Cake Layers as directed in Step 1 (page 61). Place 24 paper baking cups in 2 (12-cup) standard-size muffin pans. Spoon batter into prepared cups, filling about three-fourths full. Bake at 350°F until a wooden pick inserted in center comes out clean, 18 to 20 minutes. Remove from pans to wire racks, and cool completely, about 30 minutes. Prepare Cream Cheese Frosting as directed in Step 4 (page 61), and pipe or spread onto cupcakes. Garnish with Candied Pineapple Wedges, if desired.

Candied Pineapple Wedges

ACTIVE 15 MIN. - TOTAL 15 MIN.

MAKES 24 WEDGES

Slice 6 candied dried pineapple rings into 4 wedges each. Microwave ¼ cup light corn syrup in a small microwavable bowl on HIGH until warm, about 10 seconds. Brush wedges with warm corn syrup, and sprinkle with desired amount of yellow sparkling sugar and pale yellow sanding sugar. Use immediately.

Game Day Potatoes

Kick off the Super Bowl with these crowd-pleasing one-bite appetizers

Mini Potato Skins

These appetizers were made to travel. To take them to a party, prepare the recipe through Step 3, and place potato skins in a container. Complete Step 4 before serving.

ACTIVE 30 MIN. TOTAL 1 HOUR, 45 MIN.
SERVES 20

- 1–1 ½ lb. Baby Dutch Yellow potatoes (about 20 [2-inch] potatoes)
- 1 Tbsp. olive oil
- 4 oz. sharp Cheddar cheese, shredded (about 1 cup)
- 6 bacon slices, cooked and crumbled
- ½ cup sour cream
- 2 Tbsp. chopped fresh chives

1. Preheat oven to 425°F. Scrub potatoes, and pat dry thoroughly. Place potatoes in a large bowl, and drizzle with olive oil; toss to coat. Arrange potatoes in a single layer on a baking sheet lined with parchment paper. Bake in preheated oven until tender, 17 to 20 minutes. Cool potatoes completely on baking sheet, about 30 minutes.
2. Slice potatoes in half lengthwise, and scoop out potato flesh, leaving ⅛-inch-thick shell. Reserve potato flesh for another use (such as mashed potatoes).
3. Increase oven temperature to 450°F. Place potato skins, hollowed side down, on baking sheet lined with parchment paper. Bake at 450°F for 10 minutes; flip potatoes over, and bake until crispy, 8 to 10 minutes longer.
4. Fill potato skins evenly with Cheddar cheese, and top with bacon crumbles. Bake at 450°F until cheese melts, 1 to 2 minutes. Top each potato skin with a dollop of sour cream, and sprinkle evenly with chopped fresh chives.

The King of Cakes

Our resident queen of confections, Pam Lolley, puts a new twist on this celebratory dessert

A ribbon of Praline-Cream Cheese Filling runs through this sweet bread.

Praline-Cream Cheese King Cakes

ACTIVE 45 MIN. - TOTAL 5 HOURS

MAKES 2 CAKES

DOUGH

- 1 (16-oz.) container sour cream
- 1/4 cup butter
- 1 tsp. salt
- 1/3 cup plus 1 Tbsp. granulated sugar
- 2 (1/4-oz.) envelopes active dry yeast
- 1/2 cup warm water (100°F to 110°F)
- 2 large eggs, lightly beaten
- 6 3/4 cups bread flour

PRALINE-CREAM CHEESE FILLING

- 2 (8-oz.) pkg. cream cheese, softened
- 1/2 cup granulated sugar
- 1/4 cup packed dark brown sugar
- 2 tsp. ground cinnamon
- 2 tsp. vanilla extract
- 1 large egg
- 1 cup finely chopped toasted pecans

CREAMY VANILLA GLAZE

- 3 cups (about 12 oz.) powdered sugar
- 3 Tbsp. butter, melted
- 2 tsp. vanilla extract
- 3–4 Tbsp. whole milk

ADDITIONAL INGREDIENTS

Purple, green, and gold/yellow sparkling sugars

1. Prepare the Dough: Combine sour cream, butter, salt, and 1/3 cup of the sugar in a saucepan over medium-low. Cook, stirring, until butter melts, 5 minutes. Remove from heat; cool to 100°F to 110°F, 15 minutes.

2. Stir together yeast, water, and remaining 1 tablespoon granulated sugar in a 1-cup glass measuring cup; let stand 5 minutes.

3. Combine sour cream mixture, yeast mixture, 2 eggs, and 2 cups of the flour in the bowl of a heavy-duty electric stand mixer fitted with paddle attachment. Beat at medium speed until smooth, 1 minute. Reduce speed to low; gradually add 4 cups of the flour, beating until Dough forms.

4. Turn out onto a surface dusted with 1/4 cup of the flour. Knead, gradually adding remaining 1/2 cup flour, 2 tablespoons at a time, until smooth and elastic, about 10 minutes. (It should be tacky but release easily from surface.) Place in a well-greased bowl; turn to grease top. Cover; let rise in a warm place (85°F) until doubled in bulk, 45 minutes to 1 hour.

5. Meanwhile, prepare the Praline-Cream Cheese Filling: Beat cream cheese, sugars, cinnamon, and vanilla with an electric mixer on medium speed until smooth. Beat in egg.

6. Prepare the baked cakes: Gently punch Dough down; divide in half. On a lightly floured surface, roll 1 portion into a 22- x 12-inch rectangle (keep remaining portion covered). Spread half of the filling over rectangle, leaving a 1-inch border. Sprinkle with 1/2 cup of the pecans. Starting at 1 long side, carefully roll up rectangle in a jelly-roll fashion. Place, seam side down, on a large parchment paper-lined baking sheet. Bring ends of roll together to form a ring. Moisten ends with water; pinch together to seal. Repeat with second portion and remaining filling and pecans. Cover; let rise in a warm place (85°F) until doubled in bulk, 45 minutes to 1 hour.

7. Preheat oven to 350°F. Uncover Dough rings, and bake in preheated oven until deep golden brown and done, about 25 minutes. Cool cakes completely on pans set on wire racks, about 1 1/2 hours.

8. Prepare the Creamy Vanilla Glaze: Stir together powdered sugar, melted butter, and vanilla. Stir in 3 tablespoons milk. Add additional milk, 1 teaspoon at a time, until pourable but still opaque. Pour evenly over cakes; sprinkle with sparkling sugars, alternating colors to form bands.

COOKING (SL) SCHOOL

TIPS AND TRICKS FROM THE SOUTH'S MOST TRUSTED KITCHEN

SLOW-COOKER EDITION

STORE VEGETABLE TRIMMINGS IN THE FREEZER TO MAKE A DELICIOUS STOCK.

KNOW-HOW

Homemade Stock, Simplified

The easiest way to make flavorful stock is with your slow cooker

▲ VEGETABLES

- Use trimmings and scraps from potatoes, onions, celery, carrots, and other veggies. Be sure they are clean and still fresh.
- Toss in peppercorns, herb sprigs, and garlic cloves to give the stock complexity.

CHICKEN

- Roasted bones make a darker, richer stock than raw bones.
- Use collagen-rich chicken wings for a robust flavor and texture. The stock will congeal when chilled but will liquefy when heated.

BEEF

- Acidity helps break down the bones; tomato paste, red wine, and red wine vinegar are best for beef.
- Meaty bones make great stock. Reserve any bits of slow-cooked beef for soups, stews, and pastas.

MAKE AHEAD

Prep Freezer Meals Like a Pro

Three steps for planning ahead and stocking up

Label a ziplock plastic freezer bag with a waterproof marker. Include the recipe name, date, and cooking instructions. Note anything that should be added later, like grated cheese.

Prepare the ingredients (such as raw proteins and vegetables, seasonings, etc.) according to the recipe, and place them in the bag. Don't freeze fresh herbs, pasta, dairy products, or grains like rice.

Let out as much air as possible from each bag, and then flatten them so they can be stacked in the freezer. Defrost bags in the refrigerator before adding the contents to the slow cooker.

GREAT GEAR

Choose the Best Model for You

New styles, fun designs, brand-new tricks—pick the cooking companion that complements your lifestyle

FOR THE TECH OBSESSED
This WiFi-enabled option can conveniently be operated from your smartphone. **SL PICK:** Black+Decker WiFi Enabled 6-Quart Slow Cooker, $59.99; *walmart.com*

FOR DISPLAYING ON THE COUNTER
Get dinner on the table and brighten up the kitchen with this cheery gingham print. **SL PICK:** Hamilton Beach 3-Quart Slow Cooker, $19.99; *amazon.com*

FOR COOKING FOR TWO
A scaled-down model is the perfect size for two (or for one person who loves leftovers). **SL PICK:** Proctor Silex Portable 1.5-Quart Slow Cooker, $14.99; *amazon.com*

TEST KITCHEN TIPS

New Uses for Kitchen Items

Three surprising secret weapons that will help in a pinch

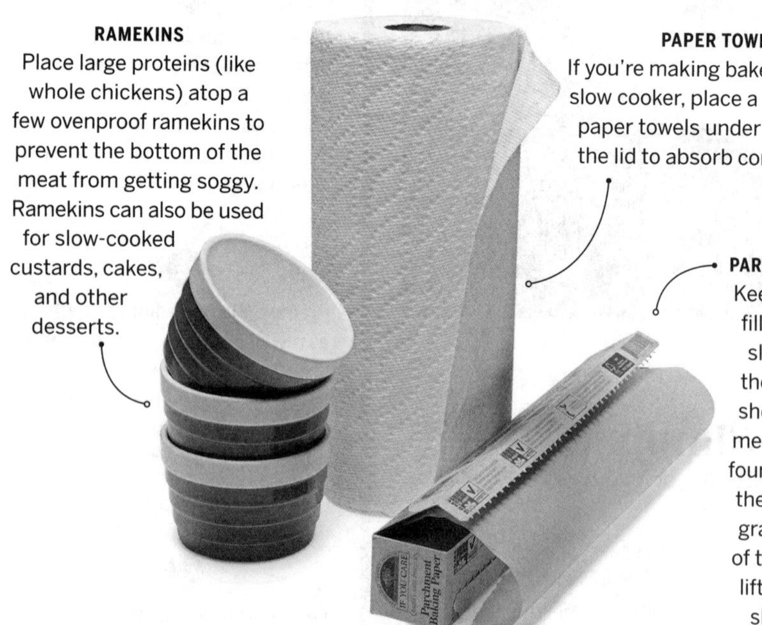

RAMEKINS
Place large proteins (like whole chickens) atop a few ovenproof ramekins to prevent the bottom of the meat from getting soggy. Ramekins can also be used for slow-cooked custards, cakes, and other desserts.

PAPER TOWELS
If you're making baked goods in a slow cooker, place a few layers of paper towels under the edge of the lid to absorb condensation.

PARCHMENT PAPER
Keep tender fish fillets intact by slow-cooking them in a large sheet of parchment folded into four layers. When the fish is done, grab the edges of the paper and lift it out of the slow cooker.

"To easily remove fat from a braising liquid or sauce, strain the liquid into a glass measuring cup, and then refrigerate it overnight. The fat will rise to the top and harden."

—Paige Grandjean
Test Kitchen Professional

March

68 **A Beautiful Easter Brunch** that's both simple and special

72 QUICK FIX **Bacon Makes Everything Better** and we've got half a dozen recipes to prove it

76 WHAT CAN I BRING? **Vegging Out** Our creamy, savory dip elevates the humble veggie platter

77 HEALTHY IN A HURRY **Wild about Salmon** These tasty croquettes are all fish and no filler

78 DINNER IN AMERICA **Pot Roast, Please** This Sunday supper classic is tailor-made for the slow cooker

79 ONE AND DONE **Luck of the Leftovers** Turn the stars of the St. Patrick's Day table into a vibrant soup that's perfect for spring

80 *SL* COOKING SCHOOL **Bring Home the Best Bacon** A buyer's guide to bacon, how to freeze leftover slices, and the proper way to store bacon grease

A BEAUTIFUL
Easter Brunch

Make this a wonderful celebration with an easy-to-prepare spread of top-your-own **BISCUITS**, springtime **SALADS**, and a festive **PUNCH**

Buttermilk Biscuits with Ham,
recipe at right

Sparkling Citrus Punch, *recipe page 71*

Buttermilk Biscuits with Ham

Our classic, melt-in-your-mouth biscuits are pretty much perfect on their own, but they make great sandwiches too. Prepare them along with our sweet and savory toppers and a few pieces of thinly sliced ham, and then allow everyone to serve themselves. Keep in mind that these biscuits are on the smaller side, so you may want to bake an extra batch for Easter brunch—they tend to disappear very quickly. Find easy make-ahead instructions below.

ACTIVE 25 MIN. - TOTAL 35 MIN.
SERVES 10

2 cups all-purpose flour
1 Tbsp. granulated sugar
2 tsp. baking powder
¾ tsp. kosher salt
½ tsp. baking soda
½ cup cold butter, cut into ½-inch pieces
¾ cup whole buttermilk
1 Tbsp. butter, melted
12 oz. thinly sliced ham
Biscuit Spreads (recipes follow)

1. Preheat oven to 450°F. Whisk together all-purpose flour, granulated sugar, baking powder, salt, and baking soda in a medium bowl. Cut cold butter pieces into flour mixture with a pastry blender until mixture is crumbly. Make a well in center of mixture. Add whole buttermilk, and stir until mixture comes together in a ball.
2. Scrape dough onto a lightly floured surface, and knead three to four times. Lightly flour top of dough and a rolling pin. Roll dough into a rectangle, and fold dough in half so short ends meet. Repeat the rolling and folding procedures one more time.
3. Roll dough to ½-inch thickness. Cut with a floured 2-inch round cutter, rerolling scraps once. (You should have 10 biscuits.) Place biscuits 1 inch apart on a baking sheet lined with parchment paper. Bake in preheated oven until golden brown and firm to the touch, about 10 minutes.
4. Brush tops of hot biscuits with melted butter, and serve with sliced ham and choice of Biscuit Spreads (recipes follow).

Make Ahead: The biscuits can be cut and frozen up to two weeks in advance. Freeze the dough solid on the baking sheet. Store in a ziplock plastic bag in the freezer. Bake frozen biscuits at 450°F for 12 to 14 minutes.

Creole Mayonnaise

ACTIVE 5 MIN. - TOTAL 5 MIN.
MAKES ABOUT ⅔ CUP

Stir together ½ cup mayonnaise, 1 Tbsp. minced shallot (from 1 small shallot), 1 Tbsp. Creole mustard, 1 tsp. white wine vinegar, and ½ tsp. Creole seasoning (such as Tony Chachere's) in a bowl. Spoon mixture into a serving bowl. Cover and chill until ready to serve.

Spicy Orange-Peach Butter

ACTIVE 10 MIN. - TOTAL 40 MIN.
MAKES ABOUT ¾ CUP

Stir together 3 Tbsp. orange marmalade, 3 Tbsp. peach preserves, ½ tsp. crushed red pepper, ½ tsp. salt, and ½ tsp. white wine vinegar in a small saucepan; bring to a boil over medium, stirring often. Cook, stirring constantly, until mixture thickens, about 4 minutes. Scrape mixture onto a lightly greased plate; cool completely, about 30 minutes. Meanwhile, place ½ cup salted butter, softened, in a bowl; beat with an electric mixer on medium speed until light and fluffy, 3 to 4 minutes. Stir in marmalade mixture until well combined. Scrape mixture into a serving bowl. Cover and chill until ready to serve.

Pecan Cheese Spread

ACTIVE 5 MIN. - TOTAL 5 MIN.
MAKES ABOUT 1 ⅓ CUPS

Beat 2 oz. cream cheese, softened; ¼ cup mascarpone cheese; 2 tsp. honey; ¼ tsp. cayenne pepper; and ¼ tsp. seasoned salt with an electric mixer on medium speed until smooth, about 3 minutes. Stir in 4 oz. white Cheddar cheese, shredded (about 1 cup), and ½ cup chopped toasted pecans. Scrape mixture into a serving bowl. Cover and chill until ready to serve.

Chive-Radish Compound Butter

ACTIVE 10 MIN. - TOTAL 10 MIN.
MAKES ABOUT ⅔ CUP

Beat ½ cup salted butter, softened, and ¼ tsp. salt with an electric mixer on high speed until light and fluffy, 3 to 4 minutes. Gently stir in 2 Tbsp. finely chopped radishes (from 2 small radishes) and 2 Tbsp. chopped fresh chives. Scrape compound butter into a serving bowl. Cover and chill until ready to serve.

Mini Cheese Grits Casseroles

Prepare the grits the night prior to serving, and then bake the casseroles before everyone arrives. If you don't have 8-ounce ramekins, our recipe can be made in a 2-quart baking dish (increase the baking time to about 50 to 55 minutes).

ACTIVE 15 MIN. - TOTAL 9 HOURS, 25 MIN., INCLUDING 8 HOURS CHILLING
SERVES 6

- **4 ½ cups water**
- **1 ½ cups uncooked quick-cooking grits**
- **2 tsp. salt**
- **1 cup half-and-half**
- **1 tsp. dry mustard**
- **¼ tsp. black pepper**
- **2 large eggs**
- **1 large egg yolk**
- **12 oz. sharp Cheddar cheese, shredded (about 3 cups)**
- **2 Tbsp. chopped fresh chives**

1. Bring water to a boil in a medium saucepan over high. Add grits and 1 teaspoon of the salt. Reduce heat to medium-low, and cook, stirring occasionally, until grits are thickened and tender, about 5 minutes. Remove pan from heat; cover and let stand 5 minutes.
2. Meanwhile, whisk together half-and-half, mustard, pepper, eggs, egg yolk, and remaining 1 teaspoon salt. Stir in grits and cheese until cheese is melted. Divide mixture evenly among 6 (8-ounce) lightly greased ramekins. Cover and chill 8 hours or overnight.
3. Preheat oven to 350°F. Uncover ramekins, and place on a baking sheet; let stand at room temperature while oven preheats, 15 to 20 minutes. Bake in preheated oven until puffed and edges are set, about 42 minutes. Let stand 10 minutes. Sprinkle with chives, and serve.

Warm Asparagus, Radish, and New Potato Salad with Herb Dressing

Potato salad gets a makeover for the season with the addition of roasted asparagus and radishes. The tangy dressing can be made up to a week in advance and stored in the refrigerator.

ACTIVE 20 MIN. - TOTAL 30 MIN.
SERVES 8

- **2 lb. new potatoes, halved (quartered, if large)**
- **2 cups large radishes, halved lengthwise (about 8 oz.)**
- **3 Tbsp. olive oil**
- **1 tsp. kosher salt**
- **¾ tsp. black pepper**
- **1 lb. fresh asparagus, trimmed and cut into 2-inch pieces**
- **¾ cup mayonnaise**
- **¼ cup whole buttermilk**
- **1 Tbsp. apple cider vinegar**
- **1 Tbsp. chopped fresh flat-leaf parsley**
- **1 Tbsp. chopped fresh chives**
- **1 Tbsp. minced shallot (from 1 small)**
- **2 tsp. chopped fresh tarragon**
- **1 tsp. whole-grain mustard**

1. Place a large rimmed baking sheet in oven. Preheat oven to 425°F. (Do not remove baking sheet while oven preheats.)
2. Place potatoes and radishes in a large bowl. Add 2 tablespoons of the oil, ½ teaspoon of the salt, and ¼ teaspoon of the pepper; toss well to coat. Arrange potato mixture in a single layer on hot baking sheet. Bake in preheated oven 15 minutes, stirring after 10 minutes. (Do not clean large bowl.)
3. Meanwhile, combine asparagus, remaining 1 tablespoon oil, and ¼ teaspoon each of the salt and pepper in large bowl; toss well to coat. Remove baking sheet from oven; stir potato mixture again. Add asparagus mixture, spreading in a single layer. Bake until potatoes are tender and asparagus is tender-crisp, about 5 minutes.
4. Whisk together mayonnaise, buttermilk, vinegar, parsley, chives, shallot, tarragon, mustard, and remaining ¼ teaspoon each salt and pepper in a small bowl. Drizzle desired amount of dressing over potato salad. Serve warm or at room temperature. (Reserve remaining Herb Dressing for another use.)

Strawberry-Rhubarb Salad

This salad is a delightfully unexpected way to use the fresh rhubarb and berries that are just coming into season. Avoid overcooking the rhubarb; it should still have some crispness.

ACTIVE 20 MIN. - TOTAL 35 MIN.
SERVES 6

- **1 cup water**
- **½ cup granulated sugar**
- **2 cups 1-inch diagonally sliced rhubarb (from 3 large stalks)**
- **1 Tbsp. fresh orange juice (from 1 small orange)**
- **1 Tbsp. fresh lemon juice (from 1 lemon)**
- **20 oz. fresh strawberries, quartered lengthwise (about 3 cups)**
- **½ cup toasted slivered almonds**
- **¼ cup small mint leaves**

1. Stir together water and sugar in a small saucepan over medium-high; bring to a boil, and cook, stirring occasionally, until sugar dissolves. Add rhubarb to pan; cook 1 minute. Remove pan from heat. Cover and let stand until rhubarb is tender-crisp, about 15 minutes. Remove rhubarb with a slotted spoon, reserving rhubarb syrup.
2. Stir together orange juice, lemon juice, and 2 tablespoons rhubarb syrup in a large bowl. Add rhubarb, strawberries, almonds, and mint; stir gently to combine. Serve at room temperature or chilled. (Reserve remaining rhubarb syrup for another use.)

Coconut-Carrot Cake with Coconut Buttercream

Why choose between carrot cake and coconut cake when both flavors work so well together? Macerating the shredded carrots makes them extra tender in the cake.

ACTIVE 1 HOUR - TOTAL 2 HOURS, 45 MIN.
SERVES 20

CAKE LAYER
- **1 lb. carrots, peeled and shredded (about 3 packed cups)**
- **1¼ cups granulated sugar**
- **1 cup sweetened shredded coconut**
- **⅔ cup unsweetened large flaked coconut (such as Let's Do... Organic)**
- **2½ cups all-purpose flour, plus more for pans**
- **2½ tsp. baking powder**
- **2 tsp. ground cinnamon**
- **1 tsp. salt**
- **½ tsp. baking soda**
- **1 cup unsalted butter, plus more for pans**
- **1 cup packed light brown sugar**
- **4 large eggs**
- **1½ tsp. vanilla extract**
- **½ cup chopped walnuts**
- **½ cup raisins**

COCONUT BUTTERCREAM
- **1 cup well-shaken canned unsweetened coconut milk**
- **3 Tbsp. cornstarch**
- **¼ tsp. salt**
- **1 cup unsalted butter, softened**
- **3¼ cups powdered sugar**
- **½ tsp. coconut extract**
- **½ tsp. vanilla extract**

ADDITIONAL INGREDIENT
- **1 large peeled carrot, peeled into 3-inch curls**

1. Prepare the Cake Layer: Preheat oven to 350°F. Grease and flour sides and bottom of a 13- x 9-inch baking pan.
2. Toss together carrots and ½ cup of the granulated sugar in a bowl. Let stand 15 minutes. Pour mixture through a mesh strainer over a bowl, pressing on solids in strainer; discard liquid. Set shredded carrots aside.
3. Spread sweetened shredded coconut in a single layer on half of a large baking sheet; spread unsweetened flaked coconut in a single layer on other half. (Keep shredded and flaked coconut separated on baking sheet.) Bake in preheated oven until unsweetened flakes are golden brown, about 5 minutes (sweetened shredded coconut will be only slightly browned). Cool completely, about 10 minutes. Reserve unsweetened flaked coconut for garnish. Reduce oven temperature to 325°F.
4. Whisk together flour, baking powder, cinnamon, salt, and baking soda.
5. Beat butter with an electric mixer on medium speed until creamy, about 1 minute. Add brown sugar and remaining ¾ cup granulated sugar, and beat until light and fluffy, about 3 minutes. Add eggs, 1 at a time, beating well after each addition (mixture may look broken). Beat in vanilla. Add flour mixture; beat on low speed until just combined, 1 to 2 minutes. Stir in shredded carrots, shredded coconut, walnuts, and raisins.
6. Spread batter in prepared pan, smoothing top. Bake at 325°F until a wooden pick inserted in the center comes out clean, 40 to 45 minutes. Transfer pan to a wire rack, and cool completely, about 1 hour.
7. Meanwhile, prepare the Coconut Buttercream: Whisk together coconut milk, cornstarch, and salt in a saucepan until completely combined and smooth. Bring mixture to a boil over medium, stirring often. Boil, stirring constantly, until mixture thickens, about 2 minutes. Scrape mixture onto a plate, and cover surface with plastic wrap. Cool completely, about 30 minutes (or about 20 minutes in the refrigerator).
8. Beat butter with an electric mixer on medium speed until creamy, 1 to 2 minutes. Add powdered sugar; beat on medium-low speed until smooth, about 2 minutes. Beat in extracts. Add coconut milk mixture, a little at a time, beating well after each addition. Increase speed to medium-high, and beat until light and fluffy, 2 to 3 minutes. Spread buttercream over top of cooled cake, and garnish with reserved toasted flaked coconut and carrot curls.

Sparkling Citrus Punch

Lemonade Ice Cubes keep this bubbly big-batch drink cold without diluting it.

ACTIVE 10 MIN. - TOTAL 10 MIN.
SERVES 6

Stir together 1 (750-milliliter) bottle sparkling Moscato, 1½ cups fresh orange juice (from 3 large oranges), ¼ cup fresh Ruby Red grapefruit juice (from 1 small grapefruit), ¼ cup (2 oz.) elderflower liqueur (such as St-Germain), 2 Tbsp. fresh lemon juice (from 1 small lemon), and 2 Tbsp. fresh lime juice (from 1 lime) in a large pitcher. If desired, add Lemonade Ice Cubes, and serve immediately.

Lemonade Ice Cubes

ACTIVE 5 MIN. - TOTAL 5 HOURS, 5 MIN., INCLUDING 5 HOURS FREEZING
MAKES 12 ICE CUBES

Arrange thinly sliced lemon, lime, and orange wedges in the bottom of a 12-compartment ice cube tray. Fill tray with 2 cups prepared lemonade, and freeze until solid, about 5 hours or overnight.

Bacon Makes Everything Better

Six new recipes for suppers that sizzle, from pork chops to pasta

Fettuccine Alfredo with Leeks and Peas, recipe at right

Fettuccine Alfredo with Leeks and Peas

Pasta with homemade Alfredo sauce is a simple weeknight meal that feels downright indulgent, especially when bacon is involved. Cook the vegetables in the drippings for extra richness. To make sure the chopped leeks are free of sand, soak them in a large bowl of cold water for five minutes and then drain.

ACTIVE 35 MIN. - TOTAL 45 MIN.
SERVES 4

1 Tbsp. plus 1 tsp. kosher salt
4 thick-cut bacon slices
2 medium leeks, chopped (about 6 oz.)
1½ cups frozen green peas, thawed
2 garlic cloves, finely sliced
1½ cups heavy cream
½ tsp. black pepper
⅛ tsp. ground nutmeg
12 oz. uncooked fettuccine
2 oz. Parmesan cheese, finely grated (about ¼ cup)

1. Bring a large pot of water and 1 tablespoon of the salt to a boil over high.
2. While water is coming to a boil, cook bacon in a large deep skillet over medium until crisp, turning occasionally, about 8 minutes. Transfer bacon to a plate lined with paper towels, reserving drippings in skillet. Set bacon aside.
3. Place skillet over medium-high. Add leeks to hot drippings, and cook until wilted and beginning to brown, about 3 minutes. Add peas and garlic, and cook, stirring often, until garlic just begins to brown. Transfer mixture to a medium bowl with a slotted spoon. Reduce heat to medium; add cream to skillet, and bring to a simmer. Cook, stirring often, until slightly reduced, about 5 minutes. Add pepper, nutmeg, and remaining 1 teaspoon salt; stir to combine.
4. Add pasta to boiling salted water, and cook according to package directions; drain well, reserving 1 cup cooking water.
5. Finely chop bacon. Toss fettuccine with leek-and-cream sauce mixture over low until heated through. Add reserved 1 cup cooking water, 2 tablespoons at a time, to reach desired consistency. Divide mixture among 4 bowls; top evenly with bacon and Parmesan.

Creamy Rice with Scallops

Smoky, salty bacon tastes delicious with naturally sweet foods like corn and scallops. Here, we combined all three ingredients in this sophisticated risotto-like dish made with Arborio rice. For a crisp, golden brown sear, ensure the pan is very hot before adding the scallops to it.

ACTIVE 30 MIN. - TOTAL 35 MIN.
SERVES 6

2 cups uncooked Arborio rice
4 cups chicken broth
1 cup water
1 thyme sprig
2 Tbsp. unsalted butter
1¾ tsp. kosher salt
½ tsp. black pepper
1 cup half-and-half
4 thick-cut bacon slices
2 cups fresh yellow corn kernels (about 3 ears)
1½ lb. dry sea scallops
2 Tbsp. chopped fresh chives

1. Combine rice, chicken broth, and water in a large pot over high, and bring to a boil. Stir in thyme sprig, butter, 1½ teaspoons of the salt, and ¼ teaspoon of the pepper. Reduce heat to medium-low, cover, and cook until rice is tender and most of the liquid is absorbed, about 15 minutes. Remove from heat, and take out thyme. Stir in half-and-half. Cover to keep warm.
2. While rice is cooking, cook bacon in a large cast-iron skillet over medium, turning occasionally, until crisp, about 10 minutes. Transfer bacon to paper towels to drain, reserving drippings in skillet. Crumble bacon, and set aside.
3. Place skillet with drippings over high, and add corn. Cook, stirring often, until corn begins to char, about 4 minutes. Using a slotted spoon, remove corn from skillet, and stir into cooked rice.
4. Place skillet with remaining drippings over medium-high. Sprinkle scallops with remaining ¼ teaspoon each salt and pepper, and sear in hot drippings until charred, about 1 minute per side. Stir bacon into warm rice. Serve scallops over creamy rice mixture sprinkled with chopped chives.

Shrimp Cobb Salad with Bacon Dressing

A Cobb salad isn't complete without bacon, but in this recipe, we went a step further and added extra bacon (and drippings) to the bright and tangy vinaigrette. Build your own Cobb salad by substituting diced chicken or ham for shrimp and trying crumbled feta instead of blue cheese.

ACTIVE 25 MIN. - TOTAL 25 MIN.
SERVES 4

4 thick-cut bacon slices
1 head romaine lettuce (about 14 oz.), chopped
2 hard-cooked eggs, peeled and cut into wedges
¾ lb. poached or steamed large peeled and deveined shrimp
1 cup halved cherry tomatoes (from 1 pt. tomatoes)
½ cup chopped red onion (from 1 onion)
1 ripe avocado, chopped
4 oz. blue cheese, crumbled (about 1 cup)
1 garlic clove, crushed
½ tsp. kosher salt
½ tsp. black pepper
¼ tsp. granulated sugar
3 Tbsp. extra-virgin olive oil
2 Tbsp. red wine vinegar

1. Cook bacon in a skillet over medium, turning occasionally, until crisp, about 10 minutes. Transfer bacon to a plate lined with paper towels, reserving drippings in skillet. Set bacon aside. Pour drippings into a small bowl; set aside to cool slightly.
2. Reserve 1 bacon slice. Roughly chop remaining 3 bacon slices, and arrange on a large platter with lettuce, eggs, shrimp, tomatoes, onion, avocado, and cheese.
3. Crumble reserved bacon slice into a food processor. Add garlic, salt, pepper, and sugar; pulse until finely chopped, about five times. Add reserved drippings, olive oil, and vinegar; process until blended. Drizzle over salad; serve immediately.

Bacon-Wrapped Chicken Breasts

If you need a break from chicken tenders, try this no-fuss, kid-friendly meal that will also please the adults around the table. The creamy sauce is a delicious companion to the chicken and potatoes, and it can be used as a salad dressing as well. Pieces of center-cut (not thick-cut) bacon will wrap around the chicken more easily.

ACTIVE 45 MIN. - TOTAL 1 HOUR, 20 MIN.
SERVES 4

- **1½ tsp. finely chopped fresh thyme**
- **½ tsp. granulated sugar**
- **⅛ tsp. cayenne pepper**
- **2 tsp. kosher salt**
- **1 tsp. black pepper**
- **4 (8-oz.) boneless, skinless chicken breasts**
- **8 bacon slices (not thick cut)**
- **1½ lb. baby Yukon Gold potatoes, halved**
- **2 Tbsp. olive oil**
- **½ cup mayonnaise**
- **2 Tbsp. Dijon mustard**
- **2 Tbsp. ketchup**
- **2 Tbsp. chopped fresh chives**

1. Preheat oven to 400°F. Stir together thyme, sugar, cayenne, 1 teaspoon of the salt, and ½ teaspoon of the black pepper in a small bowl. Sprinkle chicken evenly on both sides with thyme mixture. Wrap 1 bacon slice around each breast; tuck a second slice under wrapped slice, and wrap again, covering as much of the chicken as possible. Tuck the end of the second slice back under itself.
2. Add the bacon-wrapped chicken to a large nonstick skillet, and cook over medium, turning frequently, until all sides are browned and crispy, about 25 minutes. Remove skillet from heat.
3. While chicken is cooking, toss potatoes with oil and remaining 1 teaspoon salt and ½ teaspoon pepper; arrange on a lightly greased wire rack on a rimmed baking sheet. Bake in preheated oven until potatoes are golden brown and cooked through, about 25 minutes. Remove baking sheet from oven, and slide potatoes to one side of rack. Arrange chicken on rack; transfer potatoes, cut side down, to skillet. Bake chicken in preheated oven until a thermometer inserted into thickest portion registers 165°F, about 10 minutes. Place skillet with potatoes over medium, and cook until crispy, about 10 minutes.
4. Stir together mayonnaise, Dijon, ketchup, and 1 tablespoon of the chives in a small bowl. Garnish chicken and potatoes with remaining 1 tablespoon chives, and serve with mayonnaise-chive sauce.

Bacon-Hash Brown Quiche

Bacon-Hash Brown Quiche

Meet your new favorite dinner—or lunch or breakfast. In this crowd-pleasing recipe, we replaced the usual pastry shell with a golden crust made from shredded potatoes and bacon. We also gave the filling a flavorful boost with Gruyère cheese and a touch of Dijon mustard.

ACTIVE 20 MIN. - TOTAL 1 HOUR, 20 MIN.
SERVES 4

- **4 thick-cut bacon slices, cut into ½-inch pieces**
- **8 oz. fresh asparagus, cut into 2-inch pieces**
- **4 cups frozen shredded hash browns (about 12 oz.)**
- **1½ tsp. kosher salt**
- **¾ tsp. black pepper**
- **6 large eggs**
- **1 cup half-and-half**
- **4 oz. Gruyère cheese, shredded (about 1 cup)**
- **2 Tbsp. Dijon mustard**
- **¼ cup sliced scallions (about 2 scallions)**

1. Preheat oven to 375°F. Cook bacon in a 10-inch cast-iron skillet over medium until browned and almost crisp, but still tender, about 6 minutes. Transfer bacon to a plate lined with paper towels. Reserve drippings in skillet, and let cool slightly. Add asparagus to skillet, and cook over medium-high, stirring often, until lightly browned and just beginning to soften, about 3 minutes. Using a slotted spoon, transfer asparagus to a medium bowl.
2. Add hash browns, bacon, ½ teaspoon of the salt, and ¼ teaspoon of the pepper to hot drippings in skillet over medium-high; stir to combine. Using a wooden spoon, spread mixture into an even layer across the bottom and 1 inch up sides of skillet. Transfer to preheated oven, and bake until lightly golden, about 30 minutes.
3. Whisk together eggs, half-and-half, Gruyère, Dijon, and remaining 1 teaspoon salt and ½ teaspoon pepper in a large bowl. Stir in scallions.
4. Remove skillet from oven, and scatter asparagus over crust. Pour egg mixture over asparagus, and return to oven.
5. Bake until egg mixture is just set, 20 to 25 minutes more. Let cool 5 minutes before slicing.

Pork Chops with Tomato-Bacon Gravy

While the pork chops roast in the oven, the savory pan gravy comes together quickly on the stove-top, making a company-worthy meal in under an hour. Swap out the green beans for thin asparagus spears or sliced zucchini.

ACTIVE 40 MIN. - TOTAL 50 MIN.
SERVES 4

- **4 thick-cut bacon slices**
- **4 (1-inch-thick) bone-in center-cut pork chops (about 10 oz. each)**
- **1 tsp. kosher salt**
- **1 tsp. black pepper**
- **8 oz. fresh green beans, trimmed**
- **1 medium shallot, sliced**
- **1 Tbsp. olive oil**
- **1 pt. cherry tomatoes**
- **2 Tbsp. all-purpose flour**
- **1 cup unsalted beef stock**
- **2 Tbsp. chopped fresh flat-leaf parsley**

1. Preheat oven to 400°F. Cook bacon in a skillet over medium until crisp, turning occasionally, about 8 minutes. Remove bacon to paper towels to drain; set aside. Reserve drippings in skillet off heat. Sprinkle pork chops evenly with ½ teaspoon each of the salt and pepper. Place skillet over medium-high; add pork chops, and cook in hot drippings until well browned, 3 minutes per side. Transfer pork chops to one end of an aluminum foil-lined rimmed baking sheet; set aside. (Do not wipe skillet clean.)

2. Toss green beans, sliced shallot, and oil together with ¼ teaspoon each of the salt and pepper. Set aside.

3. Place skillet with remaining drippings over medium-high. Add tomatoes and remaining ¼ teaspoon each salt and pepper. Cook, stirring occasionally, until blistered and beginning to burst, about 3 minutes. Sprinkle with flour, and cook, stirring constantly, 1 minute. Add stock; stir until smooth. Reduce heat to medium, and simmer until thickened, 5 minutes.

4. Add green bean mixture to opposite side of baking sheet from pork chops. Place in preheated oven; cook until a thermometer inserted into thickest portion of pork chops registers 145°F and green beans just begin to brown, about 10 minutes. Chop bacon; stir into tomato gravy, and serve over pork chops with green beans. Sprinkle with parsley.

Vegging Out

The real secret to a crowd-pleasing crudités platter? A rich, tangy homemade dip

Creamy Feta-and-Herb Dip

Serve on a tray piled with colorful baby vegetables such as rainbow carrots, English cucumbers, and French Breakfast radishes.

ACTIVE 15 MIN. - TOTAL 15 MIN.
SERVES 12

- 1 (1-lb.) block feta cheese, drained
- ½ (8-oz.) pkg. cream cheese, at room temperature
- ½ cup sour cream
- ½ cup mayonnaise
- 1 Tbsp. fresh lemon juice (from 1 lemon)
- 1 garlic clove, minced (about 1 tsp.)
- ¼ tsp. black pepper
- 1½ Tbsp. chopped fresh flat-leaf parsley
- 1½ Tbsp. chopped fresh dill
- 2½ tsp. chopped fresh thyme
- ½ tsp. paprika
- 1 Tbsp. extra-virgin olive oil
- Crudités and pita chips, for serving

1. Place 12 ounces of the feta in a food processor. Crumble remaining 4 ounces; set aside. Add cream cheese, sour cream, mayonnaise, lemon juice, garlic, and pepper to processor; process until combined and creamy, about 1 minute and 30 seconds. Transfer to a medium bowl, and gently stir in parsley, dill, thyme, and remaining crumbled feta. Chill until ready to serve.
2. Just before serving, sprinkle with paprika, and drizzle with olive oil. Serve with crudités and pita chips.

TIP

Choose feta that's sold in blocks stored in brine. Crumbled feta contains an additive that prevents clumping, and it will not blend as smoothly.

TIP

For cakes with the best texture, chop the fish by hand—a food processor will quickly turn the salmon into a paste.

Wild about Salmon

With finely chopped fish and no filler, these cakes are incredibly moist and delicious

Fresh Salmon Cakes with Buttermilk Dressing

We prefer salmon from the tail of the fish, which is thinner than most fillets and also contains a little more fat for extra flavor.

ACTIVE 30 MIN. - TOTAL 30 MIN.
SERVES 4

- 1 ¼ lb. skinless salmon fillet
- ¼ cup chopped fresh chives
- ¾ tsp. kosher salt
- ½ tsp. black pepper
- 7 Tbsp. mayonnaise
- ½ cup plus 2 Tbsp. panko (Japanese-style breadcrumbs)
- 2 Tbsp. olive oil
- 2 Tbsp. chopped fresh flat-leaf parsley
- 1 Tbsp. whole buttermilk
- 1 Tbsp. reduced-sodium soy sauce
- 2 tsp. fresh lemon juice (from 1 lemon)
- ½ tsp. granulated sugar
- 1 head butter lettuce, torn
- ½ cup sugar snap peas, thinly sliced
- ½ cup thinly sliced radishes

1. Finely chop salmon on a cutting board; place in a medium bowl. Add chives, salt, pepper, and 4 tablespoons of the mayonnaise; stir to combine. Shape mixture into 8 (2 ½-inch-wide) patties. Place breadcrumbs in a shallow dish. Place each patty in breadcrumbs; press to coat all sides.
2. Heat oil in a large skillet over medium-high. Add patties to skillet; cook until golden brown and internal temperature reaches 130°F, about 3 minutes per side. Remove from skillet.
3. Whisk together parsley, buttermilk, soy sauce, lemon juice, sugar, and remaining 3 tablespoons mayonnaise in a small bowl.
4. Divide lettuce, snap peas, and radishes evenly among 4 plates. Top each with 2 salmon cakes; drizzle with dressing.

Nutritional information (per serving):
Calories: 499 - Protein: 37g - Carbs: 10g - Fiber: 1g - Fat: 36g

Pot Roast, Please

Certain comfort foods are synonymous with Sunday supper, the meal that brings the family together. The convenience of a slow cooker makes it easy to enjoy this classic any day of the week

Cut the vegetables into large, uniform pieces so they will hold up during the long cook time.

Home-Style Slow-Cooker Pot Roast

ACTIVE 15 MIN. - TOTAL 9 HOURS

SERVES 6

- 1 (2 ½- to 3-lb.) boneless chuck roast
- 3 tsp. kosher salt
- 1½ tsp. black pepper
- 2 lb. large red potatoes, quartered
- 4 medium carrots, peeled and cut diagonally into 2-inch pieces (about 1 lb.)
- 3 celery stalks, cut diagonally into 2-inch pieces (about 4 oz.)
- 1 large yellow onion, cut into ¾-inch-thick wedges
- 1 Tbsp. minced garlic (about 2 large garlic cloves)
- 2 cups beef broth
- 5 Tbsp. instant-blending flour (such as Wondra)
- 1 Tbsp. tomato paste
- 6 thyme sprigs
- ¼ cup Worcestershire sauce
- 3 Tbsp. ketchup
- 2 tsp. hot sauce
- Fresh herb sprigs (optional)

1. Sprinkle roast with 2 teaspoons of the salt and 1 teaspoon of the pepper. Combine potatoes, carrots, celery, onion, and garlic in a slow cooker. Whisk together broth, flour, and tomato paste in a medium bowl; stir into slow cooker. Add thyme. Place roast on top of vegetables; cook, covered, on LOW until tender, about 8 hours.

2. Transfer roast to a cutting board. Let rest 20 minutes before slicing; then cover with aluminum foil. Using a slotted spoon, remove thyme and transfer vegetables to a serving platter. Sprinkle with ½ teaspoon of the salt. Cover with aluminum foil.

3. Whisk together Worcestershire sauce, ketchup, hot sauce, and remaining ½ teaspoon each of the salt and pepper in a bowl; stir into slow cooker. Increase heat to HIGH, and cook, partially covered, until sauce thickens, 35 to 40 minutes. Serve sliced roast and vegetables with sauce; garnish with herb sprigs, if desired.

Luck of the Leftovers

Turn extra Saint Patrick's Day corned beef and cabbage into a hearty, homey one-pot soup

TIP

If you don't have leftovers, use store-bought cooked corned beef (choose a piece about 1 inch thick) and preboil the cabbage, potatoes, and carrots until tender, 10 to 15 minutes.

Day-After-Saint Patrick's Day Soup

Caraway seeds, fresh dill, and malt vinegar add complex flavor.

ACTIVE 15 MIN. - TOTAL 30 MIN.
SERVES 8

- 1 Tbsp. olive oil
- 1 Tbsp. unsalted butter
- 2 cups chopped yellow onion (from 1 large onion)
- 1 cup chopped celery (from 4 stalks)
- 2 tsp. minced garlic (from 2 garlic cloves)
- 1 tsp. caraway seeds
- ½ tsp. kosher salt
- ½ tsp. black pepper
- 2 bay leaves
- 8 cups beef broth
- 2 cups chopped cooked cabbage
- 2 cups chopped cooked Yukon Gold potatoes
- 2 cups chopped cooked carrots
- 1 lb. shredded cooked corned beef
- 2 Tbsp. chopped fresh dill
- 2 Tbsp. chopped fresh flat-leaf parsley
- Malt vinegar

1. Heat oil and butter in a large Dutch oven over medium-high. Add onion and celery; cook until translucent, 5 minutes. Add garlic, caraway seeds, salt, and pepper; cook until fragrant, 1 minute. Add bay leaves and beef broth; bring to a boil over high. Reduce to medium-low.

2. Stir in cooked cabbage, potatoes, carrots, and beef; cook until hot, 15 minutes. Remove bay leaves; discard. Stir in dill and parsley. Serve with vinegar on the side.

COOKING SL SCHOOL

TIPS AND TRICKS FROM THE SOUTH'S MOST TRUSTED KITCHEN

SMART SHOPPER

Bring Home the Best Bacon

Confused by the ever-growing options at the supermarket? Here's a cheat sheet

THICK CUT

WHAT IT MEANS: Hefty, meaty slices. The thickness varies depending on the brand.
BEST FOR: Sprinkling on soups and salads
OUR PICK: Hormel Black Label Original Thick Cut Bacon; *blacklabelbacon.com*

UNCURED

WHAT IT MEANS: This type of bacon has been preserved with nitrites or nitrates from natural (not artificial) sources, such as celery.
BEST FOR: Serving with eggs and pancakes
OUR PICK: Smithfield All Natural Uncured Bacon; *smithfield.com*

CENTER CUT

WHAT IT MEANS: This bacon comes from the middle portion of the pork belly. The fatty ends of the bacon have been trimmed, making leaner (and smaller) slices.
BEST FOR: Topping hamburgers and BLTs
OUR PICK: Oscar Mayer Center Cut Bacon; *oscarmayer.com*

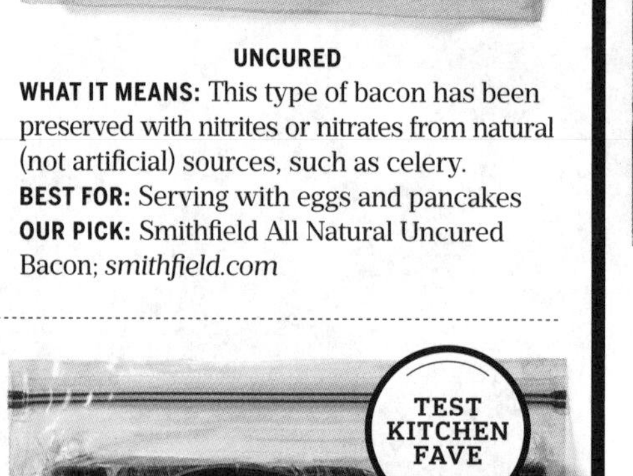

DOUBLE SMOKED

WHAT IT MEANS: Deeper, richer flavor. Look for "naturally smoked" on the label, indicating that the bacon spent time in an actual smoker.
BEST FOR: Adding to recipes like spaghetti carbonara
OUR PICK: Wright Brand Double Smoked Bacon; *wrightbrand.com*

"Although many of us grew up with a can of bacon grease on the kitchen counter, it's best to store it in the refrigerator in an airtight glass container."

—**Robby Melvin,** Test Kitchen Director

KNOW-HOW

Freeze Leftovers Like a Pro

1. SPACE OUT THE SLICES
Line up the pieces of bacon vertically on a parchment-lined baking sheet, leaving a bit of space between them.

2. GET READY TO ROLL
Form each slice into a spiral. Place the baking sheet in your freezer for 30 minutes or until the spirals have frozen solid.

3. FREEZE FOR LATER
Store the bacon in a ziplock plastic bag in the freezer. (Write the date on the bag.) Because the spirals have been individually frozen, they shouldn't stick together. Use them within one month for the best quality.

April

82 **Strawberry Sidekicks** Strawberry fields really aren't forever, so we've paired the fleeting berry with complementary fruits in desserts to help you savor them while they last

88 QUICK FIX **Chicken Salad Gets a Makeover** We've spruced up this classic in delicious ways

91 ONE AND DONE **The French Onion Casserole** The beloved ooey, gooey, savory soup is the inspiration for this equally delicious side dish

92 HEALTHY IN A HURRY **One-Pot Primavera** Springtime in a pan that's quick and company-worthy

93 SAVE ROOM **Sweet Tarts** Tastes of the tropics collide in this sunny dessert

94 *SL* COOKING SCHOOL Tips and tricks for the springtime kitchen

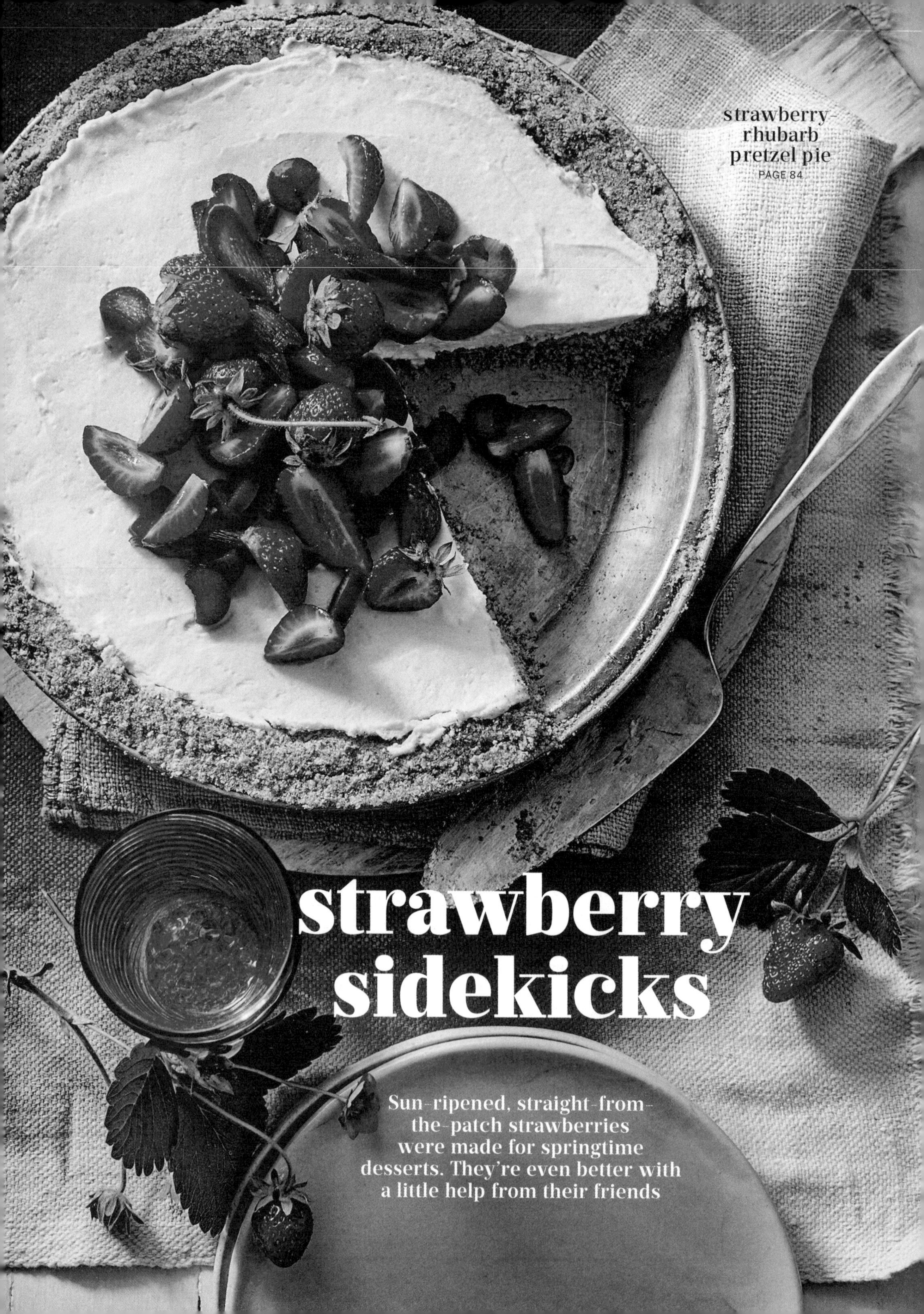

strawberry-rhubarb pretzel pie

PAGE 84

strawberry sidekicks

Sun-ripened, straight-from-the-patch strawberries were made for springtime desserts. They're even better with a little help from their friends

Strawberry season in the South is fleeting. We have only a few short weeks to enjoy the fresh, juicy gem that has been deemed the "fruit of love."

Strawberries appear suddenly at farmers' markets and you-pick farms—and then the really good ones are gone. Be mindful of when they are peaking in your region, and don't be fooled by the ones that are picked early and hit the market too soon. Unlike some fruits, strawberries don't get any sweeter after they've been harvested. The berries at the grocery store may look plump and ripe with coloring that's just a shade less than what it should be, but if they were picked too soon (green tips are a giveaway), you will be disappointed by their taste and texture.

Although they are delicious when devoured out of hand one by one, strawberries are downright heavenly when paired with other fruits. And while the tart and tangy rhubarb has been one of its longtime partners, strawberries can play well with others too. From apricots to nectarines, these surprising in-season combinations are all delightful.

strawberry-lemon crêpe cake
PAGE 85

Double the berry goodness. Blueberries can vary in size quite a bit, so we recommend mixing smaller ones in the batter because they will distribute more evenly. Choose the larger, plumper ones for garnishing the tops of the cupcakes.

Strawberry-Blueberry Cupcakes

ACTIVE 20 MIN. - TOTAL 1 HOUR, 20 MIN.
SERVES 24

- ½ cup butter, softened
- ½ (8-oz.) pkg. cream cheese, softened
- 2 cups granulated sugar
- 4 large eggs
- 1 tsp. vanilla extract
- 1 tsp. lemon zest plus 1 Tbsp. fresh juice (from 1 lemon)
- 3 cups all-purpose flour
- 1 tsp. baking powder
- ½ tsp. baking soda
- ½ tsp. salt
- 1 (8-oz.) container sour cream
- 1½ cups fresh blueberries
- Strawberry Frosting (recipe follows)
- Fresh blueberries and strawberries for topping (optional)

1. Preheat oven to 350°F. Beat butter and cream cheese with a heavy-duty stand mixer on medium speed until creamy. Gradually add sugar, and beat until light and fluffy. Add eggs, 1 at a time, beating until blended after each addition. Stir in vanilla, lemon zest, and lemon juice.
2. Stir together flour, baking powder, baking soda, and salt in a medium bowl. Gradually add to butter mixture alternately with sour cream, beating just until blended after each addition. Gently fold in blueberries. Place 24 paper baking cups in 2 (12-cup) standard-size muffin pans; spoon batter into baking cups, filling each about two-thirds full (about ¼ cup).
3. Bake in preheated oven until a wooden pick inserted in centers comes out clean, 22 to 25 minutes, switching pans from top rack to bottom rack after 15 minutes. Cool in pans on wire racks 5 minutes. Remove from pans to wire racks. Cool completely, about 30 minutes. Pipe or spread Strawberry Frosting onto cupcakes. Top with fresh blueberries and strawberries, if desired.

Strawberry Frosting

ACTIVE 10 MIN. - TOTAL 15 MIN.
MAKES ABOUT 4 CUPS

Beat **1 cup butter, softened,** with a heavy-duty stand mixer on medium speed until creamy. Gradually add **6 cups powdered sugar, 1 tsp. vanilla extract, ⅛ tsp. salt,** and **2 Tbsp. whole milk,** beating until blended. Gently fold in **6 Tbsp. chopped fresh strawberries.** Stir in up to **1 Tbsp. whole milk,** 1 teaspoon at a time, until desired consistency is reached.

STRAWBERRIES
+
RHUBARB

We turned the classic strawberry-pretzel salad into a rich and creamy pie. Rhubarb is a vegetable that needs sugar to temper its tangy flavor. Enter the strawberry for rounding out this sweet-and-salty dessert.

Strawberry-Rhubarb Pretzel Pie

ACTIVE 30 MIN. - TOTAL 4 HOURS, 20 MIN.
SERVES 8

CRUST

- 1½ cups finely crushed pretzel sticks
- ¼ cup packed light brown sugar
- 6 Tbsp. butter, melted

FILLING

- 1 (8-oz.) pkg. cream cheese, softened
- 1 tsp. vanilla extract
- ½ cup granulated sugar
- 1 cup heavy cream

TOPPING

- 2 cups water
- 6 Tbsp. granulated sugar
- 8 oz. fresh or frozen rhubarb, cut into ½-inch-thick slices (about 1 cup)
- 3 Tbsp. strawberry jam
- 2 cups sliced strawberries

1. Prepare the Crust: Preheat oven to 350°F. Stir together crushed pretzels, light brown sugar, and melted butter in a small bowl. Firmly press crumb mixture on bottom, up sides, and onto lip of a lightly greased 9-inch pie pan. Bake in preheated oven until lightly browned, about 14 minutes. Remove pan to a wire rack, and cool completely, about 1 hour.
2. Prepare the Filling: Beat softened cream cheese, vanilla, and ½ cup granulated sugar with an electric mixer on low speed until sugar dissolves and mixture is completely smooth; set aside. Beat cream at high speed using whisk attachment until medium-soft peaks form, about 2 minutes. Stir whipped cream into cream cheese mixture until fully incorporated. Spread into crust. Cover and chill 2 hours or overnight.
3. Prepare the Topping: Combine water and 6 tablespoons granulated sugar in a small saucepan; bring to a boil over high. Remove pan from heat. Add rhubarb slices; cover and let stand 5 minutes. Drain rhubarb; cool completely, about 30 minutes.
4. Microwave jam in a microwave-safe bowl on HIGH until hot, about 20 seconds. Add strawberries, and gently stir to coat. Add rhubarb slices, and gently stir to coat. Top pie with fruit, and serve.

STRAWBERRIES
+
LEMONS

If you've ever enjoyed a glass of strawberry lemonade, then you understand the power of a sweet-and-sour combination. This impressive crêpe cake is sure to wow with its delicate layers and bright lemon filling. Reserve the leftover liquid from the macerated strawberries for drizzling over each serving.

Strawberry-Lemon Crêpe Cake

ACTIVE 1 HOUR, 45 MIN. - TOTAL 5 HOURS, 15 MIN.

SERVES 8

CRÊPES

- **3 cups all-purpose flour**
- **1 tsp. baking powder**
- **1/8 tsp. salt**
- **1/4 cup granulated sugar**
- **3 cups whole milk**
- **3 large eggs**
- **1 Tbsp. lemon zest plus 2 Tbsp. fresh juice (from 1 lemon)**
- **6 Tbsp. canola oil**

FILLING

- **3 cups heavy cream**
- **1/2 cup lemon curd**
- **1/8 tsp. salt**
- **1 Tbsp. lemon zest plus 2 Tbsp. fresh juice (from 1 lemon)**
- **1/2 cup powdered sugar plus more for serving**

MACERATED STRAWBERRIES

- **1 (16-oz.) container fresh strawberries, quartered**
- **2 Tbsp. limoncello**
- **1/4 cup granulated sugar**
- **1 to 2 Tbsp. chopped fresh mint**

GARNISH

- **Lemon slices (optional)**

1. Prepare the Crêpes: Whisk together flour, baking powder, 1/8 teaspoon salt, and 1/4 cup granulated sugar in a large bowl. Whisk together milk, eggs, 1 tablespoon lemon zest, 2 tablespoons lemon juice, and 3 tablespoons of the oil in an 8-cup measuring cup. Whisk the milk mixture into the flour mixture until batter is completely smooth (with no lumps). Let stand 1 hour, or cover and chill overnight.

2. Cut 22 to 23 (12-inch) squares of wax paper. Heat a 10-inch nonstick skillet over medium. Brush a small amount of remaining oil in pan. Add 1/4 cup batter to pan, quickly tilting pan until batter covers bottom. Cook until Crêpe is set and just begins to lightly brown, 1 to 1 1/2 minutes. Turn over; cook until lightly browned, 1 to 1 1/2 minutes more. Transfer to a baking sheet, and cover with a piece of wax paper. Repeat procedure with remaining batter and oil, stacking Crêpes between wax paper. (Batter will make 22 to 23.) Cool to room temperature, about 30 minutes.

3. Meanwhile, prepare the Filling: Beat heavy cream, lemon curd, salt, and 2 tablespoons lemon juice with a heavy-duty stand mixer fitted with whisk attachment on medium speed until foamy. Gradually add powdered sugar, beating until stiff peaks form. (Do not overbeat.) Gently fold in 1 tablespoon lemon zest.

4. Prepare the Macerated Strawberries: Stir together strawberries, limoncello, and 1/4 cup granulated sugar. Let stand 10 minutes. Chill until ready to serve.

5. Assemble cake: Place 1 Crêpe on a serving platter. Using a small offset spatula, spread 1/3 cup of Filling on Crêpe, spreading almost to edge. Repeat with 19 more Crêpes, ending with a Crêpe on top. (Reserve remainder for another use.) Cover and chill 2 to 24 hours.

6. To serve, stir mint into Macerated Strawberries. Sprinkle top Crêpe with powdered sugar, and spoon Macerated Strawberries around the bottom. Garnish with lemon slices, if desired.

STRAWBERRIES
+
APRICOTS

These treats are a little jammy and a whole lot of flaky. Apricots allow the strawberries' tart side to shine in the filling. Can't find fresh apricots? Our Test Kitchen also used dried ones with the same great results.

Strawberry-Apricot Hand Pies

ACTIVE 35 MIN. - TOTAL 1 HOUR, 30 MIN.

SERVES 12

- **3 Tbsp. butter**
- **1/2 cup chopped peeled apricots (3 to 4 apricots)**
- **1 cup chopped fresh strawberries**
- **1/2 cup granulated sugar**
- **1 Tbsp. all-purpose flour**
- **2 Tbsp. fresh lemon juice**
- **2 (14.1-oz.) pkg. refrigerated piecrusts**
- **1 large egg**
- **1 Tbsp. whole milk**
- **2 Tbsp. Demerara sugar**

1. Melt butter in a small heavy-duty saucepan over medium. Add apricots, and cook, stirring constantly, until slightly softened, 2 to 3 minutes. Stir in strawberries and granulated sugar; cook, stirring constantly and crushing fruit with spoon, 8 minutes.

2. Stir together flour and lemon juice in a small bowl until smooth. Stir lemon juice mixture into strawberry mixture; bring to a boil. Boil, stirring often, until thickened, about 2 minutes. Remove from heat, and transfer mixture to a small bowl. Cover and chill about 20 minutes.

3. Meanwhile, preheat oven to 350°F. Roll 1 piecrust into a 12-inch circle on a lightly floured surface. Cut dough into 12 rectangles, using a 2 1/2- x 3-inch cutter. Repeat with remaining 3 piecrusts. Place 24 dough rectangles 2 inches apart on 2 parchment paper-lined baking sheets. Spoon about 1/2 tablespoon strawberry-apricot mixture into center of each dough rectangle, leaving a ½-inch border. Dampen edges of dough rectangles with water; top with remaining dough rectangles, pressing edges with a fork to seal.

4. Stir together egg and milk in a small bowl, and brush tops of hand pies. Cut 2 small Xs in each for steam to escape. Sprinkle each with about ¼ teaspoon Demerara sugar.

5. Bake in preheated oven until golden, 30 to 35 minutes. Transfer to a wire rack. Serve immediately, or cool completely.

STRAWBERRIES
+
MANGOES

The tangy, golden mango sorbet is a delicious contrast to the rich, milky sweetness of the strawberry ice cream. Make the semifreddo up to five days ahead, and pile on the fresh fruit just before serving.

Strawberry-Mango Semifreddo

ACTIVE 30 MIN. - TOTAL 5 HOURS, 30 MIN.
SERVES 8

- **1 cup heavy cream**
- **2 tsp. fresh lemon juice**
- **1 (16-oz.) container strawberry ice cream, softened**
- **1 (16-oz.) container mango sorbet, softened**
- **½ cup crushed shortbread cookies**
- **Diced mango and sliced strawberries**

1. Line bottom and sides of an 8½- x 4-inch loaf pan with plastic wrap, allowing 4 to 5 inches to extend over all sides.

2. Beat ½ cup of the heavy cream with an electric mixer on high speed until soft peaks form. Gently stir lemon juice into softened strawberry ice cream, and gently fold in whipped cream. Spread mixture into prepared pan, smoothing with a small offset spatula. Freeze 1 hour.

3. Beat remaining ½ cup heavy cream on high speed until soft peaks form. Gently fold whipped cream into softened mango sorbet. Spread mixture over strawberry mixture in loaf pan, smoothing with a small offset spatula, and sprinkle with cookie crumbs.

4. Pull excess plastic wrap at sides tightly over cake, gently pressing down on cookie crumbs. Freeze 4 to 24 hours.

5. Lift semifreddo from pan, using plastic wrap as handles, and transfer, crumb side down, to a serving plate. Garnish with diced mango and sliced strawberries. Cut semifreddo into 8 slices, using a serrated knife dipped in hot water and wiped dry.

Instead of cooking this compote on the stove-top, we roasted the nectarines and strawberries with the butter and sugar in the oven, which makes the fruits even juicier and sweeter.

Coconut Rice Pudding with Strawberry-Nectarine Compote

ACTIVE 55 MIN. - TOTAL 1 HOUR, 15 MIN.
SERVES 8

PUDDING
- 2 cups cooked basmati rice
- 2 cups whole milk
- 1 cup coconut milk
- 1 tsp. vanilla extract
- ¼ tsp. ground cinnamon
- ⅛ tsp. ground nutmeg
- ⅛ tsp. kosher salt
- ⅔ cup granulated sugar
- 1½ cups heavy cream
- 1 large egg
- ½ cup finely chopped unsalted pistachios

COMPOTE
- 3 cups quartered strawberries (about 1 qt.)
- 2 cups nectarine wedges, cut into 1- to 1½-inch cubes
- 2 Tbsp. butter, melted
- ¼ cup granulated sugar
- Finely chopped unsalted pistachios for topping (optional)

1. Prepare the Pudding: Stir together rice and whole milk in a sauté pan or large, deep skillet. Cook over medium, stirring often, until mixture comes to a boil, about 10 minutes. Reduce heat to low; simmer, stirring often, until mixture begins to thicken, about 10 minutes. Increase heat to medium; stir in coconut milk, vanilla, cinnamon, nutmeg, salt, ⅔ cup granulated sugar, and 1 cup of the heavy cream. Cook, stirring often, until mixture begins to bubble. Reduce heat to medium-low; cook, stirring often, until mixture thickens, about 20 minutes.
2. Whisk together egg and remaining ½ cup cream in a small bowl. Gradually whisk about ½ cup hot rice mixture into cream mixture; gradually whisk cream mixture into rest of rice mixture, and cook, stirring constantly, until thickened and creamy, about 2 minutes. Remove from heat, and stir in pistachios. Set aside.
3. Prepare the Compote: Preheat oven to 400°F. Stir together strawberries, nectarines, melted butter, and ¼ cup granulated sugar in a medium bowl. Spread mixture in an even layer in a lightly greased rimmed baking sheet. Bake in preheated oven until strawberries and nectarines are soft, about 15 minutes. Let stand 5 minutes.
4. Assemble servings: Spoon about 3 tablespoons Compote into each of 8 (6- to 8-ounce) wineglasses; top each with about ⅔ cup Pudding. Serve warm or at room temperature, or cover and chill. Top each with 2½ tablespoons Compote and chopped pistachios, if desired.

The creamy, iconic Southern dessert gets a refreshing zip from the juicy, flavorful berries. We used graham crackers instead of the usual vanilla wafers so it would slice more neatly.

Strawberry-Banana Pudding Icebox Cake

ACTIVE 40 MIN. - TOTAL 4 HOURS, 40 MIN.
SERVES 8

- 1 cup granulated sugar
- ¼ cup cornstarch
- ⅛ tsp. salt
- 4 large egg yolks
- 2 cups half-and-half
- 3 Tbsp. butter
- 1 Tbsp. lemon zest plus ¼ cup fresh juice (from 2 lemons)
- 27 graham cracker squares (about 2½ x 2½ inches)
- 4 large bananas, sliced
- 1 (16-oz.) container fresh strawberries, sliced
- 1 cup heavy cream
- ¼ cup powdered sugar
- Crumbled graham crackers and halved strawberries for topping

1. Whisk together granulated sugar, cornstarch, and salt in a heavy saucepan. Whisk together egg yolks and half-and-half in a small bowl. Add to sugar mixture; whisk until smooth. Bring mixture just to a boil over medium, whisking constantly. Boil 1 more minute, whisking constantly; remove from heat. Add butter and zest; whisk until butter melts. Gradually whisk in juice just until blended. Fill a sink or large bowl halfway with ice. Pour custard mixture into a metal bowl; place bowl on ice. Let stand, stirring occasionally, until custard is cold and slightly thickened, 8 to 10 minutes.
2. Line the bottom and sides of an 8-inch square pan with plastic wrap, allowing 4 inches to extend over all sides. Place 9 graham cracker squares in a single layer in bottom of pan to form a large square. (Crackers will not completely cover bottom.) Place a layer of banana slices, with sides touching, on graham crackers; place a layer of strawberry slices on top of bananas. Spread half of custard on top of strawberries. Repeat layers once, beginning and ending with graham crackers. Pull excess plastic wrap at sides tightly over cake; chill 4 hours or overnight.
3. Lift cake from pan, using plastic wrap as handles.
4. Beat cream with an electric mixer on high speed until foamy; gradually add powdered sugar, beating until medium-soft peaks form. Spread on top of cake. Top with crumbled graham crackers and strawberry halves.

Chicken Salad Gets a Makeover

Give your go-to recipe a rest, and get creative with these five juicy ideas

Chicken Niçoise Salad

ACTIVE 15 MIN. - TOTAL 1 HOUR

SERVES 4

- **4 bone-in, skin-on chicken breasts (about 3 lb.)**
- **3 Tbsp. olive oil**
- **3 tsp. kosher salt**
- **1 tsp. black pepper**
- **1 1/2 lb. fingerling potatoes, halved**
- **1 lb. haricots verts (thin French green beans)**
- **3 Tbsp. fresh lemon juice**
- **3 Tbsp. white wine vinegar**
- **3 Tbsp. finely chopped fresh herbs (such as dill, parsley, and chives)**
- **1 Tbsp. Dijon mustard**
- **1 tsp. granulated sugar**
- **1/2 cup olive oil**
- **1 pt. multicolored cherry tomatoes, halved**
- **4 hard-cooked eggs, halved**
- **1/4 cup Niçoise olives**

1. Preheat oven to 425°F. Rub chicken with 1 tablespoon of the olive oil. Sprinkle both sides evenly with 1 teaspoon of the salt and 1/2 teaspoon of the pepper. Place chicken, bone side down, on a rimmed baking sheet lined with aluminum foil. Set aside.

2. Toss together potatoes, 1 tablespoon of the oil, 3/4 teaspoon of the salt, and 1/4 teaspoon of the pepper on a large rimmed baking sheet lined with lightly greased aluminum foil. Bake chicken and potatoes in preheated oven 25 minutes.

3. Toss haricots verts with 3/4 teaspoon of the salt and remaining 1 tablespoon olive oil. Add haricots verts to pan with potatoes. Stir and continue baking both pans until chicken is cooked through, potatoes are tender, and haricots verts are tender-crisp, about 10 minutes. Remove pans from oven, and let chicken rest 10 minutes. Remove chicken from bone; cut into 1/2-inch to 3/4-inch slices. Discard bones.

4. While chicken rests, whisk together lemon juice, white wine vinegar, herbs, Dijon mustard, sugar, and remaining 1/2 teaspoon salt and 1/4 teaspoon pepper until combined; gradually whisk in olive oil until blended.

5. Arrange chicken, potatoes, haricots verts, tomatoes, egg halves, and olives on 4 plates. Drizzle each salad with 3 tablespoons dressing; serve remaining dressing on the side.

Oven-Fried Chicken Salad with Buttermilk Ranch Dressing

Grilled romaine lettuce gives this salad a smoky flavor.

ACTIVE 20 MIN. - TOTAL 40 MIN.
SERVES 6

- **1 cup panko (Japanese-style breadcrumbs)**
- **1/4 cup finely chopped pecans**
- **1 tsp. paprika**
- **2 1/4 tsp. kosher salt**
- **1 tsp. black pepper**
- **2 large egg whites**
- **1/2 cup all-purpose flour**
- **1 1/2 lb. chicken breast tenders**
- **Olive oil cooking spray**
- **3 romaine lettuce hearts, cut in half lengthwise**
- **3 (1/2-inch-thick) red onion slices (from 1 small onion)**
- **1 ear fresh corn, shucked**
- **1/2 cup whole buttermilk**
- **1/2 cup mayonnaise**
- **2 Tbsp. chopped fresh chives**
- **2 tsp. fresh lemon juice**
- **1 tsp. minced garlic**
- **1 pt. cherry tomatoes, halved**
- **4 bacon slices, cooked and crumbled**
- **1 cup garlic-butter seasoned croutons**
- **2 ripe avocados, chopped**

1. Preheat oven to 425°F. Place a lightly greased wire rack in an aluminum foil-lined rimmed baking sheet. Stir together panko, pecans, paprika, 1 teaspoon of the salt, and 1/2 teaspoon of the pepper in a bowl. In a separate bowl, whisk egg whites just until foamy. Place flour in another bowl.

2. Sprinkle chicken with 1/2 teaspoon of the salt. Dredge chicken in flour; dip in egg whites, and dredge in panko mixture, pressing to adhere. Coat chicken on each side with cooking spray; place on rack. Bake in preheated oven until done, 20 minutes, turning after 12 minutes. Slice chicken.

3. Meanwhile, heat a grill pan over medium-high. Coat cut sides of lettuce with cooking spray. Place lettuce, cut side down, on pan. Grill until marks appear, 3 minutes. Chop lettuce; place in a large bowl. Coat onion slices and corn with cooking spray. Grill onion until marks appear, 3 minutes per side. Grill corn, turning, until charred, 5 minutes. Cut kernels from cob; discard cob.

4. Whisk together buttermilk, next 4 ingredients, and remaining 3/4 teaspoon salt and 1/2 teaspoon pepper.

5. Toss together lettuce, tomatoes, and 1/4 cup dressing; arrange on a large platter. Top with onion, corn, chicken, bacon, croutons, and avocados. Serve remaining dressing on the side.

Chicken-Quinoa Salad with Green Goddess Dressing

Adding cooked quinoa is an easy and healthy way to make a simple salad more filling.

ACTIVE 10 MIN. - TOTAL 30 MIN.
SERVES 4

- **2/3 cup mayonnaise**
- **1 Tbsp. chopped fresh chives**
- **1 tsp. white wine vinegar**
- **1/2 tsp. anchovy paste**
- **1 tsp. lemon zest plus 1 Tbsp. fresh juice (from 1 lemon)**
- **1/4 tsp. black pepper**
- **1/2 cup loosely packed fresh parsley leaves**
- **1/3 cup loosely packed fresh tarragon leaves**
- **3/4 tsp. kosher salt**
- **3/4 cup water**
- **1/2 cup uncooked quinoa**
- **5 cups torn butter lettuce (from 1 head)**
- **3 cups pulled rotisserie chicken (from 1 chicken)**
- **1/2 cup thinly sliced English cucumber (from 1 cucumber)**
- **1/2 cup thinly sliced radishes (about 5 radishes)**

1. Process mayonnaise, chives, vinegar, anchovy paste, lemon zest, lemon juice, black pepper, 1/4 cup of the fresh parsley leaves, 1 tablespoon of the fresh tarragon leaves, and 1/4 teaspoon of the salt in a food processor until smooth, about 1 to 2 minutes. Set aside.
2. Bring water, quinoa, and remaining 1/2 teaspoon salt to a boil in a medium saucepan over medium-high. Stir and cover. Reduce heat to low, and cook until quinoa is tender and liquid is absorbed, about 15 minutes. Remove from heat; let stand 5 minutes. Remove lid, and fluff with a fork.
3. Toss together butter lettuce and remaining 1/4 cup each fresh parsley leaves and fresh tarragon leaves. Toss lettuce mixture lightly with about 1/4 cup dressing. Transfer to a serving platter. Sprinkle cooked quinoa over lettuce mixture; top with pulled rotisserie chicken. Arrange thinly sliced English cucumbers and thinly sliced radishes on top and around sides. Drizzle salad with an additional 1/4 cup dressing, and serve remaining dressing on the side, if desired.

Tropical Chicken Lettuce Wraps

Tropical Chicken Lettuce Wraps

This gluten-free chicken salad—which is livened up with jalapeño, lime zest, and honey—was a hit in the Test Kitchen. Substitute dried pineapple or avocado for the mango, if desired..

ACTIVE 15 MIN. - TOTAL 15 MIN.
SERVES 4

- **5 cups shredded rotisserie chicken (from 2 chickens)**
- **3 Tbsp. thinly sliced scallions**
- **3/4 cup mayonnaise**
- **2 Tbsp. honey**
- **2 tsp. minced jalapeño chile (from 1 chile)**
- **1 tsp. lime zest plus 1 Tbsp. fresh juice (from 1 lime)**
- **1/4 tsp. kosher salt**
- **1/8 tsp. black pepper**
- **12 butter lettuce leaves (from about 2 heads)**
- **1 cup 1/2-inch cubed mango (from 1 mango)**
- **1/2 cup coarsely chopped roasted, lightly salted cashews**
- **1/4 cup packed fresh cilantro leaves**
- **Lime wedges**

1. Toss together shredded chicken and scallions in a medium bowl. Whisk together mayonnaise, honey, jalapeño, lime zest, lime juice, salt, and pepper in a small bowl. Gently stir mayonnaise mixture into chicken mixture until combined.
2. Divide chicken mixture evenly among lettuce leaves (about 1/2 cup per leaf), and top evenly with mango, cashews, and cilantro leaves. Serve with lime wedges.

Chicken Caesar Salad Sandwiches

You can use your favorite sandwich rolls instead of mini baguettes, but be sure to spread on the garlic mayonnaise and toast the bread. The chicken-salad mixture tastes even better when prepped a day ahead, giving the flavors more time to meld.

ACTIVE 20 MIN. - TOTAL 20 MIN.
SERVES 4

- **3 cups shredded rotisserie chicken (from 1 chicken)**
- **2 oil-packed anchovy fillets, finely chopped**
- **1 garlic clove, minced**
- **1 Tbsp. fresh lemon juice**
- **1 Tbsp. red wine vinegar**
- **1 tsp. Dijon mustard**
- **1/2 tsp. Worcestershire sauce**
- **1/4 tsp. kosher salt**
- **1/8 tsp. black pepper**
- **1/3 cup extra-virgin olive oil**
- **1/2 oz. Parmesan cheese, grated (about 1/3 cup)**
- **3 Tbsp. mayonnaise**
- **1/4 tsp. garlic powder**
- **4 mini baguettes (or 1 French bread baguette cut into 4 portions), split**
- **4 romaine lettuce leaves**

1. Place chicken in a medium bowl. Process anchovy fillets, garlic, lemon juice, red wine vinegar, mustard, Worcestershire sauce, salt, and pepper in a blender until smooth. Gradually add olive oil, and process until smooth; stir in Parmesan cheese. Pour dressing over chicken, and toss to coat.
2. Stir together mayonnaise and garlic powder in a small bowl. Brush cut sides of bread evenly with mayonnaise mixture. Heat a large skillet over medium-high. Cook bread, cut side down, in hot skillet, until toasted and golden brown, about 2 minutes. Divide chicken mixture and lettuce leaves evenly among bottoms of toasted bread; cover with bread tops.

PREP AHEAD
It takes time to slice and caramelize the onions, but you can complete this step a day before and store the cooked onions in the refrigerator.

The French Onion Casserole

A rich and cheesy soup inspired this dish made with in-season Vidalia onions

French Onion Soup Casserole

Naturally sweet, Georgia-grown Vidalia onions are made for caramelizing, and this indulgent recipe with layers of bread, onions, and cheese is a great way to enjoy them.

ACTIVE 1 HOUR, 20 MIN. - TOTAL 1 HOUR, 50 MIN.
SERVES 6

- **1/4 cup unsalted butter**
- **5 medium Vidalia onions, thinly sliced (about 3 lb.)**
- **2 tsp. kosher salt**
- **1/2 tsp. black pepper**
- **3 thyme sprigs**
- **2 flat-leaf parsley sprigs**
- **2 bay leaves**
- **1 (16-oz.) baguette, thinly sliced**
- **1/3 cup all-purpose flour**
- **3 cups reduced-sodium beef broth**
- **1/2 cup sherry**
- **8 oz. Gruyère cheese, shredded (about 2 cups)**
- **1 tsp. fresh thyme leaves**

1. Melt butter in a Dutch oven over medium-low; add onions, salt, pepper, thyme and parsley sprigs, and bay leaves; cook, stirring often, until onions are golden brown, about 1 hour.

2. Meanwhile, preheat oven to 350°F. Arrange baguette slices in a single layer on a baking sheet. Bake in preheated oven until lightly toasted, 12 minutes. Set aside.

3. Remove and discard thyme and parsley sprigs and bay leaves from onion mixture. Add flour, and cook, stirring constantly, 2 minutes. Add broth and sherry; bring to a boil over high. Boil, stirring constantly, until slightly thickened, 2 to 3 minutes.

4. Layer half of the toasted baguette slices in a 13- x 9-inch baking dish. Spoon onion mixture evenly over bread. Top evenly with remaining baguette slices. Sprinkle with cheese; cover with aluminum foil. Bake in preheated oven 30 minutes. Increase heat to broil. Remove foil; broil until cheese is bubbly, about 3 minutes. Sprinkle with thyme leaves.

PASTA PICK
We prefer a twisty-shaped noodle like gemelli, which traps the flavorful sauce, but any short tubular pasta will work.

One-Pot Primavera

Step up pasta night with shrimp and seasonal veggies

Pasta Primavera with Shrimp

ACTIVE 20 MIN. - TOTAL 30 MIN.
SERVES 4

- **2 Tbsp. olive oil**
- **1 lb. peeled and deveined raw medium shrimp**
- **3/4 tsp. kosher salt**
- **1 large red bell pepper, chopped (about 1 1/4 cups)**
- **5 oz. snap peas, diagonally halved crosswise (about 1 1/4 cups)**
- **1/4 cup chopped shallot (about 1 medium shallot)**
- **10 oz. uncooked gemelli pasta**
- **4 cups unsalted chicken stock**
- **4 oz. baby spinach (about 4 cups)**
- **1 1/2 cups chopped Broccolini (about 4 oz.)**
- **2 Tbsp. white wine vinegar**
- **1/2 oz. pecorino Romano cheese, shredded (about 2 Tbsp.)**
- **1/2 tsp. crushed red pepper**

1. Heat 1 tablespoon of the oil in a Dutch oven over medium-high. Sprinkle shrimp with 1/4 teaspoon of the salt. Add shrimp to Dutch oven; cook until cooked through, 3 to 4 minutes, stirring once. Remove shrimp; set aside. Pour off any remaining drippings from Dutch oven. Add remaining 1 tablespoon oil. Add bell pepper, snap peas, and shallot, and cook, stirring often, until vegetables are tender, about 4 minutes. Add bell pepper mixture to shrimp; cover to keep warm.

2. Add pasta, stock, and remaining 1/2 teaspoon salt to Dutch oven; bring to a boil over medium-high. Boil pasta, stirring occasionally, until pasta is almost tender and stock is almost absorbed, about 9 minutes. Add spinach and Broccolini; cook until spinach is wilted, 1 to 2 minutes. Stir in shrimp mixture and vinegar. Remove from heat. Divide mixture evenly among 4 bowls; top with cheese and red pepper.

Nutritional information (per serving):
Calories: 489 - Protein: 34g - Carbs: 65g - Fiber: 5g - Fat: 10g

EASY SQUEEZE
Microwaving the Key limes for 10 seconds will help soften them so they are easier to juice.

Sweet Tarts

Lime and coconut make a delightful pair in these party-worthy pies

Mini Coconut-Key Lime Pies

ACTIVE 20 MIN. - TOTAL 3 HOURS, 35 MIN.
SERVES 12

- **1 cup graham cracker crumbs (from about 8 graham crackers)**
- **1 cup sweetened flaked coconut**
- **6 Tbsp. butter, melted**
- **5 Tbsp. granulated sugar**
- **1 (14-oz.) can sweetened condensed milk**
- **1/2 cup Key lime juice**
- **3 large egg yolks**
- **1/2 tsp. salt**
- **1 Tbsp. plus 1/2 tsp. lime zest (from 2 limes)**
- **3/4 cup heavy cream**
- **1/2 tsp. vanilla extract**
- **Key lime slices**

1. Preheat oven to 350°F. Place 12 jumbo-size (3 1/2-inch) aluminum foil baking cups in a regular-size muffin pan, and coat with cooking spray.
2. Stir together graham cracker crumbs, coconut, melted butter, and 4 tablespoons of the sugar in a bowl until combined; firmly press onto bottom and up sides of each baking cup (about 3 rounded tablespoons of mixture per cup). Bake in preheated oven until lightly browned, about 5 minutes. Set aside. Keep oven set at 350°F.
3. Whisk together sweetened condensed milk, Key lime juice, egg yolks, salt, and 1 tablespoon of the lime zest in a bowl until combined. Pour mixture evenly into prepared crusts (about 1/4 cup per crust). Bake until pies are just set, 12 to 14 minutes. Cool completely on a wire rack, about 1 hour. Refrigerate 2 hours, and then remove aluminum foil baking cups before serving.
4. Beat heavy cream with an electric mixer on medium-high speed until foamy. Gradually add vanilla and remaining 1 tablespoon sugar; beat until medium peaks form. Fold in remaining 1/2 teaspoon lime zest. Top each mini pie with a dollop of whipped cream, and garnish with a Key lime slice.

COOKING (SL) SCHOOL

TIPS AND TRICKS FROM THE SOUTH'S MOST TRUSTED KITCHEN

KITCHEN TRICKS

4 Ways To Use Past-Their-Prime Strawberries

Fast and fresh recipes for bruised or overripe fruit

STRAWBERRY FOOL
Puree 1 cup stemmed strawberries and 1 Tbsp. sugar in a food processor or blender until smooth. Gently fold the berry puree into 2 cups lightly sweetened whipped cream. Top servings with sliced berries and crushed butter cookies.

STRAWBERRY VINAIGRETTE
Puree 1 cup chopped, stemmed strawberries; 2 Tbsp. honey; 5 Tbsp. apple cider vinegar; 1/3 cup extra-virgin olive oil; 1 tsp. salt; and 1/4 tsp. black pepper in a food processor or blender until smooth.

STRAWBERRY BUTTER
Combine 1 stick softened butter; 1 cup chopped, stemmed strawberries; and 1 Tbsp. confectioners' sugar in the bowl of a stand mixer. Beat on medium speed until fluffy, about 2 minutes.

STRAWBERRY OJ
Puree 1/2 cup chopped, stemmed strawberries in a food processor or blender until smooth. Pour through a fine-mesh strainer, and discard seeds. Stir strained berry puree into 2 cups chilled freshly squeezed orange juice.

IN SEASON

Make the Most of Vidalia Onions

Our best tips for buying and storing these Georgia-grown gems

CHECK THE ORIGIN
Not all sweet onions are Vidalias. That distinction is for onions grown in or around Vidalia, Georgia (not Walla Walla or Maui onions).

STORE CAREFULLY
They'll keep well in a cool, dry place. If storing them in the refrigerator, wrap each onion in a paper towel, which will help absorb moisture.

DON'T TOSS THE TOPS
Onions sold at farm stands or farmers' markets often come with their green tops still attached. Use them as a substitute for scallions.

"Use a spatula instead of a spoon when stirring your chicken salad. This allows you to scrape up every last bit of the dressing from the bowl."

—Pam Lolley
Test Kitchen Professional

KNOW-HOW

Chicken Salad Tip

Did you know that dressing adheres better to torn meat than to chopped? Try our favorite superfast shredding method: Place cooked (skinless and boneless) chicken breasts in the bowl of a stand mixer, and mix on the lowest setting until the meat is torn.

May

96 **Gotta Love Crab** Get crackin' on these seven seasonal crab recipes

102 QUICK FIX **Next-Level Kebabs** Skewer dinnertime stress with five quick-and-easy recipes tailor-made for busy weeknights with a trio of sides to make it a meal

106 ONE AND DONE **Modern Mediterranean** An herbaceous sheet pan roast of potatoes and chicken is brightened with feta, tomatoes, and briny olives

107 WHAT CAN I BRING? **Pick a Pepper** Queso in a blanket? The new spin on the stuffed pepper popper

108 HEALTHY IN A HURRY **The Spice Is Right** Gild the pig with one of three inspired rubs created for the other white meat

109 SAVE ROOM **Thyme for Pie** The secret ingredient in this blueberry pie might surprise you

110 *SL* COOKING SCHOOL Crimp your pie! Master our four creative ways to make decorative pie crust edges

Gotta Love Crab

From a blue crab boil to soft-shell sandwiches, get crackin' on these seven seasonal recipes

Crab Boil with Beer and Old Bay

Blue crabs, once called the "pride of the Chesapeake," are typically in season from late spring to summer in most parts of the Coastal South. If you're lucky enough to get your hands on some live blue crabs, there's no better way to enjoy them than in an old-fashioned crab boil, preferably served outside with cold beer. (Pictured at left)

ACTIVE 20 MIN. - TOTAL 50 MIN.
SERVES 8

- **4 qt. water**
- **48 oz. light beer**
- **1 cup Old Bay seasoning**
- **3 Tbsp. kosher salt**
- **6 lemons, halved, plus lemon wedges for serving**
- **4 garlic heads, halved**
- **3 small yellow onions, halved with root ends intact**
- **2 lb. small red potatoes, halved**
- **2 lb. andouille sausage, cut into 3-inch pieces**
- **8 medium-size ears fresh corn, halved**
- **4 lb. live blue crabs**

1. Combine water, beer, Old Bay, salt, lemons, garlic, and onions in a large (8- to 10-quart) stockpot; bring to a boil over medium-high. Add potatoes, sausage, and corn, and cook until potatoes are tender, about 20 minutes. Using a slotted spoon; remove all solids from pot, and spread in a single layer on a large baking sheet lined with parchment paper or newspaper.
2. Return cooking liquid to a boil; add crabs, and cook until shells are bright orange and crabmeat flakes easily, about 10 minutes. Serve crabs with potatoes, sausage, corn, and lemon wedges.

Crab-and-Bacon Linguine

Crab-and-Bacon Linguine

White wine, heavy cream, and bacon combine to make an elegant pan sauce that pairs wonderfully with buttery jumbo lump crab. When draining the cooked pasta, be sure to save some of the hot cooking water. The starchy liquid adds body to the sauce.

ACTIVE 30 MIN. - TOTAL 45 MIN.
SERVES 6

- **12 oz. uncooked linguine**
- **4 oz. thick-cut bacon, coarsely chopped**
- **1 small sweet onion, finely chopped (about ½ cup)**
- **2 garlic cloves, minced**
- **1 large red Fresno chile, seeded and finely chopped**
- **½ cup dry white wine**
- **1 cup heavy cream**
- **1 lb. fresh jumbo lump crabmeat, drained and picked over**
- **¼ cup chopped fresh flat-leaf parsley**
- **2 Tbsp. unsalted butter**
- **1 Tbsp. fresh lemon juice (from 1 lemon)**
- **1 tsp. kosher salt**

1. Cook linguine according to package instructions; drain, reserving ¼ cup cooking water.
2. Add bacon to a large nonstick skillet over medium, and cook, stirring often, until bacon is browned and crisp, about 10 minutes. Add onion, garlic, and red chile to skillet, and cook, stirring often, until softened and aromatic, about 5 minutes.
3. Add white wine to skillet, and cook, stirring and scraping all bits off bottom, until reduced by half, about 5 minutes. Add cream to skillet; cook until slightly thickened, about 5 minutes. Add cooked pasta and reserved cooking water, and stir to coat. Add crabmeat, parsley, butter, lemon juice, and salt; gently toss until butter is melted and crabmeat is heated through, 2 minutes. Serve immediately.

Crab Pie

Crab Pie

Wow your brunch crowd with this creative spin on quiche made with crabmeat, sautéed spinach, and cream cheese. Save time by using a refrigerated piecrust, or make your own from scratch—either way, this savory pie is a keeper.

ACTIVE 20 MIN. - TOTAL 1 HOUR, 35 MIN.
SERVES 8

- **½ (14.1-oz.) pkg. refrigerated piecrusts**
- **1 Tbsp. olive oil**
- **1 small leek (about 5 oz.), finely chopped**
- **4 oz. baby spinach, chopped (about 3 cups)**
- **3 large eggs**
- **1 cup heavy cream**
- **4 oz. cream cheese, softened**
- **2 Tbsp. finely chopped fresh chives**
- **1 Tbsp. finely chopped garlic (about 2 garlic cloves)**
- **1 Tbsp. Dijon mustard**
- **2 tsp. finely chopped fresh thyme**
- **1½ tsp. kosher salt**
- **½ tsp. lemon zest (from 1 lemon)**
- **8 oz. fresh lump crabmeat, drained and picked over**

1. Preheat oven to 350°F. Fit piecrust into a 9-inch pie plate according to package directions. Set aside.
2. Heat oil in a skillet over medium-high; add leek, and cook, stirring often, until soft and slightly golden, about 10 minutes. Add spinach to skillet, and cook, stirring often, until spinach is wilted and all water has evaporated, about 5 minutes. Remove spinach-leek mixture from skillet.
3. Whisk together eggs, heavy cream, and cream cheese in a large bowl until smooth. Whisk in chives, garlic, mustard, thyme, salt, and lemon zest. Gently fold in spinach-leek mixture and crabmeat; carefully pour mixture into prepared piecrust. Place on middle rack of preheated oven, and bake until set in middle, about 50 minutes. Cool pie on a wire rack 15 minutes before cutting.

Deviled Crab Melts

Kick off a party with crunchy crostini topped with seasoned crabmeat, juicy tomatoes, and gooey cheese. Watch the crab melts when they are under the broiler, and pull the pan out of the oven when the cheese starts to brown.

ACTIVE 20 MIN. - TOTAL 30 MIN.
SERVES 8

- **8 sourdough bread slices**
- **24 oz. fresh lump crabmeat, drained and picked over**
- **1 cup mayonnaise**
- **2 Tbsp. chopped fresh cilantro**
- **2 Tbsp. chopped fresh basil plus basil leaves for topping**
- **1½ tsp. lime zest (from 1 lime)**
- **1 tsp. kosher salt**
- **¼ tsp. chili powder**
- **⅛ tsp. cayenne pepper**
- **5 plum tomatoes, cut into ¼-inch-thick slices**
- **8 oz. Monterey Jack cheese, shredded (about 2 cups)**

1. Preheat broiler with oven rack 6 inches from heat. Place bread on a wire rack on a baking sheet; broil until golden brown, about 3 minutes. Remove pan; set aside.
2. Gently combine crabmeat, mayonnaise, cilantro, basil, lime zest, salt, chili powder, and cayenne in a large bowl.
3. Spread crab mixture evenly over bread slices. Top evenly with tomato slices and cheese. Return pan to oven, and broil until cheese is melted and starting to brown, about 3 minutes. Let cool 5 minutes, top with basil, and serve immediately.

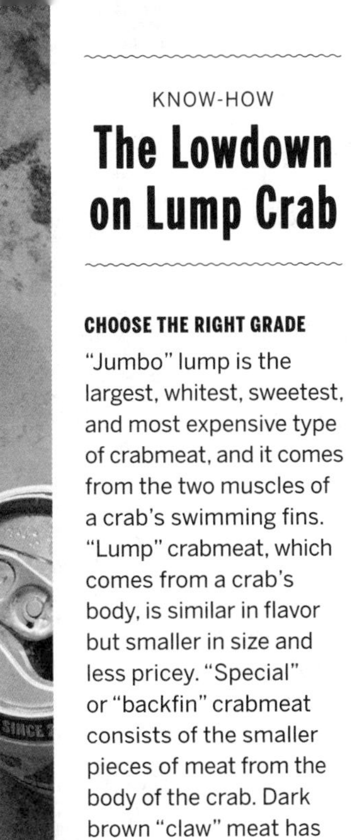

KNOW-HOW

The Lowdown on Lump Crab

CHOOSE THE RIGHT GRADE

"Jumbo" lump is the largest, whitest, sweetest, and most expensive type of crabmeat, and it comes from the two muscles of a crab's swimming fins. "Lump" crabmeat, which comes from a crab's body, is similar in flavor but smaller in size and less pricey. "Special" or "backfin" crabmeat consists of the smaller pieces of meat from the body of the crab. Dark brown "claw" meat has a stronger flavor.

STORE SMART

Fresh crabmeat (and pasteurized crabmeat that has already been opened) should be kept in the refrigerator and used within two to three days. Unopened pasteurized crabmeat can be stored in the refrigerator for up to one month.

PREP PROPERLY

It's important to remove any stray bits of shell. Spread the crabmeat on a baking sheet, and place it under the broiler for 45 seconds. The meat will barely get warm, but the shells will turn bright orange, so you'll be able to pick them out easily.

Deviled Crab Melts, page 98

SEAFOOD SMARTS

Clean Soft-Shell Crabs with Confidence

LET YOUR FISHMONGER DO THE WORK, OR FOLLOW THESE THREE EASY STEPS

1. Using a sharp pair of kitchen shears, snip off the front of the crab, about ½ inch behind the mouth and the eyes. Squeeze out and discard the gooey matter where the cut was made.

2. Carefully raise the top shell on one side of the crab. Cut and discard the feathery-looking gills; repeat on the other side.

3. Turn the crab over, and snip off the tough flap on the stomach. Rinse, pat dry, and cook or store immediately.

Crispy Soft-Shell Crab Sandwiches, page 101

Crispy Soft-Shell Crab Sandwiches

Our homemade rémoulade sauce takes this classic seafood sandwich to the next level. If you're new to cooking soft-shell crabs, many seafood counters sell crabs that are cleaned and ready to cook. (Be sure to use them the same day you purchase them.) Or follow our directions (at left) and prep them at home with kitchen shears.

ACTIVE 1 HOUR - TOTAL 1 HOUR
SERVES 6

- **½ cup mayonnaise**
- **2 Tbsp. chopped sweet-hot sandwich pickles (such as Wickles)**
- **1 Tbsp. chopped fresh flat-leaf parsley**
- **1 tsp. fresh lemon juice (from 1 lemon)**
- **½ tsp. smoked paprika**
- **½ tsp. hot sauce (such as Tabasco)**
- **1 small shallot, finely chopped (about 2 Tbsp.)**
- **1½ tsp. kosher salt**
- **1 tsp. black pepper**
- **6 live soft-shell crabs**
- **½ cup all-purpose flour**
- **4 Tbsp. unsalted butter**
- **4 Tbsp. olive oil**
- **1 small head romaine lettuce (about 4 oz.), cut into 4-inch pieces**
- **2 large tomatoes (about 1 lb.), cut into ¼-inch-thick slices**
- **6 large potato rolls, split**

1. Stir together first 7 ingredients, 1 teaspoon of the salt, and ½ teaspoon of the pepper in a bowl; set aside.
2. Using a sharp pair of kitchen shears, snip off mouth and eyes of crabs; squeeze out gooey matter where cut was made. Carefully raise top shell on far left of crab. Use shears to cut away feathery-looking gills; repeat procedure on right side of crab. Turn crab over, and remove tough flap from stomach.
3. Stir together flour and remaining ½ teaspoon each salt and pepper. Dredge crabs in flour mixture, shaking off excess. Melt 2 tablespoons butter with 2 tablespoons oil in a large skillet over medium-high until hot. Add 3 prepared crabs; cook until golden brown and aromatic, 4 to 5 minutes per side. Place crabs on paper towels to drain and cool. Repeat with remaining butter, oil, and prepared crabs.
4. Divide sauce, fried crabs, lettuce, and tomatoes evenly among potato rolls, and serve immediately.

Best-Ever Crab Cakes with Green Tomato Slaw

Flavored with fresh herbs, lemon, and a hint of hot sauce, these crunchy crab cakes live up to their name. The tangy slaw is fantastic on the side or with any fried seafood.

ACTIVE 30 MIN. - TOTAL 45 MIN.
SERVES 6

CRAB CAKES

- **12 oz. fresh jumbo lump crabmeat, drained and picked over**
- **12 oz. fresh lump crabmeat, drained and picked over**
- **4½ Tbsp. salted butter, melted and cooled**
- **4½ Tbsp. chopped scallions (from 4 scallions)**
- **1½ Tbsp. finely chopped fresh flat-leaf parsley**
- **1½ Tbsp. finely chopped fresh dill**
- **1½ tsp. lemon zest plus 1½ Tbsp. fresh juice (from 1 lemon)**
- **1½ tsp. kosher salt**
- **1½ tsp. hot sauce (such as Tabasco)**
- **3 large eggs, lightly beaten**
- **1 large garlic clove, minced (about 2 tsp.)**
- **2¼ cups panko (Japanese-style breadcrumbs), divided**
- **4 Tbsp. canola oil**

GREEN TOMATO SLAW

- **2 medium-size green tomatoes, thinly sliced and cut into matchsticks (about 2 cups)**
- **1 celery stalk, thinly sliced (about ½ cup)**
- **1 small sweet onion, thinly sliced (about 1 cup)**
- **1 small red bell pepper, thinly sliced (about 1 cup)**
- **2 Tbsp. chopped fresh flat-leaf parsley**
- **2 Tbsp. olive oil**
- **2 Tbsp. white wine vinegar**
- **1 Tbsp. granulated sugar**
- **1½ tsp. kosher salt**
- **½ tsp. black pepper**

1. Prepare the Crab Cakes: Place first 11 ingredients and 1¾ cups of the panko in a large bowl, and gently combine.
2. Shape crabmeat mixture into 6 (3-inch) cakes, about 6½ ounces each. Sprinkle remaining ½ cup panko on a large plate; gently transfer cakes to plate, pressing both sides in panko. Cover and chill until slightly firm, about 15 minutes.
3. Preheat oven to 375°F. Heat 2 tablespoons canola oil in a large nonstick skillet over medium-high. Gently reshape 3 Crab Cakes, and place in hot oil. Cook until golden brown, 4 to 5 minutes on each side. Transfer to a wire rack set in a baking sheet. Repeat with remaining oil and cakes. Place baking sheet in preheated oven, and bake cakes until heated through, about 10 minutes.
4. Prepare the Green Tomato Slaw: Toss together all slaw ingredients, and serve over Crab Cakes.

West Indies Crab Salad

Fresh lump crab doesn't need a whole lot of fuss. This little-known salad (believed to have originated in Mobile, Alabama) boosts the crabmeat's sweetness with a tangy vinaigrette.

ACTIVE 15 MIN. - TOTAL 15 MIN.
SERVES 6

- **2 lb. fresh jumbo lump crabmeat, drained and picked over**
- **⅔ cup rice vinegar**
- **½ cup finely chopped white onion (from 1 small onion)**
- **¼ cup granulated sugar**
- **¼ cup extra-virgin olive oil**
- **2 Tbsp. lemon zest (from 2 lemons)**
- **2 tsp. kosher salt**
- **1 tsp. black pepper**
- **¼ cup finely chopped fresh mint**
- **6 Bibb lettuce leaves (from 1 head)**

Place crabmeat, vinegar, onion, sugar, oil, lemon zest, salt, and pepper in a large bowl, and gently combine. Serve immediately, or chill, covered, 2 to 3 hours. (Salad is best after chilling.) Fold in mint just before serving. Spoon crab mixture and juices over lettuce leaves, and serve.

Next-Level Kebabs

Five sensational skewers—all fast, fun, and easy enough for weeknight dinners on the grill

Shrimp-Okra-and-Sausage Kebabs

ACTIVE 20 MIN. - TOTAL 20 MIN.
SERVES 4

- 8 oz. large peeled and deveined raw shrimp, tail-on
- 8 oz. andouille sausage, sliced into 1/2-inch rounds
- 6 oz. small okra pods, halved lengthwise (about 1 1/2 cups)
- 2 Tbsp. olive oil
- 2 tsp. Cajun seasoning (such as Slap Ya Mama)
- 1/2 tsp. black pepper
- 2 Tbsp. salted butter, melted
- 1 tsp. lemon juice (from 1 lemon)
- 1 tsp. hot sauce (such as Crystal)
- Lemon wedges

1. Preheat grill to high (450°F to 500°F); or heat a grill pan over high, and lightly grease. Combine shrimp, sausage, okra, olive oil, Cajun seasoning, and black pepper in a large bowl; toss to coat. Thread mixture onto 8 (8-inch) skewers, with sausage rounds inside shrimp and alternating with okra slices.

2. Place kebabs on lightly greased grill grate or in grill pan. Grill, uncovered, until okra is charred and shrimp is cooked through, about 1 1/2 minutes per side. Transfer kebabs to a serving plate. Stir together butter, lemon juice, and hot sauce; brush on kebabs. Serve with lemon wedges.

Steak-and-Potato Kebabs

Microwave the potatoes before grilling to ensure they're soft on the inside.

ACTIVE 15 MIN. - TOTAL 30 MIN.
SERVES 4

- **8 oz. baby golden potatoes, halved**
- **1 Tbsp. water**
- **2 tsp. kosher salt**
- **1 tsp. ancho chile powder**
- **1 tsp. paprika**
- **1 tsp. light brown sugar**
- **1/2 tsp. ground cumin**
- **1/2 tsp. dry mustard**
- **1/2 tsp. ground coriander**
- **2 Tbsp. olive oil**
- **1 lb. hanger steak, cut into 1-inch pieces**
- **1 medium-size red onion, cut into 1-inch pieces**
- **1 medium-size red bell pepper, cut into 1-inch pieces**

1. Preheat grill to medium-high (400°F to 450°F); or heat a grill pan over medium-high, and lightly grease. Place potatoes and water in a medium-size microwavable bowl; cover tightly with plastic wrap. Microwave on HIGH until tender, about 4 minutes. Spread potatoes on a plate lined with paper towels; let stand 10 minutes.
2. Combine salt, ancho chile powder, paprika, brown sugar, cumin, dry mustard, coriander, and oil in a large bowl. Add steak, onion, bell pepper, and potatoes; toss to coat. Thread mixture, alternating steak, onion, bell pepper, and potatoes, onto 8 (8-inch) skewers; place on lightly greased grill grate or in grill pan. Grill, uncovered, until potatoes, pepper, and onions are tender and steak is charred and cooked to desired degree of doneness (about 10 minutes per side for medium), turning occasionally.

Lemon-Herb Chicken Kebabs

Lemon-Herb Chicken Kebabs

The tangy herb-and-lemon marinade also tastes great with pork or lamb.

ACTIVE 25 MIN. - TOTAL 1 HOUR, 35 MIN.
SERVES 4

- **1/2 cup packed fresh flat-leaf parsley leaves, finely chopped**
- **1/2 cup packed fresh cilantro leaves, finely chopped**
- **2 Tbsp. lemon juice**
- **1 Tbsp. packed fresh oregano, finely chopped**
- **1 Tbsp. honey**
- **1/2 tsp. crushed red pepper**
- **6 Tbsp. olive oil**
- **2 tsp. kosher salt**
- **1 tsp. black pepper**
- **1 1/4 lb. boneless, skinless chicken thighs, cut into 1-inch-wide strips**
- **12 oz. thick asparagus, cut into 1 1/2-inch pieces**
- **2 small lemons, very thinly sliced and seeds removed**

1. Stir together first 6 ingredients, 5 tablespoons of the oil, 1 teaspoon of the salt, and 1/2 teaspoon of the black pepper in a medium bowl. Add chicken; toss to coat. Chill 1 hour.
2. Preheat grill to medium-high (400°F to 450°F). Toss asparagus and lemon slices with remaining 1 tablespoon oil. Remove chicken from marinade; discard marinade. Thread chicken, asparagus, and lemon slices tightly onto 8 (8-inch) skewers, folding chicken strips and lemon slices in half as needed. Sprinkle with remaining 1 teaspoon salt and 1/2 teaspoon black pepper. Place kebabs on lightly greased grill grate. Grill, uncovered, until asparagus is tender and chicken is charred and cooked through, 12 to 14 minutes, turning occasionally.

Grilled Pork Meatball Kebabs

Grilled Pork Meatball Kebabs

Gochujang is a spicy-sweet Korean chile paste. If you can't find it, substitute 2 tablespoons Sriracha chili sauce, and increase sugar to 2 teaspoons.

ACTIVE 25 MIN. - TOTAL 35 MIN.
SERVES 4

- 1 large egg, beaten
- 2 tsp. grated fresh ginger
- 1 tsp. finely chopped garlic (from 1 garlic clove)
- 1 1/2 tsp. kosher salt
- 1/2 tsp. black pepper
- 4 Tbsp. gochujang sauce (such as Bibigo Gochujang Hot & Sweet Sauce)
- 1 lb. ground pork
- 1/2 cup panko (Japanese-style breadcrumbs)
- 6 scallions, cut into 1 1/2-inch pieces
- 3 Tbsp. soy sauce
- 1 1/2 Tbsp. rice vinegar
- 2 tsp. toasted sesame oil
- 1 tsp. granulated sugar
- 8 Little Gem lettuce leaves or romaine lettuce heart leaves
- 1/4 cup roasted salted peanuts, chopped
- Chopped fresh cilantro
- Lime wedges

1. Preheat grill to medium-high (400°F to 450°F); or heat a grill pan over medium-high, and lightly grease. Stir together egg, ginger, garlic, salt, pepper, and 1 tablespoon of the gochujang sauce in a large bowl. Add pork and panko, and gently mix with hands until just combined. Form into 24 (1 1/4-inch) meatballs (about 1 ounce each). Thread meatballs, alternating with scallion pieces, onto 8 (8-inch) skewers.
2. Place kebabs on lightly greased grill grate or in grill pan. Grill, uncovered, until meatballs are lightly charred and cooked through, 12 to 14 minutes, turning occasionally.
3. Whisk together soy sauce, vinegar, oil, sugar, and remaining 3 tablespoons gochujang sauce in a small bowl. Place each skewer on a lettuce leaf, and spoon 2 teaspoons sauce over each kebab. Sprinkle with peanuts and cilantro. Serve with lime wedges and remaining sauce.

Halloumi-and-Summer Vegetable Kebabs

Use a Y-shaped vegetable peeler to shave the yellow squash and zucchini into long, thin strips.

ACTIVE 20 MIN. - TOTAL 1 HOUR, 20 MIN.
SERVES 4

- 6 Tbsp. olive oil
- 1/2 cup packed fresh basil plus more for garnish
- 1/4 cup packed fresh mint, plus more for garnish
- 1 garlic clove, smashed
- 1/2 tsp. black pepper
- 8 oz. Halloumi cheese, cut into 3/4-inch cubes
- 1 cup cherry tomatoes
- 1 small zucchini (about 6 oz.), shaved lengthwise
- 1 small yellow squash (about 6 oz.), shaved lengthwise
- 1/2 tsp. kosher salt

1. Process oil, basil, mint, garlic, and pepper in a blender until smooth, about 15 seconds. Pour mixture over Halloumi in a medium dish; stir to coat. Cover and chill 1 hour.
2. Preheat grill to high (450°F to 500°F); or heat a grill pan over high, and lightly grease. Add tomatoes to cheese mixture; toss to coat. Thread tomatoes, zucchini, squash, and cheese onto 8 (8-inch) skewers; sprinkle with salt. Place kebabs on lightly greased grill grate or in grill pan. Grill, uncovered, until cheese is lightly charred and vegetables are tender, about 1 1/2 minutes per side. Garnish with basil and mint leaves.

Superfast Sides

Three fresh 15-minute dishes that pair well with all of our kebabs

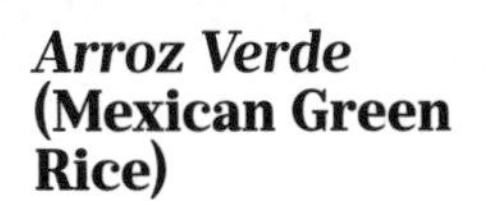

Arroz Verde (Mexican Green Rice)

ACTIVE 15 MIN. - TOTAL 15 MIN.
SERVES 4

Heat **1 tablespoon olive oil** in a large skillet over medium. Add **1 large chopped poblano chile** and **1/2 cup chopped white onion;** cook, stirring occasionally, until tender, about 8 minutes. Add **2 chopped garlic cloves** and **1/2 teaspoon cumin;** cook, stirring, until fragrant, 1 minute. Transfer mixture to a food processor, and add **1/2 cup fresh cilantro leaves, 1 teaspoon kosher salt, 1/2 teaspoon black pepper,** and **2 tablespoons olive oil.** Meanwhile, place **4 cups water** in a large microwavable bowl, and microwave on HIGH until hot, about 4 minutes. Add **5 ounces baby spinach;** let stand 1 minute. Remove spinach; squeeze between paper towels to remove excess moisture. Add spinach to mixture in food processor. Process until smooth, about 45 seconds, stopping to scrape sides as needed. Heat **2 (8.8-ounce) packages precooked microwavable rice** according to package directions. Transfer hot rice to a large bowl, and stir in cilantro mixture. Top with **1 ounce crumbled queso fresco (fresh Mexican cheese).** Serve immediately.

Couscous Pilaf

ACTIVE 10 MIN. - TOTAL 15 MIN.
SERVES 4

Heat **2 tablespoons butter** in a small saucepan over medium-high. Add **1 1/4 cups lower-sodium chicken broth;** bring to a boil. Stir in **1 cup uncooked couscous, 3/4 cup golden raisins, 1 teaspoon salt,** and **1/2 teaspoon black pepper;** cover and remove from heat. Let stand 5 minutes. Fluff couscous with a fork; stir in **1/2 cup toasted slivered almonds, 1/3 cup chopped fresh flat-leaf parsley,** and **1/4 cup thinly sliced red onion.**

Quick Pickled Slaw

ACTIVE 5 MIN. - TOTAL 15 MIN.
SERVES 4

Combine **1/2 cup rice vinegar, 1/2 cup water, 1 tablespoon granulated sugar, 1 tablespoon mustard seeds,** and **1 1/2 teaspoons salt** in a saucepan. Bring to a boil over high. Boil, stirring, until sugar dissolves, 1 minute. Place **3 cups angel hair cabbage, 1 cup matchstick carrots,** and **3 radishes (cut into matchsticks)** in a medium bowl. Pour vinegar mixture over slaw mixture; stir to combine. Chill, uncovered, 12 minutes. Drain and serve.

Modern Mediterranean

A fresh tomato-and-feta topping brightens this one-pan chicken supper

Sheet Pan Greek Chicken with Roasted Potatoes

Two baking staples, cinnamon and nutmeg, make this savory dish smell and taste heavenly.

ACTIVE 15 MIN. - TOTAL 1 HOUR
SERVES 4

- **2 tsp. onion powder**
- **2 tsp. kosher salt**
- **2 tsp. dried thyme**
- **1 tsp. black pepper**
- **1/4 tsp. ground cinnamon**
- **1/4 tsp. ground nutmeg**
- **1/4 cup chopped fresh flat-leaf parsley**
- **3 tsp. chopped fresh oregano leaves**
- **1/4 cup extra-virgin olive oil**
- **4 (12-oz.) bone-in, skin-on chicken breasts, trimmed**
- **8 thin lemon slices (from 2 lemons)**
- **1 1/2 lb. Yukon Gold potatoes (about 1 1/2 inch diameter), halved lengthwise**
- **1/2 cup chopped tomato (from 1 tomato)**
- **1/2 cup kalamata olives, coarsely chopped**
- **2 oz. feta cheese, crumbled (about 1/4 cup)**

1. Preheat oven to 400°F with rack about 8 inches from heat. Combine onion powder, salt, thyme, pepper, cinnamon, nutmeg, 2 tablespoons of the parsley, and 2 teaspoons of the oregano in a mini food processor; pulse several times until well blended. Add oil; pulse until combined.

2. Place chicken and lemons on a rimmed baking sheet; rub chicken evenly with 1/4 cup of the herb mixture. Toss potatoes with remaining 3 tablespoons herb mixture. Arrange potatoes around chicken and lemon slices. Roast in preheated oven until a thermometer inserted in thickest portion of chicken registers 155°F and potatoes are tender, about 30 minutes.

3. Increase oven temperature to broil. Broil until skin is browned and crisp, about 5 minutes. Remove from oven, and let stand 5 to 10 minutes. Sprinkle with tomato, olives, feta, and remaining 2 tablespoons parsley and 1 teaspoon oregano.

Pick a Pepper

Turn everyone's favorite party dip into a fun bite-size hors d'oeuvre

Queso-Filled Mini Peppers

ACTIVE 25 MIN. - TOTAL 1 HOUR
SERVES 10

- 2 (16-oz.) pkg. mini sweet peppers
- 1 Tbsp. canola oil
- 3/4 tsp. kosher salt
- 8 oz. pepper Jack cheese, shredded (about 2 cups)
- 1/2 cup evaporated milk
- 2 oz. cream cheese, softened
- 1/4 cup chopped pickled jalapeños
- 2 Tbsp. unsalted butter
- 1/2 cup panko (Japanese-style bread-crumbs)
- 1/4 tsp. black pepper
- 2 Tbsp. finely chopped fresh cilantro

1. Preheat broiler on HIGH with oven rack 5 inches from heat. Toss peppers with oil and 1/2 teaspoon of the salt; arrange in a single layer on an aluminum foil-lined rimmed baking sheet. Broil until tops are lightly charred, 3 to 5 minutes. Let cool to room temperature, 30 minutes. Reduce oven temperature to 425°F.

2. Flip over peppers so charred side is on bottom; cut and remove top third of each pepper (from stem end to tip). Discard cut-off part, or reserve for another use. Scoop out membranes and seeds, and discard.

3. Whisk together pepper Jack cheese and milk in the top of a double boiler over simmering water over medium. Whisk until smooth, 5 minutes. Remove from heat; stir in cream cheese, jalapeños, and remaining 1/4 teaspoon salt. Spoon a heaping teaspoon of cheese mixture into each pepper. Place on a baking sheet. Bake until tops are golden, 5 minutes.

4. Meanwhile, melt butter in a skillet over medium. Add panko and pepper; cook, stirring, until golden brown, 3 more minutes. Sprinkle peppers with panko mixture and cilantro.

MAKE AHEAD

Place filled peppers in a baking dish; cover and chill 1 day. Bake, covered, at 425°F for 5 minutes, and then uncover and bake 3 more minutes. Top with panko mixture and cilantro.

INGREDIENT SWAP

Replace the rice with cooked orzo, farro, or quinoa.

Choose Your Rub

SPICY RUB

Combine 2 tsp. ancho chile powder, 2 tsp. dried oregano, 2 tsp. ground cumin, 1 tsp. kosher salt, 1/2 tsp. black pepper, and 1/2 tsp. cayenne pepper.

MAKES ABOUT 3 TBSP.

SMOKY RUB

Combine 4 tsp. smoked paprika, 1 tsp. kosher salt, 3/4 tsp. black pepper, 1 tsp. garlic powder, 1/2 tsp. onion powder, and 1/2 tsp. sugar.

MAKES ABOUT 3 TBSP.

HERB RUB

Combine 1 Tbsp. chopped fresh oregano, 2 Tbsp. chopped fresh flat-leaf parsley, 2 tsp. chopped fresh rosemary, 1 tsp. lemon zest, 1 tsp. kosher salt, and 3/4 tsp. black pepper.

MAKES ABOUT 1/4 CUP.

The Spice Is Right

Three flavorful rubs to liven up boring boneless pork chops

Grilled Spice-Rubbed Pork Chops with Scallion-Lime Rice

ACTIVE 25 MIN. - TOTAL 25 MIN.
SERVES 4

- **4 (6-oz.) boneless center-cut pork loin chops (about 3/4 inch thick)**
- **2 Tbsp. olive oil**
- **Spicy Rub, Smoky Rub, or Herb Rub (recipes at above right)**
- **1 ear fresh corn, shucked**
- **1 bunch scallions (6 to 8 scallions), root ends trimmed**
- **1 (8.8-oz.) pouch precooked microwavable brown rice**
- **1 cup halved multicolored cherry tomatoes**
- **2 Tbsp. fresh lime juice (from 2 limes)**
- **1/2 tsp. kosher salt**
- **1/2 tsp. black pepper**

1. Preheat grill to medium-high (400°F to 450°F).

2. Place pork chops on a rimmed baking sheet or in a shallow dish; rub with 1 tablespoon of the oil. Rub chops all over with choice of rub, pressing to adhere. Place chops and corn on grill grate coated with cooking spray. Grill, covered, until a thermometer inserted into thickest portion of pork registers 140°F (temperature will continue to rise to 145°F as it rests off heat), turning occasionally at a 90-degree angle to ensure even grill marks, about 3 minutes per side. Grill corn, turning occasionally, until charred and cooked, 6 to 8 minutes. Remove chops and corn from grill.

3. Lightly coat scallions with cooking spray, and place on grate. Grill, turning often, until just softened and charred, about 90 seconds.

4. Cook brown rice according to package directions. Cut corn kernels from cob into a large bowl. Chop scallions into 1-inch pieces, and add to corn. Add rice, tomatoes, lime juice, salt, pepper, and remaining 1 tablespoon oil; toss to combine. Serve rice mixture alongside pork chops.

Nutritional information (per serving):
Calories: 429 - Protein: 40g - Carbs: 26g - Fiber: 3g - Fat: 18g

Thyme for Pie

A fresh herb adds a fragrant twist to this blueberry dessert

SERVING TIP
Let the pie cool completely before slicing it so the filling has time to set.

Thyme-Scented Blueberry Pie

Quick-cooking tapioca is our Test Kitchen's secret for a "just-right" fruit filling that's firm but not gelatinous.

ACTIVE 25 MIN. - TOTAL 5 HOURS, INCLUDING 3 HOURS COOLING
SERVES 8

- 7 cups fresh blueberries
- 1/3 cup uncooked quick-cooking tapioca
- 2 Tbsp. fresh lemon juice (from 1 lemon)
- 1/4 tsp. salt
- 1 cup granulated sugar
- 2 tsp. finely chopped fresh thyme
- 1 (14.1-oz.) pkg. refrigerated piecrusts
- 1 large egg white, beaten until frothy
- 2 Tbsp. coarse sanding sugar
- Vanilla ice cream (optional)

1. Preheat oven to 375°F. Mash 1 cup of the blueberries in a medium saucepan; stir in tapioca, lemon juice, and salt until tapioca dissolves. Stir in 1 cup of the blueberries and 1/2 cup of the sugar, and place over medium. Cook, stirring often, until blueberries begin to burst and mixture begins to thicken, 5 to 7 minutes. Remove from heat, and let cool 5 minutes. Place thyme and remaining 5 cups blueberries and 1/2 cup sugar in a large bowl; stir in cooked blueberry mixture. Set aside.

2. Unroll 1 piecrust, and fit into a lightly greased (with cooking spray) 9-inch pie plate; trim edges to lip of pie plate. Unroll a second piecrust on a very lightly floured work surface. Using a 1 1/2-inch round cutter (or a paring knife), cut out a circle in the center of top piecrust. Using a paring knife, cut 6 slits around the circle for steam to escape.

3. Spoon blueberry mixture into prepared piecrust in pie plate; cover with second prepared piecrust; turn edges under, and crimp. Brush entire piecrust with beaten egg white, and sprinkle evenly with sanding sugar.

4. Place pie on a baking sheet lined with aluminum foil. Bake in preheated oven 30 minutes. Cover edges of pie with aluminum foil. Bake pie until crust is browned and filling is bubbly, 45 to 50 minutes more, covering entire pie with aluminum foil after 20 to 25 minutes to prevent overbrowning, if necessary. Cool completely on a wire rack, about 3 hours. Top slices with ice cream, if desired.

COOKING SL SCHOOL

TIPS AND TRICKS FROM THE SOUTH'S MOST TRUSTED KITCHEN

"The key to cooking kebabs is cutting the ingredients the same size for fast, even results."

—Robby Melvin
Test Kitchen Director

TEST KITCHEN TECHNIQUES

4 Creative Ways To Crimp a Piecrust

A pretty edge makes even the most basic pie look professional

THE DOUBLE SCALLOP Carefully press a floured teaspoon, mini cookie scoop, or small melon baller around the edge of the piecrust to make evenly spaced half-moon indentations in the dough. Go around the crust two times.

THE ROPE Gently crimp a ½-inch section of crust between your index fingers at a slight angle so the dough peaks in the center and flattens out on both sides. Then repeat with the remaining dough to crimp the entire piecrust.

THE PINCH AND PRESS Make V-shaped crimps around the entire crust by pressing outward, leaving about ½ inch of space between each crimp. Once finished, use a small floured fork to press down carefully on the dough between each crimp.

THE FLUTED EDGE Press one side of a floured fluted pastry cutter around the edge of the whole piecrust to create a decorative scalloped design.

KNOW-HOW

Build a Better Kebab

USE TWO SKEWERS instead of one to keep ingredients from spinning around on them.

COAT THE SKEWERS with cooking spray to help the ingredients slide on smoothly.

THREAD LONG, THIN PROTEINS, like strips of steak, accordion style (over and under) onto skewers.

June

112 **Forgotten Fruit Desserts** These old-fashioned fruit desserts with funny names deserve a spot on your summer table

118 **The Soul of a Chef** Atlanta Chef Todd Richards shines a light on the roots of soul food and where he's taking it

121 QUICK FIX **You Say Tomato** The star of the summer garden will have you saying "yum!"

124 DINNER IN AMERICA **Lasagna Gets a New Look** A basket weave of zucchini ribbons stands in for the traditional sheets of pasta in this hearty lasagna

125 HEALTHY IN A HURRY **Salad for Supper** Whole-grain croutons add fiber and nutrition to a chicken and vegetable bread salad

126 WHAT CAN I BRING? **Let Them Eat Shrimp** A longtime Southern favorite, pickled shrimp are a make-ahead nibble that's always party perfect

127 SAVE ROOM **Twice as Nice** Peaches and bourbon collide in an upside-down cake that screams with Southern flavor

128 *SL* COOKING SCHOOL Master perfect croutons and take a peach primer

Forgotten Fruit Desserts

BUCKLE, KUCHEN, SONKER, SLUMP–
they may sound funny, but wait till you taste them. Here, six old-fashioned favorites that are making a comeback

BLUEBERRY-LEMON CRUNCH BARS
page 115

Crunch

Consider this fair warning: It may look like a bar cookie, but you'll need a fork to eat it. Similar to a crisp with baked fruit and a crumbly topping, a crunch sandwiches a jammy fruit filling between two buttery layers. The fruit is cooked down into a thick, nonsyrupy preserve. The bottom layer should be firm enough to keep from crumbling when a piece is cut from the pan, so adding toasted pecans to the mixture improves the taste as well as the texture. The top layer can duplicate the bottom, or it can be a simple streusel made with flour, sugar, and butter.

Pandowdy

Popular in the 1800s and early 1900s, a pandowdy is essentially cooked fruit underneath a layer of pastry. A fork was often used to break (or "dowdy") the crust. As the dish cooled, the pieces of broken pastry absorbed the sweet juices from the baked fruit, creating a delicious treat with a messy look. While developing this recipe, Test Kitchen pro Deb Wise was reminded of a dessert her grandmother made with gooseberries, boysenberries, or blackberries. It had a double crust that she would "break open to let the juices bubble up and spill over," recalls Deb, who used nectarines and cherries in our version. The patchwork-style crust is thick enough so it doesn't disappear into the filling.

CHERRY NECTARINE-PANDOWDY
page 115

BERRY SONKER WITH DIP
page 115

Sonker

Never heard of a sonker? You're not alone. It's a beloved dessert in a particular part of the South–Surry County, North Carolina, in the foothills of the Blue Ridge Mountains, to be precise. Those familiar with sonkers agree that they must be baked in a large, deep pan (one that's big enough to feed hungry farmhands) and then topped with a creamy vanilla sauce called "dip." And that's where the agreement ends. Opinions vary as to how the dessert is made: Some declare it must have a bottom crust, others argue it just needs a top crust, and the rest insist that a true sonker is made only with sweet potatoes–everything else is simply a cobbler.

GINGER-PLUM SLUMP
page 116

Slump

The slump (sometimes called a grunt up North) is the stovetop version of a cobbler—and it's the only thing you'll want to make when it's too hot to turn on your oven. Believed to be a variation of an English steamed pudding, a slump is simmered fruit that is topped with pillowy, lightly sweet dumplings. Cooked in a large cast-iron skillet or Dutch oven, it's also a popular treat to make on the grill or over a campfire. The fruit is boiled in the skillet until it's sweet and syrupy, topped with mounds of soft dough, and then covered. As the fruit bubbles away, the dumplings bake and "slump" down, giving this dessert its distinctive name.

Buckle

Often made with blueberries, buckles became popular in the 1960s after a recipe for the dish appeared in Elsie Masterton's 1959 *Blueberry Hill Cookbook*. These homey, streusel-topped cakes are usually prepared one of two ways: The batter can be spread on the bottom of the pan with the fruit spooned on top, or the fruit can be stirred directly into the batter. Here, we created a third method: Half of the fruit is folded into the batter, which is then poured into the pan, and the remaining fruit is arranged on top. As the cake bakes, the batter puffs up and collapses (or "buckles") around the pockets of fruit.

PEACH-RASPBERRY BUCKLE
page 116

STRAWBERRY KUCHEN
page. 117

Kuchen

The Southern dessert canon is filled with treats brought to the region from different parts of the world and adopted as our own. One of these is kuchen, which means "cake" in German. While some variations are more breadlike and made with a yeasted dough, our version has a fluffy, tender crumb and a dimpled top covered with strawberries and sliced almonds. The recipe calls for a round cake pan, but you can use a springform pan for a more impressive presentation.

Blueberry-Lemon Crunch Bars

ACTIVE 30 MIN. - TOTAL 5 HOURS, 30 MIN.
SERVES 12

FILLING
- **4 cups fresh blueberries**
- **¾ cup granulated sugar**
- **¼ cup cornstarch**
- **1 Tbsp. lemon zest plus 3 Tbsp. fresh juice (from 2 lemons)**

CRUST
- **2 ¼ cups all-purpose flour**
- **½ cup finely chopped toasted pecans**
- **1 tsp. baking powder**
- **¼ tsp. salt**
- **½ cup granulated sugar**
- **5 Tbsp. unsalted butter, softened**
- **5 Tbsp. vegetable shortening**
- **1 large egg**
- **1 tsp. vanilla extract**
- **5 Tbsp. heavy cream**

TOPPING
- **½ cup all-purpose flour**
- **¼ cup granulated sugar**
- **¼ cup packed light brown sugar**
- **⅛ tsp. salt**
- **¼ cup unsalted butter**

1. Prepare the Filling: Combine berries, sugar, cornstarch, zest, and juice in a saucepan over medium-high; bring to a boil. Reduce heat to medium-low, and simmer, mashing berries as they cook, until thick and bubbly, about 10 minutes. Cool completely, about 30 minutes.
2. Prepare the Crust: Stir together flour, pecans, baking powder, and salt in a medium bowl.
3. Combine sugar, butter, and shortening in a large bowl, and beat with an electric mixer on medium speed until light and fluffy, 2 to 3 minutes. Add egg and vanilla, beating until combined. Gradually add cream, beating on low speed until incorporated.
4. Add flour mixture to butter mixture; beat at low speed until well combined. Divide dough in half; place each half on a piece of plastic wrap. Shape each half into a 6- x 4-inch rectangle, about 1 inch thick. Wrap, and freeze 2 hours.
5. Prepare the Topping: Preheat oven to 350°F. Whisk together flour, granulated sugar, brown sugar, and salt in a medium bowl. Using a pastry blender or two knives, cut butter into mixture until it resembles small pebbles. Chill until ready to use.
6. Using a box grater or a food processor fitted with a grating blade, grate half of the dough (leave remaining half in freezer). Press grated dough into bottom of a 9-inch square pan coated with cooking spray. Bake in preheated oven until beginning to brown around edges, 12 to 14 minutes.
7. Remove pan from oven. Carefully spread Filling over Crust, from edge to edge. Grate remaining half of dough, and sprinkle over Filling; gently press. Sprinkle Topping over dough. Bake in preheated oven until well browned, 35 to 40 minutes.
8. Cool completely on wire rack, about 2 hours. Cut into 12 bars.

Cherry-Nectarine Pandowdy

ACTIVE 30 MIN. - TOTAL 3 HOURS
SERVES 12

CRUST
- **2 cups all-purpose flour**
- **1 Tbsp. granulated sugar**
- **¼ tsp. salt**
- **¾ cup cold unsalted butter, cut into ½-inch pieces**
- **¼ cup cold vegetable shortening**
- **4-5 Tbsp. ice water**

FILLING
- **2 ½ lb. nectarines, unpeeled and sliced**
- **1 ½ lb. fresh cherries, pitted**
- **1 cup granulated sugar**
- **6 Tbsp. all-purpose flour**
- **1 tsp. lemon zest plus 2 Tbsp. fresh juice (from 1 lemon)**
- **¼ tsp. salt**
- **1 large egg yolk**
- **2 tsp. water**

1. Prepare the Crust: Combine flour, sugar, and salt in a food processor; pulse until combined, 2 to 3 times. Add butter and shortening; pulse until mixture resembles small pebbles, 3 to 4 times. Drizzle in 4 tablespoons of the ice water; pulse until mixture begins to clump, 3 to 4 times, adding remaining 1 tablespoon of water, 1 teaspoon at a time as needed. Transfer mixture to a lightly floured work surface; knead until mixture is incorporated, 3 to 4 times. Shape into a 7- x 5-inch rectangle; cover with plastic wrap, and chill 1 hour.
2. Prepare the Filling: Combine nectarines, cherries, sugar, flour, lemon zest, lemon juice, and salt in a bowl; toss well. Spread mixture into a lightly greased (with cooking spray) 11- x 8-inch baking dish. Preheat oven to 400°F.
3. Roll dough into a 12-inch square (dough will be thick). Cut dough into 16 (3-inch) squares. Arrange squares over top of fruit in patchwork fashion, slightly overlapping edges. Whisk together yolk and water in a small bowl. Brush top of dough with egg mixture. Bake in preheated oven 30 minutes.
4. Without removing pandowdy from oven, reduce oven temperature to 350°F. Bake until Filling is thick and bubbly and Crust is golden, 25 to 30 minutes. (Cover after 15 minutes, if needed, to prevent overbrowning.) Cool 30 minutes before serving. Serve warm or at room temperature.

Berry Sonker with Dip

ACTIVE 30 MIN. - TOTAL 4 HOURS, 45 MIN.
SERVES 16

CRUST
- **2 cups all-purpose flour**
- **¼ cup powdered sugar**
- **⅛ tsp. salt**
- **1 cup cold unsalted butter, cut into cubes**
- **2 large egg yolks**
- **¼ cup ice water**

FILLING
- **9 cups fresh blueberries (about 2 ½ lb.)**
- **7 cups fresh blackberries (about 1 ¾ lb.)**
- **5 cups fresh raspberries (about 1 ½ lb.)**
- **1 ½ cups granulated sugar**
- **¾ cup uncooked quick-cooking tapioca**
- **1 tsp. ground nutmeg**
- **½ tsp. salt**
- **3 Tbsp. unsalted butter**
- **1 large egg yolk**
- **1 tsp. water**

DIP
- **2 cups half-and-half**
- **¾ cup granulated sugar**
- **⅛ tsp. salt**
- **1 ½ Tbsp. cornstarch**
- **1 ½ Tbsp. cold water**
- **1 tsp. vanilla extract**

1. Prepare the Crust: Add flour, powdered sugar, and salt to a food processor, and pulse until combined, 2 to 3 times. Add butter; process until mixture resembles coarse sand.

2. Whisk together egg yolks and ice water in a small bowl. With processor running, pour egg mixture through food chute, and process until mixture begins to clump.
3. Transfer to a lightly floured surface; knead until dough is smooth, 2 to 3 times. Shape dough into a 7- x 5-inch rectangle, and cover with plastic wrap. Chill 1 hour.
4. Prepare the Filling: Preheat oven to 350°F. Combine all berries in a large bowl. Stir together sugar, tapioca, nutmeg, and salt in a small bowl. Add to berries; toss gently to coat. Scoop berry mixture into a 14- x 10- x 3-inch baking dish (or a 13 ½- x 9 ⅝- x 2 ¾-inch disposable aluminum pan). Dot top of berries evenly with butter.
5. Roll dough on a lightly floured surface into a 16- x 12-inch rectangle. Use a ¾-inch round cutter or base of a piping tip to cut holes all over dough, leaving a 2-inch border around edges. Place dough on top of berry mixture; fold dough under edges of pan and crimp. Whisk together egg yolk and water; brush dough evenly with egg mixture.
6. Bake in preheated oven until Filling is bubbly and Crust is well browned, 1 hour and 10 minutes to 1 hour and 15 minutes. (Cover top with aluminum foil, if needed, to prevent overbrowning.) Let stand on a wire rack at least 2 hours before serving.
7. Prepare the Dip: Combine half-and-half, sugar, and salt in a saucepan over medium; bring to a gentle boil. Stir together cornstarch and cold water in a small bowl until smooth, and stir into half-and-half mixture. Cook until mixture is thick and bubbly, stirring constantly, 1 to 2 minutes. Strain Dip through a fine wire-mesh strainer into a small serving pitcher, and stir in vanilla. Serve sonker warm, and drizzle each serving with warm Dip.

Ginger-Plum Slump

ACTIVE 25 MIN. - TOTAL 55 MIN.
SERVES 10

FILLING
- **1 cup water**
- **1 cup granulated sugar**
- **1 ½ lb. ripe red plums, pitted and quartered**
- **1 ½ lb. ripe black plums, pitted and quartered**
- **1 ½ tsp. minced fresh ginger**

DUMPLINGS
- **1 ¾ cups all-purpose flour**
- **3 Tbsp. granulated sugar**
- **2 tsp. baking powder**
- **½ tsp. salt**
- **¾ cup whole milk**
- **¼ cup unsalted butter, melted**

TOPPING
- **1 cup heavy cream**
- **3 Tbsp. powdered sugar**
- **2 Tbsp. roughly chopped crystallized ginger**

1. Prepare the Filling: Combine water and sugar in a 12-inch cast-iron skillet with lid over medium-high. Bring to a boil, stirring until sugar dissolves. Add plums and fresh ginger; cover skillet, and bring mixture to a boil. Reduce heat to medium-low, and simmer, covered, 10 minutes.
2. Prepare the Dumplings: Whisk together flour, sugar, baking powder, and salt in a medium bowl. Add whole milk and melted butter, stirring until batter is combined and smooth.
3. Remove lid from skillet, and drop rounded spoonfuls of batter evenly over ginger-plum mixture. (You should have 10 Dumplings, about 2 tablespoons each.) Reduce heat to low; cover skillet, and simmer until a wooden pick inserted in center of Dumplings comes out clean, about 20 minutes.
4. Prepare the Topping: Combine heavy cream and powdered sugar in a medium bowl, and beat with an electric mixer on high speed until soft peaks form. Serve slump warm in shallow bowls. Top each serving with a dollop of sweetened whipped cream, and sprinkle with chopped crystallized ginger.

Peach-Raspberry Buckle

ACTIVE 20 MIN. - TOTAL 2 HOURS, 5 MIN.
SERVES 8

TOPPING
- **½ cup all-purpose flour**
- **½ cup chopped pecans**
- **¼ cup granulated sugar**
- **¼ cup packed light brown sugar**
- **¼ tsp. salt**
- **5 Tbsp. unsalted butter, melted**

CAKE
- **1 cup granulated sugar**
- **¼ cup unsalted butter**
- **1 large egg**
- **½ tsp. vanilla extract**
- **1 ¾ cups all-purpose flour**
- **2 tsp. baking powder**
- **½ tsp. salt**
- **¾ cup whole milk**
- **1 cup peeled chopped fresh peach (about 1 large peach)**
- **1 cup fresh raspberries**

1. Preheat oven to 350°F. Prepare the Topping: Stir together flour, chopped pecans, granulated sugar, brown sugar, and salt in a medium bowl. Stir in butter until well combined. Chill until ready to use.
2. Prepare the Cake: Beat sugar and butter in a medium bowl with an electric mixer on medium speed until mixture looks sandy, 2 to 3 minutes. Add egg, and beat until well combined. Beat in vanilla.
3. Whisk together flour, baking powder, and salt in a medium bowl. Alternately add flour mixture and milk to butter mixture in 5 additions, beginning and ending with flour mixture. Beat until combined after each addition. Gently fold in ½ cup each of the chopped peach and raspberries.
4. Transfer batter into a greased (with butter) and floured 9-inch springform pan. Arrange remaining ½ cup each of the chopped peach and raspberries in an even layer over top of batter.
5. Sprinkle chilled Topping evenly over the fruit. Bake in preheated oven until browned and a wooden pick inserted in center comes out clean, 40 to 45 minutes.
6. Cool in pan on a wire rack 15 minutes. Run a knife around edge of pan to loosen Cake from sides. Remove sides of pan. Cool on wire rack about 45 minutes. Serve warm or at room temperature.

Strawberry Kuchen

ACTIVE 20 MIN. - TOTAL 1 HOUR, 20 MIN.
SERVES 8

- **½ cup softened unsalted butter**
- **1 cup plus 1 Tbsp. granulated sugar**
- **2 large egg yolks**
- **1 large egg**
- **1 ½ cups all-purpose flour**
- **1 ½ tsp. baking powder**
- **⅛ tsp. salt**
- **½ cup whole milk**
- **2 cups sliced fresh strawberries**
- **¼ cup sliced almonds**
- **¼ tsp. ground cinnamon**

1. Preheat oven to 350°F. Beat butter and 1 cup of the sugar in a large bowl with an electric mixer on medium speed until light and fluffy, 3 to 4 minutes. Add yolks and egg, 1 at a time, beating well after each addition.

2. Whisk together flour, baking powder, and salt in a medium bowl. Alternately add flour mixture and milk to butter mixture in 5 additions, beginning and ending with flour mixture. Beat on low speed just until blended after each addition. Transfer batter to a greased (with butter) and floured 9-inch round cake pan.

3. Arrange sliced strawberries in an even layer over top of batter, and sprinkle evenly with sliced almonds. Sprinkle ground cinnamon and remaining 1 tablespoon sugar evenly over strawberries.

4. Bake in preheated oven until browned and a wooden pick inserted in center comes out clean, 35 to 40 minutes. Cool cake in pan on a wire rack until room temperature, about 20 minutes, or serve warm.

THE SOUL OF A CHEF

In his debut cookbook, Atlanta chef **TODD RICHARDS** puts his original stamp on soul food

Todd Richards remembers that sausage biscuit well. He was only about 4 years old then, but he can still taste the peppery meat with its crisp edges and the flaky bread layers that left butter on his fingers. The biscuit itself was nothing special, just a pit stop meal at a Bob Evans restaurant, but for a Chicago-born kid on a road trip to the South, it was a revelation. "I didn't know what biscuits were," he says. "We were a cornbread family."

Every summer, Richards and his parents drove from Chicago to Hot Springs, Arkansas, to visit his Auntie Wanda and Uncle Daniel. In Hot Springs, he ate peaches from roadside stands, drank iced sweet tea instead of hot tea, and realized that tomatoes weren't always perfectly round like at the grocery store back home.

Whether in Chicago or on those family trips, Richards was surrounded by great cooks and eaters, especially his parents. He can still see his father stirring pots of richly spiced red beans, and he can still taste his mother's crisp fried catfish as if it were yesterday. "Cooking was central to every party, every birthday, every holiday," he says. "There was always so much food–you would have thought the President was coming."

Given his background, it's not surprising that he would find his calling as a chef or that he would head South to do it. In 1993, he moved to Atlanta and

worked up to a position in the kitchen at the Occidental Grand Hotel (now the Four Seasons), where he trained under the late Darryl Evans, one of the city's most influential chefs.

In the decades that followed, Richards made his own imprint across the city's food scene—from fine dining (White Oak Kitchen & Cocktails; The Ritz-Carlton, Atlanta and Buckhead) to the airport (as culinary director of One Flew South) to Richards' Southern Fried (as the chef-owner of this hot-chicken spot in Krog Street Market).

In *Soul*, Richards' first cookbook, the chef unites his restaurant training and the seasonal, down-home cooking he grew up eating. He says the two sides of his culinary background have a lot in common. "The way my dad made pot roast is no different from how I make osso buco. My mom fried up squares of leftover grits to make croutons. That's something you see with a stiff price tag at restaurants today."

Through stories and sophisticated, globally influenced dishes (Collard Green Ramen, Stone-Ground Grits Soufflés), the book defines what "soul" means to Richards. Of course, there's a recipe for biscuits—flavored with black pepper and thyme. Old soul, meet new soul.

GET THE BOOK
Soul: A Chef's Culinary Evolution in 150 Recipes is on sale now.

CHICKEN THIGHS AND BBQ BEANS

"This is inspired by the beans my dad made as a side dish when he grilled for celebrations during the summer," says Richards. "He always fixed too much so we'd have leftover beans, and this recipe does the same."

ACTIVE 30 MIN. - TOTAL 10 HOURS, 5 MIN., INCLUDING 8 HOURS SOAKING
SERVES 2

- 4 bone-in, skin-on chicken thighs
- 4 tsp. kosher salt
- 2 tsp. coarsely ground black pepper
- 2 Tbsp. blended olive oil
- 1 lb. dried white beans, soaked in water 8 hours or overnight
- 2 cups diced yellow onions (from 2 onions)
- 1¼ cups diced green bell peppers (from 2 bell peppers)
- ½ cup diced celery (from about 2 stalks)
- 4 garlic cloves, minced
- 1½ tsp. red pepper flakes
- 6 cups chicken stock
- 2 bay leaves
- ⅛ tsp. fennel seeds
- 1 cup packed light brown sugar
- ½ cup ketchup
- ¼ cup Worcestershire sauce
- 2 Tbsp. coarse-grain mustard
- 2 Tbsp. apple cider vinegar
- 2 scallions, thinly sliced

1. Sprinkle the chicken thighs with 1½ teaspoons of the salt and 1 teaspoon of the black pepper.
2. Heat the oil in a large saucepan over medium. Sear the chicken thighs, skin side down, in the hot oil, until golden brown, about 7 minutes. Turn the chicken over, and cook until browned, about 5 more minutes. Remove the chicken from the pan; set aside.
3. Add the beans, onions, bell peppers, celery, garlic, red pepper flakes, stock, bay leaves, and fennel seeds to the pan; bring to a boil.
4. Reduce heat to medium-low, and simmer until the beans are tender, about 1 hour and 30 minutes. Stir the brown sugar, ketchup, Worcestershire sauce, mustard, vinegar, and remaining 2½ teaspoons salt into the pan. Return the chicken to the pan, and simmer until the chicken is done, about 10 minutes. Remove and discard the bay leaves.
5. Let stand 25 minutes. Sprinkle with remaining 1 teaspoon black pepper and thinly sliced scallions before serving.

CANTALOUPE SOUP WITH CHORIZO RELISH AND BLACK PEPPER-AND-HONEY WHIPPED GOAT CHEESE

Melon puree may be used as a sauce for meats, frozen for sorbet, or as in this case, enjoyed as a soup. Soups are a simple way to introduce uncommon flavors of a new cuisine. A bowlful offers the comfort of a familiar dish and inventive taste combinations simultaneously.

SERVES 4

- **2 tsp. blended olive oil**
- **1 medium shallot, diced (about ¼ cup)**
- **½ cup (4 oz.) unfiltered apple cider**
- **1 Tbsp. apple cider vinegar**
- **1 tsp. kosher salt**
- **⅛ tsp. red pepper flakes**
- **1 (4-lb.) cantaloupe, peeled and cut into chunks (about 8 cups)**
- **1 (8-oz.) cucumber, peeled, seeded, and cut into chunks (about 1 cup)**
- **¼ cup (2 oz.) extra-virgin olive oil**
- **Black Pepper-and-Honey Whipped Goat Cheese**
- **Chorizo Relish**

1. Heat the oil in a saucepan over medium. Add the shallot, and cook, stirring often, until the shallot is tender, about 5 minutes.
2. Add the apple cider, apple cider vinegar, salt, and red pepper flakes, and simmer until the liquid is reduced by half, about 10 minutes. Add the cantaloupe, and cook until the cantaloupe begins to soften, about 5 minutes. Remove from the heat.
3. Process the cantaloupe mixture, cucumber, and olive oil in a blender until smooth, 30 seconds. Refrigerate until thoroughly chilled, about 4 hours.
4. Serve the soup with the Black Pepper-and-Honey Whipped Goat Cheese and Chorizo Relish.

BLACK PEPPER-AND-HONEY WHIPPED GOAT CHEESE

MAKES ABOUT ½ CUP

Whisk together 4 oz. softened goat cheese, 2 Tbsp. honey, ½ tsp. coarsley ground black pepper, and a pinch of ground cinnamon in a bowl until the goat cheese mixture is light and airy.

CHORIZO RELISH

MAKES 1 ½ CUPS

Heat 1 Tbsp. blended olive oil, 4 oz. diced dry-cured Spanish chorizo, and ⅓ cup diced shallots in a saucepan over medium. Cook, stirring constantly, until the chorizo begins to brown and has released some oil, about 2 minutes. Add ½ cup sherry vinegar, and cook, stirring often, until the chorizo is tender, about 15 minutes. Remove from the heat, and let stand 1 hour. Fold 4 peeled and diced hard-cooked eggs into the relish, and refrigerate at least 1 hour. (The relish can be made 1 day ahead.)

POTATO CROQUETTES

SERVES 6

- **2 cups panko (Japanese-style breadcrumbs)**
- **½ cup chopped fresh flat-leaf parsley**
- **2 tsp. kosher salt**
- **½ tsp. granulated onion**
- **2 cups Mashed Potatoes, refrigerated overnight**
- **½ cup finely chopped cooked bacon (about 2 oz.)**
- **1 cup Seasoned Flour (recipe follows)**
- **½ cup (4 oz.) water**
- **1 large egg, beaten**
- **Blended olive oil**
- **Chive Sour Cream (recipe follows)**

1. Pulse the panko, parsley, salt, and granulated onion in a food processor until thoroughly combined, 6 to 10 times.
2. Stir together the potatoes and bacon in a medium bowl. Scoop the potato mixture by tablespoonfuls, and shape into 2-inch-long cylinders.
3. Place the Seasoned Flour in a shallow dish. Stir together the water and egg in a second shallow dish. Place the panko mixture in a third shallow dish. Roll the potato cylinders in the flour, and dip in the egg wash, shaking off any excess. Dredge in the panko mixture, pressing to coat. Place the coated potato cylinders on a baking sheet, and freeze until slightly firm, about 15 minutes.
4. Pour the oil to a depth of 1 inch in a deep skillet. Heat over medium until the oil reaches 350°F. Gently place the potato croquettes, 7 to 8 at a time, in the skillet. Fry the croquettes until golden brown, turning occasionally if necessary, about 3 minutes. Drain on a plate lined with paper towels. Serve hot with the Chive Sour Cream.

MASHED POTATOES

Fill a stockpot with water, and bring to a boil over high. Add 2 lb. peeled Yukon Gold potatoes (cut into 1 ½-inch. pieces) and 1 Tbsp. kosher salt; return water to a boil. Reduce the heat to medium. Cover, and simmer until a knife can easily be inserted into the potatoes, about 20 minutes. Remove from the heat, and let the potatoes stand in the cooking water 15 minutes. Remove ⅔ cup of the cooking water, and set aside. Drain the potatoes Process the potatoes with a food mill into a large bowl until smooth. Bring ½ cup heavy cream and reserved cooking water to a boil in a small saucepan over medium-high. Pour over the potatoes, and fold to combine. Fold in ½ cup cold unsalted butter, ½ tsp. fine sea salt, and ½ tsp. ground white pepper. Serve immediately with Chive Sour Cream, or refrigerate.

SEASONED FLOUR

MAKES 2 ¼ CUPS

Combine 1 cup all-purpose flour, 2 Tbsp. kosher salt, 1 ½ Tbsp. granulated onion, 1 Tbsp. coarsely ground black pepper, 1 Tbsp. granulated garlic, 1 Tbsp. chili powder, 1 tsp. curry powder, 1 tsp. ground ginger in a medium bowl, and store in an airtight container.

CHIVE SOUR CREAM

MAKES 1 ¼ CUPS

Stir together 1 cup sour cream, 1 Tbsp. mayonnaise, 1 Tbsp. plain Greek yogurt, 1 tsp. granulated onion, 1 tsp. Worcestershire sauce, ¼ bunch thinly sliced fresh chives, ¼ tsp. ground white pepper, and 1 Tbsp. lemon zest in a small bowl.

You Say Tomato

We say try one of these five great ways to use the star of summer

Sheet Pan Pizza with Corn, Tomatoes, and Sausage

Thick-walled plum tomatoes contain less liquid and hold their shape better than other types, which is why they are best for roasting and using in chunky sauces. Par-bake the pizza crust before adding the toppings for the crispiest results.

ACTIVE 25 MIN. - TOTAL 55 MIN.
SERVES 6

- **1½ lb. fresh prepared pizza dough**
- **1½ lb. plum tomatoes**
- **10 oz. hot Italian sausage, casings removed**
- **1 Tbsp. olive oil**
- **2 oz. goat cheese, crumbled (about ½ cup)**
- **6 oz. whole-milk mozzarella cheese, shredded (about 1½ cups)**
- **1 cup fresh corn kernels (from 2 ears)**
- **½ bell pepper, thinly sliced (about ½ cup)**
- **¼ cup thinly sliced fresh basil**

1. Preheat oven to 475°F. Let dough stand at room temperature 30 minutes.
2. Meanwhile, chop half of tomatoes, and place in a small bowl. Slice remaining tomatoes, and place in a separate small bowl. Cook sausage in a large skillet over medium-high, breaking it up with a wooden spoon, until well browned, about 7 minutes. Add chopped tomatoes, and cook, stirring occasionally, until the tomatoes release their juices and reduce slightly, about 7 minutes. Remove from heat.
3. Stretch dough to fit a 17- x 12-inch lightly greased rimmed baking sheet, pushing edges of dough up onto the rim. Brush oil over dough, and bake in preheated oven until the dough is lightly browned around the edges, about 8 minutes.
4. Remove from oven, and spread sausage-and-tomato mixture evenly over crust. Sprinkle with goat cheese and ¾ cup of the mozzarella; top with sliced tomatoes, corn, and bell pepper. Sprinkle with remaining ¾ cup mozzarella. Bake on middle oven rack until the cheese melts and crust is crispy, about 8 minutes. Increase oven temperature to broil, and broil 6 inches from heat until the cheese is lightly charred, 1 to 2 minutes. Sprinkle with fresh basil.

Pasta with Shrimp and Tomato Cream Sauce

Smaller tomatoes, like cherry or grape, have brighter, fruitier flavors than larger ones. Look for colorful selections such as the orange Sun Gold and the purple Black Cherry. Tarragon's anise notes complement the cherry tomatoes and cream, but you can substitute basil or oregano.

ACTIVE 25 MIN. - TOTAL 25 MIN.
SERVES 4

- **8 oz. uncooked penne pasta**
- **2 Tbsp. unsalted butter**
- **2 pt. cherry tomatoes, halved (about 1 lb.)**
- **⅔ cup minced shallot (from 1 [3-oz.] shallot)**
- **1 Tbsp. minced garlic (about 3 garlic cloves)**
- **1 lb. large peeled and deveined raw shrimp**
- **1 tsp. kosher salt**
- **½ tsp. black pepper**
- **¾ cup heavy cream**
- **1 Tbsp. chopped fresh tarragon**

1. Cook pasta according to package directions; drain and keep warm.
2. Meanwhile, melt unsalted butter in a large skillet over medium-high. Add cherry tomatoes, and cook, stirring occasionally, until they start to burst and lose their juices, about 3 to 4 minutes. Add minced shallot and garlic, and cook, stirring occasionally, until fragrant, about 1 to 2 minutes. Stir in shrimp, and cook, stirring occasionally, just until shrimp are opaque, about 2 to 3 minutes. Sprinkle the tomato-shrimp mixture with salt and pepper, and stir in heavy cream. Cook, stirring occasionally, until the sauce thickens slightly, about 1 to 2 minutes. Stir in chopped fresh tarragon and cooked pasta, and serve immediately.

Crispy Chicken Cutlets with Blistered Tomatoes

Heirloom tomatoes come in different sizes and colors and vary in flavor too. Use a few different selections in a recipe to give the dish a more complex taste. Avoid overstirring the cherry tomatoes in the hot pan; you want them to brown and caramelize.

ACTIVE 25 MIN. - TOTAL 25 MIN.
SERVES 4

- **8 (3-oz.) chicken cutlets (about 1 ½ lb.)**
- **1 Tbsp. kosher salt**
- **1 tsp. black pepper**
- **1 cup all-purpose flour**
- **2 large eggs, lightly beaten**
- **1 cup panko (Japanese-style breadcrumbs)**
- **½ cup olive oil, divided**
- **2 pt. heirloom cherry tomatoes**
- **2 Tbsp. brined capers, drained and rinsed**
- **4 scallions, with green and white parts sliced and separated**
- **⅓ cup dry white wine**
- **1 Tbsp. fresh lemon juice (from 1 lemon)**
- **2 Tbsp. unsalted butter**
- **2 Tbsp. chopped fresh flat-leaf parsley**

1. Sprinkle chicken with ¾ teaspoon of the salt and ¼ teaspoon of the black pepper. Place flour, eggs, and panko in 3 separate bowls. Stir 1 ¼ teaspoons of the salt and ¾ teaspoon of the pepper into flour, and stir remaining 1 teaspoon salt into panko. Dredge chicken in flour, dusting off any excess flour. Dip in eggs, and dredge in panko, pressing lightly to adhere.
2. Heat ¼ cup of the oil in a large skillet over medium-high until it shimmers. Cook chicken in hot oil, in batches, until chicken is cooked through and golden brown on both sides, about 3 minutes per side, adding remaining ¼ cup oil as needed when skillet begins to get dry. Transfer to a plate lined with paper towels, reserving oil in a heatproof bowl. Keep chicken warm in a 200°F oven. Wipe out skillet with a paper towel, removing any excess panko.
3. Return skillet to medium-high, and add 2 tablespoons reserved hot oil. Add tomatoes, and cook, stirring occasionally, until blistered on all sides, 3 to 4 minutes. Add capers and white parts of scallions; cook, stirring occasionally, until fragrant, 1 to 2 minutes. Add wine, and cook, stirring occasionally, until sauce starts to thicken, 1 to 2 minutes. Reduce heat to low, add lemon juice and butter, and cook, stirring constantly, until butter melts. Stir in chopped fresh parsley and green parts of scallions; serve immediately with chicken.

Grilled Steak Salad with Green Tomato Vinaigrette

Firm and tart green tomatoes can add acidic notes to a dish. Although they are most often breaded and fried, they can be blended into condiments or used in desserts such as pies. Some tomato selections (like Green Zebra) ripen to a lovely shade of green, but this dressing calls for a not-yet-ripened red tomato.

ACTIVE 35 MIN. - TOTAL 50 MIN.
SERVES 4

- **1 ½ lb. flank steak**
- **1 ½ tsp. kosher salt**
- **1 ½ tsp. black pepper**
- **5 Tbsp. olive oil**
- **1 medium-size green tomato, halved and cored (about 4 oz.)**
- **2 Tbsp. rice vinegar**
- **1 ½ tsp. honey**
- **1 tsp. Dijon mustard**
- **5 oz. mixed greens (about 3 cups packed)**
- **3 oz. arugula (about 2 cups packed)**
- **2 large heirloom tomatoes, cut into 1-inch-thick wedges (8 oz.)**
- **1 pt. heirloom cherry tomatoes, sliced (about 4 cups)**
- **¾ cup thinly sliced red onion (from ½ red onion)**

1. Preheat grill to high (450°F to 500°F). Sprinkle flank steak with 1 teaspoon each of the salt and pepper. Let stand at room temperature 30 minutes.
2. Meanwhile, spread 1 tablespoon of the oil over cut sides of green tomato halves, and sprinkle with remaining ½ teaspoon each of salt and pepper. Grill tomato halves, covered and turning halfway through, until charred on both sides and slightly tender, 12 to 14 minutes. Remove from grill; place in a large bowl. Cover with plastic wrap, and let stand until cool enough to handle, about 5 minutes.
3. Peel and discard skin from charred tomato halves; place tomato halves, vinegar, and honey in a blender or food processor. Process until tomato is finely chopped but not smooth. Pour into a medium bowl, and whisk in mustard. Add remaining 4 tablespoons oil in a slow, steady stream, whisking constantly until smooth. Set vinaigrette aside.
4. Grill steak, covered and turning once, until charred on both sides and a meat thermometer inserted into thickest portion of steak registers 120°F or to desired degree of doneness, about 4 minutes per side. Let steak rest 10 minutes. Cut diagonally across the grain into thin strips.
5. Arrange mixed greens, arugula, heirloom tomato wedges, cherry tomato slices, and red onion on a large serving platter. Top with sliced steak, and drizzle with desired amount of vinaigrette.

Bacon-Spinach-and-Couscous Stuffed Tomatoes

Ideal for stuffing because they're meaty and firm enough to hold up while baking, beefsteak tomatoes are also large enough to make a hearty supper. Brush the inside of each hollowed-out tomato with bacon drippings to make them extra smoky and savory.

ACTIVE 25 MIN. - TOTAL 50 MIN.
SERVES 6

6 large beefsteak tomatoes (about 4 lb.)
1½ tsp. kosher salt
½ tsp. black pepper
1 cup chicken broth
1 cup uncooked couscous
6 thick-cut bacon slices
5 oz. baby spinach (4 cups loosely packed)
2 oz. feta cheese, crumbled (about ½ cup)
1 Tbsp. thinly sliced fresh basil

1. Preheat oven to 375°F. Using a paring knife, remove core from tomatoes, creating a 2-inch cavity in each and being careful not to cut through skin. Sprinkle tomato cavities with ½ teaspoon of the salt and ¼ teaspoon of the pepper. Place tomatoes on a parchment paper-lined rimmed baking sheet.
2. Bring chicken broth to a boil in a small saucepan; stir in couscous. Cover and remove from heat. Let stand 5 minutes; fluff with a fork.
3. Meanwhile, cook bacon in a large skillet over medium until crispy on both sides, about 4 to 5 minutes per side. Transfer bacon to a plate lined with paper towels, reserving 1 tablespoon drippings in skillet and remaining drippings in a small heatproof bowl. When bacon is cool enough to handle, roughly chop to measure about ½ cup. Reserve 2 tablespoons chopped bacon for garnish.
4. Cook spinach in reserved 1 tablespoon bacon drippings in skillet over medium, stirring often, until wilted, about 1 minute. Stir together spinach, couscous, feta, basil, and remaining chopped bacon, 1 teaspoon salt, and ¼ teaspoon pepper in a large bowl.
5. Brush insides of tomatoes with reserved bacon drippings in bowl, and stuff cavities with couscous mixture. Bake tomatoes in preheated oven until tender, about 25 minutes. Sprinkle with reserved 2 tablespoons chopped bacon, and serve immediately.

Lasagna Gets a New Look

Three cheeses and thin, woven strips of zucchini make this one-pan classic a crowd-pleaser, whether you're cooking Sunday supper or planning for the family reunion

Zucchini Lasagna

ACTIVE 30 MIN. - TOTAL 1 HOUR, 50 MIN.
SERVES 6

- **3 large zucchini (about 1 1/4 lb.)**
- **2 tsp. kosher salt**
- **1 tsp. extra-virgin olive oil**
- **1 garlic clove, halved**
- **12 oven-ready lasagna noodles (from 1 [9-oz.] box)**
- **4 cups marinara sauce (from 1 [42-oz.] jar)**
- **1 cup whole-milk ricotta cheese**
- **1 1/4 cups Parmesan cheese, grated (about 2 1/2 oz.)**
- **8 oz. fresh mozzarella cheese, thinly sliced**
- **1/4 cup loosely packed torn basil leaves**
- **1 tsp. black pepper**

1. Preheat oven to 375°F. Line a large baking sheet with paper towels. Using a mandoline, shave zucchini lengthwise into very thin strips. Place about one-third of the strips in a single layer on paper towels; sprinkle evenly with about one-third of the salt. Top with another layer of paper towels; repeat process twice. Let stand 10 minutes; gently press strips with paper towels to remove excess moisture.

2. Rub inside of a 13- x 9-inch (3-quart) glass baking dish with olive oil; rub entire inside surface with cut sides of garlic.

3. Place 3 lasagna noodles in bottom of prepared dish. (They will not cover entire surface but will expand when cooked.) Top with 1 cup marinara sauce, spreading evenly to cover noodles. Top evenly with 1/4 cup ricotta, 1/4 cup Parmesan, and 2 ounces mozzarella. Cover with about one-fourth of the zucchini strips; sprinkle with about 4 teaspoons basil and 1/4 teaspoon pepper. Repeat layers twice. Layer with remaining 3 noodles, 1 cup marinara sauce, and 1/4 cup ricotta. Top with 1/4 cup Parmesan and remaining 2 ounces mozzarella.

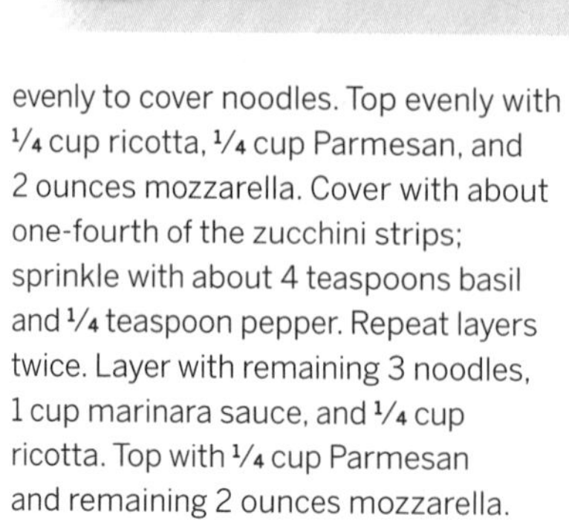

Arrange remaining zucchini strips on top in a lattice design. Sprinkle with remaining 1/4 cup Parmesan and 1/4 teaspoon pepper.

4. Cover with foil; bake in preheated oven 45 minutes. Remove foil; bake until top is lightly browned and noodles are tender, about 20 minutes more. Let stand at least 15 minutes before slicing.

Salad for Supper

Juicy tomatoes shine in this main dish that you can pull together in under an hour

Whole-Grain Panzanella

ACTIVE 30 MIN. - TOTAL 45 MIN.
SERVES 6

- **2 medium-size red onions, cut into 1/2-inch-thick wedges**
- **2 garlic cloves, smashed**
- **1/2 cup extra-virgin olive oil**
- **3/4 tsp. kosher salt**
- **3/4 tsp. black pepper**
- **1 (12-oz.) whole-grain country-style bread loaf, cut into 1-inch cubes (about 8 cups cubes)**
- **1 medium-size heirloom tomato, cut into 12 wedges**
- **3 Tbsp. red wine vinegar**
- **1 tsp. Dijon mustard**
- **10 oz. shredded rotisserie chicken breast (2 cups)**
- **1 small English cucumber, thinly sliced into half-moons**
- **1 cup multicolored cherry tomatoes, halved**
- **1/2 cup jarred sweet cherry peppers, thinly sliced**
- **1/4 cup tightly packed torn basil leaves**
- **2 Tbsp. fresh flat-leaf parsley leaves**
- **2 Tbsp. chopped fresh chives**

1. Place a rimmed baking sheet on top rack of oven; preheat oven to 450°F. (Do not remove baking sheet while oven preheats.) Toss onion wedges and garlic with 1 tablespoon of the olive oil and 1/4 teaspoon each of the salt and pepper. Spread onion mixture in a single layer on preheated baking sheet; place on top oven rack. Place bread cubes on a separate large rimmed baking sheet; place baking sheet on center rack in oven. Bake in preheated oven until bread is toasted and onions are softened and charred, 15 to 17 minutes, stirring onions after 8 minutes.

2. Meanwhile, use a spoon to scrape seeds and juices from heirloom tomato wedges into a medium bowl. Place scraped wedges in a large bowl, and set aside.

3. Whisk vinegar, mustard, and remaining 1/2 teaspoon salt and 1/2 teaspoon pepper into tomato juices and seeds. Slowly whisk in remaining 7 tablespoons olive oil until emulsified.

4. Place toasted bread, onion mixture, chicken, cucumber, cherry tomatoes, and peppers in bowl with tomato wedges. Drizzle vinaigrette over salad; toss gently to coat. Let stand 15 minutes. Top with herbs.

Nutritional information (per serving): Calories: 449 - Protein: 25g - Carbs: 35g - Fiber: 7g - Fat: 23g

IN SEASON

The tomato has been named a superfood by the American Diabetes Association. Toss two kinds with whole-grain croutons, other veggies, and chicken for a hearty take on panzanella.

Let Them Eat Shrimp

Greet guests with this make-ahead party appetizer

SERVING TIP

Let guests help themselves, or portion out the Pickled Shrimp and Vegetables into small glass bowls.

Pickled Shrimp and Vegetables

Keep the shrimp cold in the summer heat by nestling the serving bowl inside a larger bowl of crushed ice. If it's stored in the refrigerator, the mixture will stay fresh for three to four days.

ACTIVE 20 MIN. - TOTAL 8 HOURS, 20 MIN., INCLUDING 8 HOURS MARINATING
SERVES 8

- 4 qt. water
- 2 lb. medium peeled, deveined raw shrimp
- 4 1/2 oz. fresh okra, washed and halved lengthwise
- 2 1/2 cups thinly sliced sweet onion (from 1 medium onion)
- 2 cups thinly sliced sweet mini peppers (about 6 oz.)
- 3 thyme sprigs
- 3/4 cup olive oil
- 1/4 cup white balsamic vinegar
- 2 tsp. kosher salt
- 1/2 tsp. black pepper
- 1/4 tsp. crushed red pepper
- 2 large lemons
- 1/2 cup thinly sliced fresh basil

1. Bring water to a boil in a stockpot over medium-high. Add shrimp; boil until opaque and just pink, about 2 minutes. Drain and rinse under cold water until cold, about 2 minutes. Pat dry with paper towels.
2. Combine shrimp, okra, onion, peppers, and thyme sprigs in a large glass bowl or trifle dish.
3. Whisk together oil, vinegar, salt, black pepper, and red pepper in a bowl until emulsified. Thinly slice 1 lemon; add slices to shrimp mixture. Juice remaining lemon to equal 1/4 cup; whisk juice into oil mixture. Pour dressing over shrimp mixture, stirring to combine. Cover and chill at least 8 hours, stirring occasionally. Stir in basil just before serving.

SMART SWAP
One 15-ounce can of sliced peaches will work in a pinch. Drain and gently pat dry before using.

Twice as Nice

Break out the Bundt pan, and bake an upside-down cake sweetened with caramelized peaches

Peach-Bourbon Upside-Down Bundt Cake

ACTIVE 25 MIN. - TOTAL 4 HOURS, 20 MIN.
SERVES 12

- 1 3/4 cups butter, softened, divided
- 2 cups packed light brown sugar
- 4 peaches, peeled and cut into 4 slices
- 1 (8-oz.) pkg. cream cheese, softened
- 1 1/2 cups granulated sugar
- 6 large eggs
- 1 1/2 tsp. vanilla extract
- 3 cups all-purpose flour
- 1/2 tsp. salt
- 1/4 cup (2 oz.) bourbon
- 1 cup powdered sugar
- 1–2 Tbsp. milk

1. Preheat oven to 325°F. Melt 1/4 cup of the butter in a small saucepan over medium; stir in 1/2 cup of the brown sugar. Cook, whisking constantly, until sugar has dissolved and mixture is thoroughly combined, about 1 minute. Pour mixture evenly into a 15-cup (10 1/2-inch) Bundt pan that has been heavily greased with cooking spray. Place peach slices in an even layer on top of brown sugar mixture.

2. Beat cream cheese and remaining 1 1/2 cups butter with a heavy-duty stand mixer on medium speed until creamy, about 1 minute. Gradually add granulated sugar and remaining 1 1/2 cups brown sugar, beating on medium speed until light and fluffy, 3 to 5 minutes. Add eggs, 1 at a time, beating just until yolk disappears. Beat in 1 teaspoon of the vanilla.

3. Sift together flour and salt; add to butter mixture alternately with bourbon, beginning and ending with flour mixture. Spoon batter carefully over peaches in prepared pan; level with a spatula.

4. Bake in preheated oven until a long wooden pick inserted in center of cake comes out clean, 1 hour and 25 minutes to 1 hour and 30 minutes. Cool in pan on a wire rack until pan is cool enough to handle but still hot, about 25 minutes. Remove cake from pan to rack, and cool completely, about 2 hours.

5. Stir together powdered sugar, remaining 1/2 teaspoon vanilla, and 1 tablespoon of the milk in a small bowl, adding remaining 1 tablespoon milk, 1 teaspoon at a time, if needed to reach desired consistency. Drizzle over cooled cake.

COOKING SL SCHOOL

TIPS AND TRICKS FROM THE SOUTH'S MOST TRUSTED KITCHEN

GREAT DEBATE

The Case for Homemade Croutons

Two Test Kitchen pros face off about the best way to make a batch from scratch

Store croutons in a ziplock plastic bag for up to five days.

KAREN RANKIN

Swears by Stove-Top

"Sautéing the croutons in bacon drippings and olive oil creates a chewy and tender exterior with tons of flavor."

Toss **4 cups bread cubes** with **1 1/2 Tbsp. each warm bacon drippings** and **olive oil, 1/2 tsp. each salt** and **pepper,** and **1/4 tsp. garlic powder.** Cook in a large skillet over medium-high, stirring often, until browned and crisp, about 8 minutes.

DEB WISE

All About the Oven

"Toasting the bread cubes on a baking sheet gives them plenty of space so the entire surface can dry out and become crisp."

Toss **4 cups cubed bread** with **5 Tbsp. melted butter; 1/2 tsp. salt;** and **1/4 tsp. each pepper, garlic powder,** and **dried thyme** on a baking sheet. Bake at 375°F until golden brown, stirring once, 16 to 18 minutes.

IN SEASON

Reach for the Right Peach

CLINGSTONE

These smaller, sweeter peaches have flesh that clings to the pit. Choose them for eating out of hand, canning, or preserving.

FREESTONE

Slightly larger and firmer, these peaches have pits that separate easily from the flesh—best for pickling, grilling, and tossing in fruit salads.

SEMIFREESTONE

This lesser-known type has a pit that clings to the flesh until the peach is ripe. It's great for eating out of hand, baking, pickling, and freezing.

Don't Pick Pink

The rosy blush of a peach is not actually a sign of ripeness. Look for the yellow undertone, or "ground color," on the fruit's skin. Ripe peaches will have a warm, creamy yellow or yellow-orange undertone with no hint of green.

July

130 **All-American Desserts** Join the serenade to desserts in red, white, and blue

135 **Fried and True** A Mississippi chef overcomes doubts and stays true to his roots in the most delicious ways

142 QUICK FIX **Pick a Side** Cool side dish salads for the grilling days of summer

144 SOUTHERN CLASSIC **Stirring Up Controversy** Worthy variations on the pâté of the South

146 HEALTHY IN A HURRY **Summer Scallops** It just takes minutes to whip up this bright, flavorful seafood plate

147 WHAT CAN I BRING? **Ready To Roll** Sushi can't compete with Southern shrimp salad sliders

148 *SL* COOKING SCHOOL The best ways to baste, and techniques and tasty toppings for grilled corn

ALL-AMERICAN

Cherry Flag Pie
page 132

DESSERTS

Festive, fruity Fourth of July treats

clockwise from top left:
Cornmeal Cookie Berry Shortcakes, page 133; Red Velvet Ice-Cream Cake, page 132; Fourth of July Confetti Roulade, page 133; Red, White, and Blueberry-Filled Cupcakes, page 134

Red Velvet Ice-Cream Cake

A teaspoon of unflavored gelatin helps the whipped cream frosting stabilize so it doesn't lose its shape, even in the summer heat. Cooling the hot gelatin for 5 minutes is key; otherwise it may turn gummy.

ACTIVE 30 MIN. - TOTAL 9 HOURS, 15 MIN. (INCLUDING 7 HOURS FREEZING)

SERVES 12

RED VELVET CAKE

- **¾ cup unsalted butter, softened**
- **1½ cups granulated sugar**
- **3 large eggs**
- **3 Tbsp. red liquid food coloring**
- **1 Tbsp. vanilla extract**
- **2¾ cups all-purpose flour**
- **⅓ cup unsweetened cocoa**
- **2 tsp. baking powder**
- **½ tsp. baking soda**
- **¼ tsp. salt**
- **1½ cups whole buttermilk**

ICE-CREAM LAYER

- **5 cups vanilla ice cream**

FROSTING

- **1½ Tbsp. cold water**
- **1 tsp. unflavored gelatin**
- **1½ cups heavy cream**
- **3 Tbsp. powdered sugar**
- **¼ tsp. vanilla extract**

ADDITIONAL INGREDIENT

- **2 cups fresh blueberries**

1. Preheat oven to 350°F. Grease and flour 2 (9-inch) round cake pans. Place paper baking cups in 2 standard-size muffin cups, or grease and flour 2 (4-oz.) ramekins.

2. Prepare the Red Velvet Cake: Beat butter with an electric mixer at medium speed until light and fluffy, about 3 minutes. Gradually add granulated sugar, beating until blended. Add eggs, 1 at a time, beating until blended after each addition. Beat in food coloring and vanilla.

3. Whisk together flour, cocoa, baking powder, baking soda, and salt; add to butter mixture alternately with buttermilk, beginning and ending with flour mixture. Beat at low speed just until blended after each addition. Fill muffin cups or ramekins three-fourths full. Divide remaining batter between prepared cake pans.

4. Bake in preheated oven until a wooden pick inserted in the center comes out with moist crumbs, 15 to 16 minutes for cupcakes and 20 to 25 minutes for cake layers. Cool cake layers and cupcakes in pans on wire racks 15 minutes. Transfer cake layers and cupcakes from pans to wire racks, and cool completely, about 30 minutes. Wrap cupcakes in plastic wrap, and freeze 2 hours.

5. Prepare the Ice-Cream Layer: Line a 9-inch round cake pan with plastic wrap, allowing ends to extend over edge of pan to create handles. Remove cupcakes from freezer, and cut into ¼-inch cubes. Place ice cream in a large bowl; beat at medium speed until soft but not melted. Gently fold cupcake cubes into ice cream. Spread ice cream into prepared pan. Cover and place pan in freezer until frozen, at least 3 hours or overnight.

6. Prepare the Frosting: Place water in a small microwavable bowl, and sprinkle with gelatin; let stand 5 minutes. Microwave on HIGH until gelatin melts and mixture is smooth, about 10 seconds. Let stand 5 minutes.

7. Place cream, powdered sugar, and vanilla in a large bowl. Beat at medium-high speed until soft peaks form. With mixer on low, gradually add gelatin. Increase speed to high, and beat until stiff peaks form.

8. Assemble the cake: Place 1 Red Velvet Cake layer on a platter or cake stand. Using plastic wrap handles, remove Ice-Cream Layer from pan and place on top of cake layer. Top with remaining cake layer. Spread Frosting over sides and top. Loosely cover with plastic wrap, and freeze at least 2 hours.

9. Let stand at room temperature 20 minutes before serving. Top with blueberries, and serve immediately. Freeze any leftovers.

Cherry Flag Pie

Brushing the piecrust with a mixture of egg yolk and water creates a deeper golden brown crust than plain milk or a whole egg.

ACTIVE 35 MIN. - TOTAL 4 HOURS, 55 MIN. (INCLUDING 2 HOURS COOLING)

SERVES 8

CRUST

- **2 cups all-purpose flour**
- **1 Tbsp. granulated sugar**
- **½ tsp. salt**
- **¾ cup cold unsalted butter, cut into ½-inch cubes**
- **¼ cup cold vegetable shortening**
- **4-5 Tbsp. ice water**

FILLING

- **3 lb. fresh Bing cherries, pitted and halved**
- **½ cup granulated sugar**
- **¼ cup cornstarch**
- **1 tsp. vanilla extract**
- **⅛ tsp. salt**

ADDITIONAL INGREDIENTS

- **1 large egg yolk**
- **2 tsp. water**
- **1 Tbsp. turbinado sugar**

1. Prepare the Crust: Place flour, sugar, and salt in bowl of a food processor; pulse until combined, 3 to 4 times. Add butter and shortening; pulse until mixture resembles small pebbles, 4 to 5 times. Sprinkle 4 tablespoons of the water over top, and pulse until mixture becomes a shaggy mass, adding additional water, 1 teaspoon at a time, as necessary.

2. Transfer mixture to a lightly floured surface, and knead until mixture comes together, 3 to 4 times. Divide into 2 pieces (making two-thirds of the dough the first piece and the remaining one-third of dough the second piece). Shape each piece into a disk. Cover each with plastic wrap, and chill 1 hour.

3. Preheat oven to 400°F. Prepare the bottom Crust: Roll larger disk of dough on a lightly floured work surface into a 12-inch circle, and place into a 9-inch deep-dish pie plate. Fold edge of dough under rim of pie plate. Chill until ready to use.

4. Prepare the Filling: Combine cherries, sugar, cornstarch, vanilla, and salt in a large bowl, stirring well. Transfer mixture to prepared Crust.

5. Prepare the top Crust: On a sheet of lightly floured parchment paper, roll remaining disk of dough into a 10-inch circle. Use a paring knife to cut 2 (1-inch-wide) strips from the bottom one-third of the dough, leaving a semicircle of dough on top. Use a ¾-inch star-shaped cutter to cut out stars from the left half of the dough semicircle. Use a paring knife to cut out and remove 3 (1-inch-wide) strips of dough from the right half. Use the parchment to carefully transport and place the prepared semicircle on top of Filling. Place the 2 (1-inch-wide) strips across the uncovered Filling at the bottom of the pie to complete the flag design. Crimp the dough edges.

6. Whisk together egg yolk and water. Brush entire piecrust with egg mixture. Sprinkle with turbinado sugar. Place pie on a baking sheet lined with aluminum foil.

7. Bake in preheated oven on lower oven rack 20 minutes. Leaving pie in oven, reduce oven temperature to 350°F, and bake 55 to 60 minutes, until Crust is golden and Filling is bubbly throughout, shielding pie with aluminum foil to prevent overbrowning after 20 to 30 minutes, if needed. Transfer pie from baking sheet to a wire rack, and cool at least 2 hours before serving.

Cornmeal Cookie Berry Shortcakes

Bake the cookies up to two days in advance, and store them in an airtight container. The macerated berries and cream cheese whipped cream can be made the day before and refrigerated.

ACTIVE 30 MIN. - TOTAL 2 HOURS, 50 MIN.

SERVES 6

- **1 cup unsalted butter, softened**
- **¾ cup powdered sugar, divided, plus more for dusting**
- **1 tsp. vanilla extract, divided**
- **2 cups all-purpose flour**
- **½ cup fine plain yellow cornmeal**
- **½ tsp. salt**
- **1 cup fresh raspberries**
- **1 cup fresh blueberries**
- **2 Tbsp. granulated sugar**
- **1 Tbsp. raspberry liqueur (optional)**
- **4 oz. cream cheese, softened**
- **1 tsp. fresh lemon juice (from 1 lemon)**
- **1 cup heavy cream**

1. Beat butter and ½ cup of the powdered sugar with an electric mixer on medium speed until light and fluffy, about 4 minutes. Beat in ½ teaspoon of the vanilla. Whisk together flour, cornmeal, and salt in a bowl. Gradually add flour mixture to butter mixture, beating at low speed until combined, about 1 minute. Divide dough in half. Shape each half into a flat disk, and wrap in plastic wrap. Chill until firm, about 1 hour.

2. Preheat oven to 350°F. Roll 1 disk of dough ¼ inch thick on a lightly floured work surface. Cut into 6 (4-inch) circles. Cut a 2 ½-inch star from center of each circle (you should have 6 circles and 6 star cookies). Place cookies 1 inch apart on baking sheets lined with parchment paper. Bake in preheated oven until beginning to brown around edges, 12 to 14 minutes. Cool on baking sheets 5 minutes; transfer cookies to wire racks, and cool completely, about 20 minutes. Repeat process with remaining disk of dough, omitting star cutouts.

3. Gently stir together raspberries, blueberries, granulated sugar, and, if desired, liqueur. Let stand, stirring occasionally, until syrupy, about 20 minutes.

4. Meanwhile, place cream cheese, lemon juice, remaining ¼ cup powdered sugar and ½ teaspoon vanilla in a medium bowl. Beat with an electric mixer on medium speed until creamy and smooth, about 1 minute.

5. Place cream in a separate medium bowl, and beat with an electric mixer on medium-high speed until foamy. Increase speed to high, and beat until soft peaks form. Stir one-fourth of whipped cream into cream cheese mixture. Gently fold remaining whipped cream into mixture. Cover and chill until ready to use.

6. To assemble each shortcake, place 1 circle cookie (without cutout) on a plate and top with about ¼ cup whipped cream mixture. Top cream with 3 tablespoons berry mixture; top with 1 star-cutout cookie. Dust with powdered sugar before serving.

Fourth of July Confetti Roulade

A splash of orange liqueur is optional in the creamy filling, but don't skip the fresh lemon juice in the frosting—it gives the dessert brightness and zing.

ACTIVE 40 MIN. - TOTAL 1 HOUR, 50 MIN.

SERVES 8

CAKE

- **Cooking spray**
- **5 large eggs, separated**
- **¾ cup granulated sugar, divided**
- **1 tsp. vanilla extract**
- **¼ tsp. cream of tartar**
- **¾ cup unbleached cake flour**
- **½ tsp. baking powder**
- **¼ tsp. salt**
- **4 Tbsp. red, white, and blue sprinkles, divided**
- **6 Tbsp. powdered sugar, divided**

FILLING

- **1 ½ Tbsp. cold water**
- **1 tsp. unflavored gelatin**
- **1 ½ cups heavy cream**
- **¼ cup powdered sugar**
- **1 Tbsp. orange liqueur (optional)**

FROSTING

- **¼ cup unsalted butter, softened**
- **2 cups powdered sugar**
- **1 Tbsp. fresh lemon juice (from 1 lemon)**
- **¼ tsp. salt**
- **1-2 Tbsp. heavy cream**

1. Preheat oven to 400°F. Spray a 10- x 15-inch rimmed baking sheet with cooking spray; line with parchment paper. Spray paper with cooking spray.

2. Prepare the Cake: Beat egg yolks and ½ cup of the granulated sugar with an electric mixer on high speed until thick and pale, 3 to 4 minutes. Beat in vanilla.

3. Using clean, dry beaters, beat egg whites and cream of tartar in a separate bowl on medium speed until foamy. Increase speed to high, and beat until soft peaks form. Add remaining ¼ cup sugar, 1 tablespoon at a time, beating on high speed until medium peaks form. Stir one-fourth of egg white mixture into egg yolk mixture; gently fold in remaining three-fourths egg white mixture.

4. Sift together cake flour, baking powder, and salt. Sift one-third of flour mixture over egg mixture, and sprinkle with 1 tablespoon of the sprinkles. Fold gently until just blended. Repeat twice with 2 tablespoons of the sprinkles and remaining flour mixture. Spread batter gently in prepared pan, taking care not to deflate batter.

5. Bake in preheated oven until puffed and lightly browned on top, 7 to 9 minutes. Run a butter knife or offset spatula around edges of pan to loosen; cool in pan 2 minutes. Sprinkle 4 tablespoons of the powdered sugar over top. Invert onto a parchment paper-lined surface. Gently peel top layer of parchment paper from Cake; sprinkle top with remaining 2 tablespoons powdered sugar. Starting at 1 short side, roll Cake and bottom parchment together. Transfer to a wire rack, and cool completely, about 1 hour.

6. Prepare the Filling: Place water in a small microwavable bowl, and sprinkle with gelatin; let stand 5 minutes. Microwave on HIGH until gelatin melts and mixture is smooth, about 10 seconds. Let stand 5 minutes.

7. Place cream, powdered sugar, and, if desired, liqueur in a large bowl. Beat on medium-high speed until soft peaks form. With mixer on low speed, slowly drizzle in gelatin. Increase speed to high, and beat until stiff peaks form. Cover and chill until ready to use.

8. Unroll Cake onto a flat surface. Spread Filling over top, leaving a ½-inch border on all sides. Starting at 1 short side and using parchment paper as a guide, roll up Cake in a jelly-roll fashion, discarding parchment. Place on a platter, seam side down.

9. Prepare the Frosting: Beat butter with an electric mixer on medium speed until creamy and smooth. Add powdered sugar, lemon juice, and salt; beat until smooth. Beat in cream, 1 tablespoon at a time, until mixture is a spreadable consistency. Spread Frosting over top and sides of roulade, leaving ends uncovered. Sprinkle remaining 1 tablespoon candy sprinkles over top and sides of roulade.

Red, White, and Blueberry-Filled Cupcakes

The jammy blueberry filling is a sweet surprise inside each cupcake. If you prefer strawberry, simply replace the fruit and preserves.

ACTIVE 35 MIN. - TOTAL 1 HOUR, 25 MIN.

SERVES 12

BLUEBERRY FILLING

- **½ cup blueberry preserves**
- **¼ cup fresh blueberries**
- **2 Tbsp. unsalted butter**
- **1 Tbsp. cornstarch**
- **1 Tbsp. water**

CUPCAKES

- **¼ cup unsalted butter, softened**
- **2 oz. cream cheese, softened**
- **1 cup granulated sugar**
- **2 large eggs**
- **½ tsp. vanilla extract**
- **1½ cups all-purpose flour**
- **½ tsp. baking powder**
- **¼ tsp. baking soda**
- **¼ tsp. salt**
- **½ cup whole buttermilk**

FROSTING

- **6 oz. cream cheese, softened**
- **6 Tbsp. unsalted butter, softened**
- **1 Tbsp. fresh lemon juice (from 1 lemon)**
- **¼ tsp. salt**
- **3½ cups powdered sugar**
- **1 Tbsp. heavy cream**

ADDITIONAL INGREDIENTS

- **6 fresh strawberries, halved**
- **¼ cup fresh blueberries**

1. Prepare the Blueberry Filling: Combine preserves, blueberries, and butter in a small saucepan over medium-high, and bring to a boil. Cook, stirring often, until berries begin to break down, about 4 minutes. Stir together cornstarch and water in a small bowl, and add mixture to pan. Cook, stirring constantly, until thickened, 1 to 2 minutes. Transfer Blueberry Filling from pan to a bowl, and cool completely, about 20 minutes.

2. Prepare the Cupcakes: Preheat oven to 350°F. Beat butter and cream cheese with an electric mixer on medium speed until creamy and smooth, about 1 minute. Gradually add sugar, and beat until light and fluffy, 3 to 4 minutes. Add eggs, 1 at a time, beating until blended after each addition. Beat in vanilla.

3. Combine flour, baking powder, baking soda, and salt. Gradually add to butter mixture alternately with buttermilk, beating just until blended after each addition. Place 12 paper baking cups in a 12-cup standard-size muffin pan, and divide batter evenly among baking cups (filling about three-fourths full). Bake in preheated oven until a wooden pick inserted in centers comes out clean, 15 to 17 minutes. Cool in pan on a wire rack 5 minutes. Transfer from pan to wire rack, and cool completely, about 30 minutes.

4. Prepare the Frosting: Beat cream cheese and butter on medium speed until creamy and smooth. Beat in lemon juice and salt. Gradually add powdered sugar, and beat at low speed until smooth, 1 to 2 minutes. Gradually beat in cream until spreadable consistency is reached.

5. To fill Cupcakes, carefully scoop out centers, using a 1-inch melon baller and leaving a ½-inch border around edges (hole will be about 1 inch deep). Discard or reserve cake centers for another use. Spoon or pipe 1 tablespoon of Blueberry Filling into center of each Cupcake.

6. Pipe or spread Frosting on top of each. Arrange fresh strawberries and blueberries on tops of Cupcakes before serving.

FRIED AND TRUE

JACKSON, MISSISSIPPI, CHEF **NICK WALLACE** USES FOOD TO TELL HIS FAMILY'S STORY AND GIVE FRIENDS A REASON TO COME TOGETHER

Nick Wallace learned to cook from queens. Growing up in Jackson and nearby Edwards, Mississippi, the chef spent his childhood by the stove with his two grandmothers (Queen Morris, 83, and Lennell Donald, 90). Though only one of them has a royal name, Wallace regards them both as the monarchs of his family, which has been shaped and led by women.

On Donald's farm in Edwards, Wallace recalls picking buckets of blueberries for his Granny to ladle into jars that would be opened that winter and helping her prepare meals for relatives who worked in town and came home hungry after days spent cutting timber. "I was there with her slinging flour, making homemade biscuits, fixing different fruit cobblers, frying chicken—the whole nine yards," he says.

About 25 miles to the east, Morris (his Nana) lived in Jackson but still kept farm-rooted recipes simmering on the burners in her kitchen. "She wasn't a 'premade' kind of lady," says Wallace. "She always had big pots cooking something from the morning till the afternoon. The greatest thing about her was that she taught my mom to be a fabulous cook."

FAMILY AFFAIR Wallace says one of his Nana's biggest accomplishments was teaching his mother, Susie Marshall (shown at left), how to be "a fabulous cook."

Their strong influence was just as visible on the plates of pickled vegetables, cornbread, and greens covering the table at the opening of the Mississippi Civil Rights Museum in Jackson this past December, where Wallace cooked for attendees like Myrlie Evers-Williams, the widow of Medgar Evers and an icon of the movement. For Wallace, the day represented a full-circle moment. He shared the food that spoke to his family's legacy, but he also felt validated in his decision to make Mississippi his home—even when others told him he would squander his talent if he stayed there after culinary school.

"There came a point when I started to look at the Bobby Flays and Emerils of the world, and I wondered if I could be that person too," he says. "But there was always this self-doubt because I never saw anyone who looked like me."

As the chef at Jackson's King Edward Hotel, Wallace started an experiment. First, he planted a mini farm filled with tomatoes, peppers, and collards that wrapped around the hotel's outside walls and placed pots of fragrant lemon trees and herbs by the entrance. He sent his staff out daily to gather ingredients that he would prepare at a chef's table for surprised visitors who were not expecting to find a farm-to-table restaurant at a Hilton Garden Inn outpost. "That's when I knew it could actually work here," Wallace says. "From that point on, I dedicated myself to my roots. I was devoted to bringing this kind of cooking back to Mississippi."

Five years later, Wallace left the hotel and took over the cafe space at the Mississippi Museum of Art while he waited to open his own full-service French-inspired restaurant. It was set to be located in Jackson's former federal courthouse. On the wall behind a judge's bench in this building was a long-hidden 1938 mural featuring a demeaning depiction of black sharecroppers. Wallace wanted to create a place that could help the city heal from its past and where citizens could come together at the table.

But the funding from investors, who also wanted to add apartments and retail space to the courthouse's redevelopment, fell through before his dream could become a reality. Disappointed, he remembered what Nana told him before he left the King Edward Hotel: "Nick, I want you to remember where you came from."

A determined Wallace got to work creating yet another micro-incarnation of his Granny's farm. This time, it was on the grounds of the downtown art museum. During his breaks, he would walk through "The Mississippi Story" exhibit, lined with the work of the state's artists and activists.

"I saw all of these people who had brought so much change to our state," he adds. "I decided that I was going to make the most of this." Soon after green shoots appeared in the raised beds and herbs settled into the fertile soil, Wallace, who's a father of three, started inviting groups of school students to wander through his edible maze. He ultimately brought thousands of children to the museum to provide them with the same kind of knowledge and appreciation for food that his grandmothers had instilled in him. Wallace's own homegrown revolution was happening just blocks from the old Greyhound bus station where Freedom Riders had arrived and the site of the Woolworth's lunch counter sit-in.

The James Beard Foundation took notice and invited Wallace to cook at a dinner in New York City. Next, producers at the Food Network asked him to compete on an episode of Alton Brown's *Cutthroat Kitchen.* While contestants attempted to turn mystery ingredients into presentable dishes, Wallace confronted another challenge. "There was this one guy on the show who was giving me the blues about being from Mississippi, saying I could only make comeback sauce and I was just going to stand in front of the fryer," the chef recalls. Wallace didn't make it beyond the second round.

Waiting at the airport before returning home, he was reminded of his grandmother's words. As soon as the plane landed in Jackson, he sent a text to his tattoo artist. And three years later, when he returned to the Food Network on his first episode of *Chopped,* Wallace had a whiskered Mississippi channel catfish swimming down the length of his bicep in blue ink. And he won the round.

Although he left the museum cafe earlier this year, Wallace's plate is still filled with ideas—from a fast-casual franchise that uses locally sourced produce to a new restaurant with his mother working as co-chef. And as he makes these plans for the future, he is content cooking for his friends and family, especially his children. These days, you will likely find his son, Nick Wallace Jr., stationed by the stove watching his father stir a big pot of greens, just how the chef once learned from his grandmothers as a child. Etched in colorful ink down the chef's forearm is a pair of hands holding vegetables from the garden—another reminder of where he came from.

Green Goddess Dressing, page 140

SLOW COOKER

"Everything that my grandmothers made was slow," says Wallace. "That's how I've been eating for 39 years. That's the flavor of love. You have to care about what you're cooking. It has to have a story behind it, and that's the biggest impact they've had on me."

Cheddar-Caramelized Onion Bread, page 140

Watermelon Salad, page 140

NICK WALLACE'S CATFISH

FRIED DELACATA CATFISH

ACTIVE 35 MIN. - TOTAL 40 MIN.

SERVES 6

Peanut oil
6 (4-oz.) Delacata catfish fillets
1 cup whole milk or buttermilk
3/4 cup fine yellow cornmeal
1/2 cup all-purpose flour
1 tsp. garlic powder
1 tsp. black pepper
1 tsp. dried thyme
1 tsp. paprika
1/2 tsp. cayenne pepper
1/4 tsp. celery seeds
2 tsp. kosher salt, divided
Lemon wedges, for serving
Black-Eyed Pea Ranchero Sauce, for serving (recipe follows)

1. Preheat oven to 200°F. Pour enough peanut oil into a large, heavy frying pan to come 1/2 inch up sides. (Cast iron is best.) Heat over medium-high until oil reaches 350°F. (A good test is to flick a little of the dry breading into the oil. If it sizzles at once, you're good to go.)
2. While oil is heating, soak catfish in milk 5 minutes. Set a wire rack inside a large rimmed baking sheet, and place in preheated oven.
3. Combine cornmeal, flour, garlic powder, black pepper, thyme, paprika, cayenne, celery seeds, and 1 teaspoon of the salt in a shallow dish for dredging. (Or you can substitute your favorite seasoning instead.)
4. Once the oil is hot, remove catfish fillets from milk, and dredge in flour mixture, shaking off excess. Working in 2 batches, carefully place fillets in hot oil, and fry until golden brown and cooked through, about 4 minutes per side. Sprinkle remaining salt (about 1/2 teaspoon per batch) on fish when it comes out of the pan.
5. Transfer cooked catfish to wire rack in baking sheet in preheated oven. Serve catfish with lemon wedges and Black-Eyed Pea Ranchero Sauce.

BLACK-EYED PEA RANCHERO SAUCE

ACTIVE 20 MIN. - TOTAL 25 MIN.

SERVES 10

1 Tbsp. olive oil
1 (15.5-oz.) can black-eyed peas, drained and rinsed
1 cup chopped white onion (from 1 onion)
1/2 cup chopped, seeded jalapeño chiles (from 3 large chiles)
1 garlic clove, minced
1 (15-oz.) can whole peeled plum tomatoes
1 1/2 tsp. kosher salt
1/2 tsp. black pepper
1/2 tsp. ground cumin
1/2 tsp. paprika

Heat oil in a medium saucepan over medium-high. Add peas, onion, and jalapeño; cook, stirring constantly, until softened, about 5 minutes. Add garlic, and cook, stirring constantly until soft, about 1 minute. Carefully add tomatoes, breaking tomatoes up using the back of a wooden spoon. Stir in salt, pepper, cumin, and paprika. Reduce heat to medium-low, and simmer, stirring occasionally, until tomato liquid is partially thickened, about 10 minutes. Remove from heat, and cool slightly, about 5 minutes.

FRY CATFISH THE WALLACE WAY

CHOOSE CENTER CUT

Wallace prefers Delacata Style Catfish Fillets because they are thick and meaty from end to end, which helps them cook more evenly.

REMEMBER THE SOAK

Catfish has a mild flavor, but Wallace gives the fillets a bath in whole milk or buttermilk beforehand to help neutralize any fishy odors.

FLAVOR THE BREADING

Add seasonings to the cornmeal-and-flour mixture to give the fish underlying spicy and herbal tones—an easy step for next-level taste.

KEEP IT CRISPY

Transfer the fried fillets to a wire rack set over a baking sheet. Then place it in a warm oven so the fish doesn't turn soggy before hitting the table.

Crispy Potatoes, page 141

Fried Delacata Catish, page 138

Peach-and-Blackberry Crisp, page 141

Turnip Green Salad

TURNIP GREEN SALAD

ACTIVE 10 MIN. - TOTAL 25 MIN.
SERVES 6

- **¼ cup Champagne vinegar**
- **2 Tbsp. canned crushed tomatoes**
- **1 Tbsp. finely chopped shallot (from 1 shallot)**
- **1 tsp. chopped fresh sage**
- **1 tsp. fresh lime juice (from 1 lime)**
- **1 Tbsp. honey**
- **1 tsp. kosher salt**
- **1 tsp. Dijon mustard**
- **1 tsp. hot sauce (such as Tabasco)**
- **½ cup olive oil**
- **5 cups chopped fresh turnip greens (from 1 [16-oz.] pkg. or 1 bunch greens)**
- **4 cups purple cauliflower florets (from 1 head cauliflower)**
- **2 cups baby kale (2 oz.)**
- **1 cup watermelon radishes, cut into thin strips (from 2 medium radishes)**
- **1 cup heirloom grape tomatoes, halved (from 1 pt.)**

1. Stir together vinegar, crushed tomatoes, chopped shallot, sage, and lime juice in a medium bowl, and let stand 5 minutes. Whisk in honey, salt, Dijon mustard, and hot sauce. Add oil in a slow, steady stream, whisking constantly, until smooth.
2. Massage ¼ cup of the vinaigrette into turnip greens, cauliflower, baby kale, radishes, and tomatoes, and let stand 10 minutes (to help tenderize the greens). Serve salad with remaining vinaigrette.

GREEN GODDESS DRESSING

ACTIVE 10 MIN. - TOTAL 10 MIN.
SERVES 8

- **2 tsp. anchovy paste (or 3 canned anchovy fillets)**
- **1 small garlic clove, minced (about 1 tsp.)**
- **¾ cup mayonnaise**
- **¾ cup sour cream**
- **½ cup chopped fresh flat-leaf parsley**
- **¼ cup chopped fresh tarragon**
- **3 Tbsp. chopped fresh chives**
- **2 Tbsp. fresh lemon juice (from 1 lemon)**
- **½ tsp. kosher salt**
- **¼ tsp. black pepper plus more for garnish**

Place all ingredients in a blender or food processor, and process until smooth, 30 to 45 seconds. Garnish with extra black pepper, if desired. Serve as a dip, or toss with salad greens. The dressing will last a week if stored in an airtight container in the refrigerator.

WATERMELON SALAD

ACTIVE 20 MIN. - TOTAL 25 MIN.
SERVES 6

- **8 cups seedless watermelon, cut into 1-inch cubes (from 1 watermelon)**
- **3 lb. heirloom tomatoes, cored and cut into 1-inch wedges**
- **1 tsp. kosher salt**
- **4 cups arugula (4 oz.)**
- **2 satsumas (4 oz. each), peeled and cut into segments**
- **5 Tbsp. extra-virgin olive oil, divided**
- **2 Tbsp. chopped fresh mint**
- **1½ Tbsp. red wine vinegar**
- **½ tsp. black pepper**
- **2 oz. goat cheese, crumbled (about ½ cup)**
- **½ cup chopped pecans, toasted**

1. Combine watermelon and tomatoes in a large bowl. Sprinkle with salt, and toss gently to combine; let stand 10 minutes.
2. Combine arugula, satsumas, and 1 tablespoon of the oil in a medium bowl, tossing to coat. Add to watermelon mixture, and toss gently to coat. Whisk together mint, vinegar, pepper, and remaining 4 tablespoons oil in a small bowl. Drizzle over watermelon mixture. Sprinkle with goat cheese and toasted pecans, and serve.

CHEDDAR-CARAMELIZED ONION BREAD

ACTIVE 35 MIN. - TOTAL 1 HOUR, 30 MIN.
SERVES 8

- **½ cup plus 2 Tbsp. unsalted butter, divided**
- **2 tsp. caraway seeds**
- **1 Tbsp. extra-virgin olive oil**
- **1 large (9 oz.) red onion, thinly sliced**
- **1 tsp. kosher salt, divided**
- **1 cup almond flour**
- **1 cup all-purpose flour**
- **1 tsp. baking powder**
- **¼ tsp. baking soda**
- **½ cup heavy cream**
- **1 large egg**
- **2 tsp. honey**
- **4 oz. Cheddar cheese, shredded (about 1 cup)**
- **Chopped fresh thyme (optional)**
- **Whipped Sweet Potato Butter (recipe follows)**

1. Place ½ cup of the butter in freezer until solid, at least 30 minutes.
2. Preheat oven to 350°F. Heat a medium skillet over medium. Add caraway seeds, and cook, stirring constantly, until lightly toasted, about 1 minute. Remove seeds from skillet, and set aside.
3. Add oil to skillet, and heat over medium-high. Add onion, and cook, stirring often, until starting to soften, about 3 minutes. Reduce heat to medium-low, and cook, stirring occasionally, until tender and browned, about 15 minutes. Season with ¼ teaspoon of the salt. Remove onions from skillet, and let cool 10 minutes.
4. Place a 9-inch cast-iron skillet in preheated oven. Stir together flours, baking powder, baking soda, ½ teaspoon of the salt, and toasted caraway seeds in a medium bowl. Whisk together cream, egg, and honey in a separate bowl.
5. Remove butter from freezer. Using the large holes on a box grater, grate frozen butter into coarse shreds. Add shredded butter to flour mixture, stirring to combine. Add cream mixture, cheese, and caramelized onions to flour mixture; stir just until dough comes together. Turn dough out onto a lightly floured surface; pat into an 8-inch circle. Add remaining 2 tablespoons butter to hot cast-iron skillet, swirling to melt. Gently place dough in skillet; sprinkle with remaining ¼ teaspoon salt.
6. Bake bread in preheated oven until sides and top are golden brown, 20 to 25 minutes. Remove from oven, and let cool in skillet 5 minutes. Remove bread from skillet, and place on a wire rack to cool to room temperature, about 30 minutes. Sprinkle with thyme, if desired; serve with Whipped Sweet Potato Butter.

WHIPPED SWEET POTATO BUTTER

ACTIVE 15 MIN. - TOTAL 1 HOUR, 5 MIN.

SERVES 20

1 lb. sweet potatoes, peeled and cut into 2-inch chunks
2 tsp. white vinegar
2 ½ tsp. kosher salt, divided
1 cup unsalted butter, softened
¼ cup honey
¾ tsp. ground cinnamon
¼ tsp. black pepper

1. Place potatoes in a medium saucepan, and cover with cold water by 1 inch. Add vinegar and 2 teaspoons of the salt. Bring to a boil over high. Reduce heat to medium, and cook until tender, about 20 minutes.
2. Drain potatoes, and transfer to a large bowl; cool completely, about 20 minutes. Add butter, honey, cinnamon, pepper, and remaining ½ teaspoon salt to potatoes. Beat with an electric mixer, or process in a mini food processor until smooth, about 45 seconds. Chill Whipped Sweet Potato Butter until ready to serve.

CRISPY POTATOES

ACTIVE 10 MIN. - TOTAL 40 MIN.

SERVES 6

1 ½ lb. peeled russet potatoes, cut into 1-inch chunks
1 ½ lb. peeled sweet potatoes, cut into 1-inch chunks
¼ cup canola oil
2 tsp. garlic powder
2 tsp. onion powder
1 ½ tsp. kosher salt
1 ½ tsp. black pepper
4 thyme sprigs

1. Preheat oven to 425°F. Toss potatoes with oil, garlic powder, onion powder, salt, and pepper in a large bowl until well coated. Spread in a single layer on a large rimmed baking sheet, and top with thyme sprigs.
2. Bake in preheated oven until browned and crispy, about 25 minutes. Let cool 5 minutes before serving. Garnish with crispy thyme sprigs.

PEACH-AND-BLACKBERRY CRISP

ACTIVE 20 MIN. - TOTAL 1 HOUR, 25 MIN.

SERVES 8

2 lb. ripe peaches, halved, pitted, and cut into ½-inch wedges
3 cups fresh blackberries (15 oz.)
½ cup granulated sugar
2 Tbsp. cornstarch
2 tsp. fresh lemon juice (from 1 small lemon)
1 cup uncooked quick-cooking oats
1 cup all-purpose flour
⅓ cup honey
½ tsp. kosher salt
½ tsp. ground cinnamon
¼ tsp. ground cardamom
⅛ tsp. ground nutmeg
½ cup plus 1 Tbsp. cold unsalted butter, cubed
Lemon zest (optional)

1. Preheat oven to 350°F. Gently toss together peaches, blackberries, granulated sugar, cornstarch, and lemon juice in a large bowl. Transfer fruit to a lightly greased 11- x 7-inch baking dish.
2. Toss together oats, flour, honey, kosher salt, cinnamon, cardamom, and nutmeg in a medium bowl; add cubed butter. Using your hands, combine until mixture is crumbly. Sprinkle topping evenly over fruit.
3. Bake in preheated oven until top is golden brown and fruit mixture is bubbling, 45 to 50 minutes. Remove from oven, and cool 15 minutes. If desired, sprinkle with lemon zest before serving.

Pick a Side

Five flavorful salads that taste great with anything you toss on the grill

Cherry Tomato Caprese Salad

ACTIVE 15 MIN. - TOTAL 15 MIN.
SERVES 8

Combine 2 pt. **multicolored cherry tomatoes,** halved; 1 (8-oz.) container small **fresh mozzarella balls (such as bocconcini);** 1/4 cup **extra-virgin olive oil;** 2 Tbsp. **white balsamic vinegar;** 1 tsp. **kosher salt;** and 1/2 tsp. **black pepper** in a large bowl. Stir in 1 cup **small fresh basil leaves,** and serve immediately.

Spicy Grilled Corn Salad

Three jalapeños give this salad a real kick; make it milder by substituting mini sweet peppers. Serve with grilled flank steak and warm tortillas for an easy taco night.

ACTIVE 30 MIN. - TOTAL 30 MIN. - **SERVES 8**

Preheat grill to medium-high (400°F to 450°F). Remove the husks from 8 large ears **fresh yellow corn.** Brush corn with 3 Tbsp. **mayonnaise;** sprinkle with 1 tsp. **kosher salt** and 1/4 tsp. **black pepper.** Grill corn, covered, turning occasionally, until charred and tender, 10 to 12 minutes. (Kernels may pop.) Cut 1 medium-size **red onion** into 1/2-inch-thick slices, and brush with oil. Brush 3 large **jalapeño chiles,** halved lengthwise and seeds removed, with oil. Sprinkle onion and jalapeños with additional 1/2 tsp. **salt** and 1/4 tsp. **pepper.** Grill, covered, turning occasionally, until charred and tender, about 5 minutes. Cut kernels from corn into a large bowl. Chop onion and jalapeños; add to corn. Stir in 1/2 cup loosely packed **cilantro leaves** and 1/4 cup **fresh lime juice** (from 2 limes); serve immediately.

Three-Bean Pasta Salad

Swap out the canned beans for your favorite cooked field peas.

ACTIVE 30 MIN. - TOTAL 30 MIN. - **SERVES 8**

Cook 8 oz. small **shell pasta** in salted water according to package directions. Drain and rinse with cold water. Cook 8 oz. **fresh green beans,** trimmed and cut into 1-inch pieces, and 1/2 cup thinly sliced **celery** in boiling salted water to cover until tender-crisp, about 2 minutes. Drain and plunge vegetables into ice water to stop the cooking process; drain. Combine pasta; green beans; celery; 1 (16-oz.) can **pinto beans,** drained and rinsed; and 1 (16-oz.) can **red kidney beans,** drained and rinsed, in a large bowl. Combine 1 small minced **shallot** and 3 Tbsp. **rice vinegar** in a medium bowl, and let stand about 5 minutes. Add 1 tsp. **lemon zest,** 2 Tbsp. **fresh lemon juice,** 1 tsp. **Dijon mustard,** and 1 tsp. **honey,** stirring with a whisk. Gradually whisk in 3/4 cup **olive oil** until well combined, and pour over bean mixture. Sprinkle with 1 tsp. **kosher salt** and 1/2 tsp. **black pepper,** and toss gently. Sprinkle with 1/4 cup minced **fresh chives.**

Permanent Slaw

This salad is designed to be prepared in advance. The longer it sits, the more flavorful it becomes (hence the name).

ACTIVE 15 MIN. - TOTAL 12 HOURS, 15 MIN. - **SERVES 8**

Combine 1 cup **granulated sugar,** 1 cup **water,** 1 cup **apple cider vinegar,** 1 1/2 tsp. **celery seeds,** 1 1/2 tsp. **mustard seeds,** and 1 tsp. **kosher salt** in a medium saucepan; bring to a boil over high, stirring occasionally. Boil 1 minute. Combine 2 (10-oz.) pkg. **angel hair cabbage,** 1 1/4 cups shredded **carrot,** 1 cup thinly sliced **red bell pepper,** and 1 cup thinly sliced **Vidalia or other sweet onion** in a large bowl. Pour hot vinegar mixture over slaw mixture; cover with plastic wrap. Chill at least 12 hours or up to 7 days. Sprinkle with 1/4 cup thinly sliced **scallions** just before serving.

Watermelon, Cucumber, and Feta Salad

Replace the fresh mint with basil, or use a combination of both herbs. Dress the salad right before serving to prevent the melon and cucumbers from watering down the vinaigrette.

ACTIVE 30 MIN. - TOTAL 30 MIN. - **SERVES 8**

Combine 6 cups cubed **seedless watermelon;** 3 cups chopped **English cucumber;** and 1 (8-oz.) block **feta cheese,** cut into cubes, in a large bowl. Set aside. Combine 1/2 cup **red wine vinegar,** 1/4 cup thinly sliced **shallot,** 2 Tbsp. **fresh lemon juice,** 1 tsp. **fresh thyme leaves,** 1/2 tsp. **kosher salt,** and 1/4 tsp. **black pepper** in a medium bowl. Slowly drizzle in 3/4 cup **olive oil,** whisking until emulsified. Toss the watermelon mixture with 1/2 cup of the dressing. Transfer to a serving platter, and drizzle with remaining dressing. Sprinkle with 1/2 cup torn **fresh mint leaves** before serving.

Basic Pimiento Cheese

ACTIVE 15 MIN.
TOTAL 15 MIN.
MAKES 4 CUPS

- **1 (4-oz.) jar diced pimiento, drained**
- **1½ cups mayonnaise**
- **1 tsp. Worcestershire sauce**
- **1 tsp. finely grated yellow onion**
- **¼ tsp. cayenne pepper**
- **1 (8-oz.) block extra-sharp yellow Cheddar cheese, finely shredded**
- **1 (8-oz.) block sharp yellow Cheddar cheese, shredded**

1. Stir together pimiento, mayonnaise, Worcestershire, onion, and cayenne in a large bowl.
2. Stir cheeses into pimiento mixture until well combined. Store covered in the refrigerator up to 1 week.

Stirring Up Controversy

What goes into the best pimiento cheese? It depends on whom you ask

THIS COLUMN was created to give readers a definitive guide to classic Southern dishes, and we take that task seriously. We do plenty of research and put our Test Kitchen professionals through the wringer, asking them to test and retest recipes until everyone around the tasting table can confidently say: "Yes, this one is the best!" But when July rolled around, we decided to tackle pimiento cheese—and the notion of a consensus went out the window.

As it turns out, there are countless views on pimiento cheese perfection. It can be a smooth and spreadable version sandwiched between two slices of white bread. It can be chunky, spiked with hot sauce and cayenne pepper, and stuffed into celery sticks. It can be made with extra mayonnaise for a creamy cracker topper. The list goes on and on. We found that, apart from the fundamental ingredients (cheese, pimientos, and mayo), the best pimiento cheese is the one you grew up eating.

So while this is the place where we typically take a firm stance on a Southern classic, we kept the peace in the Test Kitchen and honored the "pâté of the South" in all its glorious forms, with two caveats. First, hand shred the cheese—some finely, some coarsely—for the best texture (a food processor will get the job done, but don't cheat with the pregrated stuff). Second, pick jarred pimientos that are diced, not sliced. After that, it's up to you. Keep it no-frills with our basic recipe, or spice it up with these four variations.

PIMIENTO CHEESE POINTERS

CHEESE

Use the large holes of a box grater to coarsely shred half of the Cheddar and the small holes to finely shred the rest.

PIMIENTOS

Choose diced (not sliced) jarred pimientos, which retain their shape when mixed with the other ingredients.

MAYONNAISE

Whether you prefer to add Hellmann's or Duke's, a high-quality mayonnaise is key. Skip the low-fat options.

1

Chipotle Pimiento Cheese

Prepare Basic Pimiento Cheese as directed, reducing mayonnaise to 1 1/4 cups, increasing cayenne pepper to 1/2 tsp., and substituting 2 Tbsp. minced canned chipotle chiles in adobo sauce and 1 Tbsp. fresh lime juice for Worcestershire and onion. Proceed with Step 2, substituting 8 oz. shredded sharp white Cheddar cheese and 8 oz. shredded pepper Jack cheese for sharp and extra-sharp yellow Cheddar cheeses.

2

Goat Cheese-and-Gouda Pimiento Cheese

Prepare Basic Pimiento Cheese as directed, substituting 1/2 cup chopped toasted pecans, 1 Tbsp. hot sauce, 1 tsp. seasoned salt, and 1/2 tsp. black pepper for Worcestershire, onion, and cayenne. Proceed with Step 2, substituting 8 oz. shredded sharp white Cheddar cheese, 4 oz. shredded Gouda cheese, and 4 oz. crumbled goat cheese for sharp and extra-sharp yellow Cheddar cheeses.

3

Prosciutto-Asiago Pimiento Cheese

Prepare Basic Pimiento Cheese as directed, substituting 1 1/2 Tbsp. lemon juice, 1/2 cup chopped basil, and 1 grated garlic clove for Worcestershire, onion, and cayenne. Proceed with Step 2, substituting 8 oz. shredded Asiago cheese, 4 oz. shredded mild yellow Cheddar cheese, and 4 oz. shredded Monterey Jack cheese for sharp and extra-sharp yellow Cheddar cheeses. Fold in 4 oz. prosciutto, cooked until crisp.

4

Horseradish Pimiento Cheese

Prepare Basic Pimiento Cheese as directed, reducing mayonnaise to 1 cup; omit Worcestershire, onion, cayenne, and sharp and extra-sharp yellow Cheddar cheeses. Process mayonnaise, 4 oz. softened cream cheese, 1 tsp. sugar, 1 tsp. prepared horseradish, 1/2 tsp. black pepper, 8 oz. shredded horseradish-flavored Cheddar cheese, and 8 oz. shredded sharp white Cheddar cheese in bowl of a food processor. Fold in pimiento.

Summer Scallops

A fast and fresh seafood salad for lazy beach days or busy weeknights

Grilled Scallop-and-Mango Salad

ACTIVE 25 MIN. - TOTAL 25 MIN.

SERVES 4

- **1/4 cup whole buttermilk**
- **2 Tbsp. mayonnaise**
- **1 Tbsp. white wine vinegar**
- **1 1/2 tsp. chopped fresh tarragon**
- **1 tsp. grated garlic (from 1 small garlic clove)**
- **1/2 tsp. kosher salt, divided**
- **1/4 tsp. black pepper, divided**
- **2 Tbsp. olive oil**
- **1 lb. bay scallops, drained**
- **12 (6-inch) wooden skewers**
- **1 medium-size firm ripe mango, peeled and sliced into 1/2-inch-thick planks (about 1 cup)**
- **5 oz. (about 8 heads) Little Gem lettuce, separated into leaves (5 cups)**
- **1 medium-size ripe avocado, cut into 1/2-inch cubes (1/2 cup)**
- **1 small radish, thinly sliced (1/3 cup)**

1. Whisk together buttermilk, mayonnaise, white wine vinegar, tarragon, garlic, 1/4 teaspoon of the salt, and 1/8 teaspoon of the pepper in a small bowl. Slowly drizzle oil into mixture, whisking constantly, until combined.

2. Measure 2 tablespoons of buttermilk dressing into a medium bowl. (Reserve the remaining dressing for serving.) Add scallops to bowl, and toss to coat. Marinate at room temperature 10 minutes. Thread scallops onto skewers (about 5 per skewer). Discard marinade.

3. Preheat a gas grill to high (450°F to 500°F). Place mango planks on oiled grates. Grill, uncovered, until slightly charred, 1 to 2 minutes per side. Remove mango from grill; cut into 1/2-inch cubes. Set aside. Re-oil grates; place scallop skewers on grill. Grill, uncovered, until charred, about 1 minute per side.

4. Line a platter with lettuce. Top with mango, avocado, radish, and scallop skewers. Sprinkle salad with remaining 1/4 teaspoon salt and 1/8 teaspoon pepper. Drizzle with reserved dressing, and serve immediately.

Nutritional information (per serving):
Calories: 333 - Protein: 16g - Carbs: 23g
Fiber: 5g - Fat: 21g

INGREDIENT SWAP

Substitute mixed baby greens for the Little Gem lettuce.

Ready To Roll

Porch parties call for shrimp-salad sliders with a little kick

MAKE & TAKE

Transport the prepared shrimp-salad mixture, toasted rolls, and fresh toppings separately. Then assemble the Mini Shrimp Rolls just before serving.

Mini Shrimp Rolls

ACTIVE 25 MIN. - TOTAL 25 MIN.
SERVES 6

- 1 lb. medium unpeeled raw shrimp
- 1 celery stalk, sliced (1/4 cup)
- 1/4 cup mayonnaise
- 2 Tbsp. finely chopped pickled jalapeño slices plus 1 tsp. pickled jalapeño liquid from jar (from 1 [16-oz.] jar)
- 2 tsp. fresh lemon juice (from 1 lemon)
- 3/4 tsp. kosher salt
- 1/4 tsp. black pepper
- 2 tsp. finely chopped fresh chives, divided
- 2 Tbsp. unsalted butter
- 12 oblong mini brioche rolls, top-sliced (from a bakery)
- 1 Tbsp. celery leaves

1. Bring a medium pot of water to a boil over high. Add shrimp; remove from heat. Cover; let stand until shrimp are cooked through, 2 to 3 minutes. Drain; let stand at room temperature until cooled, 10 minutes. Peel and roughly chop.
2. Stir together next 6 ingredients and 1 teaspoon of the chives in a medium bowl. Add shrimp; toss to combine.
3. Melt 1 tablespoon butter in a large nonstick skillet over medium. Place 6 rolls in skillet, top sides down, gently pulling rolls open so insides of rolls toast, about 1 minute. Remove rolls from skillet; set aside. Repeat with remaining 1 tablespoon butter and 6 rolls.
4. Fill each roll with 2 tablespoons shrimp mixture. Sprinkle with remaining 1 teaspoon chives and celery leaves; serve immediately.

COOKING (SL) SCHOOL

TIPS AND TRICKS FROM THE SOUTH'S MOST TRUSTED KITCHEN

KNOW-HOW

Grill Great Corn

Four easy steps for mastering this goes-with-anything veggie

1

Heat a charcoal grill to medium-high. Remove outer husks from corn, and then pull back the inner husks. Remove and discard silks. Rinse corn, and dry with paper towels.

2

Tie inner husks together with kitchen string (or use a longer outer corn husk), leaving the kernels exposed.

3

Brush kernels lightly with vegetable oil; sprinkle evenly with salt. Position corn so the tied husks hang over edge of grill to keep them from burning.

4

Grill corn, covered with grill lid, 20 minutes, turning with tongs every 5 minutes or until evenly charred. Serve on the cob, or slice off the kernels.

GRILLING TIPS

The Best Ways To Baste

Secrets to moist and juicy meats

Marinade

WHAT TO KNOW: If you want to add extra marinade to intensify the flavor, do it when the raw meat hits the grill so it cooks thoroughly. Or make a separate batch for basting.

Mop

WHAT TO KNOW: This thin, often vinegar-based liquid adds moisture and tanginess to meat. Apply periodically with a basting mop, spritz bottle, or brush.

Barbecue Sauce

WHAT TO KNOW: Sugary sauces can burn easily, so brush them on during the last few minutes of cooking.

INSTANT UPGRADE

3 Tasty Toppings

Corn gets a kick with these simple and surprising combos

Butter Honey Tabasco

Mayonnaise Old Bay Lemon Zest

Olive Oil Italian Seasoning Parmesan

August

150 **Soiree in the Swamp** A rustic inn nestled deep in Cajun country becomes a juke joint and secret supper club once the sun goes down

156 QUICK-FIX **No-Cook Summer Suppers** Assemble-and-serve (and perhaps a minute or two in the microwave) is all you need to get these five fresh main courses on the table

159 ONE AND DONE **Sizzling Skillet Steak** Pan drippings from cast-iron charred steaks create the flavorful pan sauce for garden veggies in this one-skillet meal

160 WHAT CAN I BRING? **Tasty Tomato Bites** A classic summer sandwich doubles as a tasty appetizer

193 SAVE ROOM **Just Chill** Have your pie and ice cream too

194 SOUTHERN CLASSIC **Summer Succatosh** A fresh twist on the South's favorite summer side dish

196 HEALTHY IN A HURRY **Pizza Night Alfresco** Keep the heat out of the kitchen with a loaded pie hot off the grill

198 *SL* COOKING SCHOOL Tips for your toaster oven and ideas for stove-free suppers

Soiree in the Swamp

Hidden in Louisiana's Cajun country, a secluded bed-and-breakfast hosts spirited celebrations of the region's culture

The turn toward Maison Madeleine Bed & Breakfast doesn't feel quite right. The road, barely wide enough for two cars, winds

When Walt Adams, a health-care design and construction consultant in Lafayette, heard about Maison Madeleine, he decided to celebrate the launch of his company there. But during the party, he found something else magical about the setting: Madeleine. Egged on by his adult daughters, Adams initiated a few subsequent meetings, but the couple (pictured below) had their first official date at the Blue Moon Saloon in Lafayette. Their eyes met as the Lost Bayou Ramblers played onstage, and not long after, Adams checked in permanently at the Maison.

through fields of towering, emerald green sugarcane before it dead-ends at a scrubby boat landing for a swamp-tour operation. This can't be the way to the place that lures visitors from as far away as France and Brazil deep into Louisiana's Cajun country.

But just a bit farther to the left on the bumpy dirt lane that circles Lake Martin, a hidden oasis of two sun-dappled cottages appears behind the spiky palmetto fronds and Spanish moss-cloaked oaks. A one-eyed marmalade tabby cat named Dude saunters up the steps to find a sunny spot on the porch; an azalea pink roseate spoonbill soars over the courtyard; and the sweet smell of pain perdu (French toast) floats from the kitchen.

When Louisiana native Madeleine Cenac decided to start her namesake inn here, she was recently divorced with three children, and the dreamy French Creole cottage from 1840 that now serves as the main guesthouse looked more like a nightmare to restore. But Cenac saw promise in the property, mere feet from Lake Martin, part of the Atchafalaya Basin where snowy egrets and blue herons perch above the alligators and frogs that skim the water.

From the rustic bousillage walls (made with a mixture of clay and Spanish moss) to the heirloom furnishings gathered from Cenac's past life as a design consultant, she resurrected the house into a destination for discerning tourists visiting nearby Lafayette and Breaux Bridge.

Seared Hanger Steak with Braised Greens and Grapes, page 154

Grilled Eggplant-and-Corn Romesco Napoleons, page 154

Kettle Chip-Crusted Fried Green Tomatoes with Tasso Tartar Sauce, page 154

Soon, the couple hosted another life-changing visitor at the B&B: Anthony Bourdain. Filming an episode of his television show *No Reservations* in 2011, the writer-host invited a collective of chefs, musicians, and locals over for a crawfish boil. After an evening of cracking tails and pouring bourbon, there was a consensus that they should do this more often, off camera. "We wanted to establish [this place] as a nexus of Acadian culture," says Adams.

Cenac and Adams renovated another building on the property to house a restaurant-style kitchen complete with a pint-size juke joint in the back for the gatherings that became known as the "Secret Supper" series. Once word got out, chefs such as Isaac Toups came to cook dinners served beneath sprawling oak trees as a rotating cadre of musicians set the scene sonically.

At a recent Secret Supper, chef Manny Augello of Bread & Circus Provisions in Lafayette (who cooked at the very first Secret Supper in 2013) had returned with chef de cuisine Chanel Gaude and chef Jeremy Conner (the co-owner of Cellar Salt Co. and Olympic Grove, a mobile event service).

While the three worked in the kitchen, tossing together crab salad and crushing Zapp's Spicy Cajun Crawtators potato chips to crust fried green tomatoes, the sound of a fiddle coming into tune cut through the humid air outside. Musicians Joel Savoy and Linzay Young (both formerly of the Red Stick Ramblers) strummed their guitars, Cedric Watson squeezed his accordion, and Kelli Jones (of Feufollet) sang in Cajun French.

An outsider might see this gathering, which includes a James Beard Award semifinalist and a Grammy winner performing traditional tunes, as a contrived display to impress out-of-towners, but this kind of overlap between music and food in Acadiana isn't unusual to those who call it home. (Nor is it uncommon to hear Cajun French spoken casually in the aisles of the Piggly Wiggly in town.)

"There's so much talent that it pushes all of us to remain parallel to each other," says Augello. "You've got to put your soul into it here, or it's nothing," echoes Conner.

Through Maison Madeleine, Cenac and Adams found a way to cultivate that community while also introducing visitors to the magic of their little piece of Louisiana. "This place is unlike any other on the planet, and people lose themselves in that," says Adams.

LOCAL LOVE
"The very heart of Cajun cooking is the idea of using ordinary, commonplace, and affordable ingredients to achieve some really extraordinary results," says chef Jeremy Conner (above). "Summer is awesome here. Crab, muscadines, corn, and okra are all in season."

Kettle Chip-Crusted Fried Green Tomatoes with Tasso Tartar Sauce

ACTIVE 30 MIN. - TOTAL 30 MIN.
SERVES 8

TASSO TARTAR SAUCE

- **3 oz. pork tasso, chopped (about ¾ cup)**
- **½ cup chopped shallots (from 2 medium shallots)**
- **¼ cup chopped red onion (from 1 onion)**
- **2 Tbsp. chopped celery (from 1 stalk)**
- **2 Tbsp. fresh lemon juice (from 1 lemon)**
- **1 garlic clove, crushed**
- **1 cup mayonnaise**
- **1 tsp. Creole mustard**
- **⅛ tsp. cayenne pepper**
- **⅛ tsp. granulated sugar**
- **⅛ tsp. kosher salt**

FRIED GREEN TOMATOES

- **Canola oil, for frying**
- **4 green tomatoes (about 1 ¾ lb.), cut into ⅓-inch-thick slices**
- **1 tsp. kosher salt**
- **½ tsp. black pepper**
- **¼ cup all-purpose flour**
- **2 large eggs, lightly beaten**
- **3 cups finely crushed spicy kettle-cooked potato chips (such as Zapp's Spicy Cajun Crawtators, from 2 [5-oz.] bags)**

1. Prepare the Tasso Tartar Sauce: Place pork tasso, shallots, red onion, celery, fresh lemon juice, and garlic in bowl of a food processor; pulse until finely chopped, 6 to 8 times. Scrape mixture into a small bowl, and fold in mayonnaise, mustard, cayenne, sugar, and salt. Cover and refrigerate until ready to serve.
2. Prepare the Fried Green Tomatoes: Heat 1 inch of oil in a large, heavy-bottomed skillet over medium to 350°F. Sprinkle tomato slices with salt and pepper. Place flour, beaten eggs, and crushed chips in 3 separate shallow bowls. Dredge tomato slices in flour; dip in egg, shaking off excess. Dredge in crushed chips until coated. Fry tomatoes, in batches, in hot oil until golden brown and crunchy, about 2 minutes per side. Serve immediately with Tasso Tartar Sauce.

Seared Hanger Steak with Braised Greens and Grapes

If you can't find Swamp Pop Noble Cane Cola, Dr Pepper has a similar spicy and moderately sweet flavor.

ACTIVE 30 MIN. - TOTAL 2 HOURS, 40 MIN.
SERVES 8

- **4 qt. water**
- **2 large bunches fresh collard greens (1 ½ lb. each), stemmed and chopped into medium-size pieces (or 4 large bunches fresh mustard greens)**
- **2 (12-oz.) bottles fig cola soft drink (such as Swamp Pop Noble Cane Cola)**
- **1 (½-lb.) smoked ham hock**
- **1 large (12 oz.) yellow onion, sliced (about 2 ½ cups)**
- **2 garlic cloves, chopped (about 2 tsp.)**
- **3 Tbsp. kosher salt**
- **1 tsp. crushed red pepper**
- **3 tsp. black pepper, divided**
- **2 lb. hanger steak, trimmed**
- **2 ½ tsp. flaky sea salt**
- **3 oz. large red table grapes or ripe muscadines (about ¾ cup)**

1. Stir together water, greens, cola, ham hock, onion, garlic, kosher salt, crushed red pepper, and 2 teaspoons of the black pepper in a large pot. Bring to a boil over medium-high; reduce heat to medium-low, and simmer until greens and ham hock meat are tender, about 2 hours. (Mustard greens will take 45 minutes.)
2. Sprinkle hanger steak with sea salt and remaining 1 teaspoon black pepper, and rub into steak. Let stand 10 minutes.
3. Heat a well-seasoned 12-inch cast-iron skillet over medium-high. Add steak; cook, turning occasionally, 10 to 12 minutes for medium-rare or until desired degree of doneness. Remove steak from skillet, and let rest until just cool enough to handle but still very warm, about 7 minutes.
4. While hanger steak rests, thinly slice or shave grapes, removing seeds as you go.
5. Using a slotted spoon, divide greens evenly among 8 serving plates. Slice steak, and place on top of greens. Top with sliced grapes, and serve immediately.

Grilled Eggplant-and-Corn Romesco Napoleons

ACTIVE 25 MIN. - TOTAL 40 MIN.
SERVES 8

- **3 ears fresh yellow corn, husked**
- **¾ cup chopped red onion (from 1 small onion)**
- **½ cup chopped almonds, toasted**
- **2 tsp. minced garlic (2 garlic cloves)**
- **½ tsp. smoked paprika**
- **2 ½ tsp. kosher salt, divided**
- **2 tsp. black pepper, divided**
- **¼ cup apple cider vinegar**
- **¼ cup plus 3 Tbsp. olive oil, divided**
- **2 medium (1 lb. each) eggplants, cut crosswise into ⅓-inch-thick slices**
- **1 oz. (1 ½ cups) watercress, torn**

1. Preheat a grill to medium-high (400°F to 450°F). Place corn on grate, and grill, covered, until tender and lightly charred, about 12 minutes, turning occasionally. Let cool 10 minutes. Cut corn kernels from cobs.
2. Place onion, almonds, garlic, smoked paprika, 1 ½ teaspoons each of the kosher salt and black pepper, and half of corn kernels (about 1 ⅓ cups) in bowl of a food processor. In a separate bowl, whisk together apple cider vinegar and ¼ cup of the olive oil. While drizzling olive oil mixture into corn mixture in processor, pulse until combined with a coarse texture, about 10 times. Set aside, and reserve remaining half of corn kernels.
3. Toss eggplant with remaining 3 tablespoons oil, 1 teaspoon salt, and ½ teaspoon pepper. Place on grate, and grill, uncovered, in batches if needed, until grill marks appear and eggplant is soft, 2 to 3 minutes per side.
4. Place 1 eggplant slice on each of 8 serving plates. Top with about 1 ½ tablespoons romesco sauce, 1 tablespoon reserved corn kernels, and a few pieces of torn watercress. Repeat layers twice to make 8 layered stacks.

Blackberry Trifles with Pecan Feuilletage and Mascarpone-Cane Syrup Mousse

The feuilletage can be served with ice cream or simply eaten on its own as an easy make-ahead dessert for any get-together.

ACTIVE 30 MIN. - TOTAL 2 HOURS
SERVES 8

PECAN FEUILLETAGE
- **2/3 cup finely chopped pecans**
- **1/4 cup granulated sugar**
- **9 frozen phyllo pastry sheets (4 oz.), thawed and separated into layers**
- **1/3 cup butter, melted**

MULLED WINE
- **1 qt. (32 oz.) dry red wine**
- **1 1/2 cups granulated sugar**
- **1 tsp. ground cinnamon**
- **1/2 tsp. ground allspice**
- **1/2 tsp. freshly grated nutmeg**
- **2 whole cloves**

MASCARPONE-CANE SYRUP MOUSSE
- **3 oz. mascarpone cheese (about 1/3 cup)**
- **3/4 cup heavy cream**
- **1 1/2 Tbsp. cane syrup (such as Steen's)**

ADDITIONAL INGREDIENT
- **4 cups (20 oz.) fresh blackberries**

1. Prepare the Pecan Feuilletage: Preheat oven to 400°F. Stir together pecans and sugar in a small bowl. Place 1 layer of phyllo on a parchment paper-lined baking sheet; brush with some of the melted butter. Sprinkle with about 1 1/2 tablespoons pecan mixture. Cover with another layer of phyllo. Repeat process with remaining phyllo sheets, butter, and pecan mixture, ending with a butter-brushed phyllo sheet on top.
2. Bake in preheated oven until layers are golden brown, bonded together, and crispy, 12 to 14 minutes. Cool completely on baking sheet, about 30 minutes. Break apart, or cut into pieces.
3. Prepare the Mulled Wine: Stir together red wine, sugar, cinnamon, allspice, nutmeg, and cloves in a large saucepan over medium-high; bring to a boil, stirring occasionally. Reduce heat to medium, and cook, stirring occasionally, until mixture is syrupy and reduced to about 1 1/2 cups, 40 to 50 minutes. Remove from heat, and cool completely, about 30 minutes. Discard cloves.
4. Prepare the Mascarpone-Cane Syrup Mousse: Beat together mascarpone cheese, heavy cream, and cane syrup in a large bowl with the whisk attachment of an electric mixer on medium-high speed until stiff peaks form, about 1 1/2 minutes.
5. To assemble trifles: Divide fresh blackberries evenly among 8 (1/2-cup) serving glasses. Pour 3 tablespoons of Mulled Wine over berries in each glass. Top with 2 to 3 tablespoons Mascarpone-Cane Syrup Mousse and pieces of Pecan Feuilletage.

Acadian Kitchen Staples

1

Steen's 100% Pure Cane Syrup

This yellow-labeled can doesn't look very different than it did when Steen's got its start in 1910, but that's what Louisianans love about it. Made with the state's sugarcane, the subtly tangy syrup is used by locals in everything from pies to cocktails.

2

Zapp's Potato Chips

Zapp's makes their cult-followed chips outside New Orleans, but they are the entire state's flagship snack. Now distributed across the South, the colorful bags are easy to find in grocery stores and gas stations.

3

Cellar Salt Co. Sea Salt

This small, Lafayette, Louisiana-based company harvests pyramid-shaped flakes of sea salt straight from the Gulf of Mexico.

4

Swamp Pop Noble Cane Cola

Flavored with summertime figs, this small-batch soda stands out with a deep, sultry sweetness.

No-Cook Summer Suppers

Step away from the stove with five fresh and fabulous recipes for getting dinner on the table in no time

Use steam-in-bag vegetables instead of boiling water on the stove-top.

Shrimp Boil Vegetable Bowls

ACTIVE 15 MIN. - TOTAL 30 MIN. -
SERVES 4

Prepare 1 (1 ½-lb.) pkg. **microwavable red potatoes (such as Side Delights Steamables)** in the microwave according to package directions, omitting seasoning from potatoes. Discard seasoning packet. Meanwhile, fill a large bowl with ice, and fill bowl three-fourths full with cold water. Plunge cooked potatoes into ice bath until completely cooled, 1 minute. Remove to a colander with a slotted spoon; drain. Repeat procedure with 1 (8-oz.) pkg. **microwavable haricots verts (French green beans, such as GreenLine Quick & Easy).** Cut potatoes into quarters; cut haricots verts in half crosswise. Combine potatoes; haricots verts; 1 lb. **large peeled, deveined cooked shrimp;** and 2 cups **fresh corn kernels (4 ears)** in a large bowl. Combine 3 Tbsp. drained, chopped **capers;** 2 Tbsp. **lemon zest** plus 3 Tbsp. **fresh juice (from 4 lemons);** 2 Tbsp. **white wine vinegar;** 1 tsp. **Old Bay seasoning;** ½ tsp. **kosher salt;** and ¼ tsp. **black pepper** in a small bowl. Whisk in ⅓ cup **olive oil** until combined. Pour caper mixture over shrimp mixture; toss to coat. Stir in ¼ cup chopped **fresh flat-leaf parsley**.

Crunchy Chicken-Peanut Chopped Salad

Slowly whisk each of the ingredients into the dressing to prevent it from breaking. If you're preparing the mixture in advance, give it an extra stir before tossing with the salad.

ACTIVE 15 MIN. - TOTAL 15 MIN.
SERVES 4

- **1 lb. deli-fried chicken tenders (about 6 large tenders), chopped**
- **3 cups shredded coleslaw mix (from 1 [10-oz.] pkg.)**
- **2 cups shredded red cabbage (from 1 head cabbage)**
- **½ cup thinly sliced scallions (from 4 scallions)**
- **½ cup coarsely chopped fresh cilantro**
- **¾ cup dry-roasted peanuts, coarsely chopped, divided**
- **5 Tbsp. fresh lime juice (from 3 limes)**
- **3 Tbsp. creamy peanut butter**
- **3 Tbsp. toasted sesame oil**
- **2 Tbsp. soy sauce**
- **2 Tbsp. seasoned rice vinegar**
- **2 Tbsp. light brown sugar**
- **Crushed red pepper, to taste**

1. Toss together chopped chicken tenders, coleslaw mix, cabbage, scallions, cilantro, and ½ cup of the chopped peanuts in a large bowl.
2. Whisk together lime juice and peanut butter in a small bowl until smooth. Slowly whisk in oil, soy sauce, vinegar, light brown sugar, and crushed red pepper, whisking until creamy.
3. To serve, pour dressing over salad mixture; toss to coat ingredients evenly. Sprinkle with remaining ¼ cup peanuts.

Yellow Gazpacho with Herbed Goat Cheese Toasts

For the best-tasting gazpacho, give the flavors plenty of time to blend. Prepare soup one day before serving, and store in the refrigerator.

ACTIVE 30 MIN. - TOTAL 1 HOUR, 30 MIN.
SERVES 4

- **1 (8-oz.) baguette**
- **1 cup water**
- **½ cup plus 1 Tbsp. extra-virgin olive oil, divided**
- **¼ cup plus 1 Tbsp. white wine vinegar, divided**
- **3 medium-size yellow bell peppers, divided**
- **1 large English cucumber, peeled and coarsely chopped (about 2 cups)**
- **1 large garlic clove, peeled**
- **3 pt. yellow cherry tomatoes, divided**
- **1½ tsp. kosher salt, divided**
- **1 tsp. paprika plus more for garnish**
- **2 oz. goat cheese (about ½ cup), softened**
- **1½ tsp. chopped fresh chives**
- **1½ tsp. chopped fresh flat-leaf parsley**

1. Tear baguette in half; tear 1 half into small pieces, and place in a blender. (Set aside remaining baguette half.) Add water, ½ cup of the oil, and ¼ cup of the vinegar to blender; let stand 10 minutes.
2. Coarsely chop 2 of the bell peppers. Add chopped peppers, cucumber, garlic, and 2 pints of the tomatoes to blender; process until smooth, about 1 minute. Stir in 1 teaspoon each of the salt and paprika. Cover and chill until cold, about 1 hour.
3. Meanwhile, chop remaining 1 bell pepper and 1 pint tomatoes; place in a small bowl. Add remaining 1 tablespoon oil, 1 tablespoon vinegar, and ½ teaspoon salt; stir to blend. Set aside.
4. Preheat toaster oven to 400°F. Cut reserved baguette half into 8 diagonal slices. Place slices on toaster oven pan; bake in preheated oven until golden brown, 5 to 7 minutes. Let cool 10 minutes.
5. Stir together goat cheese, chives, and parsley in a small bowl; spread over cooled toasts. Ladle chilled soup into 4 serving bowls. Top with chopped tomato mixture; sprinkle with paprika. Serve with toasts.

Greek Chicken Salad Wedges

Stirring the crumbled feta cheese into the chicken mixture in Step 1 will give the salad a creamier texture. Add more protein with a can of drained, rinsed chickpeas.

ACTIVE 25 MIN. - TOTAL 25 MIN.
SERVES 4

- **2 cups shredded rotisserie chicken breast (from 1 rotisserie chicken)**
- **1 cup chopped English cucumber (from 1 cucumber)**
- **1 cup chopped tomato (from 1 tomato)**
- **¼ cup halved pitted Kalamata olives**
- **¼ cup finely chopped red onion (from 1 onion)**
- **¼ cup chopped fresh flat-leaf parsley**
- **2 Tbsp. chopped fresh oregano**
- **1 tsp. kosher salt**
- **1 tsp. black pepper**
- **6 Tbsp. red wine vinegar**
- **2 Tbsp. Dijon mustard**
- **4 tsp. honey**
- **½ cup plus 2 Tbsp. olive oil**
- **4 (5-oz.) baby romaine lettuce hearts, halved lengthwise**
- **4 oz. crumbled feta cheese (1 cup)**

1. Combine chicken, cucumber, tomato, olives, and onion in a medium bowl.
2. Whisk together parsley, oregano, salt, pepper, vinegar, mustard, and honey in a small bowl. Slowly whisk in oil in a steady stream until blended. Toss chicken mixture with ½ cup of the dressing.
3. Place 2 romaine lettuce heart halves on each of 4 plates, and top each evenly with chicken mixture. Drizzle plates evenly with remaining ½ cup dressing, and sprinkle with crumbled feta.

Roasted Tomato, Salami, and Mozzarella Pasta

When a recipe calls for a small amount of an ingredient like arugula, pick up what you need from the salad bar at the grocery store instead of purchasing an entire package. Use a toaster oven to roast the tomatoes without heating up the kitchen.

ACTIVE 30 MIN. - TOTAL 30 MIN.
SERVES 4

- **1 pt. cherry tomatoes**
- **2 large garlic cloves, finely chopped (1 Tbsp.)**
- **½ tsp. black pepper**
- **6 Tbsp. extra-virgin olive oil, divided**
- **1 tsp. kosher salt, divided**
- **2 (8.5-oz.) pkg. fully cooked microwavable penne (such as Barilla Ready Pasta)**
- **3 Tbsp. balsamic vinegar**
- **8 oz. salami, chopped (2 cups)**
- **1 cup arugula (about 1 oz.)**
- **8 oz. fresh mozzarella cheese, torn**
- **⅓ cup fresh basil leaves, torn**

1. Preheat toaster oven to 400°F. Toss together tomatoes, garlic, pepper, 3 tablespoons of the oil, and ½ teaspoon of the salt on a small baking sheet lined with aluminum foil. Place in preheated toaster oven, and cook until tomatoes burst and char slightly, about 20 minutes. Meanwhile, prepare penne in microwave according to package directions; set aside.
2. Whisk together balsamic vinegar, remaining 3 tablespoons oil, and remaining ½ teaspoon salt in a large bowl. Add roasted tomato mixture, cooked penne, chopped salami, and arugula, and toss gently to coat. Arrange penne mixture on a large serving platter, and top with torn mozzarella and basil.

Sizzling Skillet Steak

Fire up the grill, and make this entire meal in your cast-iron pan

Grilled Steak with Blistered Beans and Peppers

Sprinkle the raw meat thoroughly with salt and pepper; let it stand at room temperature before hitting the hot skillet. Substitute two quartered bell peppers for the sweet mini peppers.

ACTIVE 25 MIN. - TOTAL 40 MIN.
SERVES 4

- **4 (6-oz.) boneless beef strip steaks (1 inch thick), trimmed**
- **3 large garlic cloves, minced (about 1 Tbsp.)**
- **1½ tsp. kosher salt, divided**
- **¾ tsp. black pepper, divided**
- **2 Tbsp. canola oil, divided**
- **3 Tbsp. salted butter**
- **1½ Tbsp. chopped fresh flat-leaf parsley**
- **2 tsp. chopped fresh thyme**
- **6 oz. fresh green beans, trimmed and halved on an angle (1½ cups)**
- **5 oz. sweet mini peppers, halved lengthwise (1½ cups)**
- **¾ cup sliced red onion (from 1 onion)**
- **2 Tbsp. fresh lemon juice (from 1 lemon)**

1. Pat steaks dry with a paper towel. Rub garlic evenly over steaks; sprinkle with 1 teaspoon of the salt and ½ teaspoon of the black pepper. Let stand at room temperature 15 minutes.

2. Place a 12-inch cast-iron skillet on grill grates, and preheat grill to high (450°F to 500°F). Add 1 tablespoon of the oil to skillet; immediately add steaks to skillet. Cook until well browned, 4 to 5 minutes. Add butter to skillet, and flip steaks. Cook, tilting pan and constantly spooning butter mixture over steaks, until a thermometer inserted in thickest portion registers 125°F, 1 to 2 minutes. Remove from heat. Transfer to a cutting board, and let rest 10 minutes. Transfer skillet drippings to a small bowl; stir in parsley and thyme. Set aside. Slice steak; transfer to a serving platter.

3. Wipe skillet clean; return to grill over high heat. Add remaining 1 tablespoon oil to skillet. Add green beans and peppers; cook, stirring occasionally, until charred, about 4 minutes. Stir in onion and lemon juice, and cover and cook until vegetables are tender, about 2 minutes. Sprinkle with remaining ½ teaspoon salt and ¼ teaspoon pepper. Arrange vegetables and steak on serving platter, and spoon parsley-thyme mixture over vegetables and steak.

Tasty Tomato Bites

The classic sandwich doubles as an easy appetizer

Mini Tomato Sandwiches with Bacon Mayonnaise

ACTIVE 20 MIN. - TOTAL 20 MIN.

MAKES 20

Place 4 finely chopped **bacon slices** in a small nonstick skillet over medium, and cook, stirring occasionally, until crisp, about 6 minutes. Drain on paper towels. Stir together cooked bacon, 1/2 cup **mayonnaise,** 2 tsp. chopped **fresh chives,** 1/2 tsp. **fresh lemon zest (from 1 lemon),** and 1/4 tsp. **kosher salt** in a small bowl. Spread mayonnaise mixture on 15 very thin **white bread slices (such as Pepperidge Farm),** with crusts removed. Layer 5 of the mayonnaise-coated bread slices with 1 large **red heirloom beefsteak tomato** (cut into 1/4-inch-thick slices), and sprinkle with **salt** and **black pepper.** Top with 5 mayonnaise-coated bread slices, coated side up. Layer with 1 large **yellow heirloom tomato** (cut into 1/4-inch-thick slices), and sprinkle with **salt** and **pepper.** Top with remaining 5 bread slices. Cut each sandwich into 4 pieces, and serve immediately.

MAKE AND TAKE

Prepare the sandwiches 1 hour ahead, and then refrigerate. Transport in a container lined with paper towels to keep them in place.

PASTA PRIMAVERA
WITH SHRIMP (PAGE 92)

CLOCKWISE FROM TOP LEFT:

• OVEN-FRIED CHICKEN SALAD WITH BUTTERMILK RANCH DRESSING (PAGE 89)

• TROPICAL CHICKEN LETTUCE WRAPS (PAGE 90)

• GRILLED SPICE-RUBBED PORK CHOPS WITH SCALLION-LIME RICE (PAGE 108)

MINI COCONUT-KEY LIME PIES
(PAGE 93)

ARROZ VERDE
(MEXICAN GREEN RICE)
(PAGE 105)
COUSCOUS PILAF
(PAGE 105)
QUICK PICKLED SLAW
(PAGE 105)

DEVILED CRAB MELTS
(PAGE 98)

CRAB BOIL WITH BEER AND OLD BAY (PAGE 97)

CRAB-AND-BACON LINGUINE (PAGE 97)

QUESO-FILLED
MINI PEPPERS (PAGE 107)

CLOCKWISE FROM TOP LEFT:

- GRILLED PORK MEATBALL KEBABS (PAGE 104)
- CRISPY SOFT-SHELL CRAB SANDWICHES (PAGE 101)
- LEMON-HERB CHICKEN KEBABS (PAGE 103)
- CRAB PIE (PAGE 98)

CLOCKWISE FROM TOP LEFT:

- SHRIMP-OKRA-AND-SAUSAGE KEBABS (PAGE 102)
- WHOLE-GRAIN PANZANELLA (PAGE 125)
- SHEET PAN PIZZA WITH CORN, TOMATOES, AND SAUSAGE (PAGE 121)
- BACON-SPINACH-AND-COUSCOUS STUFFED TOMATOES (PAGE 123)

SHEET PAN GREEK CHICKEN WITH ROASTED POTATOES (PAGE 106)

THYME-SCENTED BLUEBERRY PIE (PAGE 109)

PEACH-RASPBERRY BUCKLE
(PAGE 116)

STRAWBERRY KUCHEN
(PAGE 117)

CLOCKWISE FROM TOP LEFT:

• BLUEBERRY-LEMON CRUNCH BARS (PAGE 115)

• BERRY SONKER WITH DIP (PAGE 115)

• GINGER-PLUM SLUMP (PAGE 116)

• CHERRY NECTARINE PANDOWDY (PAGE 115)

ZUCCHINI LASAGNA
(PAGE 124)

PICKLED SHRIMP AND VEGETABLES (PAGE 126)

CHEDDAR-CARAMELIZED ONION BREAD (PAGE 140)

FRIED DELACATA CATFISH (PAGE 138)

GREEN GODDESS DRESSING (PAGE 140)

CLOCKWISE FROM TOP LEFT:

- CHICKEN THIGHS AND BBQ BEANS (PAGE 119)
- TURNIP GREEN SALAD (PAGE 140)
- WATERMELON SALAD (PAGE 140)
- CRISPY POTATOES (PAGE 141)

GRILLED SCALLOP-AND-MANGO SALAD (PAGE 146)

MINI SHRIMP ROLLS
(PAGE 147)

THREE-BEAN PASTA SALAD (PAGE 143)

CLOCKWISE FROM TOP LEFT:

- PERMANENT SLAW (PAGE 143)
- CHERRY TOMATO CAPRESE SALAD (PAGE 142)
- WATERMELON, CUCUMBER, AND FETA SALAD (PAGE 143)
- SPICY GRILLED CORN SALAD (PAGE 143)

BASIC PIMIENTO CHEESE
(PAGE 144)

CHIPOTLE PIMIENTO
CHEESE (PAGE 145)
GOAT CHEESE-AND-GOUDA
PIMIENTO CHEESE (PAGE 145)
PROSCIUTTO-ASIAGO
PIMIENTO CHEESE (PAGE 145)
HORSERADISH PIMIENTO
CHEESE (PAGE 145

CLOCKWISE FROM TOP LEFT:

• CORNMEAL COOKIE BERRY SHORTCAKES (PAGE 133)

• RED VELVET ICE-CREAM CAKE (PAGE 132)

• RED, WHITE, AND BLUEBERRY-FILLED CUPCAKES (PAGE 134)

• FOURTH OF JULY CONFETTI ROULADE (PAGE 133)

CHERRY FLAG PIE
(PAGE 132)

GRILLED EGGPLANT-AND-CORN ROMESCO NAPOLEONS **(PAGE 154)**

KETTLE CHIP-CRUSTED FRIED GREEN TOMATOES WITH TASSO TARTAR SAUCE (PAGE 154)

BLACKBERRY TRIFLES WITH PECAN FEUILLETAGE AND MASCARPONE-CANE SYRUP MOUSSE (PAGE 155)

Just Chill

Ice cream is the secret to this simple no-bake pie

SERVING TIP
For the neatest slices, dip the blade of a knife in a glass of hot water; wipe off before cutting into the pie. Repeat for each new piece.

No-Bake Peanut Butter-Fudge Ice-Cream Pie

ACTIVE 15 MIN. - TOTAL 8 HOURS, 40 MIN., INCLUDING 8 HOURS FREEZING
SERVES 8

Stir together 3 cups **chocolate crisp rice cereal (such as Cocoa Krispies);** ½ cup finely chopped, **salted dry-roasted peanuts;** and ⅓ cup melted **butter** in a medium bowl. Press mixture into bottom and up sides of a lightly greased 9-inch glass pie plate. Freeze until solid, 15 to 30 minutes. Microwave ½ cup **creamy peanut butter** in a small microwave-safe bowl on HIGH until melted and smooth, about 30 seconds. Let stand at room temperature 10 minutes, stirring occasionally. Place 4 cups softened **vanilla ice cream** in the bowl of a heavy-duty stand mixer; beat on medium-low until smooth, about 30 seconds. Drizzle peanut butter into ice cream, beating on low just until incorporated, about 30 seconds. Spread ice-cream mixture into frozen pie shell. Cover and freeze until firm, 8 hours or up to 24 hours. Before serving, remove pie from freezer, and leave out at room temperature 10 minutes. Meanwhile, beat 1 cup **heavy cream** and ½ tsp. **vanilla extract** with an electric mixer on medium-high speed until foamy, about 30 seconds. Gradually add 3 Tbsp. **powdered sugar,** beating until soft peaks form, 30 seconds to 1 minute. Spread whipped cream evenly over pie. Drizzle with **hot fudge topping;** sprinkle with coarsely chopped, **salted dry-roasted peanuts.**

Summer Succotash

Our Test Kitchen surprised us with a few twists on this traditional dish

TOMATOES

Cherry tomatoes add a burst of sweetness and acidity. Stir them in at the very end so they hold their shape and juiciness.

CORN

Fresh is a lot more flavorful than frozen. Don't overcook the kernels; you want them to retain a little crunch.

LIMA BEANS

Fresh or frozen baby lima beans are both fine for this dish. If using frozen, do not thaw them before adding to the pan.

NO DISH celebrates the bounty of the late-summer garden better than succotash. When done right, this colorful mix of corn, beans (typically lima beans or field peas), and other seasonal vegetables is more than just a side—it can upstage the rest of the potluck spread. But sadly, we've all encountered plenty of anemic steam table versions of the recipe at restaurants where the ingredients have, well, suffered.

While succotash is inherently flexible—it's a resourceful way to use up a surplus of corn or show off a precious handful of field peas—certain types of produce work better than others. Zucchini and yellow squash can water down the contents, so we omitted them from our recipe, along with bell peppers, which have a stronger flavor that can overwhelm the other ingredients.

One general rule of thumb to remember for succotash: Don't bother with canned vegetables. In-season produce has a much better texture and more vibrant flavor. We found that it doesn't really matter whether you throw in fresh or frozen beans—either choice will taste great. On the other hand, for the sweetest corn, make sure it's fresh. Bacon is a key ingredient in many Southern variations of this side item. We prefer center-cut slices because they are meatier than regular cut and also render just the right amount of bacon fat, which is used to sauté the vegetables.

Many succotash recipes call for a splash of heavy cream; it forms a thin sauce that helps tie the dish together but can muddy the bright colors of the ingredients. Our version replaces the cream with butter, which adds richness while still keeping the vegetables vibrant and glossy.

The last rule of this Southern classic is that it shouldn't sit around. It's best served immediately, while the crumbled bits of bacon on top are crisp and the thinly sliced basil is fragrant. Fortunately, it's pretty hard to resist.

Secret Succotash Ingredients

1
OKRA
This in-season vegetable is a delicious addition to the dish. Choose smaller pods, and cook them until tender-crisp to prevent a slimy texture.

2
BUTTER
Unlike heavy cream, butter (we prefer the salted kind) delivers rich flavor without making this side item too heavy or turning the fresh produce dull and gray.

3
BASIL
Many versions of this recipe call for soft herbs such as tarragon, chives, or parsley, but we prefer the more classic taste of fresh basil.

Make It Meatless

While pork is a traditional ingredient in many Southern variations of succotash, it's certainly not essential to this side. For a vegetarian option, follow the recipe but omit the bacon and replace the drippings with 2 tablespoons of extra-virgin olive oil. Still want a hint of spice? Sprinkle the finished dish with a little bit of smoked paprika.

Best-Ever Succotash

ACTIVE 30 MIN. - TOTAL 30 MIN.
SERVES 6

- 10 oz. fresh or frozen baby lima beans (2 cups)
- 4 center-cut bacon slices
- 1 cup chopped sweet onion (from 1 small onion)
- 4 oz. fresh okra, cut into ½-inch-thick slices (1 cup)
- 1 garlic clove, finely chopped (1 tsp.)
- 3 cups fresh corn kernels (4 ears)
- 1¼ tsp. kosher salt
- ¼ tsp. black pepper
- 3 Tbsp. butter
- 5 oz. cherry tomatoes, halved (1 cup)
- ¼ cup thinly sliced fresh basil

1. Place lima beans in a medium saucepan, and add water to cover. Bring to a boil over medium-high. Reduce to medium-low, and simmer until beans are just tender, 8 to 10 minutes. Drain and set aside.
2. While beans simmer, place bacon slices in a large cast-iron skillet over medium. Cook until crisp, about 8 minutes, turning once after 5 minutes. Transfer bacon to paper towels; crumble and set aside. Reserve drippings in skillet.
3. Add chopped onion, fresh okra, and garlic to skillet over medium, and cook, stirring often, until onion is just tender, about 6 minutes. Stir in fresh corn kernels, salt, pepper, and drained beans, and cook, stirring often, until corn is tender and bright yellow, 5 to 6 minutes. Add butter, and cook, stirring constantly, until butter is melted, about 1 minute. Remove from heat.
4. Stir in halved cherry tomatoes and sliced basil; sprinkle with crumbled bacon, and serve immediately.

Pizza Night Alfresco

This pie topped with in-season ingredients really delivers

LIGHTENED UP
Packed with protein and veggies, this pizza is a diabetic-friendly choice. For more ideas from the American Diabetes Association, visit *diabetes.org*.

Cook the vegetables in a grilling basket before adding them to the pizza.

Grilled Pizza with Summer Veggies and Smoked Chicken

ACTIVE 25 MIN. - TOTAL 25 MIN.
SERVES 4

- 1 medium zucchini, cut into ¼-inch-thick slices (1½ cups)
- 1 cup thinly sliced red onion (from 1 small onion)
- 1 ear fresh corn, husks removed
- 1 large garlic clove, finely chopped (1½ tsp.)
- 4 tsp. extra-virgin olive oil, divided, plus more for greasing
- 12 oz. fresh prepared whole-wheat pizza dough, at room temperature
- 8 oz. smoked chicken, shredded
- 8 oz. low-moisture smoked mozzarella cheese, shredded (about 2 cups)
- ¼ tsp. kosher salt
- ¼ tsp. black pepper
- Fresh basil leaves and crushed red pepper, for topping

1. Preheat grill to high (450°F to 500°F). Toss together zucchini, onion, corn, garlic, and 2 teaspoons of the oil in a large bowl. Arrange vegetables in a single layer in a metal grilling basket lightly coated with oil. Place basket on grill grate, and grill, uncovered, turning occasionally, until vegetables are charred, 4 to 6 minutes. Remove from grill. Cut corn kernels from cob; discard cob. Set aside vegetables.
2. Roll dough into a 14- x 10-inch oval on a lightly floured surface. Place on lightly oiled grates; grill over high heat, uncovered, until lightly browned, about 1½ minutes. Flip over; brush top with remaining 2 teaspoons oil. Top with chicken; sprinkle with cheese, leaving a ½-inch border around dough edges. Arrange vegetables over pizza. Grill, uncovered, until cheese is melted, about 1½ minutes. Remove from grill.
3. Sprinkle with salt and black pepper; top with basil and crushed red pepper.

Nutritional information (per serving):
Calories: 497 - Protein: 36g - Carbs: 46g - Fiber: 4g - Fat: 22g

KNOW-HOW

Grill Pizza Like a Pro

Three simple steps for a crisp, lightly charred crust

1

START WITH AN OILED GRILL

Lightly oiled grill grates will prevent the pizza dough from sticking. Set the grill temperature to high for the crispiest results.

2

FLIP, AND THEN TOP

Grill one side of the dough; turn it over with tongs. Add cheese and other toppings. Or transfer the half-cooked dough to a baking sheet, add the toppings, and slide it back onto the grill.

3

LET IT MELT

After adding the toppings, let the pizza continue to cook on the grill for one to two more minutes to melt the cheese.

EXTRA TOPPINGS

More Creative Combos

Try our summery spins on grilled pizza

Marinara sauce + roasted eggplant + mozzarella cheese + fresh oregano

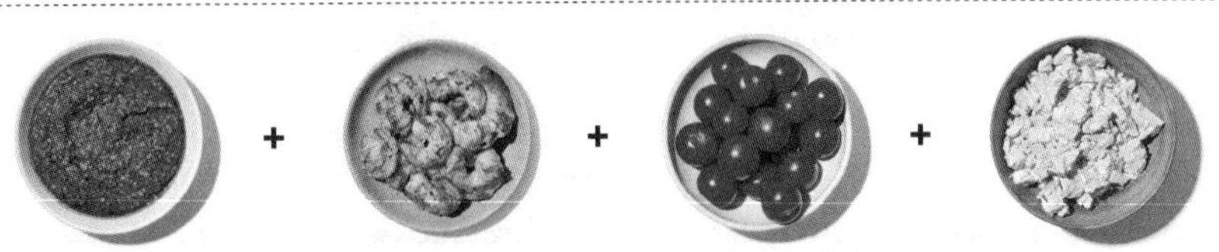

Pesto + grilled shrimp + cherry tomatoes + feta cheese

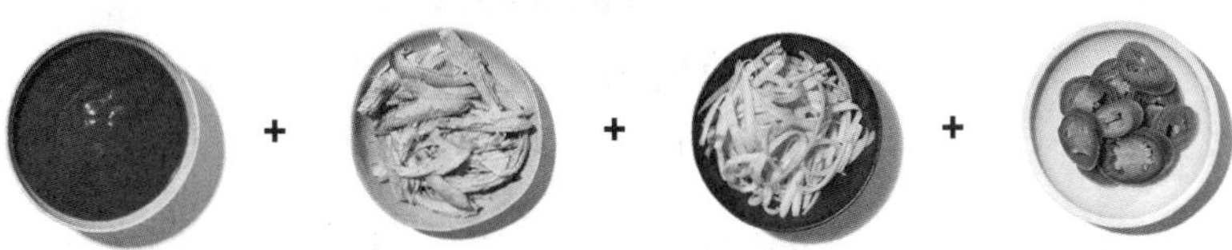

Barbecue sauce + shredded chicken + Monterey Jack cheese + pickled jalapeños

COOKING (SL) SCHOOL

TIPS AND TRICKS FROM THE SOUTH'S MOST TRUSTED KITCHEN

KNOW-HOW

Toaster Treats

Here's a sweet dessert that doesn't need the main oven

▶ Mix or replace the blackberries with any fresh summer berries.

TOASTER OVEN BLACKBERRY COBBLERS

Preheat toaster oven to 375°F. Toss 3 cups **fresh blackberries** with 1 Tbsp. **fresh lemon juice** in a medium bowl. Divide berries evenly among 6 lightly greased (8-oz.) ramekins. Stir together 1 **large egg,** 1 cup **granulated sugar,** and 1 cup **all-purpose flour** in a medium bowl. Add 6 Tbsp. melted **butter;** stir until just combined. Divide flour mixture evenly over fruit; gently press to cover the berries. Place ramekins on a baking sheet. (You may need to bake them in batches, depending on the oven size.) Bake in preheated oven 35 minutes or until golden and bubbly.

PANTRY PRIMER

Staples for Stove-Free Suppers

Keep these ingredients on hand to whip up satisfying meals in minutes

PRECOOKED RICE
Microwavable rice (such as Uncle Ben's Ready Rice) has an al dente texture, while frozen cooked rice is fluffier.

MICROWAVABLE PASTA
Forget about boiling water when you have a packet of heat-and-eat pasta (such as Barilla Ready Pasta) within reach.

STEAM-IN-BAG VEGETABLES
Microwave-ready fresh vegetables won't get soggy, unlike the frozen kind.

COOKED SALMON
Add protein to salads and pasta dishes with skinless, boneless salmon (like Bumble Bee Premium Pink Salmon).

"Not all oven-safe dishes can be used in a toaster oven, especially glass cookware. When in doubt, be sure to check with the manufacturer."

—**Paige Grandjean**
Test Kitchen Professional

GREAT GEAR

The Hottest New Oven

CUISINART TOA-60 CONVECTION TOASTER OVEN AIR FRYER

Why we love it: This roomy, multipurpose unit can roast a Sunday chicken, air-fry a batch of crispy catfish (using little to no oil), or bake a 12-inch pizza without heating up your whole kitchen or making a greasy mess. $199; *amazon.com*

September

200 **The Southern Living Tailgating Playbook** Whether you get your game on in the stadium parking lot or the comfort of your living room, we've got the recipe lineup covered

206 FALL BAKING **Bake Another Batch** The best things are worth sharing, and these big-batch recipes are no exception

210 BACK-TO-SCHOOL SPECIAL **Snack Attack** Enjoy after-school nibbles that satisfy kids and parents

212 DINNER IN AMERICA **Easier Enchiladas** Deconstructed deliciousness turns a Mexican favorite into a one-pan wonder

The Southern Living

Tailgating Playbook

Food and football go hand in hand, but what you cook at a tailgate depends on where you're watching the game. So we came up with two easy, crowd-pleasing menus: one with portable dishes that travel well and another for parties in the comfort of your own living room

Warm Cheese-and-Spicy Pecan Dip, page 204

clockwise from top left:
Sheet Pan Nachos with Chorizo and Refried Beans, page 204; Warm Spinach-Sweet Onion Dip with Country Ham, page 205; Brisket-and-Black Bean Chili with Cilantro-Lime Crema, page 205; Brined Grilled Chicken with Dipping Sauces, page 204

Spirited Cocktails

Set up a Bloody Mary bar at home with lots of creative garnishes, or make a big-batch punch and take it in a beverage dispenser.

Big-Batch Bloody Marys

ACTIVE 5 MIN. - TOTAL 5 MIN.
SERVES 10

Combine 2 (32-oz.) bottles **clam-tomato juice (such as Clamato),** 2 Tbsp. **fresh lime juice** (from 1 lime), 2 Tbsp. **fresh lemon juice** (from 1 lemon), 2 Tbsp. **prepared or freshly grated horseradish,** 2 Tbsp. **Worcestershire sauce,** 1 ½ Tbsp. **black pepper,** and 1 tsp. **celery salt** in a large punch bowl or glass dispenser, stirring until well combined. Stir in 2 cups (16 oz.) **vodka,** and serve immediately. Pour into glasses, and, if desired, garnish using **celery stalks with leaves, pickled okra,** or **lime wedges.**

Whiskey-Apple Cider Punch

ACTIVE 10 MIN. - TOTAL 1 HOUR, 10 MIN.
SERVES 10

Combine 1 cup **frozen cranberries,** thawed (about 4 oz.); ¼ cup packed **light brown sugar;** and ¼ cup **water** in a food processor. Process until cranberries are roughly chopped and sugar has almost dissolved, about 30 seconds. Transfer to a large bowl. Add 3 cups (24 oz.) **bourbon,** 1 ½ cups **fresh lemon juice** (from 14 lemons), ¾ cup **honey,** and ¼ cup **water;** stir until well combined and sugar is dissolved. Pour mixture through a fine wire-mesh strainer into a 3- to 4-qt. pitcher, discarding solids. Chill at least 1 hour or up to 8 hours. Just before serving, gently stir in 1 (24.5-oz.) bottle **sparkling apple cider,** chilled. Pour into glasses, and, if desired, garnish with **Granny Smith apple slices.**

Smoky Snack Mix, page 205

HOME

Sheet Pan Nachos with Chorizo and Refried Beans

The secret to fully loaded nachos that won't fall apart in your lap? Try a salsa-and-refried beans combo that acts like the "glue" and will help the toppings stick to the tortilla chips.

ACTIVE 20 MIN. - TOTAL 30 MIN.
SERVES 10

- 1 lb. fresh Mexican chorizo, casings removed
- ½ cup chopped yellow onion (from 1 small onion)
- 1 (15-oz.) can refried beans
- 1 (16-oz.) jar tomatillo salsa, divided
- 1 (12-oz.) pkg. tortilla chips
- 4 oz. Monterey Jack cheese, shredded (about 1 cup)
- 4 oz. sharp Cheddar cheese, shredded (about 1 cup)
- 1 ripe avocado, chopped
- 1 jalapeño chile, thinly sliced
- ¾ cup sour cream
- ½ cup loosely packed fresh cilantro leaves
- Mexican hot sauce (such as Valentina, optional)

1. Preheat oven to 400°F. Cook chorizo and onion in a large nonstick skillet over medium, stirring often with a wooden spoon to crumble, until chorizo is well browned and onion is tender, about 8 minutes. Drain on a plate lined with paper towels.
2. Stir together refried beans and 1 cup of the tomatillo salsa in a small saucepan. Cook over medium-high, stirring often, until hot, about 3 minutes.
3. Line a large rimmed baking sheet with aluminum foil. Arrange chips in a single layer on foil. Top chips evenly with chorizo mixture, bean mixture, and cheeses.
4. Bake in preheated oven until cheeses melt and just begin to brown in places, about 8 minutes. Remove from oven, and top with avocado, jalapeño, sour cream, cilantro, and remaining tomatillo salsa. Drizzle with hot sauce, if desired.

Brined Grilled Chicken with Dipping Sauces

The brine, made with herbs, garlic, brown sugar, and chiles, adds tons of flavor and keeps the chicken drumettes from drying out on the grill.

ACTIVE 30 MIN. - TOTAL 5 HOURS, 35 MIN.
SERVES 10

- 2 qt. water
- ½ cup white wine vinegar
- ¼ cup kosher salt
- ¼ cup packed light brown sugar
- 6 thyme sprigs
- 6 parsley sprigs
- 4 rosemary sprigs
- 4 garlic cloves, crushed
- 2 whole dried chiles (such as de árbol chiles)
- 2 lb. chicken drumettes
- 2 tsp. paprika
- ½ tsp. black pepper
- Dipping sauces (recipes follow)

1. Combine water, vinegar, salt, brown sugar, thyme, parsley, rosemary, garlic, and chiles in a large stockpot. Cook over medium-high, stirring occasionally, until salt and sugar dissolve, about 5 minutes. Remove brine from heat; cool completely, about 1 hour. Place chicken drumettes in cooled brine; cover and chill at least 4 hours or up to 8 hours.
2. Preheat grill to medium (350°F to 400°F). Drain chicken, discarding brine. Pat chicken dry with paper towels; sprinkle evenly with paprika and black pepper. Grill chicken, covered, until browned on all sides and a thermometer inserted into thickest part registers 170°F. Remove from grill, and let rest 5 minutes. Serve with dipping sauces.

Fiery Sweet Dipping Sauce

MAKES ABOUT 1 CUP - ACTIVE 10 MIN. - TOTAL 10 MIN.

Melt 2 Tbsp. **unsalted butter** in a small saucepan over medium-high; add ¼ cup chopped **sweet onion** (from 1 onion). Cook, stirring often, until tender and beginning to brown, about 5 minutes. Add 1 small **habanero chile,** seeded and minced; cook, stirring constantly, 30 seconds. Remove from heat; transfer onion mixture to a blender. Add ¾ cup **blackberry preserves,** ⅓ cup **fresh lime juice** (from 3 limes), and ¼ tsp. **kosher salt;** process until smooth, about 1 minute. Return onion mixture to saucepan; cook over medium, stirring often, until hot, about 2 minutes. Remove from heat. Serve immediately, or store in an airtight container in refrigerator up to 2 days. Reheat before serving.

Buttermilk-Parmesan Ranch

MAKES ABOUT 1 ¼ CUPS - ACTIVE 5 MIN. - TOTAL 5 MIN.

Combine ½ cup **mayonnaise;** 2 oz. **Parmesan cheese,** grated (about ½ cup); ¼ cup chopped **scallions,** green parts only; ¼ cup **whole buttermilk;** 2 tsp. **fresh lemon juice** (from 1 lemon); ¼ tsp. **kosher salt;** and ¼ tsp. **black pepper** in a food processor. Process until smooth. Transfer to a serving bowl; stir in 2 Tbsp. finely chopped **fresh chives** and 2 Tbsp. finely chopped **fresh flat-leaf parsley.** Serve immediately, or store in an airtight container in refrigerator up to 2 days.

Creamy Honey Mustard

MAKES ABOUT 1 ½ CUPS - ACTIVE 5 MIN. - TOTAL 5 MIN.

Stir together 1 cup **sour cream,** ½ cup **Dijon mustard,** 2 Tbsp. **olive oil,** 1 tsp. **honey,** ¼ tsp. **kosher salt,** and ⅛ tsp. **cayenne pepper** in a small bowl. Serve immediately, or store in an airtight container in refrigerator up to 2 days.

Warm Cheese-and-Spicy Pecan Dip

Classic cheese dip gets a kick from crunchy, cayenne-spiced nuts. Avoid overcooking the dip, or it could separate. Remove from the oven when it starts to bubble around the edges.

ACTIVE 10 MIN. - TOTAL 30 MIN.
SERVES 10

- 2 (8-oz.) pkg. cream cheese, softened
- 1 cup mayonnaise
- 4 oz. sharp Cheddar cheese, shredded (about 1 cup), divided
- 2 oz. Monterey Jack cheese, shredded (about ½ cup), divided
- 4 tsp. cornstarch
- 1 tsp. kosher salt
- ½ tsp. black pepper
- ½ cup Spicy Pecans (recipe follows)
- 2 Tbsp. finely chopped fresh chives
- Toasted baguette slices, for serving

1. Preheat oven to 375°F. Pulse cream cheese and mayonnaise in a food processor until smooth.
2. Toss ¾ cup of the Cheddar and ¼ cup of the Monterey Jack with cornstarch in a medium bowl until coated. Stir in cream cheese mixture, salt, and pepper. Spoon into a 1-quart baking dish, and top with remaining ¼ cup each Cheddar and Monterey Jack cheeses.
3. Bake in preheated oven until golden and bubbling around the edges, about 15 minutes. Remove from oven; sprinkle with Spicy Pecans. Cool 5 minutes; sprinkle with chives. Serve with toasted baguette slices.

Spicy Pecans

MAKES 1½ CUPS - ACTIVE 5 MIN. - TOTAL 25 MIN.

Preheat oven to 350°F. Combine 1½ cups roughly chopped **pecans,** 1 Tbsp. **olive oil,** ½ tsp. **kosher salt,** ½ tsp. **black pepper,** and ¼ tsp. **cayenne pepper** in a medium bowl, and toss to coat. Spread coated pecans in a single layer on a rimmed baking sheet, and bake in preheated oven until pecans are deeply toasted, about 15 minutes, stirring once. Let cool 5 minutes. Store in an airtight container at room temperature up to 4 days.

AWAY

Smoky Snack Mix

This recipe can be doubled or tripled easily, which we highly recommend.

ACTIVE 5 MIN. - TOTAL 20 MIN.
SERVES 10

Preheat oven to 325°F. Toss together 2 cups **crispy corn snack crackers (such as Bugles),** 2 cups **rice cereal squares (such as Rice Chex),** 2 cups **bite-size white Cheddar cheese crackers (such as Cheez-It),** 1 cup **mini pretzels,** and 1 cup **smoked almonds** in a large bowl. Melt 6 Tbsp. **unsalted butter** in a small saucepan over medium. Stir in 2 tsp. **chipotle chile powder,** 1 tsp. **smoked paprika,** 1 tsp. **kosher salt,** and ½ tsp. **garlic powder.** Drizzle over snack mixture, and toss to coat. Spread mixture in a single layer on a rimmed baking sheet lined with parchment paper. Bake in preheated oven until lightly toasted, about 10 to 12 minutes, stirring once or twice during baking. Cool completely on baking sheet. Store in an airtight container up to 5 days.

Warm Spinach-Sweet Onion Dip with Country Ham

Great for outdoor tailgates, this creamy dip can be prepared in advance and reheated in a skillet on the grill.

ACTIVE 25 MIN. - TOTAL 50 MIN.
SERVES 10

3 Tbsp. olive oil, divided
3 cups thinly sliced sweet onion (from 2 medium onions)
1 garlic clove, minced (about 1 tsp.)
1 cup diced country ham (about 6 oz.)
2 (8-oz.) pkg. cream cheese, softened
8 oz. mozzarella cheese, shredded (about 2 cups)
4 oz. Parmesan cheese, shredded (about 1 cup)
1 (1-lb.) pkg. frozen chopped spinach, thawed and well drained
Pita chips or toasted French bread slices

1. Heat 2 tablespoons of the oil in a 10-inch cast-iron skillet over medium. Add onions, and cook, stirring often, until golden brown, about 20 minutes. Stir in garlic, and cook, stirring often, 1 minute. Transfer onion mixture to a medium bowl, and wipe skillet clean.
2. Heat remaining 1 tablespoon oil in skillet over medium-high. Add ham, and cook, stirring often, until crisp, about 5 minutes. Remove ham from skillet, and drain on paper towels.
3. Add cream cheese, mozzarella, Parmesan, spinach, and ham to onion mixture in bowl, and stir until blended. Spoon mixture into cast-iron skillet. Cover and chill until ready to transport to tailgate. (Recipe can be made up to 1 day ahead. Be sure skillet cools completely before returning dip to skillet.) Transport to tailgate in a cooler.
4. Light 1 side of grill, heating to medium (350°F to 400°F), and leave other side unlit. Uncover skillet; place over unlit side of grill, and heat, covered with grill lid, stirring every 5 minutes, until cheese is melted and smooth, about 20 minutes. Serve with pita chips or toasted French bread slices.

Brisket-and-Black Bean Chili with Cilantro-Lime Crema

This hearty chili is made in a slow cooker so it's easy to prepare and transport. Instead of bowls, set out mugs and let guests help themselves to the chili and crema.

ACTIVE 30 MIN. - TOTAL 9 HOURS
SERVES 8

3 Tbsp. all-purpose flour
2 Tbsp. chili powder
1 Tbsp. ground cumin
1 Tbsp. kosher salt
1 tsp. dried oregano
2 lb. beef brisket, trimmed and cut into 1-inch cubes
4 Tbsp. olive oil, divided
2 (16-oz.) cans black beans, drained
1 (14.5-oz.) can fire-roasted diced tomatoes, drained
1 orange bell pepper, chopped
1 medium-size red onion, chopped (about 1 cup)
3 garlic cloves, minced (about 3 tsp.)
¾ cup beef broth
1 Tbsp. fresh lime juice (from 1 lime)
Cilantro-Lime Crema (recipe follows)

1. Stir together first 5 ingredients in a small bowl. Toss spice mixture with brisket cubes until well coated.
2. Heat 2 tablespoons of the oil in a large skillet over medium-high. Add half of brisket cubes, and cook, stirring often, until browned on all sides, 5 to 7 minutes. Transfer to a 6-quart slow cooker. Repeat procedure with remaining oil and brisket.
3. Stir beans, tomatoes, bell pepper, onion, garlic, and beef broth into slow cooker. Cover and cook on LOW until beef is tender, about 8 hours. Uncover and cook until slightly thickened, about 30 minutes. Stir in lime juice, and serve immediately with Cilantro-Lime Crema.

Cilantro-Lime Crema

MAKES ABOUT ¾ CUP - ACTIVE 5 MIN. - TOTAL 20 MIN.

Stir together ½ cup **sour cream;** ¼ cup chopped **fresh cilantro;** 2 Tbsp. **mayonnaise;** 1 tsp. **lime zest,** plus 1 Tbsp. **fresh juice** (from 1 lime); and ¼ tsp. **kosher salt** in a medium bowl. Cover and chill at least 15 minutes or until ready to serve. Store in an airtight container in refrigerator up to 2 days.

Bake Another Batch

What's better than a dozen treats? Two dozen, of course! Here, five seasonal surprises made for sharing

MIX IT UP
Swap out the pecans in both of these recipes for walnuts.

Toasted Oatmeal Cookies and Brown Butter-Maple-Pecan Blondies (recipes, page 209)

Sprinkle extra chopped pears and chocolate chunks on top of each muffin.

Chocolate-Pear Muffins

ACTIVE 20 MIN.
TOTAL 1 HOUR, 35 MIN.
MAKES 24

Preheat oven to 350°F. Peel and chop 2 medium **Anjou pears** (about 2 cups); set aside. Beat 1 cup softened, **unsalted butter;** 1 cup **granulated sugar;** and ½ cup packed **light brown sugar** with an electric mixer on medium speed until light and fluffy, about 4 minutes. Add 2 large **eggs,** 1 at a time, beating on low just until combined after each addition. Add 1 tsp. **vanilla extract;** beat just until smooth. Whisk together 2 ¾ cups **all-purpose flour,** ½ cup **unsweetened cocoa,** 1 ½ Tbsp. **baking powder,** ½ tsp. **baking soda,** and ½ tsp. **kosher salt** in a large bowl. Add to butter mixture in thirds alternately with ¾ cup **whole buttermilk,** beginning and ending with flour mixture, beating on low just until combined after each addition. Fold in 1 ¾ cups chopped pears and 1 cup **semisweet chocolate chunks.** Divide batter among 2 (12-cup) muffin pans lined with paper baking cups. Sprinkle tops with ¼ cup **semisweet chocolate chunks** and remaining ¼ cup chopped pears. Bake in preheated oven until a wooden pick inserted in center of muffins comes out with moist crumbs, 25 to 30 minutes. Cool in pans on wire racks 15 minutes. Remove muffins to wire racks to cool completely, about 30 minutes.

Refrigerated piecrusts make these tarts come together quickly.

Cranberry-Apple Tartlets

ACTIVE 40 MIN. - TOTAL 1 HOUR, 30 MIN. - MAKES 12

Preheat oven to 425°F. Place 1 peeled and finely chopped medium **Honeycrisp apple** (1 cup); 1 cup **fresh or frozen cranberries;** ½ cup packed **light brown sugar;** and ⅛ tsp. **kosher salt** in a medium saucepan. Cook over medium-high, stirring often, until apple is tender and cranberries burst, about 8 minutes. Whisk together 1 Tbsp. **cornstarch** and 1 Tbsp. **water** in a small bowl, and stir into apple mixture. Bring to a boil over medium-high, stirring often; cook until mixture thickens, about 1 minute. Transfer to a medium bowl; stir in 2 Tbsp. **unsalted butter,** 1 tsp. **vanilla extract,** and a pinch of **ground nutmeg.** Let cool at room temperature until butter is melted and mixture has thickened, about 20 minutes. Stir cooled mixture, and set aside. Unroll 1 piecrust from a (14.1-oz.) pkg. **refrigerated piecrusts;** cut into 4 (4-inch) squares. Reroll remaining dough; cut into 2 additional (4-inch) squares. Repeat procedure with remaining 1 piecrust. Arrange squares evenly on 2 baking sheets lined with parchment paper. Place 1 heaping Tbsp. cooled apple mixture in center of each square. Fold corners of square in toward center, pressing (or twisting) gently to seal together. Brush tartlets with 1 lightly beaten large **egg white,** and sprinkle with 1 Tbsp. **demerara sugar.** Bake in preheated oven until golden and bubbly, 14 to 16 minutes. Cool on baking sheets on wire racks 15 minutes. Serve warm or at room temperature.

Pumpkin Spice-Chocolate Marble Loaves

This delicious recipe can be divided into eight 5 ¾- x 3 ¼-inch mini loaf pans. Bake the loaves as directed, but start testing for doneness after 25 minutes in the oven.

ACTIVE 25 MIN. - TOTAL 2 HOURS, 25 MIN.
MAKES 2

BASIC BATTER
- **1 cup unsalted butter, softened**
- **2 1/2 cups granulated sugar**
- **1/2 cup packed light brown sugar**
- **4 large eggs**
- **2 large egg yolks**
- **2 tsp. vanilla extract**
- **2 1/2 cups all-purpose flour**
- **2 tsp. baking powder**
- **1 tsp. kosher salt**
- **1/2 cup sour cream**

PUMPKIN SPICE BATTER
- **1/2 cup all-purpose flour**
- **1/2 cup canned pumpkin**
- **1 tsp. pumpkin pie spice**

CHOCOLATE BATTER
- **1/2 cup unsweetened cocoa, sifted**
- **1/4 cup sour cream**
- **1 tsp. instant coffee granules**

1. Preheat oven to 350°F. Prepare the Basic Batter: Beat butter and sugars with an electric mixer on medium speed until light and fluffy, about 4 minutes. Add eggs and egg yolks 1 at a time, beating on medium-low after each addition. Add vanilla; beat just until incorporated. Whisk together flour, baking powder, and salt in a medium bowl. Add to butter mixture alternately with sour cream, beginning and ending with flour mixture, beating on low speed just until combined after each addition. Divide Basic Batter evenly between 2 large bowls.
2. Prepare the Pumpkin Spice Batter: Add flour, canned pumpkin, and pumpkin pie spice to 1 of the Basic Batter bowls; stir together until completely combined. Set aside.
3. Prepare the Chocolate Batter: Add cocoa, sour cream, and instant coffee granules to remaining Basic Batter bowl, and stir until smooth.
4. Drop large spoonfuls of the Pumpkin Spice Batter across bottom of 2 greased and floured 8- x 4-inch loaf pans. Drop large spoonfuls of the Chocolate Batter, interspersing that with the Pumpkin Spice Batter to cover the bottom of each pan. Repeat with remaining Pumpkin Spice Batter and Chocolate Batter, creating layers until all batter has been used. Swirl batters with a long pick, moving in a back-and-forth motion from one end of pan to the other.
5. Bake in preheated oven until a wooden pick inserted in center of each loaf comes out clean, 55 to 60 minutes. Cool in pans on a wire rack 15 minutes. Turn out onto rack to cool completely, about 45 minutes.

Toasted Oatmeal Cookies

ACTIVE 20 MIN. - TOTAL 1 HOUR, 45 MIN.
MAKES 36

- **3/4 cup uncooked old-fashioned rolled oats**
- **1/2 cup unsalted butter, softened**
- **1/2 cup packed light brown sugar**
- **1/4 cup granulated sugar**
- **1 large egg**
- **1 tsp. vanilla extract**
- **3/4 cup plus 2 Tbsp. all-purpose flour**
- **1/2 tsp. baking powder**
- **1/4 tsp. baking soda**
- **1/4 tsp. kosher salt**
- **1/8 tsp. ground cinnamon**
- **1/2 cup butterscotch chips**
- **1/2 cup chopped toasted pecans**

1. Preheat oven to 375°F. Spread oats in an even layer on a rimmed baking sheet. Bake in preheated oven until golden brown, about 10 minutes. Transfer baking sheet to a wire rack, and cool completely, about 20 minutes.
2. Beat butter, brown sugar, and granulated sugar with an electric mixer on medium speed until light and fluffy, about 1 minute. Beat in egg. Add vanilla, and beat on low just until incorporated. Whisk together cooled oats, all-purpose flour, baking powder, baking soda, salt, and cinnamon in a bowl. Add to butter mixture in 2 batches, beating on low just until incorporated after each addition. Fold in butterscotch chips and pecans.
3. Drop dough by tablespoonfuls, leaving 1 inch between the cookies, onto 2 baking sheets lined with parchment paper. Chill in refrigerator 10 minutes.
4. Bake in preheated oven, switching baking sheets on top and bottom racks halfway through, until cookies are golden brown, 12 to 14 minutes. Cool on baking sheets on wire racks 10 minutes, and transfer to racks to cool completely, about 20 minutes.

Brown Butter-Maple-Pecan Blondies

ACTIVE 40 MIN. - TOTAL 2 HOURS, 15 MIN.
MAKES 24

- **1 1/2 cups unsalted butter**
- **4 large eggs**
- **1 3/4 cups granulated sugar**
- **3 cups all-purpose flour**
- **1 tsp. baking powder**
- **1 tsp. kosher salt**
- **1/2 cup pure maple syrup**
- **1 tsp. vanilla extract**
- **1 1/4 cups chopped toasted pecans, divided**

1. Preheat oven to 350°F. Melt butter in a medium saucepan over medium. Cook, whisking constantly, until butter browns and smells nutty, 5 to 7 minutes. Immediately pour into a bowl. Place in freezer to cool, whisking every 5 minutes until thickened and creamy, about 20 minutes. (Butter should look like melted peanut butter.)
2. Beat eggs and sugar with an electric mixer on medium speed until thickened and pale yellow, about 3 minutes. Whisk together flour, baking powder, and salt in a bowl. Add to egg mixture in thirds, alternately with cooled butter, beginning and ending with flour mixture, beating on low after each addition. Slowly beat in maple syrup; add vanilla, and beat just until combined. Fold in 1 cup of the pecans with a spoon.
3. Pour batter into a greased and floured 13- x 9-inch baking pan, and spread into an even layer. Sprinkle with remaining 1/4 cup pecans.
4. Bake in preheated oven until golden and a wooden pick inserted in middle comes out clean, about 35 minutes. Transfer pan to a wire rack to cool completely, about 1 hour. Cut into 24 bars.

TRY THIS TWIST!
Brown Butter-Sorghum Blondies: Substitute sorghum syrup for the maple syrup and toasted walnuts for the pecans.

Snack Attack

Need an after-school bite? These three healthy treats come together in under an hour

No-Bake Granola Bars

ACTIVE 15 MIN.
TOTAL 45 MIN.
MAKES 12

Line an 8-inch square baking pan with parchment paper. Toss together 1 cup **crisp rice cereal (such as Rice Krispies)** and ¾ cup uncooked **old-fashioned regular rolled oats** in a large bowl. Place 1 cup **creamy almond butter,** ¼ cup **pure maple syrup,** ½ tsp. **ground cinnamon,** and ¼ tsp. **kosher salt** in a small saucepan; heat over medium. Cook, stirring constantly, until smooth, about 30 seconds. Pour mixture over cereal and oats; gently mix together with a spatula until combined. Spread mixture evenly into prepared pan, pressing firmly to form a compact, even layer. Chill until fully set, about 30 minutes. Cut into 12 bars.

CHERRY-PISTACHIO
Stir ½ cup chopped **roasted salted pistachios** and ½ cup chopped **dried tart cherries** into cereal-oat mixture.

APRICOT-COCONUT-CASHEW
Stir ⅓ cup chopped **roasted salted cashews,** ⅓ cup chopped **dried apricots,** and ⅓ cup **unsweetened flaked coconut** into cereal-oat mixture.

CHOCOLATE CHIP-PECAN-SEA SALT
Stir ⅓ cup chopped **roasted pecans** and ⅓ cup **miniature milk chocolate chips** into cereal-oat mixture. Before chilling, sprinkle top of granola bar mixture evenly with ¼ tsp. **flaky sea salt.**

Roasted Sweet Potato Hummus

ACTIVE 10 MIN.
TOTAL 45 MIN.
SERVES 8

Preheat oven to 400°F. Toss together 1 (12-oz.) **sweet potato,** peeled and cut into 1-inch pieces (2 ½ cups), and 1 tsp. **extra-virgin olive oil** on a large rimmed baking sheet. Bake in preheated oven until browned and very tender, about 30 minutes, stirring after 20 minutes. Remove from oven, and cool at room temperature, 5 minutes. Place cooled sweet potato; 1 (15-oz.) can **chickpeas,** drained and rinsed (1 ½ cups); 3 Tbsp. **tahini (sesame paste);** 1 Tbsp. **fresh lemon juice** (from 1 lemon); ¾ tsp. **kosher salt;** and ⅛ tsp. **black pepper** in a food processor. With processor running, pour 6 Tbsp. **water** and 2 Tbsp. **extra-virgin olive oil** through food chute. Process until smooth, about 1 minute, stopping halfway to scrape down sides as needed. Transfer to a serving bowl, and drizzle with 1 Tbsp. **extra-virgin olive oil.** Serve with **crudités** or **pita chips.**

Olive Oil Popcorn with Garlic and Rosemary

ACTIVE 15 MIN.
TOTAL 15 MIN.
SERVES 13

Place ¼ cup **extra-virgin olive oil** and 1 Tbsp. minced **garlic** (about 3 garlic cloves) in a small saucepan; heat over medium-low, undisturbed, until sizzling, about 2 minutes. Reduce heat to low. Add 1 ½ tsp. finely chopped **fresh rosemary;** stir once, and cook, undisturbed, until garlic softens and rosemary is fragrant, about 2 minutes. Remove from heat, and set aside. Place 2 Tbsp. **canola oil** in a large saucepan fitted with a lid; heat over high. Add 2 **popcorn kernels,** and cover and shake saucepan until kernels pop, 2 to 3 minutes. Add ⅓ cup **popcorn kernels,** and cover and shake constantly until kernels stop popping, about 2 minutes. Immediately pour popped popcorn into a large bowl. Drizzle with garlic-rosemary oil, stirring to coat. Add ½ cup grated **Parmesan cheese** and ¼ tsp. finely ground **sea salt;** toss to coat. Serve immediately.

Easier Enchiladas

No filling. No rolling. Serve this crowd-pleaser straight out of the skillet, and let everyone pick their own toppings for a fun family dinner

Skillet Enchiladas Suizas

Set out an assortment of flavorful fixings such as thinly sliced radishes, crumbled Cotija cheese, pickled red onions, and pickled jalapeño slices.

ACTIVE 15 MIN. - TOTAL 25 MIN.
SERVES 6

- 2 Tbsp. olive oil
- 1 medium-size yellow onion, chopped (2 cups)
- 3 garlic cloves, minced (1 1/2 Tbsp.)
- 1 1/2 tsp. ground cumin
- 1 (14.5-oz.) can diced tomatoes, drained
- 1 1/4 cups tomatillo salsa
- 4 cups shredded rotisserie chicken
- 1 cup crema or sour cream
- 6 (6-inch) corn tortillas, torn
- 8 oz. Monterey Jack cheese, shredded (about 2 cups), divided
- 1 small (6 oz.) avocado, diced
- Torn fresh cilantro leaves

1. Preheat broiler to HIGH. Place oil in a medium-size cast-iron skillet, and heat over medium, swirling to coat. Add onion, and cook, stirring occasionally, until lightly browned, about 6 minutes. Add garlic and cumin. Cook, stirring often, until fragrant, 1 to 2 minutes. Reduce heat to medium-low. Stir in drained tomatoes and salsa. Simmer over medium-low, stirring often, until slightly thickened, about 2 minutes.

2. Remove skillet from heat. Stir in chicken, crema, tortillas, and 1/2 cup of the Monterey Jack cheese. Top evenly with remaining 1 1/2 cups cheese.

3. Transfer skillet to preheated oven, and broil until cheese is lightly browned, 8 to 10 minutes. Top with avocado, and sprinkle with cilantro leaves.

TRY THIS TWIST!
BBQ Chicken Enchiladas Suizas: Use shredded barbecue chicken from your favorite pitmaster and a combination of 1/2 cup white barbecue sauce and 1/2 cup crema or sour cream in STEP 2.

October

214 **The Savory Side of Pumpkin** These delicious sides and salads are the pick of the pumpkin patch

219 **Fall Layers** Lush layer cakes with stories that warm the heart

228 QUICK FIX **More Cheese, Please** Enjoy rich flavor and gooey goodness that's fresh off the block

232 WHAT CAN I BRING? **Muffin Pan Pies** Often the most delicious things come in tiny packages

233 COMFORT FOOD **Low-and-Slow Pork Supper** Sweet-tart cider adds autumnal brightness to this long-simmered stew

234 *SL* COOKING SCHOOL Tips for saying cheese, perfecting cake layers, and apple picking

THE SAVORY SIDE OF PUMPKIN

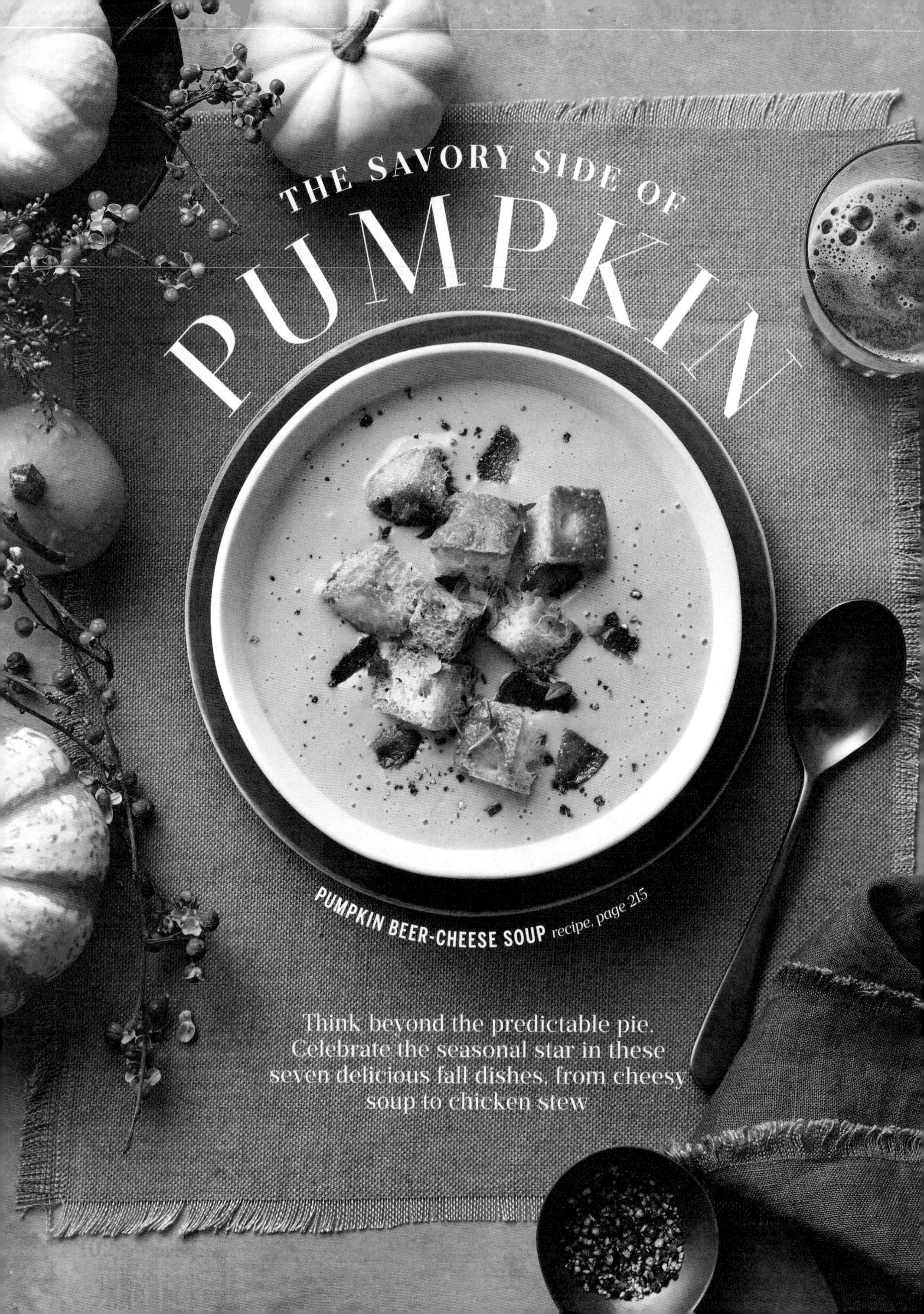

PUMPKIN BEER-CHEESE SOUP *recipe, page 215*

Think beyond the predictable pie. Celebrate the seasonal star in these seven delicious fall dishes, from cheesy soup to chicken stew

GREAT PUMPKIN RECIPES

Cut, cubed, canned—seven tasty new ideas

Pumpkin Beer-Cheese Soup

ACTIVE 25 MIN. - TOTAL 45 MIN.
SERVES 4

- 5 oz. thick-cut bacon, coarsely chopped (about 5 slices)
- 3 oz. focaccia bread, cut into ¾-inch cubes (about 2 cups)
- 1 Tbsp. unsalted butter
- 1 cup chopped carrots
- ½ cup chopped yellow onion
- 3 Tbsp. all-purpose flour
- 2 cups whole milk
- 1 cup canned pumpkin
- 1 (12-oz.) bottle pumpkin ale beer
- 1 ½ tsp. kosher salt
- 4 oz. extra-sharp Cheddar cheese, grated (about 1 cup)
- 4 oz. processed cheese (such as Velveeta), chopped
- 1 cup half-and-half
- 1 Tbsp. fresh thyme leaves
- ¼ tsp. black pepper

1. Preheat oven to 375°F. Place bacon in a large saucepan over medium-high, and cook until crisp, 8 to 10 minutes. Using a slotted spoon, transfer bacon to a plate lined with paper towels, reserving drippings in pan.
2. Place bread on a rimmed baking sheet; pour bacon drippings over bread, and toss to coat. Spread in an even layer, and bake in preheated oven until golden brown, 15 to 20 minutes.
3. Return saucepan to medium-high heat; add butter, and swirl to coat. Add carrots and onion to pan. Cook, stirring often, until carrots begin to soften, about 5 minutes. Add flour to pan, and cook, stirring constantly, 1 minute. Add milk, pumpkin, beer, and salt to pan. Bring to a boil, and cook, stirring constantly, 1 minute. Reduce heat to medium, and cook 10 minutes. Transfer soup to a blender. Remove center cap from blender lid (to allow steam to escape); secure lid on blender, and place a clean towel over opening in lid. Process until smooth. With blender on low speed, add cheeses, ½ cup at a time, processing until smooth. Stir in half-and-half. Divide soup evenly among 4 bowls. Top evenly with croutons, bacon, thyme, and pepper.

Roasted Pumpkin-and-Baby Kale Salad

ACTIVE 15 MIN. - TOTAL 40 MIN.
SERVES 4

- 1 (3-lb.) sugar pumpkin, cut into 12 (1-inch) wedges
- 1 small red onion, cut into 8 wedges
- 4 thyme sprigs
- 2 rosemary sprigs
- 6 Tbsp. extra-virgin olive oil, divided
- 2 Tbsp. honey, divided
- 1 ¾ tsp. kosher salt, divided
- 1 tsp. black pepper, divided
- 1 Tbsp. whole-grain Dijon mustard
- 1 Tbsp. apple cider vinegar
- 4 oz. baby kale greens (about 4 cups)
- ⅓ cup pomegranate arils
- ⅓ cup coarsely chopped, toasted pecans
- 3 oz. goat cheese, crumbled (about ¾ cup)

1. Preheat oven to 450°F. Combine pumpkin, red onion, thyme, rosemary, 2 tablespoons of the olive oil, and 1 tablespoon of the honey in a large bowl; toss to coat. Divide vegetables evenly between 2 rimmed baking sheets coated with cooking spray, and sprinkle with 1 teaspoon of the salt and ¾ teaspoon of the pepper. Bake in preheated oven until browned and tender, about 20 minutes (do not stir). Cool 10 minutes.
2. Whisk together Dijon, vinegar, remaining 4 tablespoons oil, 1 tablespoon honey, ¾ teaspoon salt, and ¼ teaspoon pepper in a small bowl. Toss kale with 1 tablespoon of the dressing, and arrange on a serving platter with pumpkin mixture. Sprinkle with pomegranate arils, pecans, and goat cheese; drizzle with remaining dressing.

TRY THIS TWIST!
Change things up by using butternut squash for the pumpkin and spicy arugula leaves for the kale.

Pumpkin-Buttermilk Biscuits with Crispy Ham and Honey Butter

ACTIVE 25 MIN. - TOTAL 50 MIN.
SERVES 8

- 1 Tbsp. canola oil
- 6 oz. sliced country ham, finely chopped
- 2 cups all-purpose flour
- 2 ½ tsp. baking powder
- ¼ tsp. baking soda
- ¼ tsp. salt
- 6 Tbsp. cold unsalted butter, cut into small pieces
- ¾ cup canned pumpkin
- ½ cup whole buttermilk
- 6 Tbsp. unsalted butter, softened and divided
- 3 Tbsp. honey

1. Preheat oven to 400°F. Heat oil in an 8-inch cast-iron skillet over medium-high. Add ham, and cook, stirring often, until crispy and well browned, about 8 minutes. Remove ham from pan, and let cool. Set aside. Wipe skillet clean with a paper towel, and place in oven to heat.
2. Combine flour, baking powder, baking soda, and salt in a medium bowl. Add cold butter pieces to flour. Using a pastry blender or 2 forks, cut butter into flour mixture until coarse crumbs form. Place bowl in freezer 10 minutes to chill.
3. Whisk together pumpkin and buttermilk in a small bowl. Stir in crispy ham. Add buttermilk mixture to flour mixture, stirring until just moistened. Place dough on a floured work surface, and gently pat to 1-inch thickness. Using a 2 ½-inch round cutter, cut dough into 8 biscuits. Remove skillet from oven, and melt 1 tablespoon of the softened butter in hot skillet, swirling to coat. Arrange biscuits in skillet, with sides touching. Melt another 1 tablespoon of the softened butter, and brush over tops of biscuits. Bake in preheated oven until biscuits are puffed and browned, about 15 minutes.
4. Combine honey and remaining 4 tablespoons softened butter in a small bowl. Serve honey butter with biscuits.

Pumpkin-Coconut Curry

ACTIVE 20 MIN. - TOTAL 35 MIN.
SERVES 6

- **2 Tbsp. canola oil**
- **½ cup chopped yellow onion**
- **2 Tbsp. garlic cloves, crushed (about 6 cloves)**
- **¼ cup red curry paste**
- **4 cups (about 19 oz.) sugar pumpkin or butternut squash, cut into 1-inch cubes**
- **2 cups red bell pepper slices**
- **1½ cups chicken broth**
- **1 (13.5-oz.) can coconut milk, well shaken**
- **1 tsp. kosher salt**
- **6 cups hot cooked jasmine rice**
- **½ cup plain whole-milk yogurt**
- **¼ cup fresh cilantro leaves**
- **6 lime wedges**

1. Heat oil in a medium saucepan over medium-high. Add onion and garlic to pan; cook, stirring occasionally, until starting to soften, about 4 minutes. Add curry paste; cook, stirring often, until fragrant, about 1 minute. Add pumpkin, bell pepper, chicken broth, coconut milk, and salt; bring to a boil. Cover, reduce heat to medium, and simmer until pumpkin is tender, 10 to 15 minutes. Using a slotted spoon, remove 4 cups of pumpkin-bell peppermixture from pan, and set aside.
2. Place remaining mixture in a blender. Remove center cap from blender lid (to allow steam to escape); secure lid on blender, and place a clean towel over opening in lid. Process until smooth.
3. Return pureed mixture to saucepan, and heat over medium. Stir in reserved pumpkin-bell pepper mixture. Place 1 cup rice in each of 6 shallow bowls; ladle pumpkin mixture over rice. Garnish with yogurt, cilantro, and lime wedges.

Slow-Cooker Chicken Stew with Pumpkin and Wild Rice

ACTIVE 30 MIN. - TOTAL 3 HOURS, 30 MIN.
SERVES 6

- **1 Tbsp. canola oil**
- **6 boneless, skinless chicken thighs (about 1¾ lb.)**
- **1 cup chopped celery**
- **1 cup chopped yellow onion**
- **2 Tbsp. chopped garlic (about 5 garlic cloves)**
- **⅓ cup all-purpose flour**
- **4 cups chicken broth**
- **4 cups (about 19 oz.) sugar pumpkin or butternut squash, cut into 1-inch cubes**
- **½ cup uncooked wild rice**
- **2 tsp. kosher salt**
- **1 cup half-and-half**
- **¼ cup coarsely chopped fresh flat-leaf parsley**
- **2 Tbsp. chopped fresh tarragon**
- **1 Tbsp. fresh thyme leaves**

1. Heat oil in a large skillet over medium-high. Add chicken, and cook until well browned, about 5 minutes. Turn chicken over, and cook 2 minutes.
2. Transfer chicken to a 5- to 6-quart slow cooker. Add celery, onion, and garlic to skillet. Cook, stirring often, until starting to soften, about 4 minutes. Add flour to skillet, and cook, stirring constantly, 1 minute. Add broth; bring to a boil, and cook, stirring constantly, until thickened, about 1 minute.
3. Transfer mixture to slow cooker. Add pumpkin, rice, and salt. Cover and cook on LOW until rice, chicken, and vegetables are tender, about 3 hours.
4. Stir in half-and-half, parsley, tarragon, and thyme leaves.

Pumpkin-and-Winter Squash Gratin

ACTIVE 25 MIN. - TOTAL 1 HOUR, 25 MIN.
SERVES 8

- **1 Tbsp. canola oil**
- **2 Tbsp. all-purpose flour**
- **¼ tsp. ground nutmeg**
- **⅛ tsp. ground cloves**
- **1½ cups whole milk**
- **5 oz. Gruyère cheese, shredded (about 1¼ cups), divided**
- **2 tsp. kosher salt, divided**
- **2 oz. French bread, torn into small pieces**
- **¼ cup fresh flat-leaf parsley leaves**
- **1 Tbsp. fresh thyme leaves**
- **2 Tbsp. salted butter, melted**
- **4 cups (about 20 oz.) russet potato, cut into 1-inch cubes**
- **3 cups (about 14 oz.) butternut squash, cut into 1-inch cubes**
- **3 cups (about 14 oz.) sugar pumpkin, cut into 1-inch cubes**

1. Heat oil in a medium saucepan over medium. Add flour, nutmeg, and cloves to pan. Cook, stirring constantly, 1 minute. Add milk; bring to a boil, and cook, stirring often, until thickened, about 1 minute. Remove from heat, and let stand 5 minutes. Add ¾ cup of the cheese, ¼ cup at a time, stirring with a whisk until melted after each addition. Whisk in 1½ teaspoons of the salt.
2. Preheat oven to 425°F with an oven rack about 8 inches from heat.
3. Combine bread, parsley, and thyme in a food processor; pulse until coarsely chopped. Transfer to a large bowl, and toss with melted butter. Set aside.
4. Place potato, squash, and pumpkin in a lightly greased 13- x 9-inch baking dish. Pour milk mixture over squash mixture, and sprinkle with remaining ½ teaspoon salt, pressing mixture into an even layer. Cover and bake in middle of preheated oven until squash is tender, about 1 hour. Remove baking dish.
5. Preheat broiler to HIGH. Uncover dish, and sprinkle top of gratin with bread-herb mixture and remaining ½ cup cheese. Broil on rack 8 inches from heat until top is browned, 2 to 3 minutes.

PUMPKIN POINTERS

Save Those Seeds

Three steps for cleaning, roasting, and eating

1 Pick seeds from around the pumpkin flesh; place in a bowl of water. Use your hands to swish the seeds around in the water, removing as much of the stringy bits of pumpkin as possible. Drain; pat dry with paper towels.

2 Toss seeds with melted butter or olive oil to coat; sprinkle with black pepper and salt. Amp up the flavor with your favorite spices, such as chili powder, pumpkin pie spice, or a barbecue seasoning.

3 Spread the seeds out on a parchment paper-lined baking sheet. Bake at 350°F for 10 to 15 minutes, or until crisp. Let cool on the baking sheet. Enjoy as a snack, stir into soups, or toss into salads.

clockwise from top left:

Roasted Pumpkin-and-Baby Kale Salad, page 215; Pumpkin-and-Winter Squash Gratin, page 216; Pumpkin-Buttermilk Biscuits with Crispy Ham and Honey Butter, page 215; Pumpkin Coconut Curry, page 216

PUMPKIN POINTERS

Pick the Best Pumpkin

Five tips for selecting and storing your gourd

1

CHOOSE THE RIGHT KIND

For cooking, you'll want to use sugar pumpkins (also called pie or sweet pumpkins), which are small and round. Long Island Cheese pumpkins, which are more oblong and can look like a wheel of cheese, are also good to eat. Field types are larger; have watery, stringy flesh; and are best used for decorating.

2

SEARCH FOR A HEALTHY STEM

Find a pumpkin with a well-attached, brown, dry stem (a sign it's mature enough to be harvested), but don't use it as a carrying handle. The stem can break off, tearing the shell and leaving it susceptible to rot.

3

EXAMINE THOROUGHLY

Look for deep nicks, bruises, and soft spots—all signs that rot has set in. Don't overlook the bottom of the pumpkin, which can sit for long periods of time in wet soil.

4

DON'T JUDGE BY COLOR

A pumpkin's hue will dull as it ages, but as long as the skin is unblemished and free of bruises, the flesh inside will still be sweet and edible.

5

STORE PROPERLY

Whole pumpkins should be kept in a cool, dry place. Once cut, they should be wrapped tightly, refrigerated, and used within five days. Puree or cube any that's left over, and freeze it for later use.

Pumpkin Ravioli with Sage Brown Butter

ACTIVE 35 MIN. - TOTAL 35 MIN.
SERVES 4

- **2 sage sprigs, divided**
- **½ cup butter**
- **3 Tbsp. extra-virgin olive oil, divided**
- **1¼ cups canned pumpkin**
- **3 oz. Parmigiano-Reggiano cheese, grated (about ¾ cup)**
- **2 Tbsp. fresh lemon juice (from 1 lemon)**
- **½ tsp. kosher salt**
- **1 (10-oz.) pkg. wonton wrappers (48 wrappers)**
- **1 large egg, lightly beaten**

1. Finely chop leaves from 1 sage sprig to equal about 1 tablespoon. Combine chopped sage and butter in a medium skillet over medium. Cook, swirling occasionally, until butter is lightly browned and fragrant, 4 to 5 minutes. Remove half of butter-sage mixture from skillet; combine with 2 tablespoons of the oil in a small bowl, and set aside. Remove skillet from heat, and add pumpkin, Parmigiano-Reggiano, lemon juice, and salt to skillet, stirring to combine.

2. Place 8 wonton wrappers on a cutting board. Brush outside edges with some of the beaten egg. Place 1 rounded tablespoon of pumpkin filling in center of each wrapper, leaving a ½-inch border around the edge. Place a second wrapper on top, pressing the edges together to seal. Press gently on filling to spread evenly. Move ravioli to a tray, and cover with plastic wrap. Repeat procedure with remaining wrappers, beaten egg, and pumpkin mixture.

3. Remove leaves from remaining sage sprig. Heat remaining 1 tablespoon oil in a small skillet over medium-high. Add sage leaves to skillet; cook until crispy, 2 to 3 seconds. Remove from skillet, and set aside.

4. Bring a large pot of salted water to a boil over high. Add half of the ravioli to pot, adding 1 at a time. Cook until ravioli are tender, 1 to 2 minutes. Remove from water with a slotted spoon, and drain excess water. Transfer cooked ravioli to a plate. Repeat procedure with remaining ravioli. Divide cooked ravioli evenly among 4 plates, and drizzle with reserved sage brown butter-and-oil mixture. Garnish servings with crispy sage leaves.

FALL LAYERS

As with most great Southern recipes, these three cakes come with memorable stories and sweet reminders of home

Apple Stack Cake

By Ronni Lundy

MY GREAT-AUNT RAE was an operator for Southern Bell Telephone and Telegraph Company in Corbin, Kentucky. When I was a little girl and stayed there in the summer or over Christmas, it was my great delight to make a call on the "magic phone." Not only did the heavy black object have no dial, as ours did in Louisville, but when you picked it up, instead of a strident dial tone, a kindly voice would ask, "Number, please?" to which you were to respond with the three digits that defined whatever household you were trying to reach.

More often than not, it was my great-aunt's pleasant voice that would greet me, and when she'd hear mine, she'd respond, "Well—hello, little girl. What are you doing today?" I'd tell her the newest adventure I'd gotten into, and before connecting me to one of my other kin in town, she'd sometimes whisper the location of a piece of gum she'd hidden in the house for me or give me a message for one of the grown-ups—making me feel grown-up too. She was, in a way, the communication hub of our family.

To my knowledge, Rae and her sister Johnnie always lived together, even during the too few years that Rae was married to her life's love, my great-uncle Charlie, before his death. Their house on Carter Street was where my mother and Uncle Jack lived in their teens after their parents were killed in a car wreck, and it was where my father was welcomed as friend and kin when he married my mother.

As sisters do, they seemed to work out a division of labor between themselves. Johnnie was the gardener who planted, hoed, and harvested. She wrung the chickens' necks and plucked their feathers before frying them. Rae was there for multihanded tasks such as canning, but because of her day job, she was not as regular in the kitchen. This is why, I think, it was Johnnie's task to pick the gnarly green June apples that grew on their tree, pare them, and lay them out to dry on clean sheets, while Rae was the maker of the family's favorite special-occasion dessert, apple stack cake.

A labor-intensive art that required baking each hand-rolled and patted-out layer one at a time in the same cast-iron skillet before skillfully stacking them high with steaming dried-apple puree between, it was a job for Rae's days off in cold winter. On one such day, my cousin Sparky dropped by for a cup of coffee just in time for Rae to unwrap and cut into the cake she had made three days before—a stack cake must "ripen."

As the two took their first bites of what was an especially good cake, Rae did what most Appalachians do when something pleases: She remembered. "Mmm, mmm, I wish Pap Lundy was here," she said. "There's nobody on this earth who likes a good stack cake better than he does." For a moment, she and Sparky considered my daddy, who was living over three hours away in Louisville, where there was work he couldn't find in his beloved home in Eastern Kentucky. Sparky reached for his hat and said, "Rae, wrap up some of that cake and I'll drive it up to Pap right now. Don't have a thing more important to do."

And that is how, late that afternoon, Daddy and Sparky were marveling over Rae's stack cake and telling stories from home until the laughing made tears run down their cheeks. Then Sparky put his hat on and drove all the way back, while Daddy wrapped up the rest of that cake to share with Mama and me later.

A VERY TALL TALE

According to Appalachian folklore, whenever there was a wedding in the community, women would bake single layers of this regional dessert and then bring them to the reception. There, they would stack the collected layers with a filling made from dried apples to make one tall cake big enough to feed a wedding party. The higher the cake, the more popular the bride. We hate to dispel beloved legends, but this one probably isn't true. All of the layers from the neighboring cooks, baked in pans and skillets of varying sizes, would have different diameters and thicknesses, so stacking a tall cake with even sides would be nearly impossible. What's more, an apple stack cake should be assembled while the layers and filling are still warm and then left to "ripen" for two to three days, so it's not something you could do at a wedding reception.

RONNI LUNDY
AUTHOR OF
VICTUALS: AN APPALACHIAN JOURNEY, WITH RECIPES
Like all apple stack cakes, Lundy's tastes best after a few days. This gives the layers and filling a chance to marry while solidifying the cake so it's easier to slice.

Blackberry Jam Cake

By Damaris Phillips

WHEN I WAS A GIRL GROWING UP in Louisville, Kentucky, holidays were spent at Aunt Julie's house. It was a beautiful brick home with a large front porch, pocket doors, and tiny spaces underneath the stairs where my cousins and I would play together. Family gatherings were loud, somewhat disjointed events with the adults laughing from the dining room and the kids carrying on from our own table in the nook off the kitchen.

The menu was always a potluck, always served buffet style, and the plates always seemed too small to fit all the offerings. After we overfilled our dishes, we would then scatter to enjoy the feast.

It was the desserts that brought the whole family back together after dinner. Aunt Julie would set out a parade of homemade treats, all lined up in a row on the counter: apple pie, pecan pie, pumpkin pie, chocolate cake, yellow cake, and coconut cake. They were all delicious, but I had two particular favorites—and they came out only at Christmas: mincemeat pie, which is a dessert for another story, and blackberry jam cake with caramel frosting.

Eating a slice of Aunt Julie's jam cake reminds me of sliding into a warm bed. Imagine the comfort of worn quilts, the excitement of clean sheets, and the sigh of relaxing into a soft mattress, and you'll have an idea of how a bite of this cake makes you feel. It is a moist and hearty spice cake with a zip of tartness from blackberries and a slather of slightly salty caramel frosting all over. In short, it is perfect.

I have always loved eating this cake, but it wasn't until I attempted to make it myself that I really began to understand its nuances. Here is what I learned. The spices are key elements. The amounts of cinnamon, allspice, and cloves called for in this recipe give the layers nicely balanced warmth, but you can feel free to bump up the spices if you want to create something a little more dramatic.

I also discovered that a cream cheese frosting is a must. Unlike the caramel icing that is traditionally paired with blackberry jam cake, my caramel-cream cheese version is a little bit savory, which tempers the sweetness of the cake layers.

But above all, I realized that the most important ingredient in this recipe is the jam. You can use whatever brand of seedless blackberry jam or preserves you like in the cake batter, but just make sure it doesn't contain additional pectin, which will make the jam much too thick. I made the mistake of using the wrong kind of jam once, and it produced a dense brick of a cake that even our backyard opossum, Sir Phillip, refused to eat.

I could tell you that I love this cake because it connects me to a special little piece of Kentucky's culinary history, which it does. I could tell you that it's also a crowd-pleaser, which it always is. I could even tell you that the finished product makes a subtly impressive sight when it's displayed on a milk glass cake stand—and, oh, how pretty it is. But the truth is, I love this blackberry jam cake because it reminds me of the warm, wonderful glow that shines from a home that's filled with a family's laughter.

A WELL-TRAVELED RECIPE

Kentuckians like to boast that the jam cake is as original to their state as bourbon and the Derby. While there is a proliferation of jam cakes in old community cookbooks from that area, the recipe is actually a gift from German immigrants who settled in Pennsylvania and then ventured to Kentucky, Tennessee, Ohio, and other places, bringing the European tradition of the jam-filled spice cake with them. Traditionally baked during the holidays, these confections were made using homemade berry jam, typically blackberry or blueberry, which the cook had put up in the summer. (According to an old wives' tale, if you don't use homemade jam in your cake layers, the fruit mixture will fall to the bottom of the pans.) Along with an abundance of spices, the original recipes also featured nuts of the region (such as black walnuts and pecans) and were iced with a satiny smooth caramel frosting. Jam cakes keep well and taste even better after a few days if covered and kept in the refrigerator (the waiting requires some restraint but is worth it).

DAMARIS
PHILLIPS
AUTHOR OF
SOUTHERN
GIRL MEETS
VEGETARIAN BOY
Inspired by her Aunt Julie's blackberry jam cake, Phillips created this upgraded, three-layer version with a rich caramel-cream cheese frosting.

Lemon-and-Chocolate Doberge Cake

By David Guas

HEN YOU MEET SOMEONE from your hometown, it's customary to ask them where they went to high school. But if you were born and raised in New Orleans, like me, the next question is usually, "Who made your birthday cakes?" This might seem like a weird thing to ask if you grew up somewhere else, but not to us natives. My wife, Simone, who also happens to be from New Orleans, posed the all-important question on our second date. It turns out that we both got the Half and Half Doberge Cake from Joe Gambino's Bakery—and we've been married for 19 years.

At a New Orleans birthday party, a doberge (DOH-bash) cake is as essential to the event as the presents. Gambino's, Haydel's, and nearly every bakery in the city offers its own take on this showstopping dessert. When I was growing up, it didn't matter if you had pony rides or a whole petting zoo at your birthday party. If you didn't have the right kind of cake, the other kids might talk about you the next day. "Oh, he didn't have a doberge."

The definition of a special-occasion cake, a doberge is made of six to nine thin layers of vanilla sponge cake sandwiched with a custard or creamy filling, then covered in rich frosting. While you can get a doberge in a single flavor such as chocolate (my sister Tracy's preference), the most popular option is the "half and half," which seamlessly combines two flavors into one cake.

My favorite is chocolate-lemon, which is what my mother would order from Gambino's for my birthday. It is a chocolate-filled-and-iced cake on one side and a lemon-filled-and-iced cake on the other. If chocolate and lemon sound like an odd combination, you're missing the point. The two flavors aren't meant to be eaten in the same bite but savored separately.

After singing the birthday song, everyone would crowd around my mother, the designated cake cutter, to wait for the first slice, which had to be right at the dividing line where chocolate met lemon. The goal was to get an equal amount of both flavors in one piece. Imagine trying to slice a six-layer cake with 20 pairs of eyes on you.

As a kid with a growing interest in cooking and food, I obsessed over this mysterious dessert. I couldn't figure out how Gambino's made it as one cake. I thought they must have used some fancy, specially made pans. Eventually, I wised up. I also became a pastry chef—and now know the secret to the half and half. Spread between each of the identical cake layers is a chocolate custard that covers one half and a lemon filling that covers the other half. The layers are stacked and covered halfway with lemon frosting and halfway with chocolate. It takes me a full day and requires every bowl in my kitchen—and I make desserts for a living.

My boys, Kemp and Spencer, have always thought they were from New Orleans, but truth be told, they were born in Washington, D.C. However, Simone and I thought it was cute and never wanted them to imagine anything different, so we adopted the customary New Orleans rituals, including doberge cake. Starting with their first birthdays, they got a half and half, made by me. As they grew up, they each settled on just one flavor: lemon for Kemp and chocolate for Spencer. It's interesting how DNA works.

A NEW ORLEANS ORIGINAL

As a way to improve her family's financial situation during the Depression, Beulah Levy Ledner opened Mrs. Charles Ledner's Superior Home Baking from her New Orleans home. Ledner became known for her miniature kuchens and lemon meringue pies, but there was one recipe that would make her a legend in New Orleans history. After some experimenting with the Hungarian Dobos torte, which is a multilayered sponge cake with chocolate buttercream filling, she came up with a brilliant spin-off: a nine-layer yellow cake filled with chocolate custard and covered in chocolate frosting. To make it a true New Orleans dessert, Ledner added a French twist to the name, calling it "doberge." The city fell in love with the cake and crowned her the "Doberge Queen of New Orleans." She later sold her bakery and recipes to the owners of Joe Gambino's Bakery, who continue to make the dessert the same way.

DAVID GUAS

OWNER OF BAYOU BAKERY IN ARLINGTON, VIRGINIA

A half and half is truly a labor of love. We adapted Guas' recipe to include store-bought chocolate pudding and lemon curd to save some steps in the kitchen.

Apple Stack Cake

ACTIVE 55 MIN. - TOTAL 5 HOURS, 45 MIN., PLUS 2 DAYS RESTING
SERVES 10

- **1 lb. unsulfured dried apples (about 5 cups)**
- **Vegetable shortening, for greasing**
- **6 cups all-purpose flour, divided**
- **1 tsp. baking soda**
- **1/2 tsp. salt**
- **2/3 cup butter, softened**
- **1 cup granulated sugar**
- **1 cup sorghum syrup**
- **1 cup whole buttermilk**
- **2 large eggs, beaten**
- **1 cup packed dark brown sugar**
- **1/2 tsp. ground mace**
- **Powdered sugar, for topping (optional)**

1. Start the filling first. Put the apples in a Dutch oven, and add enough water to cover the apples by 2 inches. Bring to a boil over high; then turn down the heat to low. Simmer, stirring occasionally, until apples are tender enough to mash, 1 to 1 1/2 hours. You may need to add a little more water to keep the apples from sticking, but you don't want the final mixture to be soupy.
2. While the filling continues to cook, prepare the skillet for baking, and make the dough. Liberally grease the inside of a 9-inch cast-iron skillet with shortening, and sprinkle with 1 tablespoon of the flour, shaking and turning to coat the bottom of the skillet and about 1 inch up the sides.
3. Sift 5 1/2 cups of the flour with baking soda and salt, and set aside. Place the butter and granulated sugar in a large bowl, and beat with an electric mixer on medium speed until blended, about 3 minutes. Add the sorghum syrup, and beat 1 minute to blend. Whisk together the buttermilk and the eggs in a small bowl. (This recipe does not use baking powder, so buttermilk is necessary to activate the baking soda.)
4. Add flour mixture to the butter mixture alternately with the egg mixture in 5 additions, beginning and ending with flour mixture. Beat on low speed after each addition to incorporate. Cover and chill at least 1 hour or up to 2 hours.
5. After the apples are cooked, stir the brown sugar and mace into the apples until sugar is dissolved. Remove from heat, and mash with a potato masher until a thick puree forms with lumps no larger than a pea. (You can also pulse the mixture in the bowl of a food processor 15 times.) If mixture is too runny, return to medium heat, and continue to cook, stirring constantly, until liquid evaporates and mixture is the consistency of apple butter. Cover to keep warm.
6. Preheat oven to 350°F. Generously sprinkle a flat surface with some of the remaining flour, and scrape the chilled dough onto it. With floured hands, shape dough into a log about 10 inches long. Using a sharp, floured knife, cut into 5 (2-inch) pieces. With floured hands, roll each piece lightly in the flour, and shape into a ball. Place 4 of the balls on a rimmed baking sheet lined with parchment paper, cover with plastic wrap, and chill until ready to use.
7. Pat remaining 1 ball into a disk. Place dough disk in the greased and floured skillet and, pressing lightly with floured palm and fingers, flatten it evenly so it spreads out to just touch the edges of the skillet all around. Don't pat too hard and don't press it up against the side of the skillet, or it will stick. Evenly prick the surface of the dough lightly with a fork.
8. Bake in preheated oven until the top is golden and the cake has pulled slightly away from the edges of the skillet, about 25 to 30 minutes. It will not rise like a normal cake layer but will look like a big cookie, only much more tender. Let cool in skillet on wire rack for 5 minutes. Run a butter knife around the inside edge of the skillet, and gently nudge the layer underneath to loosen. Turn cake layer out onto a rack, and allow to cool for about 5 minutes. Transfer layer to a cake plate, and spread warm apple mixture over the top, to the edges. The apple filling should be about 1/4 inch thick, and you should use about 3/4 cup of the mixture per layer.
9. Clean inside of skillet with a paper towel, and cool on rack until barely warm, 10 minutes. Repeat Steps 7 and 8 for each dough ball, greasing and flouring skillet for each. Proceed, stacking each successive layer while warm and spreading with apple mixture. Leave the top layer bare. Save remaining apple mixture for another use.
10. Allow cake to cool completely, about 30 minutes. Wrap cake in cheesecloth, and then wrap in several layers of plastic wrap. Allow to "ripen" at room temperature for 2 to 3 days before cutting and serving. Dust the top of the cake with powdered sugar, if desired.

Blackberry Jam Cake

ACTIVE 35 MIN. - TOTAL 2 HOURS, 35 MIN.
SERVES 12

CAKE LAYERS
- **2 3/4 cups all-purpose flour**
- **2 tsp. ground cinnamon**
- **1 1/2 tsp. baking soda**
- **1 1/2 tsp. baking powder**
- **1 1/2 tsp. ground cloves**
- **1 1/2 tsp. ground allspice**
- **1 tsp. salt**
- **2 cups granulated sugar**
- **5 large eggs**
- **1 1/2 cups vegetable oil**
- **1 1/4 cups seedless blackberry jam or preserves**
- **2 tsp. vanilla extract**
- **1 1/2 cups whole buttermilk**
- **1 cup finely chopped pecans or black walnuts**
- **1 cup golden raisins**

FROSTING
- **3 (8-oz.) pkg. cream cheese, softened**
- **1/4 cup granulated sugar**
- **1/2 cup jarred caramel topping**
- **1/2 cup heavy cream**
- **1/4 tsp. salt**

GARNISHES
- **1 tsp. finely chopped pecans or black walnuts**
- **Fresh blackberries**

1. Preheat oven to 350°F. Spray 3 (9-inch) round cake pans with cooking spray; line bottoms with parchment paper.
2. Prepare the Cake Layers: Whisk together first 7 ingredients in a large bowl; set aside.
3. Place sugar and eggs in bowl of a heavy-duty stand mixer fitted with whisk attachment; beat on medium speed until thick and smooth, 3 minutes. Change to paddle attachment. Add oil, jam, and vanilla extract; beat until combined, 1 minute.
4. Add half of the flour mixture to jam mixture; beat on low speed until just combined, 20 to 45 seconds. Add buttermilk; beat on low speed until just combined. Add remaining flour mixture; beat on low speed until smooth and combined, about 30 seconds. Fold in nuts and raisins; divide evenly among prepared pans.
5. Bake in preheated oven until edges of Cake Layers are just starting to pull from sides of pans and a wooden pick inserted

in center comes out clean, 35 to 40 minutes, rotating pans from top to bottom rack halfway through baking. Press gently on top of layers to flatten any doming; cool in pans 10 minutes. Remove from pans to wire racks; cool completely, about 1 hour.

6. Prepare the Frosting: Place cream cheese and sugar in bowl of a heavy-duty stand mixer fitted with whisk attachment; beat on medium-low speed until combined. Add caramel topping; beat until smooth, 1 to 2 minutes. With mixer running, slowly pour in cream and add salt. Beat on medium speed until thick and smooth, 3 to 4 minutes. (Mixture will look runny at first but will thicken as the cream is whipped.)

7. Transfer about two-thirds of the Frosting to a piping bag. Place 1 Cake Layer on a serving plate. Pipe Frosting on top of layer, using a circular motion and starting from the outside and gradually moving to the center. Repeat process with remaining layers. Cover sides with remaining Frosting. (Drag the back of a spoon in a side-to-side motion across the Frosting for a textured look.) Garnish cake with nuts and blackberries.

Lemon-and-Chocolate Doberge Cake

ACTIVE 45 MIN. - TOTAL 2 HOURS, 50 MIN.
SERVES 12

CAKE LAYERS

- **4 1/2 cups bleached cake flour**
- **1 Tbsp. baking powder**
- **3/4 tsp. salt**
- **1 1/2 cups unsalted butter, softened**
- **2 cups granulated sugar**
- **5 large eggs**
- **3 large egg yolks**
- **1 Tbsp. vanilla extract**
- **1 1/2 cups whole milk**

BUTTERCREAM FROSTINGS

- **1 cup unsalted butter, softened**
- **5 cups powdered sugar**
- **1 tsp. vanilla extract**
- **1/4 tsp. salt**
- **4 Tbsp. whole milk plus more as needed, divided**
- **1/2 Tbsp. lemon zest plus 2 tsp. fresh juice (from 1 lemon)**
- **1–2 drops yellow liquid food coloring**
- **2 tsp. unsweetened cocoa**
- **1 oz. finely chopped bittersweet chocolate**

ADDITIONAL INGREDIENTS

- **1 2/3 cups jarred lemon curd**
- **1 2/3 cups refrigerated prepared chocolate pudding**

1. Prepare the Cake Layers: Preheat oven to 350°F. Whisk together flour, baking powder, and salt in a medium bowl.

2. Beat butter and sugar with an electric mixer on medium speed until light and fluffy, about 5 minutes. Add eggs and egg yolks, 1 at a time, beating well after each addition. Beat in vanilla.

3. Add flour mixture to egg mixture alternately with milk in 5 additions, beginning and ending with flour mixture. Beat on low speed until just combined after each addition. Divide batter evenly among 3 greased and floured 9-inch round cake pans.

4. Bake in preheated oven until a wooden pick inserted in center comes out clean, 23 to 25 minutes. Cool in pans on wire racks 10 minutes. Remove Cake Layers from pans to wire racks; cool completely, about 30 minutes. When cool, gently slice each layer in half horizontally, making 6 thin layers.

5. Prepare the Buttercream Frostings: Beat butter with an electric mixer on medium speed until creamy, about 3 minutes. With mixer running on low speed, gradually add powdered sugar, and beat until smooth. Add vanilla, salt, and 3 tablespoons of the milk; beat until smooth, about 1 minute. (Add up to 1 tablespoon more milk, if needed to reach desired consistency.) Remove and reserve 1 cup of frosting in a small bowl. Divide remaining frosting evenly between 2 medium bowls.

6. Stir lemon zest and juice into 1 medium bowl of frosting. Stir in yellow food coloring to achieve desired color.

7. Add cocoa to remaining medium bowl of frosting, and stir until smooth. Place chocolate and remaining 1 tablespoon milk in a small microwavable bowl. Microwave on HIGH until chocolate melts and mixture is smooth, about 20 seconds, stirring every 10 seconds. Cool 5 minutes, and stir into chocolate frosting.

8. Place 1 Cake Layer on a serving plate. Spread about 1/3 cup lemon curd on half of layer. Spread about 1/3 cup chocolate pudding on the opposite half. Repeat process with 4 more Cake Layers. Top with remaining layer. (Indicate on a sticky note which flavor is on each side, and attach to serving plate.) Spread 1 cup reserved plain frosting in a thin layer over sides. Chill 1 hour.

9. Spread lemon frosting over top and frosted sides of lemon half of cake. Spread chocolate frosting over top and frosted sides of chocolate half of cake.

More Cheese, Please

Five simple and delicious meals that the whole family will melt over

White Calzones with Marinara Sauce, page 230

Fontina-Stuffed Pork Chops with Mashed Potatoes

Buttery, semisoft fontina melts beautifully, making it an ideal choice for a grilled cheese or an omelet. To shred it more easily, freeze this cheese for about an hour to firm it up before grating.

ACTIVE 45 MIN. - TOTAL 1 HOUR, 5 MIN.
SERVES 4

Heat 1 Tbsp. **unsalted butter** in a large nonstick skillet over medium. Add 1 thinly sliced large **yellow onion** (about 10 oz.); cook, stirring occasionally, until lightly caramelized, about 15 minutes. Stir in 1 tsp. minced **garlic** (about 1 garlic clove), 1 tsp. **fresh thyme leaves,** and ¼ tsp. each **kosher salt** and **black pepper.** Cook, stirring often, until fragrant, 1 to 2 minutes. Remove from heat; set aside. Using a paring knife, cut a 2-inch slit in sides of 4 (15-oz.) **bone-in, center-cut pork chops,** about 1 ½ inches thick, creating a pocket, cutting to the bone. Stuff each with ¼ cup shredded **fontina cheese** and 1 Tbsp. onion mixture. Set aside remaining onion mixture. Preheat oven to 375°F. Heat 1 Tbsp. **unsalted butter** in nonstick skillet over medium-high. Sprinkle both sides of pork chops evenly with 1 tsp. each **kosher salt** and **black pepper.** Cook 2 stuffed pork chops in skillet, undisturbed, until golden brown on each side, about 3 minutes per side. Transfer pork chops to a wire rack set inside a rimmed baking sheet. Repeat with 1 Tbsp. **unsalted butter** and remaining pork chops. Transfer baking sheet to preheated oven, and bake pork until a thermometer inserted in thickest portion registers 140°F, about 18 to 22 minutes. Remove from oven; let rest 10 minutes. While pork cooks, add 2 lb. **russet potatoes,** peeled and cut into 2-inch pieces, to a large saucepan; cover with cold water. Bring to boil over medium-high, and simmer until tender, about 15 minutes. Drain and return potatoes to saucepan. Stir in ¼ cup **whole milk,** ¼ cup **sour cream,** 1 cup shredded **fontina cheese,** 4 Tbsp. **unsalted butter,** 1 ½ tsp. **kosher salt,** and ¼ tsp. **black pepper** until combined. Mash to desired consistency. Cover to keep warm. Add 1 cup **chicken stock** and remaining onion mixture to skillet over medium. Cook, stirring often, until slightly reduced, 5 to 6 minutes. Remove from heat, and stir in 1 Tbsp. **apple cider vinegar** and 1 Tbsp. **unsalted butter.** Divide potatoes among 4 plates. Serve with pork chops, and top with sauce. Sprinkle with **fresh thyme leaves.**

Gnocchi Gratin with Ham and Peas

Gruyère is an aged Swiss cheese with a firm texture and slightly sweet and nutty flavor. If you can't find it, try Comté, Appenzeller, or Emmental, which are all in the same family.

ACTIVE 25 MIN. - TOTAL 45 MIN.
SERVES 4

Preheat oven to 400°F. Cook 1 (16-oz.) pkg. **potato gnocchi** according to package directions; drain and transfer to a large bowl. Melt 2 Tbsp. **unsalted butter** in a large Dutch oven over medium-high. Add 1 lb. **ham steak,** cut into ½-inch pieces, and cook, stirring often, until ham is lightly browned and any moisture has evaporated, 5 to 6 minutes. Using a slotted spoon, transfer ham to bowl with gnocchi. Wipe Dutch oven clean. Melt 4 Tbsp. **unsalted butter** in Dutch oven over medium-high. Whisk in ¼ cup **all-purpose flour.** Cook, whisking constantly, until mixture is light golden brown, 1 to 2 minutes. Slowly whisk in 2 cups **whole milk,** and bring to a boil; whisk vigorously to work out any lumps. Whisk in ¼ tsp. **kosher salt** and ¼ tsp. **black pepper.** Remove from heat, and slowly whisk in 4 oz. shredded **Gruyère cheese** (about 1 cup) and ¼ cup grated **Parmesan cheese,** until melted. Pour cheese sauce over ham and gnocchi; stir in 1 cup thawed **frozen green peas.** Transfer this mixture to a lightly greased (with cooking spray) 11- x 7-inch baking dish. Sprinkle ¼ cup grated **Parmesan cheese** on top, and bake in preheated oven until bubbly and golden brown, 20 to 25 minutes. Remove from oven, and serve warm.

Beef Stew with Cheddar Biscuits

Its sharpness, not color, is an indicator of its flavor. Mild Cheddar contains the most moisture and melts the best. Sharp Cheddar is aged longer for a tangy punch and has less moisture.

ACTIVE 25 MIN. - TOTAL 1 HOUR, 10 MIN.
SERVES 6

Preheat oven to 450°F. Heat a large (12-inch) cast-iron skillet over medium-high. Add 1 ½ lb. **lean ground beef sirloin.** Cook, breaking up and stirring with a wooden spoon, until well browned, 6 to 8 minutes. Add 1 (14-oz.) pkg. thawed **frozen pearl onions,** 2 tsp. **fresh thyme leaves,** 1 tsp. minced **garlic** (from 1 garlic clove), and ¾ tsp. each **black pepper** and **kosher salt,** and stir until combined. Cook until fragrant, 2 to 3 minutes. Stir in 3 Tbsp. **tomato paste,** and sprinkle with 1 Tbsp. **all-purpose flour.** Cook, stirring often, until well incorporated, about 2 minutes. Add 1 (12-oz.) pkg. thawed **frozen peas and carrots;** stir to combine. Stir in 3 cups **beef stock;** bring to boil. Reduce heat to medium-low; simmer until thickened, 15 to 20 minutes. Meanwhile, whisk together 2 cups **self-rising flour** and 1 tsp. **kosher salt** in a large bowl. Using your hands, work ½ cup **unsalted butter,** cut into small pieces, into mixture until it clumps together and becomes pea-size pieces. Stir in 1 cup shredded **mild Cheddar cheese.** Stir in 1 cup **whole buttermilk** just until incorporated. Using a ¼-cup ice-cream scoop, drop biscuit dough directly on top of stew, leaving about ½ inch of space between biscuits. Sprinkle top with ½ cup shredded **mild Cheddar cheese.** Place skillet on a rimmed baking sheet, and bake in preheated oven until biscuits are browned and flaky, 20 to 22 minutes. Let stand 5 minutes, and serve.

TRY THIS TWIST!
Pitmaster Stew: Use cubed **pork shoulder** in place of the beef and substitute **smoked Cheddar** for the regular Cheddar.

Baked Rigatoni with Zucchini and Mozzarella

Fresh mozzarella sold in water has a short shelf life; use it within a few days of purchase for the best flavor. If you can't find small mozzarella balls, tear a standard-size ball into pieces.

ACTIVE 15 MIN. TOTAL 1 HOUR, 15 MIN.
SERVES 8

Preheat oven to 375°F. Cook 1 lb. **rigatoni pasta** according to package directions. Drain and transfer to a large bowl. Heat 1 Tbsp. **olive oil** in a large nonstick skillet over medium-high. Add 1 ½ cups **zucchini,** cut into half-moons (from 1 [8 oz.] zucchini), and cook, stirring occasionally, until lightly browned on all sides, about 4 minutes. Stir in 5 oz. **baby spinach;** cook until wilted, about 1 minute. Sprinkle with ¼ tsp. each **black pepper** and **kosher salt.** Transfer to bowl with pasta. Whisk together ¾ cup **sour cream,** ½ cup **plain whole-milk Greek yogurt,** 1 large **egg,** and ¾ tsp. **kosher salt** in a medium bowl until well incorporated. Stir sour cream mixture into pasta mixture until well coated. Add 12 oz. small **fresh mozzarella cheese balls** and 1 oz. grated **Parmesan cheese** to pasta mixture; toss to combine. Gently stir in 1 (14.5-oz.) can **diced tomatoes,** drained. Transfer mixture to a lightly greased (with cooking spray) 9-inch springform pan, and place on a rimmed baking sheet. Bake in preheated oven until set, about 30 minutes. Top with 4 oz. small **fresh mozzarella cheese balls** and 1 oz. grated **Parmesan cheese,** and return to oven. Bake until golden brown, about 5 minutes. Remove and let stand 15 minutes. Release sides of springform pan, and cut into 8 pieces. Sprinkle with **fresh basil leaves.**

TRY THIS TWIST!
Baked Rigatoni with Sweet Red Peppers and Fontina: Substitute 1 ½ cups **red bell peppers,** cut into ½-inch pieces, for the zucchini and use 3 cups grated **fontina cheese** in place of the fresh mozzarella with the Parmesan cheese in the pasta mixture before baking. Use 1 cup grated **fontina** with the Parmesan on top when baking the last 5 minutes.

White Calzones with Marinara Sauce

White Calzones with Marinara Sauce

Ricotta often contains stabilizers, which can give it a gummy texture when baked. Choose one that's made with as few ingredients as possible—ideally milk, whey, vinegar, and salt.

ACTIVE 20 MIN. TOTAL 55 MIN.
SERVES 4

Preheat oven to 450°F. Divide 1 lb. **fresh prepared pizza dough** (at room temperature) into 4 equal pieces; form into small balls. Wrap each dough ball with plastic wrap; let rest 20 minutes. Unwrap and roll on a lightly floured surface into flat disks, about 7 inches wide. Place disks on a baking sheet lined with parchment paper. While dough balls rest, stir together 6 oz. shredded **low-moisture part-skim mozzarella cheese** (about 1 ½ cups), ¾ cup **ricotta cheese,** 1 large **egg yolk,** ½ tsp. **lemon zest** (from 1 lemon), 2 finely grated **garlic cloves,** ½ tsp. **kosher salt,** and ¼ tsp. **black pepper** in a medium bowl with a fork until well incorporated. Divide mixture among dough disks, adding mixture to 1 side of the disk and leaving a ½-inch border. Lightly beat 1 large **egg** in a small bowl. Brush outside edge of the dough with half of egg; fold into half-moons, and crimp edges with fork. Brush tops of calzones with remaining egg; sprinkle with 1 oz. grated **Parmesan cheese** (about ¼ cup) and 1 tsp. **dried Italian seasoning.** Bake in preheated oven until golden brown, 16 to 18 minutes. Serve with 1 cup warmed jarred **marinara sauce.**

clockwise from top left:

Gnocchi Gratin with Ham and Peas, page 229; Beef Stew with Cheddar Biscuits, page 229; Fontina-Stuffed Pork Chops with Mashed Potatoes, page 229; Baked Rigatoni with Zucchini and Mozzarella, page 230

Muffin Pan Pies

These savory appetizers taste great whether served warm or at room temperature

Mini Mushroom-and-Goat Cheese Pot Pies

ACTIVE 25 MIN. - TOTAL 55 MIN.
MAKES 12

- **2 Tbsp. unsalted butter**
- **1 Tbsp. olive oil**
- **1 large shallot, finely chopped**
- **8 oz. cremini mushrooms, chopped**
- **2 garlic cloves, minced**
- **1 tsp. chopped fresh thyme**
- **½ tsp. chopped fresh rosemary**
- **⅓ cup dry sherry**
- **2 oz. cream cheese, at room temperature**
- **2 oz. goat cheese, at room temperature**
- **¼ tsp. kosher salt**
- **⅛ tsp. black pepper**
- **1 (14.1-oz.) pkg. refrigerated piecrusts**
- **1 large egg, lightly beaten**
- **1 Tbsp. water**
- **Flaky sea salt**
- **Fresh thyme leaves**

1. Preheat oven to 350°F. Melt butter with olive oil in a large skillet over medium-high. Add shallot; cook, stirring often, until slightly transparent and fragrant, 1 minute. Add mushrooms; cook, stirring occasionally, until mushrooms are tender and lightly browned, about 8 minutes. Add garlic, thyme, and rosemary; cook, stirring often, until fragrant, 1 minute. Add sherry, and cook until liquid is nearly all evaporated, 2 more minutes. Remove from heat; let cool slightly, 10 minutes. Mix in cream cheese, goat cheese, kosher salt, and pepper.

2. Coat 2 (12-cup) miniature muffin pans or 1 (24-cup) miniature muffin pan with cooking spray. Unroll both piecrusts on a work surface. Using a 3 ¼-inch round cutter, cut out 12 dough rounds; using a 2 ½-inch round cutter, cut out 12 more dough rounds, combining and rolling out remaining dough once, if necessary.

3. Whisk together egg and water. Fit a 3 ¼-inch dough round into every other muffin cup in pans, leaving a small edge at top. Brush edges with some of the egg mixture. Spoon about 1 tablespoon mushroom mixture into each dough cup. Top each filled cup with a 2 ½-inch dough round, crimping edges of bottom and top crusts together to seal.

4. Brush tops of pies with remaining egg mixture, and sprinkle with flaky sea salt and thyme. Bake in preheated oven until golden brown, 25 to 30 minutes. Cool 5 minutes before serving.

BAKING TIP

This recipe calls for leaving every other cup in the muffin pans empty to allow room to crimp the dough edges.

Low-and-Slow Pork Supper

The secret to this flavorful meat is the cider-infused gravy

Hard Cider-Braised Pork

ACTIVE 30 MIN. - TOTAL 5 HOURS, 50 MIN.
SERVES 6

- **1 (3 ½-lb.) boneless pork shoulder (Boston butt)**
- **1 Tbsp. kosher salt, divided**
- **¾ tsp. black pepper, divided**
- **1 Tbsp. olive oil**
- **2 cups vertically sliced sweet onion (from 1 onion)**
- **2 Tbsp. chopped garlic (from 4 to 5 garlic cloves)**
- **4 large carrots, peeled, cut into 2-inch pieces (about 3 cups)**
- **1 ½ lb. celery root, peeled, cut into 2-inch pieces (about 3 cups)**
- **1 Honeycrisp apple, halved**
- **2 (12-oz.) bottles hard apple cider**
- **4 thyme sprigs**
- **½ cup water**
- **¼ cup cornstarch**
- **1 (8-oz.) pkg. wide egg noodles, cooked according to pkg. directions**
- **Fresh thyme leaves, for garnish**

1. Pat pork dry with paper towels; season on all sides with 1 ½ teaspoons of the salt and ½ teaspoon of the pepper. Heat oil in a large skillet over medium-high. Add pork, and cook until browned on all sides, 10 to 12 minutes. Transfer to a 6-quart slow cooker. Pour off all but 2 tablespoons drippings in skillet, and add onion and garlic to hot drippings. Cook, stirring often, until slightly softened, 3 to 4 minutes. Transfer onion mixture to slow cooker with pork.
2. Add carrots, celery root, apple, cider, thyme, and ½ teaspoon of the salt to slow cooker. Cover; cook until vegetables are tender and pork is very tender, 5 hours on HIGH or 8 hours on LOW. Remove pork, and place on a platter. Using a slotted spoon, remove vegetables from liquid in slow cooker, and place in a bowl. Discard apple and thyme sprigs.
3. Skim fat from surface of liquid; discard. Whisk water and cornstarch in a small bowl. Stir cornstarch mixture into liquid in slow cooker, and cover and cook on HIGH until thickened, 30 minutes. Meanwhile, shred pork into bite-size pieces, discarding any large pieces of fat. Sprinkle with ½ teaspoon of the salt. Stir remaining ½ teaspoon salt and ¼ teaspoon pepper into gravy in slow cooker. Serve hot cooked noodles with vegetables, pork, and gravy. Garnish with thyme.

TRY THIS TWIST!
Coffee Stout-Braised Beef: Substitute beef chuck roast for the pork shoulder, eliminate the Honeycrisp apple, and use coffee-oatmeal stout instead of hard apple cider.

SHOP SMART
A hard cider that's not too sweet works best in this recipe. Our Test Kitchen likes Woodchuck Hard Cider.

COOKING SL SCHOOL

TIPS AND TRICKS FROM THE SOUTH'S MOST TRUSTED KITCHEN

SHOPPING SMARTS

Choose the Right Cheese

Our Test Kitchen shared their small-batch and supermarket favorites

GOAT CHEESE

BEST SOUTHERN MADE
Stone Hollow Farmstead Fresh Chevre (Harpersville, Alabama)

WHY WE LOVE IT
It's ultrasmooth and spreadable with just the right amount of tanginess.
stonehollowfarmstead.com

BLUE CHEESE

BEST SOUTHERN MADE
Sweet Grass Dairy Asher Blue (Thomasville, Georgia)

WHY WE LOVE IT
With its pungent aroma and earthy, slightly salty flavor, this is a standout blue cheese.
sweetgrassdairy.com

FETA CHEESE

BEST SOUTHERN MADE
Dayspring Dairy's Classic Greek-Style Feta (Gallant, Alabama)

WHY WE LOVE IT
It combines a pleasant creaminess with feta's distinctive crumbly texture.
dayspringdairy.com

BEST GROCERY STORE PICK
Ile de France Chèvre Fresh Goat Cheese

WHY WE LOVE IT
This light and tangy cheese is delicious plain or flavored (we like Garlic & Herb) and comes in a variety of sizes.
iledefrancecheese.com

BEST GROCERY STORE PICK
Castello Traditional Danish Blue

WHY WE LOVE IT
A little sharp, a little nutty, and a little funky, this blue cheese offers big yet balanced flavor.
castellocheese.com

BEST GROCERY STORE PICK
Vigo Feta Cheese

WHY WE LOVE IT
This not-too-salty feta is sold in brine, which gives the cheese a smoother texture and keeps it from drying out.
vigo-alessi.com

"If your cake layers come out of the oven with slightly domed tops, no need to trim them with a knife. Press down gently on the warm cakes with your hands to flatten."

—Deb Wise
Test Kitchen Professional

IN SEASON

Pick Me!

Here's why we always choose the Honeycrisp

It's not only a popular choice for eating out of hand but also the apple we reach for most often when cooking and baking. The Honeycrisp offers a nicely balanced sweet-tart flavor and has a texture that doesn't turn to mush when cooked. It's ideal for pies, and cobblers.

November

236 **Thanksgiving at the Farm** Gathering to give thanks on the family homestead

240 **Friendsgiving at Joy's** A Crescent City-based cookbook author creates new holiday traditions with friends in her new hometown

246 **Let's Talk (Smoking) Turkey** Wisps of woodsy flavor and long, slow cooking make this holiday bird the hit of the Thanksgiving table

248 **It's Called Dressing, Not Stuffing** A *Southern Living* editor's aunt is the "Dressing Diva" of her family, and her unique recipe will make you your family's too

250 **Pass The Gravy** Three tricks from the pros to rich, satiny-smooth gravy

252 **Respect the Relish Tray** These mouthwatering nibbles rev the appetite for the feast to come

253 **Here Come the Casseroles** Classic Thanksgiving side dishes get gussied up in fresh new ways

258 **Old Faithfuls** A trio of Southern bakeries shares their recipes for traditional pies of the Thanksgiving sideboard

262 **"Look What Aunt Lisa Brought!"** Unexpected desserts destined to become the new family favorites

266 THE LEFTOVERS **Make the Best Sandwich of the Year** Four tasty turkey sandwiches paired with the best bags of chips

267 THE LEFTOVERS **Chili for a Crowd** Think beyond the sandwich with this big-batch chili

268 *SL* COOKING SCHOOL Quick tricks for making store-bought seem scratchmade

THANKSGIVING AT THE FARM

Every November, a grandmother's legacy calls a family back to its historic South Carolina homestead for a feast of food and memories

The moment the skillet slipped through his fingers and cracked on the brick steps, everything changed.

Dennis Powell had been given his grandmother's cast-iron pan and her butcher knife when he'd left for college and had cherished them for the 40 years that followed. When the skillet broke in two, "It was like it cracked that literal connection to her hands, her cooking, and the place we came from," he says.

That place is a farm in Sandridge, South Carolina. When repair attempts failed, Dennis (who was then an architect working in Alexandria, Virginia) set out to cast two reproductions to give his sons. He didn't know it at the time, but the quest would eventually lead him on a long, circuitous journey to build Butter Pat Industries, his own cast-iron cookware company. These efforts were about much more than replacing an heirloom–he was also seeking "a restoration of that connection to our family home," he says. Butter Pat skillets are all named after strong women in his life. The latest, an 8-inch-diameter workhorse, is named Estee.

As it turns out, cast iron is a fitting representation of Estee Hilton Rudd, his late grandmother, a hardworking self-taught butcher who ran a meat market in Charleston where she sold sausage, hog's-head cheese, chickens, and rice pudding. Dennis still remembers the sawdust-and-blood smell of her slaughterhouse and helping out by working gut-bucket detail. While Estee's husband, Hiram Eugene Rudd, raised cattle, she grew her business, often serving lunch for up to 20 work-hands, and raised seven children–Dorothy, Gertrude, Miriam, Mary (Dennis' mother), Joseph, Joyce, and Lynwood. Each Thanksgiving, those siblings and up to 100 descendants get together on the same farm, located about 45 miles northwest of Charleston, for a serious casserole show-down–and a feast of memories.

Composed of cypress logs and shingles and a sloping, Cabernet-colored tin roof, the remnants of Estee's house is the oldest cypress-log home in Berkeley County. What remains of the original structure (and nearby smokehouse) has survived the Civil War and the earthquake of 1886 that cracked open steam pits and fissures throughout the region. In 1989, Hurricane Hugo ripped off the kitchen and back porch and destroyed the pecan grove and several outbuildings.

Some family members–like Aunt Gertie, who always brings her tender and tasty boiled sieve ("sivvy") beans (small speckled limas that she's grown and put up)–still live nearby. Others travel from big cities up North, so reintroductions are in order. Before the meal, everyone gathers in a circle to hold hands, count off, and introduce new babies and guests. Uncle Joseph reads a verse from the family Bible, and Dennis' father, Dennis T. Powell, says grace.

Then it's time to line up, from the oldest to the youngest, to serve their plates from a long table laden with turkeys, casseroles, and covered dishes that they've eaten all their lives. The original sign from Estee's business now hangs over the table, looking down on the feast and family who've come to honor what she taught them about hard work and perseverance and the pleasures of sharing a meal together. In this case, that means eating at picnic tables scattered around the property or from plates on laps near the bonfire.

Perennial favorites–dubbed the "Hall of Fame"–include Aunt Dot's custardy macaroni and cheese, Denise's pineapple delight, and Mary's carrot soufflé. Newer additions like Candice's baked Brie slathered with fig-ginger preserves and Matilde's wild rice salad muscle in for attention. After a trip or three through the buffet, when it doesn't seem possible to eat another bite, a table on the front porch holding a buttery assortment of cakes (including coconut and caramel) and pies (such as pecan and sweet potato) defies anyone to throw in the towel.

At last, when all bellies are full and the afternoon sun casts long shadows from a towering magnolia tree, heaps of memories emerge. While the kids race around the lawn, the older folks talk about which old barns were where and recall a giant fig tree they used to climb. They remember the year Miriam's son Dale fell into a hog-scalding pot and how their mama didn't allow card playing because it reminded her of gambling and the time Joseph borrowed a pink convertible for a date at the drive-in but then couldn't get the top back up when it started raining. And so it continues with the soft sounds of easy laughter as the sisters tease their younger brothers with recollections, correct each other on details of their shared history, and contest the ownership of various recipes.

Meanwhile, a sputtering tractor tows a trailer for hayrides around a field, and cousins play touch football, drive four-wheelers, and shoot clay pigeons. Estee's children, all entrepreneurs like their mama, say they come together because they always have–and hope they always will. Though they might disagree about who makes the best nut cake, they're convinced that this annual gathering helps maintain their connection. "Mama was a peacemaker and taught us that nothing was worth an argument," said Aunt Dot with a laugh.

– Paula Disbrowe

Dennis cooks pinwheel sweet potatoes with pecan streusel in one of his skillets.

Stacy and Joyce's Cornbread Dressing

It's hard to single out one dish from the family's enormous Thanksgiving spread, but this dressing—a joint effort by Aunt Joyce and her daughter Stacy—is an annual favorite.

ACTIVE 30 MIN. - TOTAL 3 HOURS

SERVES 18

CHICKEN STOCK

- 32 oz. chicken broth
- ½ cup finely chopped yellow onion (from 1 small [6 oz.] onion)
- 1½ tsp. dried parsley
- ½ tsp. Jane's Krazy Mixed-Up Salt (or seasoned salt)
- ¼ tsp. salt
- ¼ tsp. black pepper
- 2 lb. boneless, skinless chicken thighs, trimmed

CORNBREAD DRESSING

- 1 cup whole milk
- 3 large eggs
- 3 (8½-oz.) pkg. Jiffy Corn Muffin Mix
- 3 Tbsp. canola or vegetable oil
- 1 Tbsp. butter
- 1 large (8 oz.) green bell pepper, finely chopped (1 cup)
- 1 large (12 oz.) yellow onion, finely chopped (2 cups)
- 4 celery stalks, finely chopped (1½ cups)
- 2 tsp. Jane's Krazy Mixed-Up Salt (or seasoned salt), divided
- ½ tsp. black pepper, divided
- 6 hard-cooked eggs, finely chopped
- 1 (12-oz.) can evaporated milk
- Fresh sage leaves or flat-leaf parsley leaves

1. Prepare the Chicken Stock: Place chicken broth, onion, dried parsley, Jane's Krazy Mixed-Up Salt, salt, and pepper in a large saucepan over medium-high. Bring to a boil; add chicken thighs. Reduce heat to medium-low; cook, uncovered, until chicken is very tender, about 1 hour. Remove chicken from stock; set aside until cool enough to handle, about 20 minutes. Cut into small pieces to measure 4 cups. (Reserve remaining chicken for another use.) Strain stock; discard solids.

2. While Chicken Stock cooks, prepare the Cornbread Dressing. Place a greased 10-inch cast-iron skillet in oven; preheat to 400°F. Whisk together milk and eggs in a large bowl until well blended; let stand 5 to 10 minutes. Gently whisk in corn muffin mix. Carefully remove hot skillet from oven; pour in corn muffin batter. Return skillet to preheated oven; bake until golden brown and a wooden pick inserted in center comes out clean, 20 to 23 minutes. Carefully invert cornbread onto a wire rack; cool completely, about 45 minutes. Reduce oven temperature to 350°F; place a large cast-iron Dutch oven or a 14-inch cast-iron skillet inside oven. (Or you can bake the dressing in a 15- x 10- x 3-inch baking dish [a lasagna dish] and skip this step.)

3. Wipe the 10-inch cast-iron skillet clean; add oil and butter, and heat over medium. Add bell pepper, onion, celery, 1 teaspoon of the Jane's Krazy Mixed-Up Salt, and ¼ teaspoon of the black pepper. Cook, stirring often, until onion is translucent and tender, about 10 minutes. Remove from heat.

4. Place cooled cornbread in a large mixing bowl, and crumble using your hands. Add chopped chicken, hard-cooked eggs, bell pepper mixture, evaporated milk, and 2½ cups of the Chicken Stock. (Reserve remaining stock for another use.) Add remaining 1 teaspoon Jane's Krazy Mixed-Up Salt and ¼ teaspoon black pepper to cornbread mixture; stir to thoroughly combine.

5. Transfer mixture to preheated cast-iron Dutch oven or skillet (or large baking dish). Bake at 350°F until set and lightly browned, 1 hour to 1 hour and 15 minutes. Garnish dressing with fresh sage or parsley leaves.

Friendsgiving at Joy's

New Orleans cookbook author Joy Wilson celebrates the holiday her way—with a playful make-ahead menu, a fabulous dessert, and a table filled with friends

Wilson greets guests with a platter of French Onion Puff Pastry Bites (left) and glasses of Thanksgiving Rum Punch (above). Recipes, page 243

I always thought Friends-giving was forced.

It felt like an ill-conceived potluck meal on a day meant to gather all of the joys and dramas of family around a big baked bird served once a year on Grandmother's good china. Friendsgiving seemed more like a hashtag than a tradition, and I didn't know what to do with it.

And then I moved. Four years ago, I packed up my car and relocated with my cat from California to New Orleans for change, for adventure, and simply because it's a magical place that called to me.

But leaving family is never easy, especially when the holiday season rolls around. It's also not always feasible to hop on a plane for Thanksgiving. So, after a few years of calling the Crescent City home, I knew it was time to create my own version of Turkey Day.

New Orleans is a place with deep traditions that involve bringing the community together, and for thousands of us in the city, the holiday starts out at the racetrack. Instead of fretting over turkey-basting all morning, we dress up in our finest fall outfits (fancy hats included) and head to the track to watch the horses, sip Bloody Marys, and reconnect with friends we may not have seen since the summer.

Because I know the morning of November 22 will involve quality time with my friends instead of the kitchen stove, I create a mostly make-ahead meal that nods to the classics but brings levity and ease. On my menu: buttery puff pastry bites filled with caramelized onions, individual pot pies featuring turkey and vegetables and covered with a savory dressing crumble, a crunchy fall salad, a top-your-own mashed potato bar, and a refreshing seasonal rum punch.

Now I understand it. Friendsgiving is all about the people sitting around the table, the friends you've chosen to become your family, and celebrating those new bonds with fresh holiday traditions—and, of course, plenty of Pumpkin Layer Cake with Caramel-Cream Cheese Frosting.

Mini Turkey Pot Pies with Dressing Tops, page 244

A Make-Ahead Game Plan

Prep the Meal in Stages So You Can Enjoy the Party Too

ONE WEEK AHEAD Assemble the pot pies, and wrap in plastic wrap or aluminum foil. Store (unbaked) in the freezer. Bake from frozen as directed. (They may need an extra 10 minutes in the oven.)
THREE DAYS AHEAD Cook the pancetta; refrigerate in an airtight container, and reheat before serving. Mix the salad dressing; store in the refrigerator. Make the cake, and store it (covered) in the refrigerator.
TWO DAYS AHEAD Prepare the mashed potatoes; refrigerate in an airtight container, and reheat before serving. Assemble the French Onion Puff Pastry Bites. Store the unbaked bites (covered) in the refrigerator, and then bake as directed. Prepare the cider syrup for the punch; store in the refrigerator.
THE DAY BEFORE Slice the apple and celery for the salad, and place in a bowl filled with lemon water; refrigerate.

Thanksgiving Rum Punch

ACTIVE 15 MIN. - TOTAL 30 MIN.
SERVES 8

Combine ⅓ cup **honey,** 12 **whole cloves,** 4 **cinnamon sticks,** and 2 cups **apple cider** in a small saucepan over medium. Cook, stirring often, until honey dissolves and mixture is fragrant, about 7 minutes. Remove cider mixture from heat; cool and steep 15 minutes. Discard cloves and cinnamon sticks. Combine spiced cider mixture; 4 cups chilled **cranberry juice;** 3 cups **spiced rum;** 2 chilled (12-oz.) bottles **ginger beer;** and 6 additional cups chilled **apple cider** in a large punch bowl. Serve over ice. Garnish with sliced **green apples, oranges,** or **lemons** and a **rosemary sprig.**

French Onion Puff Pastry Bites

ACTIVE 40 MIN. - TOTAL 1 HOUR, 10 MIN.
MAKES 25 PASTRIES

- 3 Tbsp. unsalted butter
- 1 Tbsp. olive oil
- 2 large sweet onions, sliced into ½-inch-thick half-moons
- 1 Tbsp. chopped fresh thyme
- 1 tsp. Dijon mustard
- 1 tsp. freshly cracked black pepper, plus more for topping
- ½ tsp. sea salt plus more for topping
- Pinch of granulated sugar
- 3 Tbsp. chicken stock
- 1 (17.3-oz.) pkg. frozen puff pastry sheets, thawed (such as Pepperidge Farm)
- 1 oz. Gruyère cheese, shredded (about ¼ cup)
- 1 large egg, beaten
- Dijon mustard and grainy mustard, for serving

1. Heat butter and olive oil in a heavy-bottomed saucepan over medium until butter is melted. Add sliced onions all at once; stir to coat. Cook, undisturbed, until onions begin to soften, about 4 minutes. Add thyme, mustard, pepper, salt, and sugar; stir to combine. Cook, covered, stirring every 4 minutes, until onions begin to brown, break down, and resemble onion jam, about 16 minutes. Reduce heat if onions begin to brown too quickly.
2. Add chicken stock to pan. Cook, stirring constantly with a wooden spoon to loosen browned bits from bottom of pan, until liquid evaporates, about 30 seconds. Remove pan from heat, and let stand while pastry bites are assembled.
3. Preheat oven to 375°F with rack in upper third of oven. Unfold thawed puff pastry on a lightly floured work surface. Use a rolling pin to roll out 1 sheet, creating a 10-inch square. Repeat with second sheet.
4. Spoon 25 dollops (about 1 teaspoon each) of onion filling about 1 inch apart on 1 of the pastry sheet squares (5 individual teaspoons on each of 5 horizontal rows and 5 teaspoons on each of 5 vertical rows). Top each teaspoon of onion filling with a pinch of shredded Gruyère.
5. Carefully place remaining pastry sheet square on top of onion- and cheese-topped square. Gently press pastry around onion-and-cheese filling to seal. Use a pizza cutter to slice into 25 pastry bites. Use a fork to press edges of each to seal in filling.
6. Place pastry bites about 2 inches apart on a baking sheet lined with parchment paper. Lightly brush each with egg, and sprinkle with salt and pepper.
7. Bake in preheated oven until golden brown and puffed, 12 to 15 minutes. Remove from oven; let cool 15 minutes before serving. (Unbaked bites can be made ahead, covered, and refrigerated up to 2 days or frozen up to 2 weeks ahead;

bake at 375°F for 15 to 20 minutes.) Serve the puff pastry bites with Dijon and grainy mustards on the side for dipping.

Apple, Celery, and Romaine Salad with Pancetta and Blue Cheese

ACTIVE 15 MIN. - TOTAL 15 MIN.
SERVES 8

- 1 head romaine lettuce, stripped of tough outside leaves, roughly chopped (6 cups)
- 8 celery stalks, whites to leafy greens, thinly sliced (about 3½ cups)
- 1 Granny Smith apple, thinly sliced
- 4 oz. cubed pancetta, browned, plus 1½ Tbsp. reserved drippings
- 2 oz. blue cheese, crumbled (about ½ cup)
- 3 Tbsp. fresh lemon juice (from 1 lemon)
- 2 Tbsp. finely chopped red onion
- 1 tsp. Dijon mustard
- ¾ tsp. freshly cracked black pepper, divided
- ½ tsp. flaky sea salt, divided
- 3 Tbsp. olive oil

1. Combine lettuce, celery, and apple in a large bowl. Reserve 3 tablespoons each of pancetta and blue cheese. Add remaining pancetta and blue cheese to lettuce mixture.
2. Combine fresh lemon juice, red onion, mustard, reserved pancetta drippings, ½ teaspoon of the pepper, and ¼ teaspoon of the salt in a small jar with a lid. Place lid on jar, and shake well to combine, about 30 seconds.
3. Add olive oil to jar. Place lid on jar, and shake until emulsified. Pour dressing over salad, and toss to combine. Sprinkle salad with reserved pancetta and blue cheese and remaining ¼ teaspoon each salt and pepper. Serve immediately.

Crowd-Pleasing Pot Pies

Instead of making a traditional roast turkey, Wilson likes to surprise everyone with single-serving (but filling!) turkey pot pies topped with dressing. A 6-inch cast-iron skillet is just the right size and also helps the crust bake up nice and crisp. If your Friendsgiving celebration falls after Thanksgiving, these pot pies are a great way to use up leftover turkey, vegetables, and herbs from the big holiday meal.

Mini Turkey Pot Pies with Dressing Tops

ACTIVE 1 HOUR - TOTAL 3 HOURS, 15 MIN.
SERVES 8

CRUST
- **3 ¾ cups all-purpose flour plus more for work surface**
- **1 ½ tsp. sea salt**
- **1 ½ cups cold unsalted butter, cut into cubes**
- **1 cup cold whole buttermilk**

FILLING
- **6 Tbsp. unsalted butter, divided**
- **½ cup all-purpose flour**
- **2 cups chicken stock**
- **1 ¾ cups whole milk**
- **1 ½ tsp. sea salt**
- **¾ tsp. freshly cracked black pepper**
- **1 yellow onion, finely chopped (about 1 ¼ cups)**
- **2 garlic cloves, minced (about 2 tsp.)**
- **1 ½ cups thinly sliced peeled carrots (from 4 carrots)**
- **1 ½ cups sliced fresh green beans**
- **1 cup frozen green peas, thawed**
- **1 Tbsp. chopped fresh thyme leaves**
- **1 Tbsp. chopped fresh sage leaves**
- **2 lb. cooked turkey breast, chopped (about 4 heaping cups)**

TOPPING
- **3 cups water**
- **½ cup unsalted butter**
- **2 (6-oz.) pkg. stuffing mix (such as Stove Top)**

EQUIPMENT
- **8 (6-inch) cast-iron skillets**

1. Prepare the Crust: Whisk together flour and salt in a medium bowl. Add cold cubed butter, and use your fingers to quickly work butter into flour mixture. (Some butter pieces will be the size of oat flakes, and some will be the size of peas.) Create a well in flour mixture, and pour in cold buttermilk. Use a fork to bring dough together, moistening all flour bits. Dump dough mixture onto a lightly floured work surface. Dough will be moist and shaggy. Divide dough in 2 pieces, and gently knead each piece into a disk. Wrap each disk in plastic wrap, and chill 1 hour.
2. Meanwhile, prepare the Filling: Melt 4 tablespoons of the butter in a large saucepan over medium. Whisk in flour, and cook, whisking constantly, about 1 minute (mixture will be very thick). Reduce heat to low; gradually add chicken stock, whisking constantly until no flour bits remain. Whisk in milk. Increase heat to medium-low; cook, whisking often, until mixture is consistency of thick pudding, about 20 minutes. Remove from heat, and whisk in salt and pepper; set aside.
3. Melt remaining 2 tablespoons butter in a large skillet over medium. Add onion; cook, stirring constantly, until translucent, about 3 minutes. Add garlic; cook, stirring constantly, 1 minute. Add carrots and green beans; cook, stirring occasionally, 5 minutes (vegetables will not be cooked through). Stir in peas, thyme, and sage; cook 1 minute. Remove from heat, and stir in turkey. Stir turkey-vegetable mixture into stock mixture in saucepan; cool slightly, about 5 minutes.
4. Prepare the Topping: Bring water and butter to a boil in a large saucepan over medium, stirring occasionally to melt butter. Add stuffing mix, and gently stir to combine. Cover and remove from heat. Let stand 10 minutes.
5. Remove 1 pie dough disk from refrigerator. Unwrap and roll dough into a ¼-inch-thick round on a lightly floured surface. Cut an 8-inch circle from a piece of parchment paper. Use parchment round as a guide to cut 8-inch rounds from piecrust using a sharp knife. Fit 1 piecrust round in bottom and up sides of each skillet. Repeat with remaining dough disk, rerolling scraps as needed, until all 8 skillets are lined.
6. Preheat oven to 375°F, and place racks in lower and upper third of oven. Spoon about 1 ½ cups Filling into each Crust; cover with about ¾ cup Topping. Bake in preheated oven until Crust is golden brown and Filling is lightly bubbling, 45 to 50 minutes, rotating skillets halfway through baking. Remove from oven, and let stand 20 minutes before serving.

Mashed Potato Bar

ACTIVE 25 MIN. - TOTAL 45 MIN.
SERVES 8

- **4 lb. russet potatoes, peeled and cut into quarters**
- **¾ cup unsalted butter, softened, plus more for serving**
- **4 oz. cream cheese, softened**
- **½ cup chicken stock**
- **½ cup whole milk, divided**
- **1 Tbsp. sea salt**
- **1 tsp. freshly cracked black pepper**
- **Sour cream**
- **Chopped fresh chives**
- **Shredded Cheddar cheese**
- **Crisp cooked bacon, crumbled**

1. Place potatoes in a large pot, and add cold tap water to cover. Bring to a boil over medium-high, and cook, undisturbed, until potatoes are tender, about 20 minutes.
2. Drain and return hot potatoes to pot. Immediately add butter, cream cheese, stock, and ⅓ cup of the milk. Use a potato masher to blend ingredients together. Add salt and pepper. Stir in remaining milk as necessary to reach desired consistency. Preheat oven to 250°F. Transfer mashed potatoes to a 4-quart baking dish; cover with aluminum foil, and keep warm in preheated oven until ready to serve. (Potatoes can be made up to 2 days ahead and reheated, covered, just before serving. Stir in more butter and milk if potatoes seem dry after reheating.)
3. Place sour cream, chives, cheese, bacon, and butter in small bowls; serve alongside warm potatoes.

Pumpkin Layer Cake with Caramel-Cream Cheese Frosting

ACTIVE 50 MIN. - TOTAL 8 HOURS, 10 MIN. (INCLUDING ABOUT 6 HOURS CHILLING)

SERVES 10 TO 12

CARAMEL

- ½ cup granulated sugar
- 2 Tbsp. water
- 2 Tbsp. light corn syrup
- ⅓ cup heavy cream
- 2 Tbsp. unsalted butter, softened
- ½ tsp. sea salt

CAKE LAYERS

- 2 ½ cups all-purpose flour plus more for dusting pan
- 1 cup granulated sugar
- ¾ cup packed brown sugar
- 2 tsp. pumpkin pie spice
- 2 tsp. baking powder
- 1 tsp. baking soda
- 1 tsp. sea salt
- 1 ¼ cups canned pumpkin
- 1 cup whole buttermilk
- ½ cup canola oil
- ½ cup water
- 2 large eggs
- 2 tsp. vanilla extract

FROSTING

- 1 (8-oz.) pkg. cream cheese, softened
- ½ cup unsalted butter, softened
- 4 cups powdered sugar
- 2 Tbsp. heavy cream
- 2 tsp. vanilla extract
- ¼ tsp. sea salt

1. Prepare the Caramel: Bring sugar, water, and corn syrup to a boil in a medium saucepan over medium, stirring once or twice. Continue to cook, without stirring, until mixture is a medium amber color, 8 to 9 minutes. Remove from heat, and immediately add heavy cream and butter (mixture will boil and foam). Whisk until well blended, and whisk in salt. Transfer to a bowl, cover with plastic wrap, and chill until cold, about 4 hours.

2. Meanwhile, prepare the Cake Layers: Place oven rack in center of oven; preheat oven to 350°F. Coat 2 (9-inch) round baking pans with cooking spray; lightly dust bottoms and sides of pans with flour.

3. Sift together flour, sugars, pumpkin pie spice, baking powder, baking soda, and salt in a large bowl. Whisk together pumpkin, buttermilk, oil, water, eggs, and vanilla in a medium bowl until well combined. Add pumpkin mixture to flour mixture; whisk gently until just blended but no lumps remain. Divide batter between prepared pans. Bake in preheated oven until a toothpick inserted in center comes out clean or with a few moist crumbs, 20 to 25 minutes. Cool Cake Layers in pans 20 minutes, and transfer from pans to a wire rack. Cool completely, about 1 hour.

4. Prepare the Frosting: Beat cream cheese in bowl of a stand mixer fitted with paddle attachment on low speed until softened, about 1 minute. Add butter and beat on medium speed until creamy, about 1 minute. Add powdered sugar, heavy cream, vanilla, and salt. Beat on low until incorporated; increase speed to medium until combined and thick but still spreadable, about 2 minutes. Chill 30 to 45 minutes before assembling cake.

5. Place 1 Cake Layer, top side up, on a cake plate. Dollop with about ½ cup of the Frosting, and spread evenly. Top with second Cake Layer, top side up, and dollop with another ½ cup of Frosting. Spread top and sides with a thin layer of Frosting. Chill 20 minutes. Take Caramel out of refrigerator, and let stand 20 minutes.

6. Generously swirl Caramel into remaining Frosting, keeping swirls large in mixture. Spread along top and sides of cake in a few swoops so it looks rustic. Chill 1 hour before slicing and serving.

Let's Talk (Smoking) Turkey

Start a new tradition that will free up your oven and result in a moist, juicy bird

FEW YEARS AGO, my mother called me about five days before Thanksgiving and got right to the point: "Honey, we have 30 people coming over, and I need you to smoke the turkey. I got a 20-pound bird, and my oven is going to be taken up with casseroles. I know you'll do a beautiful job." Obviously, I couldn't tell her no, so I began researching some smoked-turkey recipes—and tried not to panic.

My father started smoking turkeys for Thanksgiving years ago (he liked to fry them, too, but that's another story), and this method became popular with Mom for a few reasons. One, it gave her an extra oven. Two, it gave the men a reason to go outside. And three, it always resulted in moist, flavorful meat.

Back then, Dad was using a simple bullet smoker, but these days, there are lots of options, from a Big Green Egg to an Oklahoma Joe's. The keys to success are the same for all of them—season the bird well, use indirect heat, maintain a consistent cooking temperature, and generate smoke from a hardwood like cherry or hickory. And be sure to give yourself plenty of time, because it can take a while. Smoking a turkey means you'll be getting up early, but it's worth it.

Thanks to some research and tips from the *Southern Living* Test Kitchen, my smoked turkey was a big hit with the family that year, and now I've done it a few times, tweaking the recipe along the way.

I know most of you are going to roast a bird the old-fashioned way, and there's nothing wrong with that. But if your mother—or insert family member here—calls you in a panic about oven space, we've got you covered.

—**Sid Evans**

Herb-Rubbed Smoked Turkey

ACTIVE 30 MIN. - TOTAL 15 HOURS, 40 MIN.
SERVES 10

- **3 Tbsp. kosher salt**
- **3 Tbsp. dark brown sugar**
- **2 tsp. dried thyme**
- **2 tsp. dried rosemary, chopped**
- **2 tsp. rubbed sage**
- **1½ tsp. black pepper**
- **1 tsp. garlic powder**
- **1 (12- to 14-lb.) whole fresh or frozen turkey, thawed**
- **½ cup unsalted butter, softened**
- **3 cups hickory chips**

1. Stir together salt, brown sugar, thyme, rosemary, sage, black pepper, and garlic powder in a small bowl; set aside herb rub.
2. Remove giblets and neck from turkey; reserve for another use. Pat turkey dry with paper towels. Reserve 1 tablespoon herb rub for Step 3. Rub 1 tablespoon herb rub inside cavity, and sprinkle outside of turkey with remaining amount; massage into skin. Chill, uncovered, 10 to 24 hours.
3. Stir together butter and reserved 1 tablespoon herb rub. Loosen skin from turkey breast without totally detaching it; spread butter mixture under skin. Replace skin, securing with wooden picks. Tie ends of legs together with kitchen twine, tuck wing tips under, and let stand at room temperature 30 minutes.
4. Meanwhile, prepare charcoal fire in smoker according to manufacturer's instructions, bringing internal temperature to 225°F to 235°F. Maintain temperature inside smoker 15 to 20 minutes. Place hickory chips on coals. Smoke turkey, breast side up, covered with smoker lid, until a thermometer inserted in thickest portion of turkey registers 155°F, 5 to 6 hours.
5. Remove turkey from smoker, cover loosely with heavy-duty aluminum foil, and let stand 20 minutes before slicing.

Cajun Smoked Turkey

Stir together 3 Tbsp. **kosher salt;** 3 Tbsp. **light brown sugar;** 2 tsp. each **paprika, dried oregano,** and **cayenne pepper;** and 1 tsp. **garlic powder** in a small bowl to make Cajun rub. Prepare the recipe as directed, substituting Cajun rub for the herb rub.

3 MORE RULES FOR SMOKED TURKEY

BRINE, AND THEN BUTTER

For the most flavor, dry-brine the turkey with the rub, and refrigerate to dry the skin. Then add a layer of butter, mixed with more rub, under the skin.

DON'T SOAK THE CHIPS

Wet chips smolder over a long period of time, over-smoking the turkey. Dry chips burn instantly and die down as it cooks, giving the right amount of smoke.

PULL IT EARLY

Turkey is safe to eat when it reaches 165°F. Remove it from the smoker at 155°F, and tent with foil. It will continue to cook as it rests and will remain moist.

It's Called Dressing, Not Stuffing

Every family believes it has the best recipe for this dish. One *Southern Living* editor says we're all wrong

by **VALERIE FRASER LUESSE**

WHENEVER MY MOTHER assembles the women in the family to plan a holiday gathering, Aunt Grace gets an "of course"—as in, "Of course, Grace will make the dressing." Nobody makes better cornbread dressing than my Aunt Grace. Nobody. Not even your mama. As for my mama? I refuse to answer on the grounds that she might never make her championship fried chicken and potato salad for me again.

I guess all Southern families have their kitchen divas—women who have that one dish (or two or three) that nobody can touch. My Aunt Vivian was the family cake baker, famous especially for her chocolate, lemon cheese, and pound cakes. Aunt Joyce taught me to make her baked beans (which I finally mastered), but I've never been brave enough to attempt her peach cobbler or candied sweet potatoes. Aunt Patsy made the only congealed salad I've ever liked and the best butter beans I've ever tasted. Mama's divinity, lemon icebox pie, and banana pudding are *it*, I'm here to tell you. As for cornbread dressing? It belongs to Aunt Grace. Period. No contest. Close the recipe box.

"Nobody makes better cornbread dressing than my Aunt Grace. Nobody. Not even your mama."

Once I got serious about dressing, I booked a lesson in her kitchen, where she tutored me in the fine art of her silky smooth, ultra-moist recipe. (She explained that I should serve it in a baking dish, as a side to the turkey. It would not be stuffed anywhere.) Aunt Grace's son, Stanley, was our official taster, dipping a spoon to judge the balance of seasonings as we added each of them a little bit at a time.

I took down copious notes. Those pages, covered with hastily scribbled reminders ("Aunt Grace says to heat the soups and toast the breads"), are now spattered and smeared with cream of chicken soup because I'm still not confident enough to fly solo—even after successfully producing several batches on my own.

The recipe on the following page will get you close to Aunt Grace's dressing. Why just close? Because time spent in the kitchen with her is the secret ingredient for the real deal.

Aunt Grace says to always make a big batch. You can freeze what you don't use.

Trust us. The variety of breads gives this dressing its silky texture.

Aunt Grace's Famous Cornbread Dressing

ACTIVE 40 MIN. - TOTAL 10 HOURS

SERVES 24

- **2 (6-oz.) pkg. unsweetened cornbread mix (such as Martha White)**
- **1 (16.3-oz.) can refrigerated biscuits (such as Pillsbury Grands!)**
- **7 white sandwich bread slices, toasted**
- **6 hamburger buns, toasted**
- **1 cup unsalted butter**
- **4 cups finely chopped yellow onions (from 2 medium onions)**
- **4 cups finely chopped celery (from 1 large bunch celery)**
- **8 cups chicken broth**
- **3 (10.5-oz.) cans condensed cream of chicken soup**
- **1 (10.5-oz.) can condensed cream of celery soup**
- **1 Tbsp. poultry seasoning**
- **1 Tbsp. ground sage**
- **6 large eggs, beaten**

1. Prepare cornbread and biscuits according to package directions. Let cool, and crumble into a large bowl. Tear toasted bread slices and hamburger buns into small pieces, and add to cornbread-biscuit mixture. Combine with hands to break breads into small pieces.

2. Melt butter in a large saucepan over medium-high. Add onions and celery to pan, and cook, stirring occasionally, until softened and onions are translucent, about 10 minutes. Stir in chicken broth, cream of chicken soup, cream of celery soup, poultry seasoning, and sage. Bring broth-soup mixture to a boil, and pour over breads, stirring to combine. Let cool 20 minutes, stirring occasionally. Add eggs, stirring well to combine. Divide mixture evenly between 2 (9- x 13-inch) baking dishes. Cover and refrigerate overnight.

3. Preheat oven to 350°F. Uncover baking dishes, bring to room temperature, and bake in preheated oven until top is browned and middle is set, about 1 hour.

For smoother dressing, use the edge of a wooden spoon to break up the breads.

Season to taste, but add spices a little at a time, tasting after each addition.

The mixture should look slightly soupy before you slide it into the oven.

Pass the Gravy

The really good stuff is simple, smooth, and made from scratch

AH, THANKSGIVING—our national day of gratitude and gravy. Even when a Southern holiday table is a groaning board, it depends upon more than just the turkey. If the entire meal is stellar, excellent gravy is the crowning glory. And if things go wrong in the kitchen, it's the balm that can soothe (not to mention moisten and camouflage) any shortcomings in the rest of the menu.

Gravy isn't difficult to prepare, but it has a reputation for being intimidating, perhaps because it's often the last thing made and is rushed to the table moments before everyone gathers to eat. When hot pans, hungry guests, and the anticipated dishes are zipping in and out of the kitchen, it's challenging for any cook to focus on getting the gravy just right.

The smartest strategy is to make it ahead in stages, as time allows. Knock out the broth weeks in advance, and then whisk the gravy together a few days before, so the only thing left to do on November 22 is to warm it up and stir in the finishing touches.

Great gravy stands on the shoulders of made-from-scratch turkey broth, which can be prepared and stored in the refrigerator up to three days before T-Day or stashed in the freezer for up to three months. One of the easiest culinary luxuries is homemade broth. It has body and soul, and no other ingredient is more essential to the gravy's flavor.

Prep the gravy up to three days in advance. Heat it up and add the final ingredients moments before it hits the table.

Relying on a robust broth instead of roasting-pan drippings means that you are free to grill, smoke, or deep-fry the bird. It also means you can double or triple the recipe to make as much as you need, instead of only what you can glean from a small turkey or a lean breast. This ensures plenty for a large crowd or for carefully planned leftovers.

While guests understand that some other components of the Thanksgiving spread might need to be store-bought, good homemade gravy is liquid gold—there's just no substitute.

3 ESSENTIALS TO GOOD GRAVY

STOCK

It might seem odd to use store-bought stock in a homemade broth, but it immediately boosts flavor.

FLOUR

Instant-blending flour (such as Wondra) dissolves quickly and smoothly for the silkiest results.

SPIRITS

A splash of spirits (sherry, bourbon, or Madeira) adds a subtle but distinct taste and aroma.

Rich Turkey Broth

ACTIVE 20 MIN. - TOTAL 4 HOURS
MAKES 8 CUPS

Place 6 lb. **turkey wings;** 2 large **onions,** cut into chunks; 4 large **carrots,** cut into chunks; 4 **celery stalks,** cut into chunks; 2 Tbsp. **apple cider vinegar;** 1 tsp. **kosher salt;** ½ tsp. **black peppercorns;** 2 large **thyme sprigs;** and 2 **bay leaves** in a large stockpot. Add 12 cups store-bought **turkey stock,** chicken stock, or water. Bring to a boil over medium-high; reduce heat to low, and cook, uncovered, at a bare simmer until wings fall apart, about 2 hours. Strain and discard solids. Return strained broth to stockpot; simmer over medium-low until reduced to 8 cups, about 1 hour. (The broth should be golden brown and taste like turkey soup.) Transfer to a large metal or plastic bowl; place bowl on top of a separate large bowl filled with ice. Let stand, stirring occasionally, until broth cools to room temperature, about 30 minutes. Store, covered, in refrigerator up to 3 days, or divide into 2 (1-quart) containers and freeze up to 3 months.

Make-Ahead Gravy

ACTIVE 15 MIN. - TOTAL 45 MIN.
MAKES ABOUT 4 ½ CUPS

Melt ¼ cup **butter** or bacon fat in a large saucepan over medium-high until sizzling, 1 to 2 minutes. Sprinkle with ¼ cup **instant-blending flour,** whisking until smooth. Cook, whisking constantly, 2 minutes. (Flour will brown; if it starts to burn, reduce heat as needed.) Add 4 cups warmed **Rich Turkey Broth** (recipe above) in a slow, steady stream, whisking constantly. Cook, whisking often, until gravy comes to a simmer and thickens, 6 to 9 minutes. Remove from heat; cool 30 minutes. Pour into a bowl or jar; cover and refrigerate up to 3 days. To serve, reheat gravy over low. Stir in 2 Tbsp. **heavy cream;** 2 Tbsp. (1 oz.) **sherry,** bourbon, or Madeira; 1 Tbsp. **fresh thyme leaves;** ¾ tsp. **black pepper;** and ½ tsp. **kosher salt.**

Respect the Relish Tray

For our Test Kitchen Director, it wouldn't be Thanksgiving without this Southern appetizer. Here's his take on the classic

Round out the spread with store-bought pickled cherry peppers, olives, and okra. Halve the okra pods lengthwise, and wrap them in prosciutto or country ham.

SOMETHING TANGY

Pickled Beets

Trim ends of 1 ½ lb. small **red beets,** leaving roots and 1-inch stems; scrub with a brush. Place in a medium saucepan with water to cover; bring to a boil over high. Cover, reduce heat to medium, and simmer until tender, about 45 minutes. Drain and rinse with cold water, and drain completely. Cool 5 minutes. Trim roots, and rub off skins. Cut beets into ¼-inch-thick slices, and place in a large bowl. Stir together 1 cup each **apple cider vinegar** and **water;** ½ cup each **sugar** and thinly sliced **red onion;** 2 tsp. **dried thyme;** and 1 tsp. each **kosher salt, dried oregano,** and **black peppercorns** in a medium saucepan. Bring to a boil over medium-high, stirring to dissolve sugar and salt. Pour hot liquid over beets; cover and chill at least 4 hours or up to overnight.

ACTIVE 20 MIN. - TOTAL 5 HOURS
SERVES 10

SOMETHING CREAMY

Cream Cheese-Walnut Stuffed Celery

Cut each of 5 **celery stalks** into 2 (3-inch) pieces. Stir together 8 oz. softened **cream cheese,** ½ cup chopped toasted **walnuts,** 1 Tbsp. **honey,** ¼ tsp. **kosher salt,** and ⅛ tsp. **ground cinnamon** until well blended. Spoon mixture into a piping bag or a ziplock plastic bag with a ½-inch corner cut off, and pipe into celery pieces. Sprinkle with 1 Tbsp. thinly sliced **fresh chives,** and serve immediately. Or cover and chill until ready to serve.

ACTIVE 10 MIN. - TOTAL 10 MIN.
SERVES 10

SOMETHING SPICY

Fiery Pickled Carrots

Trim tops of 1 lb. small **carrots** to ½ inch; place carrots in a medium saucepan with water to cover, and bring to a boil over high. Reduce heat to medium, and simmer just until tender, 8 to 10 minutes. Drain and rinse with cold water; drain completely, and place in a large bowl. Stir together 1 ½ cups **white vinegar,** 1 cup **water,** ¼ cup **sugar,** 1 ½ tsp. **kosher salt,** 1 tsp. each **onion powder** and **crushed red pepper,** and ½ tsp. **mustard seeds** in a medium saucepan. Bring to a boil over medium-high, stirring to dissolve sugar and salt. Pour hot liquid over carrots; cover and chill at least 4 hours or up to overnight.

ACTIVE 10 MIN. - TOTAL 4 HOURS, 10 MIN.
SERVES 10

Here Come the Casseroles

Green Bean Casserole with Crispy Leeks, page 256

What happens when you break out the 13- by 9-inch dish for the holiday? Something spectacular. Dig into these six crowd-pleasers

Corn Pudding,
page 256

Broccoli-Cheese
Casserole, page 256

Brussels Sprouts with Bacon and Shallots, page 257

Hasselback Sweet Potato Casserole

ACTIVE 30 MIN. - TOTAL 1 HOUR, 45 MIN.
SERVES 12

- 3 ½ lb. sweet potatoes
- 2 cups heavy cream
- ⅛ tsp. black pepper
- 4 Tbsp. light brown sugar, divided
- 1 ½ tsp. kosher salt, divided
- ½ cup all-purpose flour
- 3 Tbsp. unsalted butter, melted
- ⅓ cup chopped hazelnuts

1. Peel and cut sweet potatoes into ⅛-inch-thick slices, using a mandoline or a knife. Bring a large pot of water to a boil over high. Add sweet potato slices, and cook until slightly softened, 3 to 4 minutes. Drain and spread in a single layer on a paper towel-lined baking sheet. Let potatoes stand until cool and dry, about 20 minutes. Arrange slices, standing vertically on edges, in a lightly greased 13- x 9-inch broiler-proof baking dish.
2. Bring cream to a simmer in a medium saucepan over medium. Whisk in black pepper, 2 tablespoons of the brown sugar, and 1 teaspoon of the salt. Cook, stirring occasionally, until thickened slightly, about 10 minutes. Pour over potatoes. Cover and chill until ready to bake, up to 1 day ahead.
3. Stir together flour, butter, remaining 2 tablespoons brown sugar, and remaining ½ teaspoon salt in a small bowl. Stir in hazelnuts, and set aside.
4. Preheat oven to 350°F. Remove casserole from refrigerator while oven preheats. Bake, covered, 45 minutes. Uncover and top evenly with hazelnut mixture. Return to oven, and bake 15 minutes. Increase oven temperature to broil, and broil until topping is golden brown, about 5 minutes. Let stand 10 minutes before serving.

Hasselback Sweet Potato Casserole

Green Bean Casserole with Crispy Leeks

ACTIVE 1 HOUR, 15 MIN. - TOTAL 2 HOURS
SERVES 10

- 3 lb. green beans, trimmed and halved crosswise
- 2 Tbsp. olive oil
- 1 cup chopped yellow onion (from 1 large onion)
- 1 Tbsp. minced garlic (about 3 garlic cloves)
- ¼ cup dry white wine
- ¼ cup all-purpose flour
- 2 cups whole milk
- ½ (8-oz.) pkg. cream cheese, softened
- 1 ½ tsp. kosher salt
- ½ tsp. black pepper
- ⅛ tsp. freshly ground nutmeg
- 2 medium leeks (about 1 ½ lb.)
- 1 cup canola oil

1. Bring a large pot of water to a boil over high. Add green beans; return to a boil, and cook 2 minutes. Drain green beans, and rinse under cold running water to cool. Spread in a single layer on paper towels to drain. Let stand at room temperature until completely dry, about 45 minutes.
2. Meanwhile, heat olive oil in a large skillet. Add onion, and cook, stirring often, until softened, about 8 minutes. Add garlic and wine, and cook until most of the wine evaporates, about 2 minutes. Sprinkle flour over onion mixture, and cook, stirring constantly, 1 minute. Add milk, and bring to a simmer, stirring constantly. Cook, stirring constantly, until thickened, about 2 minutes. Stir in cream cheese, salt, pepper, and nutmeg until smooth.
3. Transfer green beans to a lightly greased 13- x 9-inch baking dish. Pour milk mixture evenly over green beans, and stir to coat. Spread in an even layer; cover with aluminum foil. Chill until ready to bake, up to 1 day ahead.
4. Preheat oven to 350°F. Remove casserole from refrigerator while oven preheats. Bake, covered, until hot and bubbly around the edges, about 1 hour.
5. While beans bake, cut leeks in half lengthwise; cut each half into 2- to 3-inch pieces. Thinly slice into long strips (about 2 cups thin strips). Heat canola oil in a small saucepan over medium-high to 350°F. Fry leeks in hot oil, in 2 to 3 batches, until golden, 1 to 2 minutes per batch. Remove with a slotted spoon, and drain on paper towels. Sprinkle fried leeks over hot casserole just before serving.

Corn Pudding

ACTIVE 20 MIN. - TOTAL 1 HOUR, 15 MIN.
SERVES 10

- 4 large eggs
- 2 ½ cups half-and-half
- 2 (15-oz.) pkg. frozen corn, thawed
- 8 oz. fontina or Swiss cheese, shredded (about 2 cups)
- ½ cup grated yellow onion (from 1 large onion)
- 6 Tbsp. all-purpose flour
- 2 tsp. minced garlic (about 2 garlic cloves)
- 2 Tbsp. chopped fresh chives plus more for garnish
- 1 Tbsp. chopped fresh thyme plus more for garnish
- 2 tsp. kosher salt
- 1 tsp. black pepper

1. Whisk together eggs and half-and-half in a large bowl. Pulse corn, in 2 batches, in a food processor until coarsely chopped, about 5 times. Add to egg mixture along with cheese, grated onion, flour, garlic, chives, thyme, salt, and pepper. Stir to combine. Transfer to a lightly greased 13- x 9-inch baking dish; cover and chill until ready to bake, up to 1 day ahead.
2. Preheat oven to 350°F. Remove casserole from refrigerator while oven preheats. Bake, uncovered, until golden and bubbly around edges and center is just set, about 45 minutes. Let stand 10 minutes before serving. Garnish with thyme and chives.

Broccoli-Cheese Casserole

ACTIVE 45 MIN. - TOTAL 2 HOURS
SERVES 10

- 2 (12-oz.) pkg. fresh broccoli florets
- ¼ cup water
- 4 Tbsp. unsalted butter, divided
- 1 cup chopped yellow onion (from 1 medium onion)
- 2 tsp. chopped garlic (about 2 garlic cloves)
- ¼ cup all-purpose flour

- 2 cups whole milk
- ½ cup mayonnaise
- 1 Tbsp. Dijon mustard
- 1½ tsp. kosher salt
- 1 tsp. black pepper
- 8 oz. sharp Cheddar cheese, shredded (about 2 cups)
- 1½ cups crushed rectangular buttery crackers (about 40; such as Club)
- 2 Tbsp. chopped fresh flat-leaf parsley

1. Place broccoli and water in a large microwavable bowl. Cover loosely with plastic wrap, and microwave on HIGH until tender, about 8 minutes. Set aside.
2. Melt 3 tablespoons of the butter in a Dutch oven over medium-high. Add onion, and cook, stirring occasionally, until softened, about 5 minutes. Add garlic, and cook, stirring occasionally, 1 minute. Sprinkle flour evenly over onion mixture, and cook, stirring constantly, 1 minute. Whisk in milk, and cook, stirring constantly, until thickened, about 2 minutes. Reduce heat to medium, and whisk in mayonnaise, mustard, salt, and pepper until smooth. Add cheese, and stir until melted and smooth. Add broccoli, and stir to coat. Transfer to a lightly greased 13- x 9-inch broiler-proof baking dish, and cool to room temperature, about 30 minutes. Cover with aluminum foil, and chill until ready to bake, up to 1 day ahead.
3. Preheat oven to 350°F. Remove casserole from refrigerator while oven preheats. Bake, covered, until hot and bubbly, about 1 hour.
4. Place remaining 1 tablespoon butter in a medium-size microwavable bowl, and microwave on HIGH until melted, about 15 seconds. Add crackers and parsley, and stir to combine. Sprinkle evenly over casserole. Increase oven temperature to broil on HIGH, and broil casserole until top is golden brown, about 1 minute. Let stand 10 minutes before serving.

Cheesy Potato Casserole

ACTIVE 20 MIN. - TOTAL 2 HOURS, 25 MIN.
SERVES 12

- 3 lb. russet potatoes, peeled and cut into 1-inch pieces (about 9 small potatoes)
- 1 Tbsp. plus 2 tsp. kosher salt, divided
- 6 large egg yolks, at room temperature
- 1 cup heavy cream, at room temperature

Cheesy Potato Casserole

- ¼ cup unsalted butter, melted
- 8 oz. white Cheddar cheese, shredded (about 2 cups)
- 2 oz. Parmesan cheese, grated (about ½ cup)
- ½ tsp. ground white pepper

1. Place potatoes and 1 tablespoon of the salt in a Dutch oven with water to cover by 1 inch. Bring to a boil over high, and cook until potatoes can be pierced easily with a knife, about 15 minutes. Remove from heat. Drain well, and return potatoes to Dutch oven. Mash potatoes with a potato ricer or potato masher until very smooth. Stir in egg yolks, 1 at a time. Stir in cream, butter, both cheeses, white pepper, and remaining 2 teaspoons salt until smooth. (Cheese may not melt completely.) Transfer mixture to a lightly greased 13- x 9-inch broiler-proof baking dish, and let cool to room temperature, about 1 hour. While potatoes are still soft, smooth top with an offset spatula or create a decorative pattern with a spoon, if desired. Cover with aluminum foil, and chill until ready to bake, up to 1 day ahead.
2. Preheat oven to 350°F. Remove casserole from refrigerator while oven preheats. Bake, covered, until heated through, about 45 minutes. Uncover and bake 15 minutes. Increase oven temperature to broil on HIGH, and broil until topping is browned, 3 to 4 minutes.

Brussels Sprouts with Bacon and Shallots

ACTIVE 45 MIN. - TOTAL 1 HOUR, 25 MIN.
SERVES 10

- 4 thick-cut bacon slices
- 2 small shallots, chopped (about ¼ cup)
- 2 tsp. minced garlic (about 2 garlic cloves)
- 3 Tbsp. sherry vinegar
- 3 lb. fresh Brussels sprouts, halved (about 10 cups)
- 2 Tbsp. canola oil
- 1½ tsp. kosher salt, divided
- ¾ tsp. black pepper, divided
- ½ cup panko (Japanese-style breadcrumbs)
- 1 Tbsp. unsalted butter, melted

1. Cook bacon in a large skillet over medium, turning occasionally, until browned and crisp, about 10 minutes. Transfer to a plate lined with paper towels; reserve drippings in skillet.
2. Add shallots to hot drippings, and cook over medium, stirring often, until shallots are softened and start to brown, about 8 minutes. Add garlic, and cook, stirring often, 1 minute. Add vinegar, and cook until thick and syrupy, about 2 minutes. Remove from heat, and pour into a small microwavable bowl. Crumble bacon, and stir into shallot mixture. Cool to room temperature, cover, and chill until ready to use, up to 1 day ahead.
3. Preheat oven to 400°F. Toss Brussels sprouts with canola oil, 1 teaspoon of the salt, and ½ teaspoon of the pepper. Transfer to 2 aluminum foil-lined rimmed baking sheets. Roast Brussels sprouts in preheated oven until golden and tender, about 25 minutes, stirring halfway through baking. Set aside for up to 1 hour.
4. Combine breadcrumbs, melted butter, and remaining ½ teaspoon salt and ¼ teaspoon pepper in a small bowl. Set aside.
5. Microwave bacon-shallot mixture on MEDIUM (50% power) until mixture can be stirred, about 30 seconds. Toss roasted Brussels sprouts with bacon-shallot mixture, and transfer to a lightly greased 13- x 9-inch baking dish. Sprinkle evenly with breadcrumb mixture, and bake at 400°F until heated through and breadcrumbs are golden brown, about 15 minutes. Let stand 10 minutes before serving.

Old Faithfuls

Apple. Pumpkin. Pecan. All eyes are on this trio displayed on mama's sideboard. To celebrate the season, We asked three of the South's most beloved bakeries to share their best versions of our favorites. The results are a sweet reminder of what we've always known: You can't beat the classics

Back in the Day Bakery Southern Pumpkin Pie, page 261

Buxton Hall Ultimate Apple Pie, page 260

Oxbow Bakery Pecan Pie, page 259

David and Becky Wolfe at Oxbow Bakery

BECKY WOLFE NEEDED one more draw that would encourage customers to stay a spell longer at her Palestine, Texas, antiques store. "That's when I thought: Pies!" she says. She made one coconut and one chocolate and set them out on the counter. The slices quickly disappeared, and (soon after) so did the antiques. Today, with the help of her son and co-owner David, Becky sells pies exclusively. Though they're open only Thursday through Saturday, they bake between 60 and 100 each day in their mule barn turned country store in Old Town Palestine.

Born and raised in the restaurant business, Becky credits her parents with teaching her to "use the best," a lesson that she and her son carry almost 45 miles up State 155 to the Sam's Club in Tyler, the closest store that stocks the shortening brand responsible for that crispy Oxbow Bakery crust. David estimates that 60% of their business comes from out of town–and even from outside of Texas. "A lady from Houston just grabbed me and hugged me with tears in her eyes," says Becky. "She said she hadn't had pie like this since her mother passed."

Oxbow Bakery Pecan Pie

ACTIVE 30 MIN. - TOTAL 4 HOURS, 45 MIN.

SERVES 8

PIECRUST

- ½ tsp. salt
- ¼ cup plus 1 to 2 Tbsp. ice water, if needed
- 2 cups all-purpose flour plus more for work surface
- 10 Tbsp. vegetable shortening
- 1 large egg, lightly beaten

FILLING

- 6 Tbsp. unsalted butter
- 1 cup plus 2 Tbsp. granulated sugar
- 1 cup plus 2 Tbsp. light corn syrup
- 4 extra-large eggs, beaten
- 1 tsp. vanilla extract
- ⅜ tsp. salt
- 2 cups chopped pecans

1. Prepare the Piecrust: Place salt and ¼ cup of the water in a glass measuring cup. Stir to dissolve salt; chill 30 minutes.

2. Place flour in a large bowl. Cut in shortening, using a pastry blender, until crumbly. Drizzle cold salted water over flour mixture. Toss lightly with a fork until dough comes together, adding 1 to 2 tablespoons ice water, if needed.

3. Form dough into a disk. Wrap with plastic wrap, and chill 30 minutes.

4. Preheat oven to 425°F. Roll dough disk into a 14-inch circle on a lightly floured surface. Carefully transfer to a 9½-inch deep-dish pie plate, and press into bottom and up sides of pie plate. Trim Piecrust, leaving about 1 inch around edges; reserve dough scraps. Fold edges under and crimp. Bake in preheated oven just until crust is set, about 4 minutes. Let cool 2 to 3 minutes on a wire rack, and fill in any cracks with leftover dough scraps so there are no openings in any of the crust. Cool 30 minutes. Brush lightly with beaten egg. Reduce oven temperature to 350°F.

5. Prepare the Filling: Melt butter in a medium saucepan over medium. Add sugar, and cook, stirring occasionally, until mixture starts bubbling, 3 to 4 minutes. Add corn syrup, and cook, stirring occasionally, until mixture starts bubbling, 3 to 4 minutes.

6. Remove from heat, and cool 5 minutes. Slowly whisk about 1 cup hot mixture into beaten eggs; slowly whisk beaten egg mixture back into hot sugar mixture, and whisk until thoroughly incorporated. Whisk in vanilla and salt. Stir in pecans.

7. Pour Filling into cooled crust. Bake at 350°F until pie is cooked through and set in the middle, 40 to 45 minutes. Cover edges with aluminum foil after 30 to 35 minutes to prevent overbrowning. (The center will rise a little at the end but will settle when cooled.) Let cool completely (about 2 hours) before slicing.

WHEN CUSTOMERS WALK through the door of Buxton Hall Barbecue in Asheville, North Carolina, they are not only greeted by the sweet smell of smoke from whole hogs cooking over oak and hickory but also by "the pie table" showcasing the current desserts. Ashley Capps, the pastry chef behind the restaurant's in-house Buxton Hall Bakery, crowns the long table's vintage stands with flavors like Bourbon Chocolate Chess and her sellout hit, Banana Pudding Pie. With a background in both pastry making and fine art, Capps looks at the ingredients she and her team use—like leaf lard rendered from the barbecued pork or apples from a local orchard—with the eye of a painter and a sculptor. "Making desserts is poetic, artistic, and meaningful," she says. Even though the bakery has more than 150 orders for Thanksgiving alone, Capps says, "Every piece of pie we send out is like a tiny piece of art."

Buxton Hall Ultimate Apple Pie

ACTIVE 30 MIN. - TOTAL 8 HOURS, 15 MIN.
SERVES 8

FLAKY PIE DOUGH

- **6 Tbsp. unsalted butter**
- **2 ⅓ cups all-purpose flour plus more for dusting**
- **⅔ cup whole-wheat pastry flour**
- **½ tsp. kosher salt**
- **10 Tbsp. cold unsalted butter, cut into small pieces**
- **½ cup cold whole buttermilk plus 2 to 3 Tbsp. more, if needed**

FILLING

- **3 lb. mixed apples (such as Winesap, Mutsu, Granny Smith, and Honeycrisp), cored, peeled, and cut into ½-inch-thick slices (about 6 apples)**
- **4 oz. dried apples, coarsely chopped**
- **¼ cup unsalted butter**
- **¼ cup apple butter**
- **3 Tbsp. fresh lemon juice (from 2 lemons)**
- **1 tsp. orange zest (from 1 orange)**
- **½ tsp. grated fresh ginger**
- **½ tsp. vanilla extract**
- **¼ tsp. ground cinnamon**
- **⅛ tsp. ground nutmeg**
- **⅛ tsp. ground cloves**
- **⅛ tsp. ground cardamom**
- **2 cups packed light brown sugar**
- **¼ cup all-purpose flour**
- **½ tsp. kosher salt**

ADDITIONAL INGREDIENTS

- **1 large egg, lightly beaten**
- **1 ½ Tbsp. demerara sugar**

1. Prepare the Flaky Pie Dough: Line a small metal or plastic bowl with aluminum foil. Place 6 tablespoons butter in a small heavy saucepan; cook over medium, stirring constantly, until butter begins to turn golden brown, 6 to 8 minutes. Remove from heat; immediately pour butter into prepared bowl. Freeze until butter has solidified, about 1 hour. Lift foil from bowl; remove foil from butter, and cut into small pieces.
2. Stir together flours and salt in a medium bowl. Sprinkle browned butter pieces and cold butter pieces over flour mixture. (Do not mix into flour.) Place bowl in freezer 10 minutes.
3. Remove from freezer. Using your hands, pinch and smear butter pieces into the flour mixture to evenly distribute. (Return bowl to freezer for 10 minutes if butters begin to soften.)
4. Add ½ cup cold buttermilk, and stir just until dough begins to come together, stirring in more buttermilk, 1 tablespoon at a time, if needed. Dough should be dry and formed into a mass; pieces of butter should be visible.
5. Divide dough in half. Press each half into a round, flat disk; wrap in plastic wrap, and refrigerate until thoroughly chilled, at least 1 hour.
6. Remove 1 dough disk from refrigerator and unwrap. Roll dough into a 13-inch circle on a lightly floured surface. Fit dough into a 9-inch pie plate, making sure dough is evenly draped with no stretching or pockets. Place pie plate in refrigerator.
7. Remove remaining dough disk from refrigerator and unwrap. Roll dough to ⅛-inch thickness on lightly floured parchment paper. Cut into about 8 (1-inch-wide) strips. Transfer dough strips, with parchment paper, onto a large plate or baking sheet, and chill until ready.
8. Prepare the Filling: Stir together apple slices, dried apples, butter, and apple butter in a large skillet. Cook apple mixture over medium-high, stirring often, until apples are tender-crisp, 10 to 15 minutes. Remove from heat. Add lemon juice, orange zest, grated ginger, and vanilla. Gently stir to combine. Sprinkle cinnamon, nutmeg, cloves, and cardamom over apple mixture, and gently stir to combine. Sprinkle with brown sugar, flour, and salt, and gently stir to combine.
9. Spoon Filling into chilled pie shell. Arrange dough strips in a lattice pattern on top. Trim excess dough, and discard. Press edges with a fork or crimp by pinching with your fingers to make a decorative pattern. Freeze 20 minutes.
10. Preheat oven to 425°F. Brush crust with beaten egg, and sprinkle lightly with demerara sugar. Bake in preheated oven 15 minutes; reduce oven temperature to 350°F, and bake until Filling is bubbly and crust is golden brown, about 45 more minutes. Cover pie with aluminum foil after 30 minutes to prevent overbrowning. Let cool completely (4 to 6 hours) before slicing.

Ashley Capps at Buxton Hall Barbecue

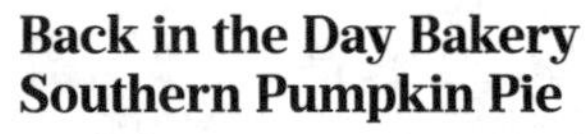

AS A GIRL GROWING UP in Los Angeles, Cheryl Day unearthed her Southern roots by way of pie. Day watched her mother, Janie Queen, stir spices into pureed sweet potatoes and hand-whip egg whites into a mighty meringue to stand atop a lemon custard made from their backyard citrus. "I lost my mom when I was 22," says Day. "That time in the kitchen with her was invaluable. It was our opportunity to talk, and she would tell me stories about growing up in the South. Pie was our thing."

Pie is still Day's thing at Back in the Day Bakery, which she currently runs with her husband, Griffith, in Savannah. Around Thanksgiving, they stock their cases with different varieties like Salted Caramel Apple and Cranberry-Orange Crumble. After the pickup rush is done (350 pies later!), she begins cooking her own Turkey Day dinner and returns to the flavors of her childhood: sweet potato (which is an easy swap in her pumpkin pie recipe) and lemon meringue. She enjoys sharing these memories of her mother with family, friends, and any "Sugarnauts" (her nickname for bakery employees) in need of a home for the holiday.

Cheryl Day at Back in the Day Bakery

Back in the Day Bakery Southern Pumpkin Pie

ACTIVE 30 MIN. - TOTAL 6 HOURS, 15 MIN.
SERVES 8

EXTRA-FLAKY CRUST

- **2 ½ cups all-purpose flour plus more for work surface**
- **1 Tbsp. granulated sugar**
- **1 tsp. baking powder**
- **1 tsp. fine sea salt**
- **1 cup cold unsalted butter, cut into ½-inch cubes**
- **1 Tbsp. apple cider vinegar**
- **½ cup ice water plus 2 to 3 Tbsp., if needed**
- **1 large egg, lightly beaten**
- **2 Tbsp. demerara sugar**

FILLING

- **2 cups canned pumpkin**
- **1 cup heavy cream**
- **3 large eggs, lightly beaten**
- **2 Tbsp. pure cane syrup or sorghum syrup**
- **½ cup granulated sugar**
- **½ cup light brown sugar**
- **1 tsp. ground cinnamon**
- **1 tsp. vanilla extract**
- **½ tsp. fine sea salt**
- **¼ tsp. ground cardamom**
- **¼ tsp. ground cloves**
- **¼ tsp. ground ginger**

1. Prepare the Extra-Flaky Crust: Whisk together flour, granulated sugar, baking powder, and salt in a medium bowl. Cut in butter using a pastry blender. Stir together vinegar and ½ cup ice water; drizzle over flour mixture, and stir lightly with a fork until flour is moistened. (If dough seems dry, add ice water, 1 to 2 tablespoons at a time, until a small piece of dough mostly holds together when slightly pressed.)

2. Turn dough out onto a lightly floured work surface, and gather into a tight mound. Using the heel of your hand and working from side to side, smear dough by pushing away from you a little at a time and working your way down the mass of dough, creating flat layers. Once complete, use a dough scraper to bring both short ends of dough up and over, folding so ends meet in the middle and creating 2 layers. Repeat smearing-and-folding process once.

3. Divide dough in half; shape each half into a flat disk. Wrap disks in plastic wrap, and chill at least 1 hour or up to overnight.

4. Remove chilled dough disks from refrigerator; let stand at room temperature 10 to 15 minutes. Place 1 dough disk on a lightly floured surface; dust top of dough with flour. Using a lightly floured rolling pin, roll disk into a 12-inch circle (2 to 3 inches larger than pie plate and about ⅛ inch thick). Repeat process with second disk.

5. Fit 1 piecrust into a 9-inch pie plate. Trim dough to allow about 1 ½ inches of excess to extend over sides. Reserve scraps. Fold dough edges under and crimp. Cover with plastic wrap, and chill at least 30 minutes or up to 3 days, or freeze for up to 1 month.

6. Cut designs, using small leaf-shaped cookie cutters, from reserved scraps of dough and remaining dough round. Place leaf cutouts on a parchment paper-lined baking sheet, and chill 30 minutes.

7. Preheat oven to 400°F. Line chilled pie shell with aluminum foil or parchment paper; fill with dried beans or pie weights. Bake in preheated oven until edges are very lightly browned, 10 to 15 minutes. Remove foil and beans; return to oven. Continue baking until lightly golden, about 10 more minutes. Cool completely on a wire rack, about 30 minutes.

8. Brush leaf cutouts with egg; sprinkle with demerara sugar. Bake at 400°F until golden, 8 to 10 minutes. Set aside. Reduce oven temperature to 350°F.

9. Prepare the Filling: Whisk together all Filling ingredients in a large bowl. Pour into cooled crust. Bake at 350°F until Filling is firm around edges but still jiggles slightly in center, 45 to 50 minutes. Cover edges with foil after 35 minutes, if needed, to prevent overbrowning. Cool completely, about 3 hours. (Filling will continue to firm up as it cools.) Decorate with baked leaf cutouts.

"Look What Aunt Lisa Brought!"

Three sensational desserts that (dare we say it?) could upstage the pumpkin pie

Butterscotch-Spice Trifle, page 263

Pumpkin-Spice Magic Cake

Silky flan teams up with moist pumpkin-spice cake and buttery caramel sauce in one incredible confection that's inspired by chocoflan, a Mexican dessert. While this treat isn't difficult to make, our Test Kitchen recommends using a light-colored Bundt pan to achieve the best results. A darker pan may get too hot and overbake the cake.

ACTIVE 25 MIN. - TOTAL 2 HOURS, 40 MIN.
SERVES 12

CAKE
- **½ cup butter, softened**
- **½ cup granulated sugar**
- **½ cup packed light brown sugar**
- **1 large egg, at room temperature**
- **2 ¼ cups all-purpose flour**
- **1 tsp. pumpkin pie spice**
- **¾ tsp. baking powder**
- **¾ tsp. baking soda**
- **¼ tsp. salt**
- **½ cup canned pumpkin**
- **⅓ cup whole buttermilk**
- **1 tsp. vanilla extract**
- **½ cup jarred cajeta (Mexican caramel sauce) or caramel sauce, divided**

FLAN
- **1 (14-oz.) can sweetened condensed milk**
- **1 (12-oz.) can evaporated milk**
- **4 oz. cream cheese, softened**
- **3 large eggs**
- **1 Tbsp. vanilla extract**

ADDITIONAL INGREDIENTS
- **⅓ cup chopped toasted pecans**
- **Cajeta (Mexican caramel sauce) or caramel sauce, for serving**

1. Prepare the Cake: Fill a large roasting pan with hot water to a depth of 2 inches; place on rack in lower third of oven. Preheat oven to 350°F. Generously coat a 14-cup light-colored Bundt pan with cooking spray.
2. Beat butter, granulated sugar, and brown sugar in bowl of a heavy-duty stand mixer on medium speed until light and fluffy, about 3 minutes. Add egg; beat just until blended. Sift together flour, pumpkin pie spice, baking powder, baking soda, and salt in a bowl. Whisk together pumpkin, buttermilk, and vanilla in a separate bowl. Add flour mixture to butter mixture alternately with pumpkin mixture, beginning and ending with flour mixture, beating on low speed after each addition (batter will be thick).
3. Evenly pour ¼ cup of the cajeta into prepared Bundt pan. Gently spoon batter over cajeta; smooth top of batter. Set aside.
4. Prepare the Flan: Place condensed milk, evaporated milk, cream cheese, eggs, and vanilla in a blender. Process on high speed until completely combined, about 30 seconds, stopping to scrape down sides as needed. Pour mixture over batter in Bundt pan. Cover loosely with aluminum foil.
5. Carefully remove roasting pan with hot water from preheated oven. (Water should be steaming when removed from oven.) Gently place Bundt pan in prepared roasting pan, and return to oven. Bake at 350°F until a wooden pick inserted in center comes out clean, 1 hour and 30 minutes to 1 hour and 45 minutes, rotating Bundt pan halfway through bake time.
6. Remove Bundt pan from roasting pan; transfer to a wire rack to cool until slightly warm, about 45 minutes. Gently invert onto a rimmed serving plate. Spoon remaining ¼ cup cajeta over top; sprinkle with pecans. Serve additional cajeta on the side.

Pumpkin-Spice Magic Cake

Butterscotch-Spice Trifle

Thin layers of spice cake give the old-fashioned trifle a modern look, but you can cut the cake into cubes if you like. Make the dessert a day ahead, and top with whipped cream before serving.

ACTIVE 50 MIN. - TOTAL 11 HOURS, 10 MIN., INCLUDING 8 HOURS CHILLING
SERVES 12

BUTTERSCOTCH CUSTARD
- **¾ cup packed light brown sugar**
- **¼ cup cornstarch**
- **¼ tsp. salt**
- **2 ½ cups half-and-half**
- **4 large egg yolks**
- **3 Tbsp. butter**
- **2 tsp. vanilla extract**

SPICE CAKE
- **1 cup butter, softened**
- **2 cups granulated sugar**
- **3 large eggs**
- **3 ¼ cups all-purpose flour plus more for pans**
- **1 tsp. baking soda**
- **1 tsp. ground cinnamon**
- **½ tsp. ground allspice**
- **½ tsp. salt**
- **¼ tsp. ground cloves**
- **1 ½ cups whole buttermilk**
- **1 tsp. vanilla extract**

VANILLA WHIPPED CREAM
- **3 cups heavy cream**
- **2 tsp. vanilla extract**
- **½ cup plus 2 Tbsp. unsifted powdered sugar**

ADDITIONAL INGREDIENTS
- **1 cup heavy cream**
- **Ground cinnamon**

1. Prepare the Butterscotch Custard: Whisk together brown sugar, cornstarch, and salt in a large heavy saucepan. Whisk together half-and-half and egg yolks in a 4-cup glass measuring cup. Gradually whisk half-and-half mixture into brown sugar mixture. Cook over medium, whisking constantly, until mixture just begins to bubble, 8 to 10 minutes. Simmer, whisking constantly, 1 minute. Remove from heat; whisk in butter and vanilla until butter is melted. Spoon mixture into a bowl; place plastic wrap directly on top of mixture in bowl (to prevent a film from forming). Set aside to cool to room temperature, about 30 minutes. Chill at least 4 hours or up to 24 hours. (While Butterscotch Custard chills, prepare the Spice Cake and Vanilla Whipped Cream.)

2. Prepare the Spice Cake: Lightly coat 3 (8-inch) round cake pans with cooking spray, and dust with flour. Preheat oven to 350°F. Beat butter in bowl of a heavy-duty stand mixer on medium speed until creamy, about 2 minutes. Gradually add sugar, beating until light and fluffy, about 4 minutes. Add eggs, 1 at a time, beating until just blended after each addition. Stir together flour, baking soda, cinnamon, allspice, salt, and cloves in a bowl; add to butter mixture alternately with buttermilk, beginning and ending with flour mixture, beating on low speed until just blended after each addition. Add vanilla; beat on low speed until just blended. Pour batter evenly into prepared cake pans.

3. Bake cake layers in preheated oven until a wooden pick inserted in centers comes out clean, about 25 minutes. Cool cake layers in pans on wire racks 10 minutes. Remove from pans, and transfer to wire racks to cool completely, about 1 hour.

4. Prepare the Vanilla Whipped Cream: Beat cream and vanilla in bowl of a heavy-duty stand mixer fitted with whisk attachment on high speed until foamy, about 1 minute. With mixer running, gradually add powdered sugar; beat until stiff peaks form, 1 to 2 minutes. Cover and chill until ready to assemble trifle.

5. Assemble the trifle: Beat 1 cup heavy cream with an electric mixer on high speed until stiff peaks form, about 2 minutes. (Do not overbeat.) Gently fold into chilled custard. Horizontally slice ⅛ to ¼ inch off the tops of each cooled cake layer using a serrated knife, creating an even, flat surface. Place 1 cake layer, cut side up, in an 18-cup trifle dish. (You will need to slightly push it into place to fit in bottom of dish.) Top cake layer with one-third of the custard mixture (about 1⅓ cups); top custard with 1⅓ cups whipped cream. Top whipped cream with 1 cake layer; repeat layering process with 1⅓ cups custard and 1⅓ cups whipped cream. Top with third cake layer and then with remaining custard. (Cover and refrigerate remaining Vanilla Whipped Cream until ready to serve.)

6. Cover assembled trifle; chill at least 4 hours or up to 24 hours. To serve, dollop remaining whipped cream over top. Sprinkle with ground cinnamon.

Fudge Layer Cake with Caramel Buttercream

The trick to mastering this dessert's deliciously messy look? Let it spend a short spell in the freezer to allow the ganache to set over the cake layers so the buttercream can be spread on top of it. Make sure there is enough space in your freezer before assembling.

ACTIVE 1 HOUR - TOTAL 3 HOURS, 10 MIN.
SERVES 16

FUDGE CAKE

- **1½ cups bittersweet chocolate chips**
- **½ cup butter, softened**
- **1 (1-lb.) pkg. light brown sugar**
- **3 large eggs**
- **2 cups all-purpose flour plus more for pans**
- **1 tsp. baking soda**
- **½ tsp. salt**
- **½ tsp. ground cinnamon**
- **1 (8-oz.) container sour cream**
- **1 cup strong brewed coffee, hot**
- **1 Tbsp. (½ oz.) bourbon**

CARAMEL BUTTERCREAM

- **1 cup granulated sugar**
- **⅓ cup water**
- **⅓ cup heavy cream**
- **¼ cup butter, chilled and cut into ½-inch pieces**
- **1 cup butter, softened**
- **4 oz. cream cheese, softened**
- **½ tsp. vanilla extract**
- **¼ tsp. salt**
- **4 cups unsifted powdered sugar, divided**

CHOCOLATE GANACHE

- **8 oz. semisweet baking chocolate (2 [4-oz.] baking chocolate bars), chopped**
- **6 oz. bittersweet baking chocolate (from 2 [4-oz.] baking chocolate bars), chopped**
- **1½ cups heavy cream**

ADDITIONAL INGREDIENTS

Shaved bittersweet chocolate

1. Prepare the Fudge Cake: Coat 2 (9-inch) square cake pans with cooking spray; lightly dust with flour. Preheat oven to 350°F. Place chocolate chips in a microwavable bowl; microwave on MEDIUM (50% power) until melted, about 2 minutes, stopping to stir every 30 seconds. Stir melted chocolate until completely smooth.

2. Beat butter and brown sugar in bowl of a heavy-duty stand mixer on medium speed until well combined, about 5 minutes. Add eggs, 1 at a time, beating until just combined after each addition. Add melted chocolate, beating until just combined.

3. Sift together flour, baking soda, salt, and cinnamon in a bowl. Gradually add to melted-chocolate mixture alternately with sour cream, beginning and ending with flour mixture, beating on low speed until just blended after each addition. Gradually add coffee, beating on low speed until just blended. Stir in bourbon. Pour batter evenly into prepared cake pans.

4. Bake cake layers in preheated oven until a wooden pick inserted in centers comes out clean, 22 to 25 minutes. Cool in pans on wire racks 10 minutes. Remove cake layers from pans; transfer to wire racks to cool completely, about 1 hour.

5. Prepare the Caramel Buttercream: Place granulated sugar and water in a small saucepan; cook, stirring often, over medium-high, until sugar dissolves, about 1 minute. Bring to a boil over medium-high. Cook, without stirring but swirling pan occasionally, until mixture is deep amber in color, about 10 minutes. Remove from heat; quickly add cream in a thin, steady stream, stirring constantly with a wooden spoon. Stir in chilled butter until mixture is smooth. Transfer caramel to a small bowl to cool completely, about 1 hour.

6. Beat softened butter and cream cheese in bowl of a heavy-duty stand mixer on medium speed until creamy, 3 minutes. Stir in vanilla and salt. Gradually add 2 cups of the powdered sugar, beating on low speed until smooth, 2 minutes. Add cooled caramel; beat on medium speed until combined, 2 minutes. Gradually add remaining 2 cups powdered sugar, beating on low speed until combined.

7. Prepare the Chocolate Ganache: Place semisweet and bittersweet baking chocolates and cream in a microwavable bowl; microwave on MEDIUM (50% power) for 1 minute. Remove and stir. Microwave until melted, 3 to 3½ minutes, stopping to stir every 30 seconds.

8. Assemble the cake: Place 1 cooled cake layer on a serving platter; pour half of ganache over top, allowing some to drip down sides. Freeze until just set, about 5 minutes. Dollop with half of buttercream; spread gently to edges of cake layer. Top with remaining cake layer; repeat process with remaining ganache and buttercream. Garnish with shaved chocolate.

Fudge Layer Cake with
Caramel Buttercream, page 264

Make the Best Sandwich of the Year

Four delicious ways to gobble up leftovers

Turkey and Pimiento Cheese Club Sandwich

MAKES 1 SANDWICH

Cook 2 slices **thick-cut bacon** in a small skillet over medium until crisp, turning occasionally, 8 minutes. Drain on paper towels. Spread 1 Tbsp. **mayonnaise** each over 2 slices **multigrain bread.** Top first bread slice with 2 slices **tomato,** 2 **Bibb lettuce leaves,** and bacon; cover with second slice of bread, mayonnaise side down. Top second slice of bread with 2 ½ oz. sliced **roasted turkey.** Spread 3 Tbsp. **pimiento cheese** on third slice **multigrain bread,** and place on top of turkey (pimiento cheese side down) to make a sandwich. Cut into triangles, and secure with toothpicks. Serve immediately.

PAIR WITH

Dill Pickle Flavored Potato Chips; *goldenflake.com*

Turkey, Caramelized Onion, and Gruyère Grilled Cheese

MAKES 1 SANDWICH

Spread 2 tsp. **whole-grain mustard** on 1 slice **sourdough bread;** top with ⅓ cup shredded **Gruyère cheese,** 2 ½ oz. sliced **roasted turkey,** ¼ cup **caramelized sweet onion,** and an additional ⅓ cup shredded **Gruyère cheese.** Cover with second slice of **sourdough bread** to make a sandwich. Melt 2 Tbsp. **unsalted butter** in a small skillet over medium until beginning to foam. Add sandwich to skillet, and cook until first side is browned, about 2 minutes. Flip sandwich, and cover pan with aluminum foil. Cook until cheese is melted and second side is browned, about 2 more minutes. Serve immediately.

PAIR WITH

Sour Cream & Creole Onion chips; *zapps.com*

Turkey, Apple, and Brie Sandwich

MAKES 1 SANDWICH

Preheat oven to 400°F. Place 1 **ciabatta roll,** halved horizontally, on a baking sheet. Spread bottom half with 2 tsp. **hot pepper jelly.** Place 2 ½ oz. sliced **roasted turkey,** 3 slices **Gala apple,** and 1 oz. **Brie cheese** (sliced into ½-inch-thick pieces) on top of jelly. Bake in preheated oven until Brie melts and top half of roll is light golden brown, about 3 minutes. Remove from oven, and place ½ oz. **baby arugula** on top of Brie. Brush top half of roll with 1 tsp. **Dijon mustard,** and place on top of arugula to make a sandwich. Serve hot or at room temperature.

PAIR WITH

Sweet Potato with Sea Salt chips; *terrachips.com*

Turkey, Pesto, and Fresh Mozzarella Sandwich

MAKES 1 SANDWICH

Cut ⅓ of a French **baguette** in half horizontally. Spread 3 Tbsp. **pesto** evenly over cut sides of baguette. Layer 2 ½ oz. sliced **roasted turkey,** 4 sliced **pickled cherry peppers,** and 2 oz. **fresh mozzarella** (torn into large pieces) on bottom of baguette. Replace baguette top to make a sandwich. Cut in half, if desired. Serve immediately.

PAIR WITH

Rosemary & Olive Oil Kettle Cooked Potato Chips; *deepriver-snacks.com*

Chili for a Crowd

Consider dinner on November 23 covered. This comforting one-pot dish is made with yesterday's turkey and will feed a full house

Secret Ingredient Fine yellow cornmeal thickens the chili and also adds a hint of toasty flavor.

Slow-Cooker White Chili with Turkey

ACTIVE 15 MIN. - TOTAL 7 HOURS, 25 MIN.
SERVES 8

- **2 cooked turkey bones (such as leg or breast bones from leftover turkey), meat removed**
- **2 cups dried great Northern beans, rinsed**
- **½ cup chopped poblano chile (about 1 medium chile)**
- **1 tsp. ground cumin**
- **½ tsp. garlic powder**
- **8 cups chicken stock or turkey stock**
- **2 cups shredded cooked turkey meat (1-inch pieces)**
- **2 (4-oz.) cans chopped green chiles, drained**
- **2 Tbsp. fine yellow cornmeal**
- **1½ tsp. kosher salt**
- **1 cup frozen corn kernels**
- **1 cup sour cream, divided**
- **1 jalapeño chile, minced**
- **½ cup loosely packed fresh cilantro leaves**
- **4 oz. sharp white Cheddar cheese, shredded (about 1 cup)**

1. Place turkey bones, beans, chopped poblano, cumin, garlic powder, and stock in a 5- to 6-quart slow cooker. Cover and cook on LOW until beans are tender, about 7 hours.

2. Remove bones and 1½ cups cooked beans from slow cooker. Discard bones, and coarsely mash beans with a fork or potato masher. Return mashed beans to slow cooker; add turkey meat, chopped green chiles, cornmeal, and salt. Stir to combine; cover and cook on LOW until thickened, about 10 minutes. Add corn kernels and ½ cup of the sour cream, stirring to combine. Serve chili topped with jalapeño, cilantro leaves, cheese, and remaining ½ cup sour cream.

TRY THIS TWIST!
Southwest Stew: Use a mix of red and green chiles—a combo referred to as "Christmas" in the Southwest.

COOKING SL SCHOOL

TIPS AND TRICKS FROM THE SOUTH'S MOST TRUSTED KITCHEN

Bake a nutty piecrust

START WITH

Refrigerated Pie Dough

Dust work surface with **powdered sugar.** Unroll **dough;** place on top of sugar. Sprinkle evenly with ⅓ cup toasted, finely chopped **pecans.** Gently roll over dough with a rolling pin. Place in a pie plate; bake as directed.

Make a tangy relish

START WITH

Jellied Cranberry Sauce

Whisk 1 can **cranberry sauce** with ½ cup toasted chopped **walnuts,** ½ tsp. **fresh orange zest,** and 2 tsp. each **fresh orange** and **lemon juices** in a medium bowl until combined.

Top your casserole with a crunchy layer

START WITH

Herb-Seasoned Stuffing Mix

Process 2 cups dry **stuffing mix** in a food processor until coarsely ground. Combine with ¼ cup melted **unsalted butter** in a bowl. Use as a topping for green bean casserole or scalloped potatoes; bake as directed.

Update your bread basket

START WITH

Frozen Rolls

Stir together 2 tsp. **seeds** (such as sesame, fennel, or caraway) and a pinch of **garlic powder** in a bowl. In a second bowl, whisk 1 **egg white** until foamy. Brush tops of **frozen rolls** with beaten egg white, and sprinkle with seed mixture. Bake as directed.

"For fast turkey and dumplings, cut 6-inch flour tortillas into 1-inch-wide strips, drop into simmering broth, and add shredded turkey."

—Pam Lolley
Test Kitchen Professional

December

270 **Simply Spectacular** Super-simple recipes created to impress

289 **Merry Christmas, Sugar!** Festive seasonal treats to savor or share

294 **Gingerbread Takes the Cake** Gingerbread cookies and houses endure, but this take on the quintessential holiday staple is destined to become a classic

302 **Peace of Cake** Check out our stunningly simple layer cake that anyone can make

SIMPLY SPECTACULAR

The best holiday recipes impress your friends and family without keeping you in the kitchen for hours. We created 12 festive yet delightfully easy dishes for every occasion on your calendar, from cookie swaps to Hanukkah dinner to Christmas morning breakfast.

1 Cheddar Shortbread Crackers, *page 285*
2 Bacon, Bourbon, and Benne Seed Shortbread Crackers, *page 285*
3 Pecan-and-Thyme Shortbread Crackers, *page 285*
4 Pimiento Cheese Shortbread Crackers, *page 285*

*

Skip the bottle of wine, and dazzle the party hosts with fancy **CHEDDAR CRACKERS**

Root Vegetable Fritters, page 286

*

This big-batch, no-effort **FRUIT BUTTER** is the go-to gift for leaving on your neighbors' porches

Slow-Cooker Cranberry-Pear Butter, page 285

Slow-Cooker Bolognese Sauce, page 286

*
Keep a full house of guests happy with this hearty **MAKE-AHEAD SUPPER**

*

Nobody will miss the marshmallows after digging into this goes-with-everything **SIDE DISH**

Savory Sweet Potato Casserole, page 287

*

The **BREAKFAST CASSEROLE** at the top of everyone's Christmas morning wish list

Make-Ahead Croissant Breakfast Casserole, page 286

Ombré Citrus Salad,
page 286

*
A fresh **FRUIT SALAD** that's Instagram-worthy and a cinch to bring to a potluck brunch

*
Even your mother-in-law will request the recipe for this incredible **HOLIDAY ROAST**

Pork Crown Roast, page 287

Cornmeal Crescent Rolls,
page 287

*

Frozen yeast rolls are not going to cut it on Meemaw's table. Make her proud with **HOMEMADE CRESCENTS**

Potato Puffs with Toppings, page 288

*

The New Year's Eve **PARTY APP** that can be dressed up or down for any crowd

*
A crowd-pleasing **PUNCH** that makes your cocktail party the talk of the town

Spicy Bourbon-Citrus Punch, page 285

*

Roll out this **FIVE-IN-ONE DOUGH** when you forget the cookie exchange is tonight. (Yikes!)

1 Chocolate-Peppermint Swirl Sandwich Cookies, *page 284*
2 Chocolate-Caramel Cookie Cups, *page 284*
3 Christmas Tree Bar Cookies, *page 284*
4 Mexican Hot Chocolate Cookies, *page 285*
5 Festive Dog Cookies, *page 284*

Chocolate Sugar Cookie Dough

ACTIVE 10 MIN. - TOTAL 2 HOURS, 10 MIN.

- ¾ cup unsalted butter, softened
- 1½ cups granulated sugar
- 2 large eggs
- 1 tsp. vanilla extract
- 2 cups all-purpose flour
- ¾ cup unsweetened cocoa
- 1 tsp. baking powder
- ¾ tsp. salt

1. Beat butter and sugar with a heavy-duty electric stand mixer on medium-high speed until light and fluffy, about 3 minutes. Add eggs and vanilla. Beat on medium until combined, stopping to scrape down sides of bowl as needed.

2. Stir together flour, cocoa, baking powder, and salt in a medium bowl. With mixer running on low speed, add flour mixture to butter mixture, beating until just incorporated.

3. Shape dough into a disk, wrap tightly in plastic wrap, and chill at least 2 hours or up to 2 days.

Christmas Tree Bar Cookies

ACTIVE 30 MIN. - TOTAL 3 HOURS, 55 MIN.
MAKES 1½ DOZEN COOKIES

Prepare **Chocolate Sugar Cookie Dough** as directed. Preheat oven to 350°F. Lightly grease an 8-inch square baking pan with cooking spray. Line bottom and sides of pan with parchment paper, allowing 2 to 3 inches to extend over 2 sides. Press chilled dough into an even layer in prepared pan. Bake in preheated oven until dry to the touch, about 22 minutes. Cool completely in pan on a wire rack, about 1 hour. Lift baked cookie dough from pan using parchment paper as handles; place on a cutting board. Beat ¼ cup softened, unsalted **butter** and 2 oz. softened **cream cheese** with a heavy-duty electric stand mixer on medium speed until creamy, 1 to 2 minutes. Reduce speed to low, and, with mixer running, gradually add 2 cups **powdered sugar,** beating until smooth. Add 1 Tbsp. **heavy cream** and ¼ tsp. **vanilla extract;** beat on medium-high speed until blended, about 20 seconds. Spread frosting on baked cookie dough; cut into 18 triangles. Sprinkle with **nonpareils.**

Festive Dog Cookies

ACTIVE 35 MIN. - TOTAL 4 HOURS, 45 MIN.
MAKES ABOUT 2 DOZEN (4-INCH) COOKIES

Prepare **Chocolate Sugar Cookie Dough** as directed. Preheat oven to 350°F. Roll chilled dough to ¼-inch thickness on a lightly floured surface. Cut with desired dog-shaped cutters, rerolling scraps as needed. (If dough becomes warm and sticky, place in refrigerator for 15 minutes.) Place cookies 2 inches apart on 2 parchment paper-lined baking sheets; chill 20 minutes. Bake in preheated oven until tops of cookies are dry to the touch, about 10 minutes. Cool on baking sheets 2 minutes. Transfer to a wire rack to cool completely, about 30 minutes. Meanwhile, beat 3 cups **powdered sugar,** ¼ cup warm **water,** and 1½ Tbsp. **meringue powder** with a heavy-duty electric stand mixer on medium speed until smooth and glossy, about 2 minutes. Add ¾ tsp. **vanilla extract** and ¼ tsp. **almond extract;** beat until combined, adding up to 2 Tbsp. **water,** 1 tsp. at a time, until desired consistency is reached. Divide frosting between 2 small bowls. Tint 1 bowl of frosting with desired amount of **red food coloring gel;** tint remaining bowl with desired amount of **green food coloring** gel. Decorate cookies with icing and **candy sprinkles.** Let dry completely, about 1 hour.

Chocolate-Peppermint Swirl Sandwich Cookies

ACTIVE 30 MIN. - TOTAL 3 HOURS, 5 MIN.
MAKES 2 DOZEN SANDWICH COOKIES

Prepare **Chocolate Sugar Cookie Dough** as directed in Step 1, substituting **light brown sugar** for granulated sugar. Melt 1 cup **semisweet chocolate chips** according to package directions; cool. Add to butter-sugar mixture; beat on low until blended. Proceed as directed in Step 2, reducing flour to 1½cups. Cover dough; chill 1 hour. Preheat oven to 350°F. Shape dough into 48 (1-inch) balls. Place ½ cup **sparkling sugar** in a shallow bowl. Roll each ball in sparkling sugar; place 2 inches apart onto 2 parchment paper-lined baking sheets. Gently flatten dough balls to ½-inch thickness. Bake in preheated oven until cookies are dry to the touch, about 8 minutes. Cool on baking sheets 2 minutes. Transfer cookies to a wire rack to cool completely, about 30 minutes. Meanwhile, beat ½ cup softened, **unsalted butter** and 4 oz. softened **cream cheese** with a heavy-duty electric stand mixer on medium speed until creamy, 1 to 2 minutes. Reduce speed to low, and, with mixer running, gradually add 4 cups **powdered sugar,** beating until smooth. Beat in 1½ Tbsp. **heavy cream,** ½ tsp. **vanilla extract,** and ¼ tsp. **peppermint extract.** Using a small food-safe paintbrush, paint 3 lengthwise stripes of **red food coloring gel** on the inside of a piping bag fitted with a large star tip. Fill bag with frosting. Pipe frosting onto half of cookies; sandwich with remaining cookies. Refrigerate 15 minutes before serving to firm up frosting.

Chocolate-Caramel Cookie Cups

ACTIVE 45 MIN. - TOTAL 3 HOURS, 50 MIN.
MAKES 40 COOKIE CUPS

Prepare **Chocolate Sugar Cookie Dough** as directed. Divide dough into 40 (1-Tbsp.) balls (about ½ oz. each). Place 1 ball in each cup of 2 (24-cup) lightly greased miniature muffin pans. Using a teaspoon measure, press dough into bottom and up sides of muffin cups. (You will only use 40 cups.) Chill 20 minutes. Preheat oven to 350°F. Bake in preheated oven until cookies are dry to the touch and shape is set, about 10 minutes. Immediately press cookies again with teaspoon. Cool cookie cups in pans on a wire rack 5 minutes. Transfer cookie cups to wire rack to cool completely, about 30 minutes. Meanwhile, beat ½ cup softened, **unsalted butter;** 4 oz. softened **cream cheese;** and 2 Tbsp. jarred **caramel sauce** or topping with a heavy-duty electric stand mixer on medium speed until creamy, 1 to 2 minutes. Reduce speed to low, and, with mixer running, gradually add 2½ cups **powdered sugar,** beating until smooth. Beat in ½ tsp. each **vanilla extract** and flaky **sea salt.** Transfer filling to a piping bag fitted with a large star tip; evenly pipe into cooled cookie cups. Drizzle about 1 tsp. jarred **caramel sauce** or topping on each filled cookie cup. Sprinkle each cookie with desired amount of flaky **sea salt;** top each with a toasted **pecan** half.

Mexican Hot Chocolate Cookies

ACTIVE 30 MIN. - TOTAL 2 HOURS, 45 MIN.
MAKES 2 DOZEN

Prepare **Chocolate Sugar Cookie Dough** as directed in Step 1, substituting **light brown sugar** for granulated sugar. Melt 1 cup **semisweet chocolate chips** according to package directions; cool. Add to butter-sugar mixture; beat on low until blended. Proceed as directed in Step 2, reducing flour to 1½ cups and adding 1 tsp. ground **cinnamon** and ¼ tsp. **cayenne** pepper to flour mixture. Cover dough; chill 1 hour. Meanwhile, cut 12 large **marshmallows** in half. Preheat oven to 350°F. Using a 1¾-inch scoop, drop dough 2 inches apart onto 2 parchment paper-lined baking sheets. Roll each into a ball; flatten to a ½-inch thickness. Bake in preheated oven until cookies are almost set, about 8 minutes. Increase heat to high broil, with oven rack 4 inches from heat. Top each cookie with 1 marshmallow half, cut side down. Broil until marshmallows are lightly browned, 1 to 2 minutes. Cool cookies on baking sheets 2 minutes. Transfer cookies to a wire rack. Sprinkle cookies evenly with ⅛ tsp. ground cinnamon and a pinch of cayenne pepper. Serve warm, or cool completely.

Cheddar Shortbread Crackers

ACTIVE 20 MIN. - TOTAL 2 HOURS
MAKES ABOUT 50

- **8 oz. extra-sharp white Cheddar cheese, finely shredded (about 2 cups)**
- **1 cup all-purpose flour**
- **½ cup fine plain white cornmeal**
- **1 Tbsp. cornstarch**
- **½ tsp. kosher salt**
- **½ tsp. dry mustard**
- **¼ tsp. black pepper**
- **½ cup cold unsalted butter, cut into ½-inch pieces**
- **3 Tbsp. water**

1. Process cheese, flour, cornmeal, cornstarch, salt, dry mustard, and pepper in a food processor until combined, about 5 seconds. Add butter; process until mixture resembles wet sand, about 20 seconds. With processor running, add water through food chute; process until dough forms a ball, 10 to 15 seconds.

2. Divide dough in half, and shape each half into a 6-inch log, about 1¾ inches in diameter. Wrap logs individually in plastic wrap; chill at least 1 hour or up to 2 days.

3. Preheat oven to 350°F with oven racks in upper and lower thirds. Unwrap logs, and slice into ⅛-inch-thick rounds. Place dough rounds, ½ inch apart, on 2 parchment paper-lined baking sheets.

4. Bake in preheated oven until edges are golden brown, about 14 minutes, rotating baking sheets top to bottom halfway through bake time. Cool crackers on baking sheets 5 minutes. Transfer to a wire rack to cool completely, about 20 minutes.

Pimiento Cheese Shortbread Crackers

Prepare recipe as directed through Step 1, substituting finely shredded sharp **yellow Cheddar cheese for extra-sharp** white Cheddar. Knead ¼ cup diced, well-drained **pimientos** and ¼ cup chopped fresh **chives** into dough. Proceed with recipe as directed in Steps 2 through 4.

Pecan-and-Thyme Shortbread Crackers

Prepare recipe as directed through Step 1. Knead ½ cup finely chopped toasted **pecans** and 1½ Tbsp. chopped fresh **thyme** into dough. Proceed with recipe as directed in Steps 2 through 4.

Bacon, Bourbon, and Benne Seed Shortbread Crackers

Prepare recipe as directed in Step 1, adding 1 Tbsp. **dark brown sugar** with cheese mixture and substituting **bourbon** for water. Knead ½ cup chopped cooked **bacon** into dough. Proceed with recipe as directed in Steps 2 and 3, rolling dough logs in ⅓ cup **benne seeds** before wrapping and chilling. Just before baking, sprinkle 2 Tbsp. **benne seeds** evenly over crackers. Proceed with recipe as directed in Step 4.

Spicy Bourbon-Citrus Punch

ACTIVE 20 MIN. - TOTAL 2 HOURS, 20 MIN.
SERVES 10

- **5 oz. fresh ginger, unpeeled and thinly sliced (from 1 [5-inch] piece)**
- **1 cup granulated sugar**
- **¾ cup water**
- **¼ tsp. kosher salt**
- **3 cups fresh orange juice (from 10 oranges)**
- **1½ cups (12 oz.) bourbon**
- **1½ cups sparkling mineral water (such as Topo Chico)**
- **¾ cup fresh lemon juice (from 6 lemons)**
- **Orange slices**

1. Combine ginger, sugar, water, and salt in a saucepan. Cook over medium, stirring occasionally, until sugar is dissolved, about 8 minutes. Remove from heat, and cool completely, about 2 hours. Pour through a fine wire-mesh strainer into a small glass measuring cup, discarding solids.

2. Combine orange juice, bourbon, sparkling water, lemon juice, ginger syrup, and orange slices in a large pitcher. Stir to combine. Serve over ice.

Slow-Cooker Cranberry-Pear Butter

ACTIVE 30 MIN. - TOTAL 9 HOURS, 30 MIN., PLUS 8 HOURS CHILLING
MAKES 16 (4-OZ.) JARS

- **4 lb. (9 to 10 medium-size) ripe Bartlett pears, peeled, cored, and chopped (about 9 cups)**
- **1 lb. (4 cups) fresh or frozen cranberries**
- **1½ cups granulated sugar**
- **½ cup apple cider**
- **2 Tbsp. fresh lemon juice (from 1 lemon)**
- **1 Tbsp. grated fresh ginger (from 2-inch piece)**
- **1 tsp. ground cinnamon**
- **¼ tsp. kosher salt**

1. Stir together all ingredients in a 6-quart slow cooker. Cover and cook on LOW until pears and cranberries are very soft, about 4 hours. Transfer mixture, in batches, to a blender. Remove center piece of blender lid (to allow steam to escape); secure lid on blender, and place a clean towel over opening in lid to avoid splatters. Process until smooth, about 1 minute. Transfer to a bowl. After processing all cranberry mixture, return all mixture to slow cooker.

2. Increase heat to HIGH, and cook, uncovered, stirring occasionally with a wooden spoon, until mixture has thickened, 2 ½ to 3 hours. Spoon mixture into 16 (4-ounce) jars, and let cool to room temperature, about 2 hours. Cover with jar lids, and chill overnight or up to 2 weeks.

Root Vegetable Fritters

ACTIVE 40 MIN. - TOTAL 40 MIN.
MAKES 20

- **2 medium (1 lb. total) russet potatoes, peeled and quartered lengthwise**
- **2 large carrots, peeled**
- **2 medium parsnips, peeled**
- **1 small yellow onion, cut into wedges**
- **⅓ cup all-purpose flour**
- **1 large egg, beaten**
- **2 tsp. kosher salt**
- **½ tsp. black pepper, plus more for topping**
- **½ tsp. baking powder**
- **Canola oil**
- **½ cup sour cream**
- **2 Tbsp. fresh dill sprigs**

1. Grate potatoes, carrots, parsnips, and onion in a food processor fitted with a large shredding blade. Transfer mixture to a clean dish towel, and squeeze well to remove excess liquid; discard liquid. Transfer potato mixture to a large bowl. Add flour, egg, salt, pepper, and baking powder; stir well.

2. Preheat oven to 200°F. Pour oil to a depth of about ⅓ inch in a large skillet; heat over medium-high. Working in batches, drop spoonfuls (about 2 ½ tablespoons each) of batter into skillet, leaving 2 inches between. Using back of spoon, gently flatten batter into disks. Cook, flipping once, until golden brown and crisp, 4 to 5 minutes. Place fritters on a plate lined with paper towels to drain. Transfer fritters to a wire rack set in a rimmed baking sheet; keep warm in preheated oven while frying remaining batches.

3. Arrange fritters on a serving platter; top evenly with sour cream and dill. Sprinkle with black pepper.

Ombré Citrus Salad

ACTIVE 15 MIN. - TOTAL 15 MIN.
SERVES 6

- **2 medium-size blood oranges, peeled and cut into ¼-inch rounds**
- **1 medium Cara Cara orange, peeled and cut into ¼-inch rounds**
- **1 medium-size Ruby Red grapefruit, peeled and cut into ¼-inch rounds**
- **1 medium navel orange, peeled and cut into ¼-inch rounds**
- **¾ cup pomegranate arils**
- **¼ cup toasted hazelnuts, coarsely chopped**
- **2 tsp. honey**
- **2 tsp. extra-virgin olive oil**
- **¾ tsp. flaky sea salt (such as Maldon)**
- **⅛ tsp. black pepper**
- **Fresh small mint leaves**

Arrange citrus rounds, slightly overlapping, on a serving platter, grouping colors from dark to light. Top with pomegranate arils and hazelnuts. Drizzle with honey and olive oil. Sprinkle evenly with sea salt and pepper. Garnish with mint.

Slow-Cooker Bolognese Sauce

ACTIVE 25 MIN. - TOTAL 6 HOURS, 25 MIN.
SERVES 12

- **1 lb. 90/10 lean ground beef**
- **12 oz. (3 links) hot Italian sausage, casings removed**
- **8 oz. diced pancetta (1 ½ cups)**
- **1 medium yellow onion, chopped (2 cups)**
- **2 celery stalks, chopped (1 cup)**
- **2 large carrots, chopped (1 ¼ cups)**
- **3 garlic cloves, chopped (about 1 Tbsp.)**
- **3 Tbsp. tomato paste**
- **½ cup dry red wine**
- **2 tsp. granulated sugar**
- **2 tsp. dried Italian seasoning**
- **1 ½ tsp. kosher salt**
- **½ tsp. black pepper**
- **1 fresh bay leaf**
- **2 (28-oz.) cans whole peeled tomatoes, drained and rinsed**
- **2 lb. uncooked ziti or penne pasta**
- **Freshly shaved Parmigiano-Reggiano cheese**
- **Fresh basil leaves**

1. Combine ground beef, sausage, and pancetta in a large skillet. Cook over medium-high, stirring to break into small pieces, until browned, about 8 minutes. Using a slotted spoon, transfer meat to a 6-quart slow cooker; reserve drippings in skillet.

2. Add onion, celery, and carrots to hot drippings; cook over medium-high, stirring occasionally, until tender, about 10 minutes. Add garlic and tomato paste; cook, stirring constantly, until fragrant, about 30 seconds. Add red wine; cook, stirring occasionally, until liquid has almost completely evaporated, about 2 minutes. Add onion mixture to slow cooker with meat. Stir in sugar, Italian seasoning, salt, pepper, and bay leaf. Using your hands, crush tomatoes to break apart; add to slow cooker and stir. Cover and cook on LOW until flavors meld, about 6 hours. Remove and discard bay leaf.

3. Cook pasta in salted water according to package directions. Drain well. Serve sauce over pasta; top with cheese and basil. Sauce can be refrigerated in an airtight container up to 5 days or frozen up to 3 months.

Make-Ahead Croissant Breakfast Casserole

ACTIVE 40 MIN. - TOTAL 1 HOUR, 40 MIN., PLUS 8 HOURS CHILLING
SERVES 8

- **2 (5-oz.) country ham steaks, trimmed, bone discarded**
- **2 Tbsp. olive oil, divided**
- **1 ½ lb. Vidalia onions or other sweet onions (2 medium onions), chopped (4 cups)**
- **3 oz. baby spinach, roughly chopped (3 cups)**
- **6 large eggs**
- **2 cups whole milk**

- 2 tsp. Dijon mustard
- 1 tsp. kosher salt
- 1 tsp. black pepper
- 6 oz. fontina cheese, shredded (about 1 ½ cups)
- 1 lb. (about 15) day-old mini croissants

1. Coarsely chop ham. (You should have 1 ½ cups.) Heat 1 tablespoon of the oil in a large skillet over medium. Add ham; cook, stirring occasionally, until fat is rendered, about 4 minutes. Using a slotted spoon, transfer ham to a large bowl, reserving drippings in skillet. Add remaining 1 tablespoon oil to skillet; stir in onions. Cook, stirring occasionally, until deeply browned, about 30 minutes. Add spinach; cook, stirring often, until wilted, 1 to 2 minutes. Transfer onion mixture to bowl with ham; let cool 10 minutes.

2. Whisk together eggs, milk, mustard, salt, and pepper. Add egg mixture and 1 cup of the cheese to bowl with onion mixture; stir to combine. Arrange croissants, slightly overlapping, in 2 rows in a lightly greased 11- x 7-inch baking dish. Pour custard mixture over croissants. Sprinkle with remaining ½ cup cheese. Cover with aluminum foil, and chill 8 hours or up to overnight.

3. Preheat oven to 375°F. Uncover casserole; and place on a large rimmed baking sheet. Bake in preheated oven until golden brown and center is set, about 1 hour. If needed to prevent excess browning, shield with foil after 25 minutes.

Pork Crown Roast

ACTIVE 25 MIN. - TOTAL 4 HOURS, 20 MIN., PLUS 8 HOURS CHILLING

SERVES 10

- 1 (10-bone) pork crown rib roast (about 7 ½ to 8 ½ lb.), frenched, chine bone removed
- 3 Tbsp. country-style Dijon mustard
- 10 garlic cloves, grated (1 Tbsp.)
- 2 Tbsp. chopped fresh thyme
- 2 Tbsp. chopped fresh rosemary
- 2 Tbsp. kosher salt
- 2 Tbsp. olive oil
- 1 Tbsp. black pepper
- 2 tsp. granulated sugar

1. Trim fat on roast to ¼-inch thick. Place roast on work surface, meat side down with ribs curved up. Cut 1 ½-inch-long slits (about ¾ inch deep) between rib bones on bony side of roast. Stand rack with ribs pointed up and slits facing away from you. Curve rack so that ends meet and form a crown. Tie roast with kitchen twine at bottom, in middle, and around bones to secure. (You can ask a butcher to do this step.) Wrap top of each rib bone, individually, with aluminum foil to prevent burning.

2. Stir together mustard, garlic, thyme, rosemary, salt, oil, pepper, and sugar in a small bowl. Rub mixture on roast, working it into slits and avoiding frenched bones. Place roast on a rack set in a foil-lined rimmed baking sheet. Chill, uncovered, 8 hours or up to overnight.

3. Remove roast from refrigerator; let stand at room temperature 1 hour. Preheat oven to 450°F with oven rack in lower third of oven. Bake roast in preheated oven 15 minutes. Reduce oven temperature to 325°F and continue baking until a thermometer inserted into thickest part of rib registers 135°F for medium, 1 hour and 50 minutes to 2 hours and 10 minutes. Remove roast from oven; tent with foil. Let rest 30 minutes (internal temperature will rise to 145°F as the meat rests). Remove kitchen twine and foil caps before slicing between bones and serving.

Savory Sweet Potato Casserole

ACTIVE 25 MIN. - TOTAL 2 HOURS, 55 MIN.

SERVES 12

- 5 lb. sweet potatoes (5 to 6 large potatoes)
- 1 large (1 ½ oz.) shallot, grated (1 ½ Tbsp.)
- ⅓ cup whole milk
- 2 large eggs, beaten
- 1 ½ tsp. chopped fresh sage
- ¼ tsp. ground nutmeg
- 1 cup unsalted butter, melted, divided
- 2 ½ tsp. kosher salt, divided
- 1 ¼ tsp. black pepper, divided
- 1 ½ cups pecan halves, roughly chopped
- 1 ½ cups coarsely ground day-old sourdough breadcrumbs (2 ½ oz.)
- 2 oz. Parmigiano-Reggiano cheese, shredded (about ½ cup)
- Chopped fresh flat-leaf parsley

1. Preheat oven to 350°F. Place potatoes on an aluminum foil-lined baking sheet. Bake in preheated oven until very tender when pierced with a knife, about 1 ½ hours. Cool 30 minutes. Peel and discard skins.

2. Stir together potatoes, shallot, milk, eggs, sage, nutmeg, ½ cup of the melted butter, 2 teaspoons of the salt, and 1 teaspoon of the pepper with a fork until mostly smooth. Pour mixture into a lightly greased 13- x 9-inch baking dish.

3. Combine pecans, breadcrumbs, cheese, and remaining ½ cup butter, ½ teaspoon salt, and ¼ teaspoon pepper in a medium bowl. Sprinkle pecan mixture in an even layer over potato mixture.

4. Bake, uncovered, at 350°F until topping is golden brown, 28 to 30 minutes. Sprinkle with parsley.

Note: To make ahead, prepare recipe through Step 3. Cover and chill overnight. Let baking dish sit at room temparature while oven preheats. Proceed with recipe as directed in Step 4, increasing bake time to about 45 minutes.

Cornmeal Crescent Rolls

ACTIVE 30 MIN. - TOTAL 2 HOURS, 35 MIN., PLUS 8 HOURS CHILLING

MAKES 16

- 1 cup whole milk
- ⅔ cup plus 1 ½ Tbsp. fine plain yellow cornmeal, divided
- 1 (¼-oz.) envelope active dry yeast
- ½ cup warm water (100°F to 110°F)
- ⅓ cup plus 1 tsp. granulated sugar, divided
- 2 large eggs, beaten
- 1 ½ tsp. kosher salt
- ¾ cup butter, melted, divided
- 4 cups bread flour plus more for work surface

1. Bring milk to a simmer in a small saucepan over medium, stirring occasionally. Gradually add ⅔ cup of the cornmeal, whisking constantly. Reduce heat to low, and cook, whisking constantly, until mixture thickens to a porridge-like consistency, about 30 seconds. Transfer mixture to a medium bowl. Let cool 10 minutes.

2. Meanwhile, combine yeast, water, and 1 teaspoon of the sugar in a small bowl. Let stand until foamy, about 5 minutes.

3. Place eggs, salt, and remaining ⅓ cup sugar in the bowl of a heavy-duty electric stand mixer fitted with a dough hook; stir to combine. Add cornmeal mixture, yeast mixture, and ½ cup of the melted butter; beat on medium speed until combined, about 1 minute. Reduce speed to low, and, with mixer running, gradually add flour, beating until dough pulls away from sides of bowl, about 6 minutes. (Dough will be lumpy.) Transfer to a lightly floured surface, and knead until dough is smooth, 3 to 4 minutes. Place dough in a large, lightly greased bowl, turning to grease top. Cover with plastic wrap, and chill 8 hours or up to overnight.

4. Turn dough out onto a lightly floured surface. Divide dough in half, and shape each half into a ball. Roll dough ball into a 13-inch circle; cut into 8 wedges. Brush excess flour from wedges. Roll or stretch each wedge into a 9-inch-long triangle. Starting from wide end, roll up each triangle, and place, point side down, 3 inches apart on 2 parchment paper-lined baking sheets. Curve ends to form crescents. Repeat with remaining dough half. Cover loosely with plastic wrap, and let rise in a warm place (80°F to 85°F) until doubled in volume, 1 hour to 1½ hours.

5. Preheat oven to 350°F. Bake rolls until golden brown, 18 to 20 minutes. Brush with remaining ¼ cup butter, and sprinkle with remaining 1½ tablespoons cornmeal. Serve warm.

Potato Puffs with Toppings

ACTIVE 40 MIN. - TOTAL 2 HOURS, 10 MIN.
MAKES 6 DOZEN

- **2 lb. (4 medium) russet potatoes, peeled and cut into 2-inch pieces**
- **1 Tbsp. plus 2 tsp. kosher salt, divided**
- **½ cup all-purpose flour plus more for work surface**
- **1 large egg, beaten**
- **1 large egg yolk**
- **2 Tbsp. unsalted butter, melted**
- **2 Tbsp. heavy cream**
- **4 garlic cloves, grated (about 1½ tsp.)**
- **Canola oil**
- **Topping of choice (recipes follow)**

1. Place potatoes and 1 tablespoon of the salt in a large saucepan; add cold water to cover by 2 inches. Bring to a boil over high. Reduce heat to medium-low, and simmer until potatoes are tender when pierced with a fork, 15 to 20 minutes. Remove from heat. Drain and return potatoes to saucepan. Let stand 5 minutes to dry.

2. Pass potatoes through a potato ricer into a large bowl. Add flour, egg, egg yolk, butter, cream, garlic, and remaining 2 teaspoons salt, and stir well to combine.

3. Using a 1¼-inch scoop, drop mounds of potato mixture onto a lightly floured surface. Using lightly floured hands, roll each mound into a ball, and place on a parchment paper-lined baking sheet. Cover loosely with plastic wrap, and chill 1 hour.

4. Pour canola oil to a depth of 1 inch in a large Dutch oven. Heat over medium-high to 350°F. Working in batches, fry potato balls, turning occasionally, until golden brown and crispy, about 3 minutes. Transfer to a paper towel-lined rimmed baking sheet to drain. Garnish Potato Puffs with desired Topping. Transfer to a serving platter, and serve immediately.

THE TOPPINGS

Truffle Oil-and-Rosemary

ACTIVE 10 MIN. - TOTAL 10 MIN.
MAKES ENOUGH FOR 18 PUFFS

Toss together fried **Potato Puffs** and 2 tsp. **truffle oil** in a large bowl. Transfer to a serving platter. Sprinkle with ½ tsp. finely chopped fresh **rosemary** and ¼ tsp. flaky **sea salt.**

Parmesan-and-Black Pepper

ACTIVE 10 MIN. - TOTAL 10 MIN.
MAKES ENOUGH FOR 18 PUFFS

Toss together fried **Potato Puffs** and 2 tsp. melted **butter.** Transfer to a serving platter. Sprinkle with 1 Tbsp. finely shredded **Parmigiano-Reggiano cheese** and ¼ tsp. **black pepper.**

Cream Cheese-and-Caviar

ACTIVE 10 MIN. - TOTAL 10 MIN.
MAKES ENOUGH FOR 18 PUFFS

Top each fried **Potato Puff** with ¼ tsp. each softened **cream cheese** and **caviar.**

Smoked Salmon-and-Chives

ACTIVE 10 MIN. - TOTAL 10 MIN.
MAKES ENOUGH FOR 18 PUFFS

Evenly top fried **Potato Puffs** with 1½ oz. thinly sliced **smoked salmon** pieces. Sprinkle with 1½ tsp. chopped fresh **chives.**

Merry Christmas,

SUGAR!

Make a batch (or two, or three) of good, old-fashioned Southern sweets

THE RECIPES

DIVINITY

How could a plump, snowball-shaped confection with the celestial name "divinity" fall completely out of favor, losing its prized spot on the holiday dessert table in a few decades' time? Studded with pecans and swiftly made from a few simple ingredients, divinity is a delightful turn-of-the-century heirloom worth restoring to its former lofty place. We've tweaked the traditional rendition by swapping out the nuts for a kiss of crushed candy canes, making them extra pretty and delicious.

Peppermint Divinity

Divinity requires advance preparation and dry, sunny weather to turn out well. Once made, the candies hold nicely for up to 1 week, so check the forecast and choose your "divinity day."

ACTIVE 30 MIN. - TOTAL 1 HOUR, 40 MIN.
MAKES ABOUT 24 CANDIES

- **2 cups granulated sugar**
- **½ cup light corn syrup**
- **¼ cup water**
- **¼ tsp. kosher salt**
- **2 large egg whites, at room temperature**
- **1 tsp. pure vanilla extract**
- **¾ cup finely chopped hard peppermint candies or candy canes, divided**

1. Stir together sugar, corn syrup, water, and salt in a heavy, 2-quart saucepan; attach a candy thermometer to side of pan. Place pan over medium-high, and cook, gently stirring occasionally with a wooden spoon, until sugar dissolves and mixture boils. Once sugar syrup is clear and thickened, cook, undisturbed, until thermometer reaches 255°F (hard-ball stage), about 6 to 8 minutes. Remove from heat.

2. Place egg whites in bowl of a stand mixer fitted with whisk attachment. Beat egg whites on medium speed until foamy. Increase speed to high, and beat until egg whites are thick and stiff, and able to hold a soft peak.

3. With mixer running on low speed, carefully pour hot syrup down side of bowl into beaten egg whites, pouring slowly and steadily. Use only the syrup that pours easily out of pan into bowl (no need to scrape pan). (Expect steam and the aroma of egg whites cooking in the syrup's heat.)

4. Increase speed to high, and continue beating until syrup is well incorporated into egg whites. Stop just long enough to scrape down sides of bowl, and add vanilla. Continue beating on high speed until mixture begins to lose its gloss and shine and is thick enough to hold its shape rather than pool into a puddle, 6 to 10 minutes.

5. Add ½ cup chopped peppermint candy, and beat on medium speed just until evenly combined. Remove bowl from mixer, and use 2 spoons to quickly scoop out small balls of candy (about 1 tablespoon each), placing them on prepared baking sheets; don't allow candies to touch.

6. Garnish candies quickly with remaining ¼ cup chopped peppermint. Let divinity cool, undisturbed, until set with a matte finish, 1 to 2 hours.

7. Carefully transfer candies to an airtight container or candy tin, placing parchment paper or wax paper between layers and handling candies gently.

Fruitcake Bark

Prepare everything ahead so that you can quickly add a beautiful array of toppings while the chocolate is still hot and glossy.

ACTIVE 20 MIN. - TOTAL 2 HOURS
MAKES ABOUT 1 LB.

- **2 (4-oz.) bittersweet chocolate, semisweet chocolate, or milk chocolate baking bars**
- **2 (4.4-oz.) high-quality white chocolate bars (such as Lindt White Chocolate)**

FRUITCAKE

Peppermint bark appeared in the Christmas-season marketplace a few years back and quickly claimed a spot at holiday celebrations everywhere. Buying a tin of it is simple enough, but making a batch of bark is easy and fun and allows you to take it in a Southern direction, like our fruitcake-inspired version. Layering white chocolate with dark adds flavor and beauty, as does finishing your tasty creation with components of a classic Southern fruitcake. Go old-school with candied cherries, pecans, and pineapple, or change things up by throwing in pistachios, cranberries, and dried figs that are cut lengthwise to show off a Dickensian bit of stem. Can't decide? Fruitcake Bark is so quick and easy to make that you can prepare multiple batches to nibble and share.

2 ½ cups mixed, chopped fruitcake toppings (such as ¾ cup each of toasted pecan halves and toasted walnut halves and ⅓ cup each of candied cherries, candied orange peel, and candied pineapple)

1. Line a 13- x 9-inch baking pan with parchment paper, allowing about 2 inches to extend over the long sides of pan.

2. Break bittersweet chocolate bars into small to medium chunks. Microwave chocolate in a medium-size microwavable bowl on MEDIUM (50% power) for 30 seconds; stir. Continue to microwave until chocolate is completely smooth, shiny, and fluid, about 1 minute, stirring at 15-second intervals. To melt on the stove, bring 2 to 3 inches of water to a gentle boil in a saucepan over medium-high. Reduce heat to medium-low, and maintain a gentle simmer without steam. Place chocolate in a heatproof bowl, and set it over saucepan, making sure bowl does not touch water. Cook chocolate, stirring occasionally, until chocolate is melted, completely smooth, shiny, and fluid, 2 to 4 minutes.

3. Quickly pour melted bittersweet chocolate all over bottom of prepared pan. Using an offset spatula or the back of a large spoon, spread chocolate into a fairly even layer, covering bottom of pan completely. Place in refrigerator, and chill until chocolate is cold and set, 30 minutes to 1 hour.

4. Break white chocolate bars into small to medium chunks, and repeat melting process. Quickly spread melted white chocolate over firm bittersweet chocolate layer. (Or leave a border around the edges, if you like.) Working quickly, sprinkle and scatter toppings in a single layer all over melted white chocolate, making sure every topping piece touches the melted chocolate so that it will adhere to cooled white chocolate layer.

5. Cover and refrigerate until bark is firmly set, about 1 hour. To serve, use parchment paper handles to remove bark from pan. Use a sharp knife to cut bark into irregular chunks, or break into large pieces by hand. Store bark in an airtight container at room temperature for up to 7 days.

TRY THIS TWIST!

Boozy Fruitcake Bark: Stir 1 teaspoon natural bourbon flavor (extract) into the chocolate in Step 2.

PRALINES

New Orleans' favorite candy is a true marriage of old-world European tradition combined with Southern ingenuity. When the French settled New Orleans in the 1700s, they brought their version of pralines, a simple sweet made by cooking whole almonds with granulated sugar until they became crisp and caramelized. African-American cooks transformed the French treat by using abundant, native-grown pecans in place of the more costly almonds; they eventually stirred butter and milk or cream into the original recipe. These innovative bakers created a new, richer, and more irresistible confection, and their pralines—simultaneously crunchy, creamy, fudgy, and sweet—have become a true American classic.

Buttermilk-Pecan Pralines

For ease in shaping big, beautiful pralines, portion the mixture into paper baking cups, removing them once the candies are set.

ACTIVE 20 MIN. - TOTAL 1 HOUR, 40 MIN.
MAKES 16 LARGE PRALINES

- 1 ½ cups granulated sugar
- 1 ½ cups packed dark brown sugar
- ½ cup whole buttermilk
- ½ cup heavy cream
- 2 Tbsp. light corn syrup
- ½ tsp. salt
- 3 Tbsp. cold unsalted butter, chopped into small pieces, at room temperature
- 2 tsp. vanilla extract
- 2 ½ cups pecan halves, toasted
- 2 Tbsp. (1 oz.) bourbon, rum, or Tennessee whiskey

1. Line 2 baking sheets with parchment paper. (If using paper cupcake liners, place 16 liners on baking sheet or on a tray.)

2. Stir together sugars, buttermilk, cream, corn syrup, and salt in a heavy, 2-quart saucepan; attach a candy thermometer to side of pan. Place pan over low, and cook, stirring constantly, until sugars are melted and mixture is smooth, 5 to 8 minutes.

3. Increase heat to medium-high, and bring mixture to a boil. Boil gently until thermometer reaches about 236°F (soft-ball stage), 10 to 12 minutes. Remove from heat, and let cool to 220°F, 6 to 8 minutes.

4. Using a wooden spoon, vigorously stir in butter and vanilla, stirring until mixture turns creamy and opaque. Stir in pecans and bourbon, and quickly spoon out ¼-cup portions onto prepared baking sheet or into paper baking cups, if using.

5. Let pralines stand until completely cool, about 1 hour. Serve immediately, or wrap each praline individually in wax paper or plastic wrap, and store in an airtight container for up to 1 week.

Ginger-Pecan Bourbon Balls

We suggest melting chocolate, such as Ghirardelli Melting Wafers, which come in 10-ounce bags and are available at many supermarkets in the baking aisle. They need no tempering and will not become streaky as they dry.

ACTIVE 45 MIN. - TOTAL 4 HOURS, 45 MIN.
MAKES ABOUT 5 DOZEN CANDIES

- 2 ½ cups coarsely ground or crushed gingersnaps (from a 10-oz. pkg., 40 to 50 gingersnaps)
- ½ cup granulated sugar
- 2 Tbsp. finely chopped crystallized ginger
- 1 tsp. ground ginger
- ¼ tsp. salt
- 1 ¼ cups pecans, coarsely chopped
- ⅓ cup evaporated milk or half-and-half
- ¼ cup light corn syrup
- 3 Tbsp. (1 ½ oz.) bourbon

8 **oz. semisweet or bittersweet baking chocolate bars**
3 **(10-oz.) pkg. dark chocolate melting wafers (such as Ghirardelli Dark Chocolate Melting Wafers)**
¼ **cup chopped crystallized ginger**

1. Preheat oven to 350°F. Stir together gingersnap crumbs, sugar, finely chopped crystallized ginger, ground ginger, and salt in a large bowl until well combined.

2. Spread pecans in a single layer in a baking pan, and toast in preheated oven until fragrant and slightly darkened, 5 to 7 minutes, stirring halfway through baking. Add pecans to bowl with gingersnap mixture; do not stir.

3. Stir together evaporated milk, light corn syrup, and bourbon in a medium bowl until well combined, and set aside.

4. Break chocolate bars into small to medium chunks. Microwave chocolate in a medium-size microwavable bowl on MEDIUM (medium 50%) for 30 seconds; stir. Continue to microwave until chocolate is completely smooth, shiny, and fluid, about 1 minute, stirring at 15-second intervals. To melt on the stove, bring 2 to 3 inches of water to a gentle boil in a saucepan over medium-high. Reduce heat to medium-low, and maintain a gentle simmer without steam. Place chocolate in a heatproof bowl, and set it over saucepan, making sure bowl does not touch water. Cook chocolate, stirring occasionally, until chocolate is melted, completely smooth, shiny, and fluid, 2 to 4 minutes.

5. Add gingersnap mixture to melted chocolate, and stir once. Quickly stir in evaporated milk mixture until evenly and well combined. Cover and chill mixture 1 hour. Roll gingersnap-chocolate mixture into about 60 (1-inch) balls. Place balls in a single layer in a large container with a tight-fitting lid or on a large rimmed baking sheet lined with parchment paper. Attach lid or cover tightly with aluminum foil, and freeze until frozen solid, about 2 hours.

6. Melt melting wafers in microwave or over simmering water, as directed in Step 4. Line 2 large baking sheets with parchment paper.

7. Remove bourbon balls from the freezer. Drop bourbon balls into bowl of melted chocolate, and, using the tines of a fork, roll in melted chocolate until completely covered. Transfer to prepared baking sheets, and quickly and carefully garnish with chopped crystallized ginger. Chill bourbon balls in the refrigerator until set, about 1 hour.

8. Transfer bourbon balls to an airtight container, and store in the refrigerator for up to 1 week. To serve, remove from refrigerator, and let stand until room temperature. Transfer to paper candy cups.

BOURBON

This boozy confection headlines many a list of classic Christmas candies, but not everyone knows that it comes in three distinct styles. Chocolate, pecans, and a splash of bourbon figure in each of them, but variations commence from there. Vanilla-wafer-driven orbs flavored with cocoa powder and rolled in sugar claim first place in the hearts of fans. Second in line are the cakelike powdered sugar-and-butter-based balls of sweetness that are dipped in melted chocolate. Least known but at the top of our list are those made with melted chocolate rather than cocoa. Seeking a combination of the three with an extra twist, we used gingersnaps for the cookie component, added ground and crystallized ginger, and dunked them in chocolate for an elegant end note. We guarantee you'll earn compliments throughout the holiday season with this dessert, no matter how your bourbon balls roll.

BRITTLE

Tall tales surround the invention of peanut brittle. Some trace the history of this crunchy, sweet-and-salty candy to a resourceful Southern housewife who, in the late 1800s, added roasted peanuts and baking soda to a failed batch of taffy, creating brittle instead. Whatever its true origins are, homemade nut brittle became a well-loved holiday tradition, not only for its tempting flavor but also for how easy it is to prepare—even for a novice candy maker. Brittle made with peanuts grew even more popular in the 1900s as farmers in Virginia and Georgia increased their production of the protein-rich nut. We added that other Southern powerhouse—pecans—to our modern version of nut brittle, as well as a handful or two of cashews and whole almonds for a tasty change of pace.

Salty-Sweet Nut Brittle

Nut brittle is easy to make, travels well, and the flavor actually improves with age, making it the perfect treat to stir together and give as gifts or to fill your candy dish at home.

ACTIVE 20 MIN. - TOTAL 1 HOUR, 30 MIN.
MAKES ABOUT 2 LB.

2 ¼ **cups granulated sugar**
½ **cup water**
½ **cup light corn syrup**
½ **tsp. fine sea salt**
6 **Tbsp. butter, cut into pieces, plus more for baking sheet**

2 cups mixed nuts (such as toasted pecan halves; lightly salted, toasted pistachios; lightly salted, toasted almonds; cashews; or pumpkin seeds)

1 cup salted, dry-roasted peanuts

2 tsp. baking soda

1½ tsp. vanilla extract

2 tsp. flaky finishing salt (such as fleur de sel)

1. Rub an 18- x 13-inch baking sheet lightly with butter, or coat with cooking spray. Set aside.

2. Stir together sugar, water, corn syrup, and fine sea salt in a heavy, 2-quart saucepan; attach a candy thermometer to side of pan. Place pan over medium-high, and cook, gently stirring occasionally with a wooden spoon, until sugar dissolves and mixture boils. Once sugar syrup is clear and thickened, cook, undisturbed, until thermometer reaches 230°F to 235°F (soft-ball stage), 5 to 7 minutes. Stir in butter, and continue cooking over medium-high, stirring occasionally, until butter melts, syrup starts to caramelize, and thermometer reaches 300°F to 305°F (hard-crack stage), 6 to 8 minutes. Immediately remove pan from heat, and, working very quickly, vigorously stir in mixed nuts and peanuts just until completely coated in caramelized syrup.

3. Immediately stir in baking soda and vanilla. Once baking soda hits hot, caramelized syrup, it will lighten and start to get foamy. As soon as ingredients are combined, pour hot candy onto prepared baking sheet. Using the back of a wooden spoon, quickly and gently spread mixture, pushing into a fairly thin layer that covers most of baking sheet. (A few holes are fine. It doesn't need to be a solid sheet of candy.) Quickly sprinkle entire surface with flaky finishing salt. Let stand until brittle hardens, about 1 hour. Break into pieces. Store brittle in an airtight container or a ziplock plastic bag for up to 2 weeks.

Note: For a thinner, more delicate brittle, you can "stretch" it: After spreading the brittle onto the baking sheet, cool slightly for a minute or two just until the candy is pliable but still too hot to touch with your bare hands. Run a long, thin spatula under the candy to loosen it from the baking sheet, and, wearing clean rubber gloves, lift the edges and gently pull and stretch the candy. Move into the middle, pulling gently without tearing it, to make the brittle slightly thinner. You can leave it on the baking sheet to do this, stretching over the sides of the pan, or turn it out onto a marble or granite countertop or cutting board to make it easier to work with.

Christmas Buttermints

When freshly made, buttermint candy has the consistency of modeling clay. You can color it with food coloring, roll it and cut it with fanciful cookie cutters, press into candy molds, or simply roll into logs and cut into pieces with a sharp knife.

ACTIVE 30 MIN. - TOTAL 24 HOURS, 30 MIN.
MAKES ABOUT 1½ LB.

½ cup unsalted butter, at room temperature

1 lb. powdered sugar, plus more for work surface

2 Tbsp. evaporated milk

1 tsp. peppermint extract (or 6 to 8 drops pure peppermint oil)

⅛ tsp. vanilla extract

⅛ tsp. fine sea salt

Red food coloring gel (such as Christmas Red or Super Red)

1. Line a large baking sheet with parchment paper. Beat butter with a stand mixer or hand mixer on medium speed until light and creamy, 1 to 2 minutes. With mixer on low speed, gradually add powdered sugar, and beat until mixture forms a stiff, crumbly dough, 1 to 2 minutes, stopping to scrape down sides of bowl as needed. Add evaporated milk, peppermint extract, vanilla extract, and salt. (If using peppermint oil, start with 6 drops and taste the dough to see if a stronger peppermint flavor is desired before adding more oil.) Beat on medium speed until mixture is smooth and soft and has the consistency of modeling clay, 2 to 3 minutes.

2. Remove dough from mixer bowl, and shape into a smooth ball. Cut ball in half; wrap 1 dough ball half in plastic wrap, and set aside. To color the remaining dough ball half, use a wooden pick to deposit a little of the red food coloring gel onto dough; massage in with your fingers until evenly blended. Keep adding food coloring gel, a little at a time, until you reach desired shade of red.

3. Divide red dough portion and reserved white dough portion into 4 equal portions each to make 8 equal portions (4 red and 4 white). On a flat work surface sprinkled with powdered sugar, gently knead together 2 red portions of dough with 2 white portions of dough until mixture looks marbled. (Do not overmix.) Roll into a long, smooth, ½-inch-thick log with visible swirls of red and white color showing. Using a sharp knife, cut log into 60 (½-inch-thick) pieces. Repeat process with remaining 2 red dough portions and 2 white dough portions. Transfer buttermints to prepared baking sheet.

4. Let buttermints dry at room temperature, uncovered, 24 hours. (They will develop a crisp outer shell with a sweet, creamy, minty middle.) At this point, buttermints can be bagged up for giving as gifts, spooned into a candy dish, or stored in an airtight container or ziplock plastic bag for up to 2 weeks.

TRY THIS TWIST!
Red Hot Buttermints: Subsitute cinnamon extract for the vanilla extract in Step 1.

BUTTERMINTS

No proper Southern tea party, wedding reception, or baby shower is complete without a candy dish brimming with delicate buttermints. Traditionally colored in a rainbow of pastel hues, they are light and crisp with a sweet, buttery richness and a refreshing minty flavor that melts in your mouth. The classic recipe is a little tricky and requires expert candy-making skills. Our simplified version, however, requires no cooking and only a few pantry staples and an electric mixer to whip up a batch of delicious mints in no time at all.

Gingerbread TAKES THE CAKE

Candy-covered houses and cookies are fun to decorate, but when it comes to flavor, this is the real holiday treat

NOTHING MAKES A HOUSE smell more like Christmas than the sweet and spicy aroma of a freshly baked pan of gingerbread. We're not talking about the crisp cookies or the houses covered in icing and candy. Those holiday delights are fun to decorate, but their taste can't compare to a slice of tender, richly spiced gingerbread cake.

The practice of baking and sharing gingerbread originated in Europe several hundred years ago, and it made its way to the colonial South as families immigrated to the region and brought their recipes and traditions with them. Ginger from Asia and dried spices such as cinnamon, nutmeg, mace, allspice, and cloves arrived by ship into Southern ports and traveled inland because they were easy to transport and store. Whole dried spices kept well and retained their flavor and aroma for months.

When combined with affordable sweeteners (like molasses or honey) and farmstead staples (such as butter and eggs), gingerbread could be made by home bakers when more expensive ingredients were not an option, which is why it became a wildly popular dessert. *American Cookery* by Amelia Simmons, the first cookbook published in America in 1796, featured several recipes for it. Gingerbread may be old-fashioned, but the four creative treats that follow show it can be just as special today.

Classic Gingerbread, page 300

Gingerbread-and-Pear Upside-Down Cake, page 301

Gingerbread Cheesecake with Lemon-Ginger Glaze, page 300

Gingerbread Roulade and
Eggnog Cream

Gingerbread Roulade and Eggnog Cream

ACTIVE 45 MIN. - TOTAL 2 HOURS, PLUS 8 HOURS CHILLING
SERVES 12-16

CAKE
- **3/4 cup unbleached cake flour**
- **1 1/2 tsp. ground ginger**
- **1 tsp. ground cinnamon**
- **1/2 tsp. baking powder**
- **1/2 tsp. ground allspice**
- **1/2 tsp. ground nutmeg**
- **1/4 tsp. baking soda**
- **1/4 tsp. kosher salt**
- **5 large eggs, separated**
- **1/4 cup granulated sugar**
- **1/2 cup molasses (not black strap) or sorghum syrup**
- **1/4 cup packed dark brown sugar**
- **2 Tbsp. finely grated fresh ginger**
- **1/2 cup powdered sugar, divided**

FILLING
- **1 (8-oz.) pkg. cream cheese, at room temperature**
- **6 Tbsp. unsalted butter, at room temperature**
- **1 cup powdered sugar**
- **2 Tbsp. (1 oz.) dark rum or bourbon**
- **1 tsp. vanilla extract**
- **1/2 tsp. ground cinnamon**
- **1/4 tsp. ground nutmeg or mace**

EGGNOG CREAM
- **2 cups cold heavy cream**
- **1 cup cold eggnog**
- **1 Tbsp. (1 oz.) dark rum or bourbon**
- **1/2 tsp. ground nutmeg**

1. Prepare the Cake: Preheat oven to 325°F. Spray a 12- x 17-inch rimmed baking sheet with baking spray. Line baking sheet with parchment paper, and spray parchment paper.

2. Whisk together flour, ground ginger, cinnamon, baking powder, allspice, nutmeg, baking soda, and salt in a medium bowl. Set aside.

3. Beat egg whites in a medium bowl with an electric mixer on low speed until opaque, about 5 minutes. Increase speed to high, and beat until soft peaks form, about 3 minutes. With mixer running, add granulated sugar in a slow, steady stream. Continue beating until glossy, stiff peaks form, about 2 more minutes. Set aside.

4. Beat egg yolks in a large bowl with mixer on high speed until thick and pale, about 2 minutes. Add molasses, brown sugar, and fresh ginger, and beat on medium speed until combined, about 1 minute. Add flour mixture, and beat on low speed just until smooth. Fold in one-third of beaten egg whites. Add remaining egg whites, and fold until just combined. Spread batter evenly in prepared pan.

5. Bake at 325°F until cake is firm on top and springs back when lightly pressed, 13 to 15 minutes. Cool in pan on a wire rack 1 minute.

6. Dust a clean tea towel with 1/4 cup of the powdered sugar. Run a thin knife around edge of cake to loosen from pan. Invert cake onto prepared tea towel. Peel off, and discard parchment paper. Dust cake generously with remaining 1/4 cup powdered sugar. Starting with 1 short side, roll up cake and towel, jelly-roll fashion. Let stand until cooled completely, about 1 hour.

7. Prepare the Filling: Beat cream cheese and butter in a medium bowl with mixer on medium-high speed until smooth and fluffy, about 4 minutes. Add powdered sugar, rum, vanilla, cinnamon, and nutmeg, and beat until smooth.

8. Carefully unroll cake on a cutting board or work surface; remove tea towel, and spread Filling over cooled cake. Starting with short end, roll up cake, jelly-roll fashion. Wrap cake tightly in plastic wrap, sealing both ends. Refrigerate at least 8 hours or up to 2 days before serving.

9. Prepare the Eggnog Cream: Fit electric mixer with whisk attachment. Beat cream in a chilled bowl with mixer on high speed until stiff peaks form, about 5 minutes. Fold in eggnog, rum, and nutmeg with a rubber spatula. Beat on high speed until medium peaks form, about 30 seconds. (Consistency of the cream should be midway between whipped cream and a thick sauce.) Chill until ready to serve.

10. Trim ends of roulade. Slice roulade using a serrated knife. Spread about 3 tablespoons Eggnog Cream on each plate, and top with a roulade slice. Serve immediately.

HOW TO

Roulade Cake

1 Invert the warm cake onto a clean tea towel dusted with powdered sugar. Peel off, and discard parchment paper. Dust cake generously with powdered sugar. Starting with 1 short side, roll up cake and towel, jelly-roll fashion. Let stand until cooled completely, about 1 hour.

2 Carefully unroll cake; remove tea towel, and spread Filling over cooled cake.

3 Starting with short end, roll up cake, jelly-roll fashion. Wrap cake tightly in plastic wrap, sealing both ends. Refrigerate at least 8 hours or up to 2 days before serving.

Classic Gingerbread

ACTIVE 20 MIN. - TOTAL 1 HOUR, 50 MIN.
SERVES 9

- **2/3 cup packed dark brown sugar**
- **2/3 cup molasses or sorghum syrup**
- **2/3 cup boiling water**
- **1/4 cup cold unsalted butter, cubed**
- **1 tsp. baking soda**
- **1/2 tsp. kosher salt**
- **1 large egg**
- **1 1/2 cups all-purpose flour plus more for pan**
- **2 tsp. ground ginger**
- **1 tsp. ground cinnamon**
- **1/4 tsp. ground nutmeg**
- **1/4 tsp. ground allspice**
- **1/4 tsp. ground cloves**
- **1/4 tsp. black pepper**
- **Powdered sugar, for dusting**
- **Brown Sugar-and-Ginger Whipped Cream (recipe follows)**

1. Preheat oven to 350°F. Whisk together brown sugar, molasses, boiling water, and butter in a medium bowl until butter melts. Whisk in baking soda and salt. Let stand until lukewarm, about 25 minutes. Whisk in egg.

2. Whisk together flour, ginger, cinnamon, nutmeg, allspice, cloves, and black pepper in a small bowl; add to brown sugar mixture, and whisk until smooth. Pour into a generously greased (with butter or cooking spray) and floured 9-inch square pan.

3. Bake in preheated oven until a toothpick inserted in center comes out clean, 20 to 25 minutes. Cool in pan 10 minutes. Transfer gingerbread to a wire rack, and cool completely, about 1 hour. (For the best texture, wrap tightly in plastic wrap or place in an airtight container, and let stand at room temperature overnight before serving.) Store in an airtight container up to 3 days.

4. Just before serving, sprinkle with powdered sugar, and cut into 9 squares. Serve with Brown Sugar-and-Ginger Whipped Cream.

Brown Sugar-and-Ginger Whipped Cream

ACTIVE 10 MIN. - TOTAL 1 HOUR, 10 MIN.
MAKES ABOUT 2 CUPS

Beat 1 cup cold heavy **cream** in a chilled bowl with an electric mixer on high speed until soft peaks form, about 5 minutes. Add 1/4 cup packed **light brown sugar,** 1/2 tsp. ground **ginger,** and 2 tsp. **vanilla** extract, and beat until stiff peaks form, about 3 more minutes. Cover and chill 1 hour before serving.

Gingerbread Cheesecake with Lemon-Ginger Glaze

ACTIVE 50 MIN. - TOTAL 3 HOURS, PLUS 12 HOURS CHILLING
SERVES 12-16

CRUST

- **2 cups (8 oz.) finely crushed gingersnap cookie crumbs**
- **1 Tbsp. dark brown sugar**
- **1/2 tsp. ground ginger**
- **1/4 tsp. kosher salt**
- **5 Tbsp. unsalted butter, melted**

FILLING

- **3 (8-oz.) pkg. cream cheese, at room temperature**
- **1 1/4 cups packed dark brown sugar**
- **1 tsp. ground ginger**
- **1 tsp. ground cinnamon**
- **4 large eggs, at room temperature**
- **1 cup sour cream, at room temperature**
- **1/2 cup finely chopped crystallized ginger**
- **4 tsp. lemon zest (from 1 lemon)**
- **2 tsp. vanilla extract**

GLAZE

- **1/2 cup granulated sugar**
- **4 tsp. lemon zest plus 1/3 cup fresh juice (from 3 lemons)**
- **4 large egg yolks**
- **3 Tbsp. very finely chopped fresh ginger**
- **1/4 cup cold unsalted butter, cut into 4 pieces**

1. Prepare the Crust: Preheat oven to 325°F. Tightly wrap bottom and outside of a 9-inch springform pan with 3 or 4 layers of heavy-duty aluminum foil. (This will protect the cheesecake as it bakes in the water bath.)

2. Stir together cookie crumbs, dark brown sugar, ginger, and salt in a medium bowl. Drizzle melted butter over crumb mixture, and toss with a fork to moisten evenly. Press mixture across bottom and about 1/2 inch up inside of prepared springform pan. (Press corners with bottom of a straight-sided measuring cup to ensure they are not too thick.)

3. Bake in preheated oven until set and fragrant, about 10 minutes. Cool on a wire rack until ready to use.

4. Prepare the Filling: Beat cream cheese in a large bowl with an electric mixer on medium-high speed until smooth, light, and fluffy, 4 to 5 minutes, stopping to scrape down sides of bowl as needed. Add brown sugar, ground ginger, and cinnamon, and beat until well-combined and smooth, about 2 minutes. Add eggs, 1 at a time, beating well and stopping to scrape down sides of bowl after each addition. Add sour cream, crystallized ginger, lemon zest, and vanilla, and beat just until combined, about 1 minute. Pour into cooled crust. Firmly tap pan several times on countertop to remove any air bubbles. Place springform pan inside a large roasting pan. Add very hot tap water to roasting pan to come halfway up outside of springform pan.

5. Bake cheesecake in water bath at 325°F until edges of filling are set and center jiggles slightly when pan is gently jostled, about 1 hour. Turn off oven, and prop door open about 1 inch. Let cheesecake stand in oven 1 hour.

6. Remove cheesecake from oven, lift springform pan from water bath, and remove foil. Run a thin knife around edge of cheesecake to loosen from pan. Chill, uncovered, 8 hours or up to 2 days.

7. Prepare the Glaze: Whisk together sugar and lemon juice in a small, heavy saucepan until smooth. Whisk in yolks until smooth. Whisk in ginger and lemon zest; add butter. Cook over medium-low heat, stirring constantly with a heatproof spatula, until mixture is thick and begins to bubble around edge of pan, 8 to 10 minutes.

8. Pour through a fine wire-mesh strainer into a small bowl, pressing firmly on solids with spatula; discard solids. Place plastic wrap directly on surface of Glaze to prevent a film from forming. Chill at least 4 hours or up to 2 days. (Glaze will continue to thicken slightly as it cools.)

9. Just before serving, remove outer ring from springform pan. Spoon Glaze over top of chilled cheesecake, and spread to edges. Slice and serve immediately.

Gingerbread-and-Pear Upside-Down Cake

ACTIVE 30 MIN. - TOTAL 1 HOUR, 50 MIN.
SERVES 12

TOPPING

- **6 Tbsp. unsalted butter**
- **¾ cup packed dark brown sugar**
- **1 tsp. ground ginger**
- **1 tsp. ground cardamom**
- **1 tsp. ground cinnamon**
- **2 ripe Bosc pears (1 lb. total)**

CAKE

- **1½ cups all-purpose flour**
- **2 tsp. baking powder**
- **2 tsp. ground ginger**
- **1½ tsp. ground cinnamon**
- **½ tsp. ground cardamom**
- **¼ tsp. ground allspice**
- **¼ tsp. ground cloves**
- **¼ tsp. kosher salt**
- **6 Tbsp. unsalted butter, softened**
- **¾ cup packed light brown sugar**
- **2 large eggs**
- **½ cup whole milk**
- **2 Tbsp. molasses or sorghum syrup**
- **1 tsp. vanilla extract**

1. Prepare the Topping: Cook butter in a 10-inch cast-iron skillet over medium until butter is lightly browned and has a nutty and toasted aroma, about 5 minutes. Remove from heat. Immediately add brown sugar, ginger, cardamom, and cinnamon, and stir until smooth.

KNOW YOUR GINGER

FRESH GINGER

Choose clean knobs of fresh ginger root with smooth, shiny skin. Store in the crisper drawer of the refrigerator and use it before it begins to shrivel. Remove the peel with a vegetable peeler or the tip of a metal spoon.

CRYSTALLIZED GINGER

Look for packaged rounds or strips of ginger (also called candied ginger), and press them inside the package. The pieces should bend easily without snapping, similar to gummy bears. Prechopped "baker's cut" ginger tends to be hard and will not soften when cooked.

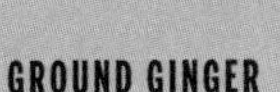

GROUND GINGER

Before you kick your holiday baking into high gear, take a moment to give your ground ginger (and other spices) the sniff test: If the aroma isn't bold and pungent, the spice is past its prime.

2. Peel, halve, and core pears. Cut halves from top to bottom into ¼-inch-thick slices, and press gently to fan the slices. Carefully place pears on Topping in skillet. (Don't pack them in—you might have a few left over.) Set skillet aside.

3. Prepare the Cake: Preheat oven to 350°F. Whisk together flour, baking powder, ginger, cinnamon, cardamom, allspice, cloves, and salt in a medium bowl.

4. Beat butter and brown sugar in a large bowl with mixer on high speed until light and fluffy, about 2 minutes, stopping to scrape down sides of bowl. Add eggs, 1 at a time, beating well after each addition.

5. Add half of flour mixture to butter mixture, and beat on medium speed until smooth, about 2 minutes. Add milk, molasses, and vanilla, and beat until smooth, about 3 minutes. Add remaining flour mixture, and beat 2 minutes, stopping twice to scrape down sides of bowl. Pour batter over Topping in skillet, and gently spread to edges.

6. Bake in preheated oven until cake is golden brown and springs back when touched lightly in center, 30 to 40 minutes. Cool on a wire rack 5 minutes.

7. Carefully invert warm cake onto a serving platter. (Some pear slices might stick to the skillet; gently loosen and replace on cake.) Cool cake completely, about 45 minutes.

PEACE *of* CAKE

This year we decided to trade in the bells, whistles, and bling for a layer cake that's as simple as a walk in the woods. Whether you dress it up or dress it down, we promise it'll get you in the spirit.

Best White Cake

ACTIVE 35 MIN. - TOTAL 1 HOUR, 55 MIN.
SERVES 10

CAKE LAYERS
- **1 cup unsalted butter, softened**
- **2 cups granulated sugar**
- **7 large egg whites, at room temperature**
- **1 tsp. vanilla extract**
- **1 tsp. almond extract**
- **2 ¾ cups all-purpose flour**
- **2 tsp. baking powder**
- **1 tsp. kosher salt**
- **1 cup whole milk**

VANILLA BUTTERCREAM
- **2 cups unsalted butter, softened**
- **7 cups powdered sugar**
- **1 tsp. vanilla extract**
- **⅛ tsp. kosher salt**
- **⅔ cup heavy cream**

GARNISHES
- **Rosemary sprigs**
- **Powdered sugar**
- **Gingerbread Fawn Cookies**

1. Prepare the Cake: Preheat oven to 350°F. Lightly grease 3 (8-inch) round cake pans with cooking spray. Line bottom of pans with parchment paper rounds; spray paper.

2. Combine butter and sugar in bowl of a heavy-duty stand mixer fitted with paddle attachment. Beat on medium-high speed until creamy and fluffy, 3 to 5 minutes. Stop mixer; scrape down sides. With mixer running on low speed, add egg whites, 1 at a time, stopping to scrape down sides as needed. Add extracts, beating on low speed just until combined.

3. Whisk together flour, baking powder, and salt in a bowl. Gradually add flour mixture to egg mixture, alternating with milk, in 3 parts, beginning and ending with flour mixture. Beat until blended after each addition. Divide batter evenly among prepared pans.

4. Bake in preheated oven until a wooden pick inserted in center comes out clean and edges begin to pull away from pans, 24 to 26 minutes.

5. Cool Cake Layers in pans on wire racks 15 minutes. Invert onto wire racks, remove pans, and cool completely before frosting, 30 minutes. (Alternatively, wrap in plastic wrap, and freeze 2 hours or refrigerate 4 to 6 hours before frosting.)

6. Prepare the Vanilla Buttercream: Beat butter in bowl of a heavy-duty stand mixer fitted with paddle attachment on medium speed until creamy, 1 to 2 minutes. Reduce speed to low. With mixer running, gradually add powdered sugar, beating until smooth, about 2 minutes, stopping to scrape down sides as needed. Beat in vanilla and salt. With mixer running on medium speed, gradually add cream, beating until fluffy and spreadable, about 30 seconds.

7. Place 1 Cake Layer on a serving plate or cake stand. Spoon about half of Vanilla Buttercream into a large 16-inch disposable piping bag. Cut a ½-inch opening in tip of bag. Pipe Buttercream, ⅓-inch high, in concentric circles starting from the outside and working your way in. Top with second Cake Layer and repeat process, refilling bag as needed. Top with third Cake Layer, and repeat process. Smooth Buttercream on top of cake, using an offset spatula. Use remaining Buttercream to thinly cover sides of the cake, allowing some of the cake itself to peek through.

8. Insert rosemary sprigs into top of cake; dust with powdered sugar. Top with Gingerbread Fawn Cookies.

Gingerbread Fawn Cookies

ACTIVE 40 MIN. - TOTAL 2 HOURS, 30 MIN.
MAKES 4 DOZEN 2- TO 4-INCH COOKIES

COOKIES
- **1 cup butter, softened**
- **1 cup granulated sugar**
- **½ tsp. baking soda**
- **¼ cup hot water**
- **1 cup molasses**
- **5 ½ cups all-purpose flour plus more for work surface**
- **1 ½ Tbsp. ground ginger**
- **1 ½ tsp. ground cinnamon**
- **¼ tsp. salt**
- **¼ tsp. ground allspice**

ROYAL ICING
- **1 (16-oz.) pkg. powdered sugar**
- **3 Tbsp. meringue powder**
- **6 to 8 Tbsp. warm water**

1. Prepare the Cookies: Beat butter and sugar with a heavy-duty electric stand mixer on medium speed until fluffy, about 3 minutes. Set aside.

2. Stir together baking soda and hot water in a bowl until dissolved; stir in molasses.

3. Stir together flour, ginger, cinnamon, salt, and allspice in a large bowl. Add flour mixture to butter mixture alternately with molasses mixture, in 3 parts, beginning and ending with flour mixture. Beat on medium speed until incorporated after each addition. Shape mixture into a flat disk; wrap in plastic wrap; chill 1 hour.

4. Preheat oven to 350°F. Roll dough to ⅛-inch thickness on a lightly floured surface. Cut dough with 3-inch and 4-inch deer- or fawn-shaped cookie cutters. Gather scraps; reroll as desired. Place Cookies 2 inches apart on parchment paper-lined baking sheets. Bake until edges are lightly browned, 15 to 18 minutes. Cool on baking sheets 2 minutes; transfer to wire racks. Cool completely, 30 minutes.

5. Prepare the Royal Icing: Beat powdered sugar, meringue powder, and 6 tablespoons of the warm water with an electric mixer on low speed until blended, 1 minute. Increase speed to medium; beat until well blended and smooth, 2 minutes. Beat in remaining warm water, ¼ teaspoon at a time, until desired consistency is reached.

6. Spoon Royal Icing into a small ziplock plastic freezer bag with 1 corner snipped; pipe on Cookies.

TRY THIS TWIST!
All-Occasion Cookie Toppers: Don't limit this cake to Christmas. Use leaf cookie cutters in autumn, flower cookie cutters in spring, number cookie cutters for birthdays ... you get the idea!

THE ICING ON THE CAKE

GO FULLY FROSTED

For a textured "ribbon" look, repeat the same process of frosting the cake, adding a second, thicker layer of buttercream to the top and sides of the cake. Then, use an offset spatula to smooth the top and sides.

2

Drag a 1-inch-wide offset spatula around the sides of the cake, starting from the bottom and ending at the top. Leave the top smooth.

MAKE A NAKED CAKE

For a rustic, lightly frosted look, use a 1-inch-wide offset spatula to cover the top and sides of the cake with a layer of buttercream. Then, use the spatula to smooth the top and sides.

2

Drag a metal bench scraper (or offset spatula) around the sides of the cake to remove excess frosting and let the cake layers peek through.

HOW TO

Rosemary Trees

SELECT THE RIGHT SPRIGS

A rosemary bush will have bigger, bushier, more treelike sprigs. If you don't have a live plant, choose precut sprigs that are as wide as possible.

FAN OUT THE NEEDLES

Use your fingers to fluff out the leaves on all sides. The bottom stem of the sprig will be the top of the tree; you want the leaves to be shorter at the top and wider at the bottom.

GIVE IT A TRIM

If necessary, use kitchen shears to trim the leaves into a triangular, treelike shape. Then dust with powdered sugar for a snowy look.

SHEET PAN NACHOS WITH CHORIZO AND REFRIED BEANS (PAGE 204)

ROASTED PUMPKIN-AND-
BABY KALE SALAD (PAGE 215)

PUMPKIN RAVIOLI WITH SAGE BROWN BUTTER (PAGE 218)

CHOCOLATE-PEAR
MUFFINS (PAGE 207)

TOASTED OATMEAL COOKIES AND BROWN BUTTER-MAPLE-PECAN BLONDIES (PAGE 209)

BAKED RIGATONI WITH ZUCCHINI AND MOZZARELLA (PAGE 230)

WHITE CALZONES WITH MARINARA SAUCE (PAGE 230)

CLOCKWISE FROM TOP LEFT:

- BRUSSELS SPROUTS WITH BACON AND SHALLOTS (PAGE 257)
- HASSELBACK SWEET POTATO CASSEROLE (PAGE 256)
- GREEN BEAN CASSEROLE WITH CRISPY LEEKS (PAGE 256)
- CHEESY POTATO CASSEROLE (PAGE 257)

TURKEY, CARAMELIZED ONION, AND GRUYÈRE GRILLED CHEESE (PAGE 266)

HERB-RUBBED SMOKED TURKEY (PAGE 247)

AUNT GRACE'S FAMOUS CORNBREAD DRESSING (PAGE 249)

CLOCKWISE FROM TOP LEFT:

- PUMPKIN-SPICE MAGIC CAKE (PAGE 263)
- BUTTERSCOTCH-SPICE TRIFLE (PAGE 263)
- FUDGE LAYER CAKE WITH CARAMEL BUTTERCREAM (PAGE 264)
- PUMPKIN LAYER CAKE WITH CARAMEL-CREAM CHEESE FROSTING (PAGE 245)

MINI TURKEY POT PIES WITH DRESSING TOPS (PAGE 244)

BLACKBERRY JAM CAKE
(PAGE 226)

LEMON-AND-CHOCOLATE
DOBERGE CAKE (PAGE 227)

APPLE STACK CAKE
(PAGE 226)

OUR BEST BREAKFAST & BRUNCH

In the South, it's hard to define the favorite meal. Is it Sunday supper at Mom's . . . a backyard barbecue in summer . . . or a tailgate outside the stadium on game day? We don't think you should have to pick favorites, but we do think that lazy weekend family breakfasts or a leisurely brunch with friends are all occasions worth celebrating. Over the years we've developed, tested, and tasted more muffins, sweet rolls, and breakfast casseroles than we can count, but some recipes endure as memorable standouts. Get ready to love the morning meal anytime of day. Whether you want breakfast for dinner or brunch at lunch, these are the recipes guaranteed to impress.

CASSEROLES

Bacon Mushroom Frittata

ACTIVE 24 MIN. - TOTAL 46 MIN.
SERVES 6-8

- **1/2 cup sliced fresh mushrooms**
- **2 Tbsp. olive oil**
- **1 garlic clove, minced**
- **1/2 (6-oz.) package fresh baby spinach**
- **1 (10-oz.) can mild diced tomatoes and green chiles, drained**
- **3 cooked and crumbled bacon slices**
- **1/4 tsp. table salt**
- **1/4 tsp. black pepper**
- **12 large eggs, beaten**
- **1/2 cup crumbled garlic-and-herb feta cheese**

1. Preheat oven to 350°F.
2. Cook mushrooms in hot oil in a 10-inch (2-inch-deep) ovenproof nonstick skillet over medium-high until browned, 2 to 3 minutes. Add the garlic, and cook 1 minute. Stir in spinach, and cook, stirring constantly, just until the spinach begins to wilt 1 minute.
3. Add tomatoes and green chiles, bacon, and next 2 ingredients; cook, stirring frequently, until spinach is wilted, 2 to 3 minutes. Add eggs, and sprinkle with cheese. Cook 3 to 5 minutes, gently lifting edges of frittata with a spatula and tilting pan so uncooked portion flows underneath.
4. Bake in preheated oven until set and lightly browned, about 12 to 15 minutes. Remove from oven, and let stand 5 minutes. Slide frittata onto a large platter, and cut into 8 wedges.

Variations:

Tomato-Sausage Frittata: Omit the mushrooms and bacon. Cook ½ lb. ground pork sausage in a 10-inch (2-inch-deep) ovenproof nonstick skillet over medium-high until browned and crumbled, 6 to 8 minutes ; remove from skillet, and drain on paper towels. Wipe skillet clean. Proceed with recipe as directed in Step 2, adding garlic to hot oil in skillet, and adding sausage with tomatoes and green chiles in Step 3.

Spicy Tomato Frittata: Omit mushrooms and bacon. Proceed with recipe as directed in Step 2, adding garlic to hot oil in skillet.

Eggplant-and-Olive Frittata: Omit mushrooms and bacon. Proceed with recipe as directed in Step 2, cooking 1 cup peeled and chopped eggplant until tender, 5 minutes, and stirring ½ cup sliced black olives in with tomatoes in Step 3.

Breakfast in a Skillet

The best of breakfast comes together here in a big cast-iron skillet. It's lovely enough to take straight from the oven to the table, even for company. Starting out the day this way sets a pretty high standard for lunch and supper. Preheating the skillet helps the biscuit crumbs stay crisp.

ACTIVE 20 MIN. - TOTAL 45 MIN., NOT INCLUDING BISCUITS
SERVES 6

- **1 lb. ground pork sausage**
- **1 cup diced onion**
- **2 garlic cloves, minced**
- **2 cups crumbled homemade biscuits**
- **6 oz. extra-sharp Cheddar cheese, freshly grated (1 1/2 cups)**
- **1 cup grape tomatoes, quartered**
- **1/8 tsp. freshly ground black pepper**
- **6 large eggs**

1. Preheat oven to 350°F. Heat a 10-inch cast-iron skillet in oven 5 minutes.
2. Meanwhile, cook sausage, onion, and garlic in a large lightly greased skillet over medium, stirring frequently, 10 minutes or until sausage is browned and onion is tender; drain. Transfer to a large bowl. Add biscuit crumbles and next 3 ingredients. Stir until blended. Transfer to hot cast-iron skillet.
3. Make 6 indentations in sausage mixture using back of a spoon. Break 1 egg into each indentation.
4. Bake in preheated oven just until eggs are set, 23 to 25 minutes. Serve immediately.

TRY THIS TWIST!
Country Breakfast in a Skillet: Substitute 2 cups cubed cornbread in place of the crumbled biscuits.

Brie-and-Veggie Strata

ACTIVE 40 MIN. - TOTAL 10 HOURS, INCLUDING CHILL TIME
SERVES 8

- **1 large sweet onion, halved and thinly sliced**
- **1 large red bell pepper, diced**
- **1 large Yukon Gold potato, peeled and diced**
- **2 Tbsp. olive oil**
- **1 (8-oz.) Brie round**
- **1 (12-oz.) sourdough bread loaf, cubed**
- **4 oz. Parmesan cheese, shredded (1 cup)**
- **8 large eggs**
- **3 cups milk**
- **2 Tbsp. Dijon mustard**
- **1 tsp. seasoned salt**
- **1 tsp. black pepper**

1. Cook first 3 ingredients in hot oil 10 to 12 minutes or just until vegetables are tender.
2. Trim and discard rind from Brie. Cut cheese into ½-inch cubes.
3. Layer a lightly greased 13- x 9-inch baking dish with half each of bread cubes, onion mixture, Brie cubes, and Parmesan cheese.
4. Whisk together eggs and next 4 ingredients; pour half of egg mixture over cheeses. Repeat layers once. Cover with plastic wrap, and chill 8 to 24 hours.
5. Preheat oven to 350°F. Meanwhile, let strata stand at room temperature 30 minutes. Remove plastic wrap, and bake in preheated oven until set, 45 to 50 minutes. Serve immediately

TRY THIS TWIST!
Make it Italian: Substitute a wheel of Italian Paglietta—similar to French Camembert—for the Brie and 2 tablespoons prepared pesto for the Dijon mustard in Step 4.

Savory Ham-and-Swiss Breakfast Pie

ACTIVE 35 MIN. - TOTAL 1 HOUR, 50 MIN.

SERVES 8

- 1 2/3 cups water
- 1 cup whipping cream
- 2 garlic cloves, pressed
- 2 Tbsp. butter
- 1 tsp. table salt
- 1/4 tsp. black pepper
- 2/3 cup uncooked quick-cooking grits
- 5 oz. Swiss cheese, shredded and divided (1 1/4 cups)
- 8 large eggs
- 1/2 lb. cooked ham, diced
- 4 scallions, chopped
- 1/2 cup milk
- Garnish: chopped fresh chives

1. Preheat oven to 350°F. Bring first 6 ingredients to a boil in a medium saucepan; gradually whisk in grits. Cover, reduce heat, and simmer, whisking occasionally, 5 to 7 minutes. Add ½ cup of the cheese, stirring until cheese melts. Remove from heat, and let stand 10 minutes.
2. Lightly beat 2 eggs, and stir into grits mixture; pour into a lightly greased 10-inch deep-dish pie plate.
3. Bake in preheated oven until golden, 20 minutes; remove from oven. Increase oven temperature to 400°F.
4. Sauté ham and scallions in a nonstick skillet over medium-high until scallions are tender, 5 minutes. Layer ham mixture over grits crust. Whisk together milk and remaining 6 eggs; pour over ham mixture. Sprinkle remaining ¾ cup cheese over egg mixture.
5. Bake until just set, 35 minutes. Let stand 10 minutes, and cut into wedges. Garnish, if desired.

TRY THIS TWIST!
Savory Bacon-and-Cheddar Breakfast Pie: Swap the ham for cooked crumbled bacon and Cheddar for the Swiss for a crowd-pleasing variation.

Individual Country Grits-and-Sausage Casseroles

Individual Country Grits-and-Sausage Casseroles

ACTIVE 30 MIN. - TOTAL 9 HOURS, 45 MIN., INCLUDING CHILL TIME

SERVES 8-10

- 2 lb. mild ground pork sausage
- 4 cups water
- 1 1/4 cups uncooked quick-cooking grits
- 12 oz. sharp Cheddar cheese, shredded (3 cups)
- 1 cup milk
- 1/2 tsp. garlic salt
- 4 large eggs, lightly beaten
- Paprika
- Garnish: chopped fresh chives

1. Cook sausage in a large skillet, stirring often, until browned, 6 to 8 minutes. Transfer to a plate lined with paper towels to drain well.
2. Bring 4 cups water to a boil in a large saucepan; gradually stir in grits. Return to a boil; cover, reduce heat, and simmer, stirring occasionally, 5 minutes. Remove from heat; add cheese and next 2 ingredients, stirring until cheese melts. Stir in sausage and eggs. Spoon mixture into 10 lightly greased 8-oz. ramekins; sprinkle with paprika.
3. Cover ramekins with plastic wrap, and chill 8 to 24 hours.
4. Preheat oven to 350°F. Uncover and let casseroles stand at room temperature 30 minutes. Bake in preheated oven until golden and mixture is set, 45 to 50 minutes. Garnish, if desired.

Variations:

Hot 'n' Spicy Grits-and-Sausage Casseroles: Substitute 2 lb. hot ground pork sausage for mild ground pork sausage and 12 oz. (3 cups) shredded pepper Jack cheese for sharp Cheddar cheese. Prepare recipe as directed.

Country Grits-and-Sausage Casserole: Prepare Step 2 as directed. Proceed as directed, substituting a lightly greased 13- x 9-inch baking dish for ramekins.

Hash Brown Breakfast Casserole

ACTIVE 15 MIN. - TOTAL 9 HOURS, 30 MIN., INCLUDING CHILL TIME

SERVES 8

- **1 lb. hot ground pork sausage**
- **1/4 cup chopped onion**
- **2 1/2 cups frozen cubed hash browns**
- **5 large eggs, lightly beaten**
- **8 oz. sharp Cheddar cheese, shredded (2 cups)**
- **1 3/4 cups milk**
- **1 cup all-purpose baking mix**
- **1/4 tsp. table salt**
- **1/4 tsp. black pepper**
- **Toppings: picante sauce or green hot sauce, sour cream**

1. Cook sausage and onion in a large skillet over medium-high 5 minutes. Stir in hash browns, and cook until sausage is browned and potatoes are lightly browned, 5 to 7 minutes. Transfer to a plate lined with paper towels to drain well; spoon into a greased 13- x 9-inch baking dish.
2. Stir together eggs, cheese, and next 4 ingredients; pour over sausage mixture, stirring well. Cover with nonstick foil, and chill at least 8 hours or overnight.
3. Preheat oven to 350°F. Meanwhile, let casserole stand at room temperature 30 minutes.
4. Bake, covered with nonstick foil, in preheated oven for 45 minutes. Uncover and bake until a wooden pick inserted in center comes out clean, 10 to 15 more minutes. Remove from oven; let stand 5 minutes. Serve with desired toppings.

Ham-and-Cheese Croissant Casserole

Nutmeg is optional, but it adds a subtle note of spice.

ACTIVE 15 MIN. - TOTAL 9 HOURS, 25 MIN., INCLUDING CHILL TIME

SERVES 8

- **3 (5-inch) large croissants**
- **1 (8-oz.) package chopped cooked ham**
- **1 (5-oz.) package shredded Swiss cheese**
- **6 large eggs**
- **1 cup half-and-half**
- **1 Tbsp. dry mustard**
- **2 Tbsp. honey**
- **1/2 tsp. table salt**
- **1/2 tsp. black pepper**
- **1/4 tsp. ground nutmeg (optional)**

1. Cut croissants in half lengthwise, and cut each half into 4 or 5 pieces. Place croissant pieces in a lightly greased 10-inch deep-dish pie plate. Top with chopped ham and Swiss cheese.
2. Whisk together eggs, next 5 ingredients, and, if desired, nutmeg in a large bowl.
3. Pour egg mixture over mixture in pie plate, pressing croissants down to submerge in egg mixture. Cover tightly with aluminum foil, and chill 8 to 24 hours.
4. Preheat oven to 325°F. Bake, covered, in preheated oven 35 minutes. Uncover and bake until browned and set, 25 to 30 more minutes. Let stand 10 minutes before serving.

TRY THIS TWIST!
Ham-and-Cheese Brioche Casserole: Use brioche rolls in place of croissants for another French spin on this breakfast casserole.

Veggie Frittata

This easy frittata is a great way to increase your vegetable intake. We use fresh baby spinach for a boost of vitamins and minerals, but you can get the same benefits from frozen chopped spinach. A combination of whole eggs and egg whites helps keep the fat and cholesterol content down.

ACTIVE 20 MIN. - TOTAL 35 MIN.

SERVES 8

- **1 medium-size yellow onion, chopped**
- **1/2 (8-oz.) package sliced fresh mushrooms**
- **1 Tbsp. olive oil**
- **1 (6-oz.) package fresh baby spinach**
- **4 large eggs**
- **6 large egg whites**
- **4 oz. shredded 2% reduced-fat sharp Cheddar cheese (1 cup)**
- **1 oz. freshly grated Parmesan cheese (1/4 cup)**
- **2 Tbsp. fat-free milk**
- **1/2 tsp. black pepper**
- **1/4 tsp. table salt**
- **1/4 tsp. ground nutmeg**

1. Preheat oven to 350°F. Sauté onion and mushrooms in hot oil in an oven-proof nonstick 10-inch skillet over medium-high until tender, 10 minutes. Stir in spinach, and cook until water evaporates and spinach wilts, 3 minutes. Remove from heat, and set aside.
2. Whisk together eggs, egg whites, Cheddar cheese, and next 5 ingredients.
3. Pour egg mixture into skillet with onion mixture, stirring to combine.
4. Bake in preheated oven until just set, 12 to 15 minutes. Let stand 3 minutes. Cut into 8 equal wedges.

TRY THIS TWIST!
For a bit of Louisiana flavor, use 1 (8-oz.) package fresh trinity blend in place of the yellow onion (or make you own using ¾ cup each chopped onion and celery, and ½ cup chopped bell pepper). Use ½ teaspoon Creole seasoning in place of the table salt and nutmeg.

Italian Brunch Casserole

ACTIVE 30 MIN. - TOTAL 9 HOURS, 45 MIN., INCLUDING CHILL TIME

SERVES 8

- **1 (8-oz.) package sweet Italian sausage**
- **8 scallions, sliced (1 cup)**
- **1 1/2 lb. zucchini, diced (about 3 cups)**
- **1 tsp. table salt**
- **1/2 tsp. black pepper**
- **1 (12-oz.) jar roasted red bell peppers, drained and chopped**
- **1 (16-oz.) Italian bread loaf, cut into 1-inch cubes (about 8 cups)**
- **8 oz. sharp Cheddar cheese, shredded (2 cups)**
- **6 large eggs***
- **1 1/2 cups milk**

1. Remove and discard casings from sausage. Cook sausage in a large nonstick skillet, stirring often, until browned and crumbled, 10 minutes; transfer to a plate lined with paper towels to drain well, reserving 1 Tbsp. drippings in skillet.
2. Cook scallions and next 3 ingredients in hot drippings until tender, 6 to 8 minutes. Stir in bell peppers. Drain and cool slightly. Stir in sausage.
3. Arrange 4 cups of the bread cubes in a lightly greased 13- x 9-inch baking dish. Top with half each of sausage mixture and cheese. Repeat with remaining bread, sausage, and cheese. Whisk together eggs and milk. Pour egg mixture over cheese. Cover and chill 8 hours.
4. Bake, covered, in preheated oven until bubbly and hot, 1 hour and 5 minutes; uncover and bake 10 more minutes.

Note: 1 ½ cups egg substitute may be substituted for 6 large eggs.

Sweet Potato and Edamame Hash

Hash is a morning mainstay on many Southern tables. This recipe offers a new twist with nutrient-packed ingredients such as sweet potato and edamame.

ACTIVE 42 MIN. - TOTAL 42 MIN.

SERVES 8

- **1 (8-oz.) package diced smoked lean ham**
- **1 medium-size sweet onion, finely chopped**
- **1 Tbsp. olive oil**
- **2 medium-size sweet potatoes, peeled and cut into 1/4-inch cubes**
- **1 garlic clove, minced**
- **1 (12-oz.) package frozen shelled edamame (green soybeans)**
- **1 (12-oz.) package frozen whole kernel corn**
- **1/4 cup chicken broth**
- **1 Tbsp. chopped fresh thyme**
- **1/2 tsp. kosher or table salt**
- **1/2 tsp. freshly ground black pepper**
- **4 cups arugula**
- **8 large eggs, poached**

1. Sauté ham and onion in hot oil in a nonstick skillet over medium-high until onion is tender and ham is lightly browned, 6 to 8 minutes. Stir in sweet potatoes, and cook 5 minutes. Add garlic; cook 1 minute. Stir in edamame and next 3 ingredients. Reduce heat to medium. Cover and cook, stirring occasionally, 10 to 12 minutes or until potatoes are tender. Stir in salt and pepper.
2. Place ½ cup arugula on each of 8 plates. Top each with 1 cup hash. Place 1 poached egg onto each serving. Serve immediately.

TRY THIS TWIST!
Old World Hash: Substitute russet potatoes for the sweet potatoes, green peas for the edamame, and parsley for the thyme in Step 1 .

Grillades and Grits

Journey to New Orleans and you'll find this popular combo served up at many a breakfast or brunch. Lean cutlets like pork, veal, or beef are cooked alongside fresh vegetables, then served over creamy grits for a hearty meal.

ACTIVE 20 MIN. - TOTAL 1 HOUR, 10 MIN., INCLUDING GRITS

SERVES 4

GRILLADES

- **3 Tbsp. all-purpose flour**
- **1 tsp. Creole seasoning, divided**
- **1 lb. lean breakfast pork cutlets, trimmed**
- **2 tsp. olive oil, divided**
- **1 cup finely diced onion**
- **1 cup finely diced celery**
- **1/2 cup finely diced green bell pepper**
- **1 (14.5-oz.) can no-salt-added diced tomatoes**
- **1 (14-oz.) can reduced-sodium fat-free chicken broth**

CREAMY GRITS

- **1 (14-oz.) can reduced-sodium fat-free chicken broth**
- **1 cup fat-free milk**
- **1/2 cup uncooked quick-cooking grits**

1. Prepare the Grillades: Combine flour and ½ tsp. of the Creole seasoning in a shallow dish. Dredge pork in flour mixture.
2. Cook pork, in 2 batches, in ½ tsp. of the hot oil per batch in a large skillet over medium-high on each side or until done, 2 minutes. Remove from skillet, and keep warm.
3. Add remaining 1 tsp. oil to skillet. Cook diced onion, celery, and bell pepper in hot oil 3 to 5 minutes or until vegetables are tender. Stir in remaining ½ tsp. Creole seasoning. Stir in diced tomatoes and chicken broth, and cook 2 minutes, stirring to loosen browned bits from bottom of skillet. Simmer until liquid reduces to about 2 Tbsp., 15 to 18 minutes .
4. Prepare the Creamy Grits: Bring chicken broth and milk to a boil in a medium saucepan over medium-high; reduce heat to low, and whisk in grits. Cook, whisking occasionally, 15 to 20 minutes or until creamy and thickened.
5. Serve tomato mixture over Creamy Grits and pork. Serve immediately.

Creamy Cheese Grits

ACTIVE 10 MIN. - TOTAL 15 MIN.

SERVES 6-8

- **5 cups water**
- **1 tsp. table salt**
- **1 1/4 cups uncooked quick-cooking grits***
- **1/2 (8-oz.) block sharp Cheddar cheese, shredded (about 1 cup)**
- **1/2 (8-oz.) block Monterey Jack cheese, shredded (about 1 cup)**
- **1/2 cup half-and-half**
- **1 Tbsp. butter**
- **1/4 tsp. black pepper**
- **Garnishes: butter, freshly ground black pepper**

Bring 5 cups water and 1 tsp. salt to a boil in a medium saucepan over medium-high. Gradually whisk in grits; bring to a boil. Reduce heat to medium-low, and simmer, stirring occasionally, until thickened, 10 minutes. Stir in Cheddar cheese and next 4 ingredients until cheese is melted and mixture is blended. Garnish, if desired. Serve immediately.

Note: Stone-ground grits may be substituted for quick-cooking grits. Increase liquid to 6 cups, and increase cook time to 50 minutes.

Sausage Tostadas

Low-fat ground pork sausage, egg whites, and reduced-fat cheese and Greek yogurt slash the calorie and saturated fat count of this satisfying breakfast.

ACTIVE 20 MIN. - TOTAL 33 MIN.

SERVES 6

- **6 (6-inch) corn tortillas**
- **Cooking spray**
- **1/8 tsp. table salt**
- **6 oz. reduced-fat ground pork sausage**
- **1 (8-oz.) package refrigerated prechopped tricolor pepper mix**
- **1/2 cup vertically sliced onion**
- **1/2 tsp. crushed red pepper**
- **6 large egg whites**
- **4 large eggs**
- **6 oz. shredded 2% reduced-fat Mexican four-cheese blend (1 1/2 cups)**
- **1/2 cup 2% reduced-fat Greek yogurt**
- **1/2 cup refrigerated prepared salsa**
- **3 scallions, chopped**

1. Preheat oven to 425°F. Arrange tortillas in a single layer on a baking sheet coated with cooking spray; spray tortillas with cooking spray, and sprinkle with salt. Bake in preheated oven until crisp and lightly golden, 13 minutes, turning after 8 minutes.
2. Meanwhile, cook sausage in a large nonstick skillet over medium-high, stirring often, until browned and crumbled, 5 minutes. Add pepper mix, onion, and crushed red pepper; sauté 5 minutes or until vegetables are tender.
3. Whisk together egg whites and eggs; pour over sausage mixture. Cook, without stirring, 1 minute or until eggs begin to set on bottom. Gently draw cooked edges away from sides of skillet to form large pieces. Cook, stirring occasionally, 3 to 4 minutes or until eggs are thickened and moist. (Do not overstir.)
4. Spoon about ½ cup egg mixture onto each tortilla; sprinkle each with ¼ cup cheese. Bake in preheated oven until cheese is melted, 2 to 3 minutes.
5. Top each tostada with 4 tsp. yogurt and 4 tsp. salsa. Sprinkle scallions over tostadas. Serve immediately.

Migas Tacos

In Tex-Mex cuisine, migas combine scrambled eggs with crunchy tortilla strips, peppers, onions, tomato, and cheese. Enjoy the mix in a soft breakfast taco; cilantro would be a nice addition.

ACTIVE 15 MIN. - TOTAL 23 MIN.

SERVES 2

- **1/3 cup lightly crushed tortilla chips**
- **1/4 cup chopped onion**
- **1/4 cup diced tomatoes**
- **2 Tbsp. chopped jalapeño peppers**
- **1 tsp. vegetable oil**
- **2 large eggs, lightly beaten**
- **1/16 tsp. table salt**
- **1/8 tsp. black pepper**
- **2 (8-inch) soft taco-size flour tortillas, warmed**
- **1/2 cup (2 oz.) shredded 2% reduced-fat Mexican four-cheese blend**

1. Cook first 4 ingredients in hot oil in a medium-size nonstick skillet over medium just until onion is tender, 3 to 4 minutes.
2. Whisk together eggs, salt, and pepper. Add to skillet, and cook, without stirring, 1 to 2 minutes or until eggs begin to set on bottom. Gently draw cooked edges away from sides of pan to form large pieces. Cook, stirring occasionally, 2 minutes or until eggs are thickened and moist. (Do not overstir.) Spoon egg mixture into warm tortillas, and sprinkle each with ¼ cup cheese; serve immediately.

WAFFLES, FRENCH TOAST & PANCAKES

Buttermilk and Brown Sugar Waffles

When the waffle iron is out on the counter, children are probably in the kitchen, squirming with excitement. It's almost as if they are willing the waffles to cook faster. Freeze any leftover waffles to liven up a weekday breakfast. They reheat nicely in the toaster.

ACTIVE 15 MIN. - TOTAL 25 MIN.

MAKES 12 (4-INCH) WAFFLES

- **2 cups all-purpose flour**
- **3 Tbsp. light brown sugar**
- **1 tsp. baking powder**
- **1/2 tsp. table salt**
- **1/4 tsp. baking soda**
- **2 large eggs**
- **3/4 cup buttermilk**
- **3/4 cup milk**
- **1/3 cup unsalted butter, melted**
- **Garnishes: butter, syrup, blueberries**

1. Whisk together first 5 ingredients in a large bowl.
2. Whisk together eggs and next 2 ingredients in a medium bowl. Add to flour mixture, and whisk just until blended. Whisk in melted butter.
3. Cook batter, in batches, in a preheated, oiled Belgian-style waffle iron until golden. (Cook times will vary.) Garnish, if desired.

Cinnamon Roll Waffles with Bananas Foster Sauce

Cinnamon roll waffles are easy to make and have a wonderful chewy texture. Top with decadent bananas Foster sauce for a special Christmas brunch treat. Double the recipe for a crowd.

ACTIVE 20 MIN. - TOTAL 20 MIN.
SERVES 10

- **2 (17.5-oz.) cans refrigerated jumbo cinnamon rolls**
- **1 cup heavy cream**
- **1/2 tsp. vanilla extract**
- **1/2 cup butter**
- **1 cup packed light brown sugar**
- **1/3 cup dark rum**
- **4 medium-size ripe bananas, sliced**
- **1 cup chopped toasted walnuts or pecans**

1. Preheat a Belgian waffle iron to medium. Line a baking sheet with aluminum foil.
2. Separate the cinnamon rolls; reserve icing. Lightly flatten each roll to ½-inch thickness with your fingers. Lightly grease the preheated Belgian waffle iron with cooking spray. Place 1 flattened roll in the center of each cavity of the prepared waffle iron. Cook until golden brown and done. Transfer the waffles to the prepared pan. Keep warm in a 200°F oven.
3. Beat the cream, vanilla, and icing from 1 can of the cinnamon rolls with an electric mixer on high speed until soft peaks form, reserving the remaining container of frosting for another use. Cover and chill.
4. Melt the butter in a large skillet over medium-high; add the brown sugar, and cook, stirring constantly, until the sugar melts, 2 minutes.
5. Remove from heat. Stir in the rum, then carefully ignite the fumes just above the mixture with a long match or long multipurpose lighter. Let the flames die down.
6. Return the skillet to heat. Cook, stirring constantly, until sauce is smooth, 2 minutes. Add the banana slices; cook 1 minute, turning slices to coat.
7. Top each waffle with about ⅓ cup of the banana sauce and a large dollop of the whipped cream mixture. Sprinkle with the walnuts. Serve immediately.

Hot Chicken-and-Waffle Sandwiches

ACTIVE 40 MIN. TOTAL 40 MIN.
SERVES 6

HOT CHICKEN
- **9 fried chicken breast tenders**
- **1 Tbsp. cayenne pepper**
- **1 tsp. paprika**
- **1/2 tsp. garlic powder**
- **2 Tbsp. sugar, divided**
- **1/2 cup peanut oil**

WAFFLES
- **2 cups all-purpose flour**
- **1 1/2 tsp. baking powder**
- **3/4 tsp. baking soda**
- **3/4 tsp. table salt**
- **1 1/2 cups buttermilk**
- **1/4 cup salted butter, melted**
- **2 large eggs**

CHIVE CREAM
- **1/2 cup sour cream**
- **2 Tbsp. thinly sliced chives**
- **1 tsp. water**

1. Prepare Hot Chicken: Preheat oven to 200°F. Place chicken tenders in a single layer on a baking sheet, and keep warm in oven until ready to use.
2. Stir together cayenne pepper, paprika, garlic powder, and 1 Tbsp. of the sugar in a small saucepan. Whisk in peanut oil, and cook over low, whisking constantly, until well combined, about 5 minutes. Set aside.
3. Prepare Waffles: Whisk together flour, next 3 ingredients, and remaining 1 Tbsp. sugar in a medium bowl. Whisk together buttermilk, butter, and eggs in a small bowl. Stir buttermilk mixture into flour mixture until combined. Cook batter, in batches, in a preheated, lightly greased waffle iron until golden brown, 4 to 5 minutes.
4. Prepare Chive Cream: Stir together sour cream, chives, and 1 teaspoon water in a small bowl.
5. Assemble Sandwiches: Toss tenders and cayenne mixture in a large bowl. Place 1 ½ tenders on each of 6 waffles; top each with 2 tablespoons Chive Cream and 1 waffle. Serve immediately.

TRY THIS TWIST!
Hot Fish-and-Waffle Sandwiches: Substitute 9 breaded fish sticks cooked according to package directions for the chicken tenders in this recipe.

Hot Chicken-and-Waffle Sandwiches

Praline-Pecan French Toast

A short-order breakfast special gets an easy hands-off finish in the oven.

ACTIVE 20 MIN. - TOTAL 8 HOURS, 55 MIN., INCLUDING CHILL TIME

SERVES 8-10

- 1 (16-oz.) French bread loaf
- 1 cup packed light brown sugar
- 1/3 cup butter, melted
- 2 Tbsp. maple syrup
- 3/4 cup chopped pecans
- 4 large eggs, lightly beaten
- 1 cup 2% reduced-fat milk
- 2 Tbsp. granulated sugar
- 1 tsp. ground cinnamon
- 1 tsp. vanilla extract

1. Cut 10 (1-inch-thick) slices of bread. Reserve remaining bread for another use.
2. Stir together brown sugar and next 2 ingredients; pour into a lightly greased 13- x 9-inch baking dish. Sprinkle with chopped pecans.
3. Whisk together eggs and next 4 ingredients. Arrange bread slices over pecans; pour egg mixture over bread. Cover and chill 8 hours.
4. Preheat oven to 350°F. Bake bread until golden brown, 35 to 37 minutes. Serve immediately.

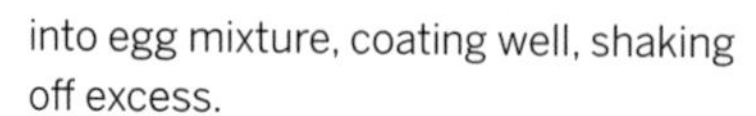

Praline-Pecan French Toast

Croissant French Toast with Fresh Strawberry Syrup

ACTIVE 25 MIN. - TOTAL 1 HOUR, INCLUDING SYRUP

SERVES 4

CROISSANT FRENCH TOAST

- 4 large day-old croissants
- 3/4 cup milk
- 2 large eggs
- 1 tsp. vanilla extract
- 2 Tbsp. butter
- 3 Tbsp. powdered sugar

FRESH STRAWBERRY SYRUP

- 1 qt. fresh strawberries, sliced
- 1/2 cup granulated sugar
- 1/4 cup orange liqueur or orange juice
- 1 tsp. orange zest
- Sweetened whipped cream (optional)

1. Prepare the Croissant French Toast: Slice croissants in half lengthwise. Whisk together milk, eggs, and vanilla in a shallow dish. Dip croissant halves into egg mixture, coating well, shaking off excess.
2. Melt 1 Tbsp. of the butter in a large nonstick skillet over medium. Add 4 croissant halves, and cook until golden brown, 2 minutes on each side. Repeat procedure with remaining butter and croissant halves. Sprinkle evenly with powdered sugar.
3. Prepare the Fresh Strawberry Syrup: Stir together first 4 ingredients in a microwave-safe bowl, and let stand 30 minutes or until sugar is dissolved. If desired, microwave at HIGH 1 to 2 minutes or until warm. Spoon over French toast, and, if desired, top with whipped cream.

Note: 1 (16-oz.) package frozen whole strawberries may be substituted for fresh strawberries. Place frozen strawberries in a colander in a bowl, and let stand at room temperature 2 hours or until completely thawed. Discard juice. Stir together strawberries and next 3 ingredients in a microwave-safe bowl; let stand 5 minutes. If desired, microwave at HIGH 1 to 2 minutes or until warm. Garnish, if desired.

English Muffin French Toast

French toast doesn't have to be limited to Sunday brunch. Make it quick and easy by using whole-grain English muffins.

ACTIVE 20 MIN. - TOTAL 8 HOURS, 20 MIN., INCLUDING CHILL TIME

SERVES 6

- 4 large eggs
- 1 cup fat-free buttermilk
- 2 tsp. orange zest
- 1 tsp. vanilla extract
- 6 English muffins, split
- 1 cup fat-free Greek yogurt
- 2 Tbsp. maple syrup
- 1 1/2 cups chopped fresh strawberries, blueberries, or nectarines

1. Whisk together first 4 ingredients in a bowl. Place English muffins in a

13- x 9-inch baking dish, overlapping edges. Pour egg mixture over muffins. Cover and chill 8 to 12 hours.
2. Remove muffins from remaining liquid, discarding liquid.
3. Cook muffins, in batches, in a large skillet coated with cooking spray over medium-high until muffins are golden, 2 to 3 minutes on each side. Stir together yogurt and syrup until blended; serve with muffin French toast and fruit toppings.

Overnight Blackberry French Toast

ACTIVE 21 MIN. - TOTAL 8 HOURS, 51 MIN., INCLUDING CHILL TIME

SERVES 8-10

- **1 cup blackberry jam**
- **1 (12-oz.) French bread loaf, cut into 1 1/2-inch cubes**
- **1 (8-oz.) package 1/3-less-fat cream cheese, cut into 1-inch cubes**
- **4 large eggs**
- **2 cups half-and-half**
- **1 tsp. ground cinnamon**
- **1 tsp. vanilla extract**
- **1/2 cup packed brown sugar**
- **Toppings: maple syrup, whipped cream**

1. Cook jam in a small saucepan over medium until melted and smooth, stirring once, 1 to 2 minutes.
2. Place half of bread cubes in bottom of a lightly greased 13- x 9-inch baking dish. Top with cream cheese cubes, and drizzle with melted jam. Top with remaining bread cubes.
3. Whisk together eggs and next 3 ingredients. Pour over bread mixture. Sprinkle with brown sugar. Cover tightly with aluminum foil, and chill 8 to 24 hours.
4. Preheat oven to 325°F. Bake, covered, 20 minutes. Uncover and bake until bread is golden brown and mixture is set, 10 to 15 more minutes. Serve with desired toppings.

Variation:

Overnight Blueberry French Toast: Substitute 1 cup blueberry jam for blackberry jam. Prepare recipe as directed.

Sweet Peach Pancakes

The sweetness of the peaches combined with the natural sweetness of the cornmeal makes for a delicious morning. A well-seasoned griddle or skillet won't need much butter and oil; use only as much as you need to keep the pancakes from sticking.

ACTIVE 1 HOUR, 5 MIN. - TOTAL 1 HOUR, 5 MIN.

MAKES 10 PANCAKES

- **3/4 cup all-purpose soft-wheat flour (such as White Lily)**
- **3/4 cup plain yellow cornmeal**
- **2 Tbsp. granulated sugar**
- **1/2 tsp. baking powder**
- **1/2 tsp. baking soda**
- **1/2 tsp. table salt**
- **1 1/4 cups buttermilk**
- **2 large eggs**
- **2 Tbsp. unsalted butter, melted**
- **Butter**
- **Canola oil**
- **3 medium peaches (about 1 1/4 lb.), unpeeled and cut into 10 thin wedges each**
- **Garnishes: sweetened whipped cream, syrup, fresh mint**

1. Sift together first 6 ingredients in a large bowl. Whisk together buttermilk, eggs, and melted butter in a medium bowl. Add buttermilk mixture to flour mixture, and whisk just until combined.
2. Melt a small amount of butter with oil on a griddle or large nonstick skillet over medium. Place 3 peach wedges for each pancake on griddle; starting at outside edge of peach slices, carefully pour 1/4 cup batter over each group of slices to form a circle.
3. Cook pancakes 3 to 4 minutes or until tops are covered with bubbles and edges look dry and cooked. Turn and cook other sides until golden, 2 to 3 minutes. Transfer to a baking sheet; keep warm in a 300°F oven. Repeat procedure with remaining peach slices and batter, adding more butter and oil to griddle as needed. Garnish, if desired.

Note: Two medium peaches, unpeeled and diced, may be substituted. Stir into batter at end of Step 1. Cook pancakes as directed, using 1/4 cup batter per pancake.

Hummingbird Pancakes

The South's favorite cake takes a breakfast turn as Hummingbird Pancakes.

ACTIVE 30 MIN. - TOTAL 45 MIN., INCLUDING SAUCE

MAKES ABOUT 18 PANCAKES

PANCAKES

- **1 1/2 cups all-purpose flour**
- **2 tsp. baking powder**
- **3/4 tsp. table salt**
- **1/2 tsp. ground cinnamon**
- **1 1/2 cups buttermilk**
- **1 cup mashed very ripe bananas**
- **1/2 cup drained canned crushed pineapple in juice**
- **1/3 cup granulated sugar**
- **1 large egg, lightly beaten**
- **3 Tbsp. canola oil**
- **1/2 cup chopped toasted pecans**

CREAM CHEESE ANGLAISE

- **1 1/2 cups half-and-half**
- **1/2 (8-oz.) package cream cheese, softened**
- **1/3 cup granulated sugar**
- **3 large egg yolks**
- **1 Tbsp. cornstarch**
- **1/8 tsp. table salt**
- **2 Tbsp. butter**
- **1 tsp. vanilla extract**
- **Garnishes: sliced bananas, chopped fresh pineapple**

1. Prepare the Pancakes: Preheat griddle to 350°F. Stir together first 4 ingredients in a large bowl. Whisk together buttermilk and next 5 ingredients in another bowl. Gradually stir buttermilk mixture into flour mixture just until dry ingredients are moistened. Fold in toasted pecans.
2. Pour about 1/4 cup batter for each pancake onto a hot, buttered griddle or large nonstick skillet. Cook until tops are covered with bubbles and edges look dry and cooked, 3 to 4 minutes. Turn and cook until done, 3 to 4 minutes. Place in a single layer on a baking sheet, and keep warm in a 200°F oven up to 30 minutes.
3. Prepare the Cream Cheese Anglaise: Process first 6 ingredients in a blender until smooth. Bring mixture to a boil in a medium saucepan over medium, whisking constantly. Boil, whisking constantly, 1 minute. Remove from heat, and whisk in butter and vanilla. Serve immediately with pancakes. Garnish, if desired.

CAKES & BREADS

Sweet Potato Coffee Cake

ACTIVE 30 MIN. - TOTAL 3 HOURS, 15 MIN., INCLUDING GLAZE

MAKES 2 (10-INCH CAKES)

SWEET POTATO COFFEE CAKE

- **2 (1/4-oz.) envelopes active dry yeast**
- **1/2 cup warm water (100°F to 110°F)**
- **1 tsp. granulated sugar**
- **5 1/2 cups bread flour**
- **1 1/2 tsp. table salt**
- **1 tsp. baking soda**
- **1 cup mashed cooked sweet potato**
- **1 large egg, lightly beaten**
- **1 cup buttermilk**
- **1/2 cup granulated sugar**
- **1/4 cup butter, melted**
- **1 Tbsp. orange zest**
- **2/3 cup granulated sugar**
- **2/3 cup packed brown sugar**
- **1 Tbsp. ground cinnamon**
- **1/4 cup butter, melted**

CARAMEL GLAZE

- **1 cup packed brown sugar**
- **1/2 cup butter**
- **1/4 cup evaporated milk**
- **1 cup powdered sugar, sifted**
- **1 tsp. vanilla extract**

1. Prepare the Sweet Potato Coffee Cake: Stir together first 3 ingredients in a 1-cup glass measuring cup; let stand 5 minutes.
2. Stir together 4 ½ cups of the bread flour, salt, and baking soda. Beat yeast mixture and ½ cup bread flour with a stand mixer on medium speed until well blended. Gradually add sweet potato, next 5 ingredients, and flour mixture, beating until well blended. Turn dough out onto a well-floured surface, and knead until smooth and elastic, gradually adding remaining ½ cup bread flour. Place dough in a lightly greased large bowl, turning to coat all sides. Cover and let rise in a warm place (80°F to 85°F), free from drafts, 1 hour or until doubled in size.
3. Stir together ⅔ cup granulated sugar and next 2 ingredients. Punch dough down; turn out onto a well-floured surface. Divide dough in half. Roll 1 portion into a 16- x 12-inch rectangle. Brush with half of ¼ cup melted butter. Sprinkle with half of sugar mixture. Cut dough lengthwise into 6 (2-inch-wide) strips using a pizza cutter or knife.
4. Loosely coil 1 strip (sugared side facing inward), and place in center of a lightly greased 10-inch round pan. Loosely coil remaining dough strips, 1 at a time, around center strip to make a single large spiral. Repeat with remaining dough half, butter, and sugar mixture. Cover and let rise in a warm place (80°F to 85°F), free from drafts, 30 minutes or until doubled in size.
5. Preheat oven to 350°F. Bake in preheated oven until lightly browned, 30 minutes. Cool in pans on a wire rack 10 minutes. Remove from pans to serving plates.
6. Meanwhile, prepare the Caramel Glaze: Bring first 3 ingredients to a boil over medium, whisking constantly. Boil, whisking constantly, 1 minute. Remove from heat; whisk in powdered sugar and vanilla until smooth. Stir gently until mixture begins to cool and thicken, 3 to 5 minutes. Use immediately, brushing Caramel Glaze over swirls.

Chocolate-Cream Cheese Coffee Cake

A swirl of cream cheese is the perfect contrast against the intense chocolate in this treat.

ACTIVE 35 MIN. - TOTAL 1 HOUR, 20 MIN.

MAKES 2 (9-INCH) CAKES

CRUMBLE TOPPING

- **1 1/3 cups all-purpose flour**
- **1/2 cup packed brown sugar**
- **1/2 cup cold butter, cut up**
- **1 cup chopped pecans**

CREAM CHEESE BATTER

- **1 (8-oz.) package cream cheese, softened**
- **1/4 cup granulated sugar**
- **1 Tbsp. all-purpose flour**
- **1 large egg**
- **1/2 tsp. vanilla extract**

CHOCOLATE VELVET CAKE BATTER

- **1 1/2 cups semisweet chocolate chips**
- **1/2 cup butter, softened**
- **1 (16-oz.) package light brown sugar**
- **3 large eggs**
- **2 cups all-purpose flour**
- **1 tsp. baking soda**
- **1/2 tsp. table salt**
- **1 (8-oz.) container sour cream**
- **1 cup hot water**
- **2 tsp. vanilla extract**

VANILLA GLAZE

- **1 cup powdered sugar**
- **2 Tbsp. milk**
- **1/2 tsp. vanilla extract**

1. Prepare the Crumble Topping: Preheat oven to 350°F. Stir together 1 ⅓ cups flour and brown sugar in a medium bowl. Cut butter into flour mixture with a pastry blender (or use your fingers) until mixture is crumbly; stir in pecans; set aside.
2. Prepare the Cream Cheese Batter: Beat cream cheese with a mixer on medium speed until smooth; add granulated sugar and 1 Tbsp. flour, beating until blended. Add egg and ½ tsp. vanilla, beating until blended; set aside.
3. Prepare the Chocolate Velvet Cake Batter: Microwave chocolate in a microwave-safe bowl at HIGH 1 to 1 ½ minutes or until melted and smooth, stirring at 30-second intervals. Beat butter and brown sugar with a mixer on medium speed until well blended. Add eggs, 1 at a time, beating just until blended after each addition. Add melted chocolate, beating just until blended. Sift together flour, baking soda, and salt. Gradually add to chocolate mixture alternately with sour cream, beginning and ending with flour mixture. Beat on low speed just until blended after each addition. Gradually add 1 cup hot water in a slow, steady stream, beating on low speed just until blended. Stir in vanilla.
4. Spoon Chocolate Velvet Cake Batter evenly into 2 greased and floured 9-inch springform pans. Dollop cream cheese mixture evenly over cake batter, and swirl batter gently with a knife. Sprinkle reserved pecan mixture evenly over cake batter.
5. Bake in preheated oven 45 minutes or until set. Cool on a wire rack.
6. Prepare the Vanilla Glaze: Whisk together powdered sugar, milk, and ½ tsp. vanilla. Drizzle evenly over tops of coffee cakes.

TRY THIS TWIST!

Mocha-Cream Cheese Latte Cake: Add 1 teaspoon espresso powder to the Chocolate Velvet Cake Batter in Step 3.

Caramel Apple Coffee Cake

ACTIVE 35 MIN. - TOTAL 4 HOURS, 50 MIN.

SERVES 8 TO 10

- 2 Tbsp. butter
- 3 cups peeled and sliced Granny Smith apples (about 3 large)

STREUSEL TOPPING

- 1 1/2 cups all-purpose flour
- 1 cup chopped pecans
- 1/2 cup melted butter
- 1/2 cup packed light brown sugar
- 1/4 cup granulated sugar
- 1 1/2 tsp. ground cinnamon
- 1/4 tsp. table salt

CARAMEL SAUCE

- 1 cup packed light brown sugar
- 1/2 cup butter
- 1/4 cup whipping cream
- 1/4 cup honey

CARAMEL APPLE COFFEE CAKE

- 1/2 cup butter, softened
- 1 cup granulated sugar
- 2 large eggs
- 2 cups all-purpose flour
- 2 tsp. baking powder
- 1/2 tsp. table salt
- 2/3 cup milk
- 2 tsp. vanilla extract

1. Preheat oven to 350°F. Melt 2 Tbsp. butter in a large skillet over medium-high; add apples; sauté 5 minutes or until softened. Remove from heat; cool completely, about 30 minutes.

2. Prepare the Streusel Topping: Stir together 1 ½ cups all-purpose flour, chopped pecans, ½ cup melted butter, brown sugar, ¼ cup granulated sugar, cinnamon, and ¼ tsp. salt until blended. Let stand 30 minutes or until firm enough to crumble into small pieces.

3. Prepare the Caramel Sauce: Bring 1 cup firmly packed light brown sugar, ½ cup butter, ¼ cup whipping cream, and ¼ cup honey to a boil in a medium saucepan over medium-high, stirring constantly; boil, stirring constantly, 2 minutes. Remove from heat, and cool 15 minutes before serving. Store in an airtight container in refrigerator up to 1 week. (Reserve ½ cup Caramel Sauce for another use.) To reheat, microwave at HIGH 10 to 15 seconds or just until warm; stir until smooth.

4. Prepare the Caramel Apple Coffee Cake: Preheat oven to 350°F. Beat butter with a mixer on medium speed until creamy; gradually add sugar, beating well. Add eggs, 1 at a time, beating until blended after each addition.

5. Combine flour, baking powder, and salt; add to butter mixture alternately with milk, beginning and ending with flour mixture. Beat on low speed until blended after each addition. Stir in vanilla. Pour batter into a greased and floured shiny 9-inch springform pan; top with apples. Drizzle with ½ cup Caramel Sauce; sprinkle with Streusel Topping.

6. Bake in preheated oven for 45 minutes. Cover loosely with aluminum foil to prevent excessive browning; bake until center is set, 25 to 30 more minutes. (A wooden pick inserted in center of cake will not come out clean.) Cool in pan on a wire rack 30 minutes; remove sides of pan. Cool completely on wire rack, about 1 ½ hours. Drizzle with ½ cup Caramel Sauce.

Caramel Apple Coffee Cake

Cream-Filled Grilled Pound Cake

We didn't think pound cake could get any better until we grilled it. Choose homemade, frozen, or fresh store-bought cake.

ACTIVE 5 MIN. - TOTAL 11 MIN.

SERVES 8

- **1/2 cup pineapple cream cheese**
- **16 (1/2-inch-thick) pound cake slices**
- **Sweetened whipped cream**
- **Fresh strawberries**

Preheat a grill to medium-high (about 450°F). Spread pineapple cream cheese over 1 side of 8 pound cake slices. Top with remaining 8 pound cake slices. Grill, covered, 2 to 3 minutes on each side. Top with whipped cream and fresh strawberries. Serve immediately.

TRY THIS TWIST!
Bananas Foster Grilled Pound Cake: Swap plain cream cheese for the pineapple cream cheese, and top finished dessert with banana slices, a drizzle of caramel sauce, and the whipped cream.

Iced Cinnamon Rolls

Cream cheese adds richness and body to the icing spread on these warm breakfast favorites.

ACTIVE 30 MIN. - TOTAL 3 HOURS, 40 MIN., INCLUDING ICING

MAKES 16 ROLLS

CINNAMON ROLLS

- **1 (1/4-oz.) envelope active dry yeast**
- **1/4 cup warm water (100°F to 110°F)**
- **1 tsp. granulated sugar**
- **1 cup butter, softened, divided**
- **1 cup granulated sugar, divided**
- **1 tsp. table salt**
- **2 large eggs, lightly beaten**
- **1 cup milk**
- **1 Tbsp. fresh lemon juice**
- **1/4 tsp. ground nutmeg**
- **4 1/2 cups bread flour**
- **1/4 to 1/2 cup bread flour**
- **1/2 cup packed light brown sugar**
- **1 Tbsp. ground cinnamon**
- **1 cup chopped toasted pecans**

CREAM CHEESE ICING

- **1 (3-oz.) package cream cheese, softened**
- **2 Tbsp. butter, softened**
- **2 1/4 cups powdered sugar**
- **1 tsp. vanilla extract**
- **2 Tbsp. milk**

1. Prepare the Cinnamon Rolls: Combine first 3 ingredients in a 1-cup glass measuring cup; let stand 5 minutes.
2. Beat ½ cup butter with a mixer on medium speed until creamy. Gradually add ½ cup of the granulated sugar and table salt, beating until light and fluffy. Add eggs and next 3 ingredients, beating until blended. Stir in yeast mixture.
3. Gradually add 4 ½ cups flour to butter mixture, beating on low speed 1 to 2 minutes or until well blended.
4. Sprinkle about ¼ cup bread flour onto a flat surface; turn dough out, and knead until smooth and elastic (about 5 minutes), adding up to ¼ cup bread flour as needed to prevent dough from sticking to hands and surface. Place dough in a lightly greased large bowl, turning to coat all sides. Cover and let rise in a warm place (80°F to 85°F), free from drafts, or until dough doubles in size, 1 ½ to 2 hours.
5. Punch dough down; turn out onto a lightly floured surface. Roll into a 16- x 12-inch rectangle. Spread with remaining ½ cup butter, leaving a 1-inch border around edges. Stir together brown sugar, cinnamon, and remaining ½ cup granulated sugar, and sprinkle sugar mixture over butter. Top with pecans. Roll up dough, jelly-roll fashion, starting at 1 long side; cut into 16 slices.
6. Place rolls, cut sides down, in 2 lightly greased 10-inch round pans. Cover and let rise in a warm place (80°F to 85°F), free from drafts, until rolls double in size, 1 hour.
7. Preheat oven to 350°F. Bake in preheated oven until rolls are golden brown, 20 to 22 minutes. Cool in pans 5 minutes.
8. Prepare the Cream Cheese Icing: Beat first 2 ingredients with a mixer on medium speed until creamy. Gradually add powdered sugar, beating on low speed until blended. Stir in vanilla and 1 Tbsp. milk. Add remaining 1 Tbsp. milk, 1 tsp. at a time, stirring until icing is smooth and creamy. Brush rolls with Cream Cheese Icing. Serve immediately.

Apricot-Pecan Cinnamon Rolls

You can also prepare these rolls as directed, but place one slice in each of 12 lightly greased 3-inch muffin cups. Bake at 375°F until golden brown, 20 to 25 minutes.

ACTIVE 10 MIN. - TOTAL 1 HOUR, 45 MIN.

MAKES 1 DOZEN ROLLS

- **1 (26.4-oz.) pkg. frozen biscuits**
- **1 (6-oz.) pkg. dried apricots**
- **All-purpose flour**
- **1/4 cup butter, softened**
- **3/4 cup packed brown sugar**
- **1 tsp. ground cinnamon**
- **1/2 cup chopped toasted pecans**
- **1 cup powdered sugar**
- **3 Tbsp. milk**
- **1/2 tsp. vanilla extract**

1. Arrange frozen biscuits, with sides touching, in 3 rows of 4 biscuits on a lightly floured surface. Let stand 30 to 45 minutes or until biscuits are thawed but still cool to the touch.
2. Pour boiling water to cover over dried apricots, and let stand 10 minutes; drain well. Chop apricots.
3. Sprinkle thawed biscuits lightly with flour. Press biscuit edges together, and pat to form a 12- x 10-inch rectangle of dough; spread evenly with softened butter. Stir together brown sugar and cinnamon; sprinkle evenly over butter. Sprinkle chopped apricots and pecans over brown sugar mixture.
4. Preheat oven to 375°F. Roll up dough, starting at one long end; cut into 12 (about 1-inch-thick) slices. Place rolls into a lightly greased 10-inch cast-iron skillet, 10-inch round pan, or 9-inch square pan.
5. Bake in preheated oven until center rolls are golden brown and done, 35 to 40 minutes; cool slightly.
6. Stir together 1 cup powdered sugar, 3 Tbsp. milk, and ½ tsp. vanilla; drizzle over rolls.

Orange Rolls

ACTIVE 45 MIN. - TOTAL 4 HOURS, INCLUDING TOPPING AND GLAZE

MAKES 24 ROLLS

ORANGE ROLLS

- **1 (1/4-oz.) envelope active dry yeast**
- **1/4 cup warm water (100°F to 110°F)**
- **1 tsp. granulated sugar**
- **1/2 cup butter, softened**
- **1/2 cup granulated sugar**
- **1 tsp. table salt**
- **2 large eggs, lightly beaten**
- **1 cup milk**
- **1 Tbsp. fresh lemon juice**
- **4 1/2 cups bread flour**
- **1/4 tsp. ground nutmeg**
- **1/4 to 1/2 cup bread flour**

HONEY TOPPING

- **1 1/3 cups powdered sugar**
- **1/2 cup butter, melted**
- **1/4 cup honey**
- **2 large egg whites**

FRESH ORANGE GLAZE

- **2 cups powdered sugar**
- **2 Tbsp. butter, softened**
- **2 tsp. orange zest**
- **3 Tbsp. fresh orange juice**
- **1 Tbsp. fresh lemon juice**

1. Prepare the Orange Rolls: Combine first 3 ingredients in a 1-cup glass measuring cup; let stand 5 minutes.
2. Beat butter with a heavy-duty mixer fitted with the paddle attachment on medium speed until creamy. Gradually add ½ cup sugar and 1 tsp. salt, beating until light and fluffy. Add eggs, milk, and lemon juice, beating until blended. Stir in yeast mixture.
3. Combine 4 ½ cups bread flour and ¼ tsp. nutmeg. Gradually add to butter mixture, beating on low speed 2 minutes or until well blended.
4. Turn dough out onto a surface floured with about ¼ cup bread flour; knead dough 5 minutes, adding additional bread flour as needed. Place dough in a lightly greased large bowl, turning to coat all sides. Cover and let rise in a warm place (80°F to 85°F), free from drafts, until rolls double in size, 1 ½ to 2 hours.
5. Punch dough down; turn out onto a lightly floured surface. Divide dough in half. Divide 1 dough half into 12 equal pieces; shape each piece, rolling between hands, into a 7- to 8-inch-long rope. Wrap each rope into a coil, firmly pinching end to seal. Place rolls in a lightly greased 10-inch round cake pan. Repeat procedure with remaining dough half. Let rise, uncovered, in a warm place (80°F to 85°F), free from drafts, until rolls doubles in size, 1 hour.
6. Preheat oven to 350°F. Bake rolls until lightly browned, 20 to 22 minutes. Cool in pans 2 minutes.
7. Prepare the Honey Topping: Stir together all ingredients.
8. Prepare the Fresh Orange Glaze: Beat powdered sugar and butter with a mixer on medium speed until blended. Add orange zest, orange juice, and lemon juice, and beat until smooth.
9. Drizzle Honey Topping over rolls. Spoon or brush Fresh Orange Glaze over warm rolls, and serve immediately.

Ham-and-Swiss Sticky Buns

ACTIVE 20 MIN. - TOTAL 1 HOUR, 10 MIN.

MAKES 16 ROLLS

- **9 oz. deli ham, finely chopped**
- **8 oz. shredded Swiss cheese (2 cups)**
- **2 Tbsp. spicy brown mustard**
- **½ cup packed light brown sugar**
- **2 (16.3-oz.) cans refrigerated jumbo biscuits**
- **Maple syrup**

1. Preheat oven to 325°F. Stir together first 3 ingredients.
2. Sprinkle brown sugar into a 12-inch square on a clean surface. Arrange biscuits in 4 rows on sugar, covering sugar completely. Pinch biscuits together to form a square. Roll dough into a 16- x 12-inch rectangle (about ¼ inch thick), pinching dough together as needed. Spread ham-and-cheese mixture over dough. Roll up tightly, starting at 1 long side, pressing brown sugar into dough as you roll. Pinch ends to seal. Cut into 16 slices using a serrated knife. Lightly grease a 24-cup muffin pan with cooking spray. Fit each slice into a muffin cup. (Dough will extend over tops of cups.)
3. Bake in preheated oven until golden and centers are completely cooked, 40 minutes. Cool on a wire rack 10 minutes. Drizzle with syrup.

New Orleans Beignets

ACTIVE 43 MIN. - TOTAL 4 HOURS, 48 MIN.

MAKES ABOUT 6 DOZEN

- **1 (1/4-oz.) envelope active dry yeast**
- **1 1/2 cups warm water (105°F to 115°F), divided**
- **1/2 cup granulated sugar**
- **1 cup evaporated milk**
- **2 large eggs, lightly beaten**
- **1 tsp. table salt**
- **1/4 cup shortening**
- **6 1/2 to 7 cups bread flour**
- **Vegetable oil**
- **Sifted powdered sugar**

1. Combine yeast, ½ cup of the warm water, and 1 tsp. granulated sugar in bowl of a heavy-duty stand mixer; let stand 5 minutes. Add milk, eggs, salt, and remaining granulated sugar.
2. Microwave remaining 1 cup water until hot, about 115°F; stir in shortening until melted. Add to yeast mixture. Beat on low speed, gradually adding 4 cups flour, until smooth. Gradually add remaining 2 ½ to 3 cups flour, beating until a sticky dough forms. Transfer to a lightly greased bowl, turning to coat all sides. Cover and chill 4 to 24 hours.
3. Turn dough out onto a floured surface; roll to ¼-inch thickness. Cut into 2 ½-inch squares.
4. Pour oil to a depth of 2 to 3 inches into a Dutch oven; heat to 360°F. Fry dough, in batches, until golden brown, 2 to 3 minutes on each side. Drain on a wire rack over a paper towel-lined baking sheet. Dust immediately with powdered sugar. Serve immediately.

Blueberry Kolaches

Don't overwork the dough. You can use a cookie scoop for easy portioning in Step 4, if desired.

ACTIVE 45 MIN. - TOTAL 10 HOURS, 10 MIN., INCLUDING CHILL TIME

MAKES ABOUT 3 DOZEN

1 (1/4-oz.) envelope active dry yeast
1/2 cup warm water (100°F to 110°F)
1/2 cup butter, softened
1 1/3 cups granulated sugar
2 1/2 tsp. table salt
2 large eggs
8 1/2 cups all-purpose flour
2 cups milk
3 (6-oz.) containers fresh blueberries (about 3 cups)
1/3 cup blueberry preserves
1/3 cup all-purpose flour
1/3 cup granulated sugar
3 Tbsp. cold butter, cut up

1. Combine yeast and warm water in a bowl; let stand 5 minutes.
2. Beat butter with a mixer on medium speed until creamy; gradually add 1 1/3 cups sugar and 2 1/2 tsp. salt. Add eggs, 1 at a time, beating just until blended after each addition. Stir in yeast mixture.
3. Add 8 1/2 cups flour to butter mixture alternately with milk, beginning and ending with flour mixture. Beat on low speed just until blended, stopping to scrape bowl as needed. Place dough in a bowl coated with cooking spray, turning to coat all sides. Cover with plastic wrap; chill 8 to 24 hours.
4. Shape dough into 35 (2-inch) balls (about 1/4 cup per ball), using floured hands. Place 1 1/2 inches apart on 2 lightly greased baking sheets. Cover and let rise in a warm place (80°F to 85°F), free from drafts, until balls double in size, 1 hour.
5. Preheat oven to 375°F. Stir together blueberries and preserves. Combine 1/3 cup flour and next 2 ingredients with a pastry blender until crumbly. Press thumb into each dough ball, forming an indentation; fill each with 1 Tbsp. berry mixture. Sprinkle with flour mixture. Bake in preheated oven until golden, 20 to 25 minutes.

Lemon Tea Bread

Tart lemons give intense flavor to this quick bread with a dense, cake-like texture. A sweet glaze ensures every slice is something worth savoring.

ACTIVE 20 MIN. - TOTAL 2 HOURS, 30 MIN.
MAKES 1 (8-INCH) LOAF

- **1/2 cup butter, softened**
- **1 cup granulated sugar**
- **2 large eggs**
- **1 1/2 cups all-purpose flour**
- **1 tsp. baking powder**
- **1/2 tsp. table salt**
- **1/2 cup milk**
- **2 Tbsp. lemon zest, divided**
- **1 cup powdered sugar**
- **2 Tbsp. fresh lemon juice**
- **1 Tbsp. granulated sugar**

1. Preheat oven to 350°F. Beat softened butter with a mixer on medium speed until creamy. Gradually add 1 cup granulated sugar, beating until light and fluffy. Add eggs, 1 at a time, beating just until blended after each addition.
2. Stir together flour, baking powder, and salt; add to butter mixture alternately with milk, beating on low speed just until blended, beginning and ending with flour mixture. Stir in 1 Tbsp. of the lemon zest. Spoon batter into a greased and floured 8- x 4-inch loaf pan.
3. Bake in the preheated oven until golden brown and a wooden pick inserted in center of bread comes out clean, 1 hour. Let cool in pan 10 minutes. Remove bread from pan, and cool completely on a wire rack.
4. Stir together powdered sugar and lemon juice until smooth; spoon over top of bread, letting excess drip down sides. Stir together remaining 1 Tbsp. lemon zest and 1 Tbsp. granulated sugar; sprinkle on top of bread.

Variation:

Lemon-Almond Tea Bread: Stir ½ tsp. almond extract into batter in Step 2. Proceed as directed.

Cream Cheese-Banana-Nut Bread

Enjoy banana bread without all the guilt with this healthy recipe. Expect a denser bread: It won't rise as much as traditional breads, and the texture will be very moist.

ACTIVE 15 MIN. - TOTAL 2 HOURS
MAKES 2 (8-INCH) LOAVES

- **1/4 cup butter, softened**
- **1 (8-oz.) package 1/3-less-fat cream cheese, softened**
- **1 cup granulated sugar**
- **2 large eggs**
- **1 1/2 cups whole wheat flour**
- **1 1/2 cups all-purpose flour**
- **1/2 tsp. baking powder**
- **1/2 tsp. baking soda**
- **1/2 tsp. table salt**
- **1 cup buttermilk**
- **1 1/2 cups mashed very ripe bananas (1 1/4 lb. unpeeled bananas, about 4 medium)**
- **1 1/4 cups chopped toasted pecans, divided**
- **1/2 tsp. vanilla extract**

1. Preheat oven to 350°F. Grease and flour 2 (8- x 4-inch) loaf pans. Beat butter and cream cheese with a mixer on medium speed until creamy. Gradually add sugar, beating until light and fluffy. Add eggs, 1 at a time, beating just until blended after each addition.
2. Combine whole wheat flour and next 4 ingredients; gradually add to butter mixture alternately with buttermilk, beginning and ending with flour mixture. Beat on low speed just until blended after each addition. Stir in bananas, ¾ cup of the toasted pecans, and vanilla. Spoon batter into prepared pans. Sprinkle with remaining ½ cup pecans.
3. Bake in the preheated oven until golden, a long wooden pick inserted in center comes out clean, and sides of bread pull away from pan, shielding with aluminum foil during last 15 minutes to prevent excessive browning, if necessary, 1 hour. Cool bread in pans on wire racks 10 minutes. Remove from pans to wire racks. Let cool 30 minutes.

Note: If you've never worked with whole wheat flour, accurate measuring is everything. Be sure to spoon the flour into a dry measuring cup (do not pack), rather than scooping the cup into the flour, and level it off with a straight edge.

Variations:

Cinnamon-Cream Cheese-Banana-Nut Bread: Prepare recipe as directed through Step 2, omitting pecans sprinkled over batter. Stir together ¼ cup packed brown sugar, ¼ cup chopped pecans (not toasted), 1 ½ tsp. all-purpose flour, 1 ½ tsp. melted butter, and ¼ to ½ tsp. ground cinnamon. Lightly sprinkle mixture over batter in pans. Bake and cool as directed.

Peanut Butter-Cream Cheese-Banana-Nut Bread: Prepare recipe as directed through Step 2, omitting pecans sprinkled over batter. Combine ¼ cup all-purpose flour and ¼ cup packed brown sugar in a small bowl. Cut in 2 Tbsp. creamy peanut butter and 1 ½ tsp. butter with a pastry blender or fork until mixture resembles small peas. Lightly sprinkle mixture over batter in pans. Bake and cool as directed.

Low-Fat Banana Bread

ACTIVE 20 MIN. - TOTAL 2 HOURS, 30 MIN.
MAKES 1 (8-INCH) LOAF

- **2 cups all-purpose flour**
- **3/4 tsp. baking soda**
- **1/2 tsp. salt**
- **1 cup granulated sugar**
- **1/4 cup butter, softened**
- **2 large eggs**
- **1 1/2 cups mashed ripe bananas (about 3 medium)**
- **1/3 cup plain low-fat yogurt**
- **1 tsp. vanilla extract**

1. Preheat oven to 350°F.
2. Combine flour, baking soda, and salt, stirring with a whisk.
3. Place sugar and butter in a large bowl, and beat with an electric mixer at medium speed until well blended. Add eggs, 1 at a time, beating well after each addition. Add banana, yogurt, and vanilla; beat until blended. Add flour mixture; beat at low speed just until moistened. Spoon batter into an 8- x 4-inch loaf pan coated with cooking spray.
4. Bake at 350°F for 1 hour or until a wooden pick inserted in center comes out clean. Cool in pan on a wire rack 10 minutes. Remove from pan, and cool on wire rack 1 hour.

Blueberry-Orange Bread

Serve these loaves bursting with berries year-round by using frozen berries when fresh are not available at a reasonable price.

ACTIVE 12 MIN. - TOTAL 1 HOUR
MAKES 4 MINI LOAVES

- **1/2 cup wheat bran cereal, crushed**
- **1/2 cup water**
- **2 tsp. orange zest**
- **1/4 cup orange juice**
- **1/2 tsp. vanilla extract**
- **1 1/2 cups all-purpose flour**
- **1/3 cup granulated sugar**
- **1 Tbsp. vegetable oil**
- **3/4 tsp. baking powder**
- **1/4 tsp. baking soda**
- **1/4 tsp. salt**
- **1 large egg, lightly beaten**
- **1/2 cup fresh or frozen blueberries**
- **1 Tbsp. all-purpose flour**

1. Preheat oven to 350°F. Stir together first 5 ingredients in a large bowl; let stand 10 minutes or until cereal softens.
2. Stir in 1 ½ cups flour and next 6 ingredients, stirring just until dry ingredients are moistened. Toss blueberries with 1 tablespoon flour; gently fold into batter.
3. Spoon batter into 4 greased 4 ½- x 2 ½-inch loaf pans. Bake in preheated oven 25 to 30 minutes or until a wooden pick inserted in center comes out clean. Cool in pans on a wire rack 10 minutes; remove from pans, and cool completely on wire rack.

TRY THIS TWIST!
Blackberry-Lemon Bread: Use Meyer lemon zest and juice in place of the orange, and swap frozen blackberries for the blueberries.

Lemon-Poppy Seed Zucchini Bread

The tender, fine-crumbed texture and bright citrus flavor offer a refreshing change from traditional spiced zucchini breads.

ACTIVE 20 MIN. - TOTAL 1 HOUR, 40 MIN.
MAKES 3 (5- X 3-INCH) LOAVES

- **1/2 cup butter, softened**
- **1 1/3 cups granulated sugar**
- **3 large eggs**
- **1 1/2 cups all-purpose flour**
- **1/2 tsp. table salt**
- **1/8 tsp. baking soda**
- **1/2 cup sour cream**
- **1 cup shredded zucchini**
- **1 Tbsp. lemon zest**
- **2 tsp. poppy seeds**

1. Preheat oven to 325°F. Beat butter with a heavy-duty stand mixer on medium speed until creamy. Gradually add sugar, beating until light and fluffy. Add eggs, 1 at a time, beating just until blended after each addition.
2. Stir together flour, salt, and baking soda. Add to butter mixture alternately with sour cream, beginning and ending with flour mixture. Beat on low speed just until blended after each addition. Stir in zucchini and next 2 ingredients. Spoon batter into 3 greased and floured 5- x 3-inch disposable aluminum foil loaf pans (about 1 ⅓ cups batter per pan).
3. Bake in preheated oven until golden and a wooden pick inserted in center comes out clean, 40 to 45 minutes. Cool in pans on wire racks 10 minutes; remove from pans to wire racks, and cool completely, about 30 minutes.

Whole Wheat-Raisin-Nut Bread

Don't be surprised by the weight of this healthy, hearty bread when you remove it from the pans. Even though the batter has no egg or oil, it still produces moist and tender loaves.

ACTIVE 12 MIN. - TOTAL 50 MIN.
MAKES 4 MINI LOAVES

- **1 1/3 cups whole wheat flour**
- **2/3 cup all-purpose flour**
- **2/3 cup chopped walnuts, toasted**
- **1/2 cup raisins**
- **1/3 cup granulated sugar**
- **1/2 tsp. salt**
- **1/2 tsp. baking soda**
- **1 cup milk**
- **1/3 cup molasses**

1. Preheat oven to 325°F. Stir together first 6 ingredients in a large bowl; make a well in center of mixture
2. Stir together baking soda, milk, and molasses. Add to flour mixture, stirring just until dry ingredients are moistened. Spoon batter into 4 greased and floured 4 ½- x 2 ½-inch loaf pans.
3. Bake at 325°F for 26 minutes or until a wooden pick inserted in center comes out clean. Cool in pans on wire rack; remove from pans, and cool completely on wire rack.

Pumpkin-Pecan Bread

No need to wait until the holidays to enjoy these tender loaves that are sweet enough for dessert.

ACTIVE 11 MIN. - TOTAL 50 MIN.
MAKES 4 MINI LOAVES

- **1 cup all-purpose flour**
- **3/4 cup granulated sugar**
- **1/2 cup canned pumpkin**
- **1/4 cup vegetable oil**
- **1 large egg**
- **1/2 tsp. baking soda**
- **1/2 tsp. salt**
- **1/2 tsp. ground cinnamon**
- **1/2 tsp. ground allspice**
- **1/2 tsp. ground nutmeg**
- **1/4 tsp. ground cloves**
- **3 Tbsp. water**
- **3/4 cup chopped pecans, toasted and divided**

1. Preheat oven to 350°F. Beat first 11 ingredients with an electric mixer at low speed 3 minutes or until blended. Add water, beating until blended; stir in ½ cup pecans.
2. Spoon batter into 4 greased and floured 4 ½- x 2 ½-inch loaf pans. Sprinkle tops evenly with remaining ¼ cup pecans.
3. Bake in preheated oven for 30 minutes or until a wooden pick inserted in center comes out clean. Cool in pans on a wire rack 10 minutes; remove from pans, and cool completely on wire rack.

Quick Buttermilk Biscuits

Try our Walnut-Honey Butter, Blackberry Butter, or Lemon-Herb Butter with these decadent biscuits.

ACTIVE 10 MIN. - TOTAL 22 MIN.
MAKES ABOUT 3 DOZEN

- 1 cup shortening
- 4 cups self-rising soft-wheat flour (such as White Lily)
- 1 3/4 cups buttermilk

1. Preheat oven to 425°F. Cut shortening into flour with a pastry blender until crumbly (or use your fingers). Add buttermilk, stirring just until dry ingredients are moistened.
2. Turn dough out onto a lightly floured surface, and knead lightly 4 or 5 times. Pat or roll dough to ¾-inch thickness, cut with a 1 ½-inch round cutter, and place on 2 lightly greased baking sheets.
3. Bake in preheated oven until lightly browned, 12 to 14 minutes.

Walnut-Honey Butter

ACTIVE 5 MIN. - TOTAL 25 MIN.
MAKES ABOUT ¾ CUP

Bake ¼ cup finely chopped walnuts at 350°F in a single layer in a pan 5 to 7 minutes or until lightly toasted, stirring halfway through. Cool 15 minutes. Stir together ½ cup softened butter, 2 Tbsp. honey, and walnuts.

Blackberry Butter

ACTIVE 5 MIN. - TOTAL 5 MIN.
MAKES ABOUT ¾ CUP

Stir together ½ cup softened butter and 3 Tbsp. blackberry preserves.

Lemon-Herb Butter

ACTIVE 5 MIN. - TOTAL 5 MIN.
MAKES ABOUT ½ CUP

Stir together ½ cup softened butter, 2 tsp. lemon zest, 1 tsp. chopped fresh chives, 1 tsp. chopped fresh oregano, and 1 tsp. chopped fresh parsley.

Basic Buttermilk Biscuits

Soft-wheat flour and buttermilk cause these biscuits to rise and to taste ultralight. Brush them with butter while hot out of the oven.

ACTIVE 10 MIN. - TOTAL 33 MIN.
MAKES ABOUT 2 ½ DOZEN

- **½ cup cold butter**
- **2 ¼ cups self-rising soft-wheat flour**
- **1 ¼ cups buttermilk**
- **Self-rising soft-wheat flour**
- **2 Tbsp. melted butter**

1. Preheat oven to 450°F. Cut butter with a sharp knife or pastry blender into ¼-inch-thick slices. Sprinkle butter slices over flour in a large bowl. Toss butter with flour. Cut butter into flour with a pastry blender until crumbly. Cover and chill 10 minutes. Add buttermilk, stirring just until dry ingredients are moistened.
2. Turn dough out onto a lightly floured surface; knead 3 or 4 times, gradually adding additional flour as needed. With floured hands, press or pat dough into a ¾-inch-thick rectangle (about 9 x 5 inches). Sprinkle top of dough with additional flour. Fold dough over onto itself into 3 sections, starting with 1 short end. (Fold dough rectangle as if folding a letter-size piece of paper.) Repeat entire process 2 more times, beginning with pressing into a ¾-inch-thick dough rectangle (about 9 x 5 inches).
3. Press or pat dough to ½-inch thickness on a lightly floured surface; cut with a 2-inch round cutter, and place, side by side, on a parchment paper-lined or lightly greased jelly-roll pan. (Dough rounds should touch.)
4. Bake at 450°F for 13 to 15 minutes or until lightly browned. Remove from oven; brush with 2 Tbsp. melted butter.

Variations:

Black Pepper-Bacon Biscuits: Combine ⅓ cup cooked and crumbled bacon slices (about 5 slices) and 1 tsp. black pepper with flour in a large bowl. Proceed with recipe as directed. Makes 30 biscuits.

Feta-Oregano Biscuits: Combine 1 (4-oz.) package crumbled feta cheese and ½ tsp. dried oregano with flour in a large bowl. Proceed with recipe as directed. Makes 30 biscuits.

Pimiento Cheese Biscuits: Combine 1 cup (4 oz.) shredded sharp Cheddar cheese with flour in a large bowl. Reduce buttermilk to 1 cup. Stir together buttermilk and 1 (4-oz.) jar diced pimiento, undrained. Proceed with recipe as directed. Makes 30 biscuits

Cinnamon-Raisin Biscuits

Plump raisins and a hint of cinnamon permeate each bite of these glazed breakfast favorites.

ACTIVE 16 MIN. - TOTAL 31 MIN.
MAKES ABOUT 1 DOZEN

- **1 ½ cups all-purpose flour**
- **1 ½ cups sifted cake flour**
- **1 Tbsp. baking powder**
- **1 tsp. salt**
- **¼ cup sugar**
- **1 ½ tsp. ground cinnamon**
- **¾ cup butter**
- **1 cup raisins**
- **1 cup milk**
- **1 ½ Tbsp. butter, melted**
- **1 cup sifted powdered sugar**
- **1 ½ Tbsp. milk**

1. Preheat oven to 400°F. Combine first 6 ingredients in a large bowl; cut in ¾ cup butter with a pastry blender until mixture is crumbly. Add raisins and 1 cup milk, stirring until dry ingredients are moistened. Turn dough out onto a lightly floured surface, and knead 4 or 5 times.
2. Roll dough to 1-inch thickness; cut with a 2-inch biscuit cutter. Place on greased baking sheets; brush with melted butter. Bake at 400°F for 15 minutes or until biscuits are lightly browned.
3. Combine powdered sugar and 1 ½ Tbsp. milk, stirring until smooth. Drizzle glaze over warm biscuits.

TRY THIS TWIST!
Cranberry-Spiced Biscuits: Trade the cinnamon for pumpkin pie spice, and use dried cranberries in place of the raisins.

Sour Cream-Praline Biscuits

Pecans add a nice crunch in these slightly sweet biscuits.

ACTIVE 7 MIN. - TOTAL 25 MIN.
MAKES 9 BISCUITS

- **¾ cup chopped pecans**
- **½ cup firmly packed brown sugar**
- **⅓ cup butter, melted**
- **2 cups all-purpose baking mix**
- **1 (8-oz.) container sour cream**

1. Preheat oven to 400°F. Combine first 3 ingredients, stirring well. Pour into a lightly greased 9-inch square pan.
2. Combine baking mix and sour cream; stir 30 seconds. Drop batter by ¼ cupfuls over pecan mixture. Bake in preheated oven for 18 minutes or until biscuits are golden. Invert pan immediately onto a serving platter. Serve immediately.

MUFFINS & SCONES

Bacon-and-Cheddar Corn Muffins

Heating the pan beforehand results in a nice crispy bottom.

ACTIVE 22 MIN. - TOTAL 52 MIN.
MAKES 1 DOZEN

- **6 bacon slices**
- **2 cups self-rising white cornmeal mix**
- **1 Tbsp. granulated sugar**
- **1 ½ cups buttermilk**
- **1 large egg**
- **4 Tbsp. butter, melted**
- **4 oz. shredded sharp Cheddar cheese (1 cup)**

1. Preheat oven to 425°F. Cook bacon in a large skillet over medium-high 12 to 14 minutes or until crisp; remove bacon, and drain on paper towels. Discard drippings in pan. Crumble bacon.
2. Heat a 12-cup muffin pan in oven 5 minutes.
3. Combine cornmeal mix and sugar in a medium bowl; make a well in center of mixture.

4. Stir together buttermilk and egg; add to cornmeal mixture, stirring just until dry ingredients are moistened. Stir in melted butter, cheese, and bacon. Remove pan from oven, and coat with cooking spray. Spoon batter into hot muffin pan, filling almost completely full.
5. Bake in preheated oven until golden, 15 to 20 minutes. Remove from pan to a wire rack, and let cool 10 minutes.

Variations:

Scrambled Egg Muffin Sliders: Prepare recipe as directed. Whisk together eggs, water, and Creole seasoning in a medium bowl. Melt 1 Tbsp. butter in a large nonstick skillet. Add egg mixture, and cook, without stirring, 2 to 3 minutes or until eggs begin to set on bottom. Gently draw cooked edges away from sides of pan to form large pieces. Cook, stirring occasionally, 4 to 5 minutes or until eggs are thickened and moist. (Do not overstir.) Cut muffins in half, and spoon eggs over bottom halves. Cover with top halves of muffins.

Ham-and-Swiss Corn Muffins: Substitute Swiss cheese for Cheddar cheese and 1 cup diced cooked ham for bacon. Reduce butter in batter to 3 Tbsp. Brown ham in remaining 1 Tbsp. melted butter in a nonstick skillet over medium-high 5 to 6 minutes. Proceed as directed, whisking in 2 Tbsp. Dijon mustard with buttermilk and egg.

Southwestern Chile-Cheese Corn Muffins: Omit bacon. Substitute pepper Jack cheese for Cheddar cheese. Proceed as directed, stirring in 1 (4.5-oz.) can chopped green chiles, drained, with cheese and butter.

Scrambled Egg Muffin Sliders

Blueberry Muffins with Lemon-Cream Cheese Glaze

These aren't your ordinary blueberry muffins! The tart-and-sugary glaze turns plain blueberry muffins into extraordinary ones.

ACTIVE 15 MIN. - TOTAL 40 MIN.

MAKES 1 ½ DOZEN MUFFINS

BLUEBERRY MUFFINS

- **3 ½ cups all-purpose flour**
- **1 cup granulated sugar**
- **1 Tbsp. baking powder**
- **1 ½ tsp. table salt**
- **3 large eggs**
- **1 ½ cups milk**
- **½ cup butter, melted**
- **2 cups fresh or frozen blueberries**
- **1 Tbsp. all-purpose flour**

LEMON-CREAM CHEESE GLAZE

- **1 (3-oz.) package cream cheese, softened**
- **1 tsp. lemon zest**
- **1 Tbsp. fresh lemon juice**
- **¼ tsp. vanilla extract**
- **1 ½ cups sifted powdered sugar**
- **Garnish: lemon zest**

1. Prepare the Blueberry Muffins: Preheat oven to 450°F. Lightly grease 1 ½ (12-cup) muffin pans with cooking spray. Stir together first 4 ingredients. Whisk together eggs and next 2 ingredients; add to flour mixture, stirring just until dry ingredients are moistened. Toss blueberries with 1 Tbsp. flour, and gently fold into batter. Spoon mixture into prepared pans, filling three-fourths full.
2. Bake in the preheated oven until golden and springy when touched lightly on top, 14 to 15 minutes. Immediately

remove from pans to wire racks, and let cool 10 minutes.

3. Meanwhile, prepare the Lemon-Cream Cheese Glaze. Beat cream cheese with a mixer on medium speed until creamy. Add lemon zest and next 2 ingredients; beat until smooth. Gradually add powdered sugar, beating until smooth. Drizzle over warm muffins.

Banana-Toffee Coffee Cake Muffins

These decadent little coffee cakes were developed to combine the best traits of a top-rated crumb-topped coffee cake with a homemade banana bread.

ACTIVE 15 MIN. - TOTAL 42 MIN.
MAKES 1 DOZEN

- **3 Tbsp. unsalted butter, melted**
- **1/2 cup firmly packed light brown sugar**
- **1/3 cup all-purpose flour**
- **1/4 tsp. ground cinnamon**
- **2 (1.4-oz.) chocolate-covered toffee candy bars, finely chopped**
- **2 cups all-purpose baking mix**
- **1/3 cup granulated sugar**
- **1 cup mashed ripe bananas (about 2 medium)**
- **2/3 cup milk**
- **1 large egg, lightly beaten**
- **1/2 tsp. ground allspice**
- **1/2 cup white chocolate morsels**
- **2 Tbsp. whipping cream**

1. Preheat oven to 400°F.
2. Stir together first 5 ingredients in a medium bowl. Set aside.
3. Stir together baking mix, granulated sugar, bananas, milk, egg, and allspice in a medium bowl until blended. Spoon batter evenly into 12 greased muffin cups; sprinkle batter evenly with candy bar mixture.
4. Bake in preheated oven for 17 minutes or until a wooden pick inserted in center comes out clean. Cool in pan on a wire rack 10 minutes. Gently run a knife around edges, and remove from pans immediately to cool completely.
5. Microwave white chocolate morsels and cream in a small microwave-safe bowl 30 to 60 seconds or until melted; stir until smooth. Place wire rack with cakes on a large piece of wax paper. Drizzle white chocolate mixture over tops of muffins with tines of a fork.

Peanut Butter-Banana Muffins

These muffins are a hit for breakfast, as a snack, or as a light dessert.

ACTIVE 25 MIN. - TOTAL 1 HOUR, 5 MIN.
MAKES 1 1/2 DOZEN

- **2 cups all-purpose flour, divided**
- **1/2 cup firmly packed light brown sugar**
- **1/4 cup butter**
- **2 Tbsp. peanut butter**
- **2 cups shreds of wheat bran cereal**
- **1 3/4 cups milk**
- **3/4 cup granulated sugar**
- **1 Tbsp. baking powder**
- **1/4 tsp. salt**
- **1/2 cup mashed ripe banana (about 1 medium)**
- **1/2 cup crunchy peanut butter**
- **1/4 cup vegetable oil**
- **1 large egg**

1. Preheat oven to 350°F. Combine 1/2 cup flour and brown sugar. Cut butter and peanut butter into flour mixture with a pastry blender or fork until crumbly. Set streusel topping aside.
2. Preheat oven to 350°F.
3. Stir together cereal and milk; let stand 5 minutes.
4. Combine remaining 1 1/2 cups flour, granulated sugar, and next 2 ingredients in a large bowl; make a well in center of mixture. Combine banana and next 3 ingredients; add to dry ingredients, stirring just until moistened. Spoon into greased muffin pans, filling two-thirds full. Sprinkle streusel topping evenly over batter.
5. Bake in preheated oven for 25 to 30 minutes. Remove from pans immediately, and cool 10 minutes on wire racks.

Morning Glory Muffins

As their name implies, these muffins make a glorious breakfast. They keep well in the freezer, so you can quickly microwave one or two just before you head out the door.

ACTIVE 20 MIN. - TOTAL 1 HOUR, 20 MIN.
MAKES 2 DOZEN

- **3 cups all-purpose flour**
- **1 tsp. table salt**
- **1 tsp. baking soda**
- **1 tsp. ground cinnamon**
- **1/2 tsp. ground nutmeg**
- **2 cups granulated sugar**
- **3/4 cup canola oil**
- **3 large eggs**
- **2 1/2 tsp. vanilla extract**
- **1 (8-oz.) can crushed pineapple, undrained**
- **1 cup finely grated carrot (about 2 medium carrots)**
- **1 cup chopped toasted pecans**
- **1 cup golden raisins**

1. Preheat oven to 350°F. Lightly grease 2 (12-cup) muffin pans with cooking spray.
2. Whisk together the flour, salt, baking soda, cinnamon, and nutmeg in a large bowl; make a well in center of mixture.
3. Whisk together sugar, canola oil, eggs, and vanilla in a large bowl. Fold in crushed pineapple and carrots. Add to flour mixture, stirring just until dry ingredients are moistened. Fold in toasted pecans and raisins.
4. Spoon into prepared pans, filling each cup two-thirds full.
5. Bake in preheated oven until golden and springy when touched lightly on top, 23 to 25 minutes. Cool in pans on wire rack 5 minutes. Remove from pans to wire rack, and cool completely, about 30 minutes.

Note: Baked and cooled muffins can be frozen in a ziplock plastic freezer bag up to 1 month. Remove from bag, and let thaw at room temperature.

Sausage and Cheese Muffins

These hearty muffins are impressively moist and tender. They might remind you of the popular and beloved baked sausage balls. They make substantial breakfast bread, but are also great with supper or a bowl of hot soup. For an easy variation, substitute condensed broccoli-cheese soup.

ACTIVE 20 MIN. - TOTAL 40 MIN.
MAKES 18 MUFFINS

- **1 lb. ground pork sausage**
- **3 cups all-purpose baking mix**
- **6 oz. shredded Cheddar cheese (1 1/2 cups)**
- **1 (10 1/2-oz.) can condensed cheese soup**
- **3/4 cup water**

1. Preheat oven to 375°F. Lightly grease 3 (6-cup) muffin pans with cooking spray.
2. Cook sausage in a large skillet, stirring often, until browned, about 10 minutes. Drain and cool.
3. Combine sausage, baking mix, and shredded cheese in a large bowl; make a well in center of mixture.
4. Stir together soup and ¾ cup water; add to sausage mixture, stirring just until dry ingredients are moistened. Spoon batter into prepared pans, filling each cup three-fourths full.
5. Bake in preheated oven until lightly browned and springy when touched lightly on top, 20 minutes.

Best-Ever Scones

When our Test Kitchen first baked this simple scone recipe, we thought they were the best we had ever tasted. Never fearing too much of a good thing, we created eight sweet and savory variations.

ACTIVE 15 MIN. - TOTAL 48 MIN.
MAKES 8 SCONES

- **2 cups all-purpose flour**
- **1/3 cup granulated sugar**
- **1 Tbsp. baking powder**
- **1/2 tsp. table salt**
- **1/2 cup cold butter, cut into 1/2-inch cubes**
- **1 cup whipping cream, divided**
- **Parchment paper**

1. Preheat oven to 450°F. Lightly coat a baking sheet with cooking spray. Stir together first 4 ingredients in a large bowl. Add butter, and, using your fingertips, blend quickly and lightly into flour mixture. (Don't let it melt on your fingers.) Freeze 5 minutes. Add ¾ cup plus 2 Tbsp. of the cream, stirring just until dough holds together without crumbling.
2. Transfer dough to center of prepared baking sheet, and using parchment paper or oiled hands, shape dough into a 7-inch round (mixture will be crumbly). Cut round into 8 wedges, pulling them apart slightly as you cut. Place wedges 2 inches apart on prepared baking sheet. Brush tops of wedges with remaining 2 Tbsp. cream.
3. Bake in the preheated oven until lightly browned, 13 to 15 minutes. Cool on baking sheet on a wire rack 20 minutes. Store scones in an airtight container.

Variations:

Chocolate-Cherry Scones: Stir in ¼ cup dried cherries, coarsely chopped, and 2 oz. coarsely chopped semisweet chocolate with the cream in Step 1.

Cranberry-Pistachio Scones: Stir in ¼ cup sweetened dried cranberries and ¼ cup coarsely chopped roasted salted pistachios with the cream in Step 1.

Brown Sugar-Pecan Scones: Substitute brown sugar for granulated sugar. Stir in ½ cup chopped toasted pecans with the cream in Step 1.

Bacon, Cheddar, and Chive Scones: Omit sugar. Stir in 3 oz. (¾ cup) shredded sharp Cheddar cheese, ¼ cup finely chopped cooked bacon, 2 Tbsp. chopped fresh chives, and ½ tsp. freshly ground black pepper with the cream in Step 1.

Ham-and-Swiss Scones: Omit sugar. Stir in 3 oz. (¾ cup) shredded Swiss cheese and ¾ cup finely chopped baked ham with the cream in Step 1. Serve warm with Mustard Butter: Stir together ½ cup softened butter, 1 Tbsp. spicy brown mustard, and 1 Tbsp. minced sweet onion.

Pimiento Cheese Scones: Omit sugar. Stir in 3 oz. (¾ cup) shredded sharp Cheddar cheese and 3 Tbsp. finely chopped pimiento with the cream in Step 1.

Rosemary, Pear, and Asiago Scones: Omit sugar. Stir in ¾ cup finely chopped fresh pear, ½ cup grated Asiago cheese, and 1 tsp. chopped fresh rosemary with the cream in Step 1.

Bite-Size Scones: Shape dough into 2 (4-inch) rounds. Slice each round into 8 wedges, pulling them apart slightly as you cut . Bake as directed for 12 to 13 minutes in Step 3.

Cranberry-Pistachio Scones

Oatmeal Scones with Pecans

Scones originated in Scotland and were first made with unleavened oats. Oatmeal remains key in this recipe, and pecans add a Southern touch.

ACTIVE 10 MIN. - TOTAL 31 MIN.

MAKES 8 SCONES

- **3/4 cup uncooked quick-cooking oats**
- **1/3 cup granulated sugar**
- **1 3/4 cups all-purpose flour**
- **2 tsp. baking powder**
- **1/2 tsp. baking soda**
- **1/4 tsp. table salt**
- **2 Tbsp. cold butter, cut up**
- **2/3 cup fat-free buttermilk**
- **1 large egg**
- **3 Tbsp. granulated sugar**
- **1/2 tsp. ground cinnamon**
- **1 1/2 Tbsp. fat-free buttermilk**
- **2 Tbsp. chopped toasted pecans**

1. Preheat oven to 400°F. Bake oats in preheated oven in a 15- x 10-inch jelly-roll pan until lightly browned, 6 minutes. Cool.
2. Combine oats and next 5 ingredients.
3. Add butter, and, using your fingertips, blend quickly and lightly into oats mixture. (Don't let it melt on your fingers.) Stir together 2/3 cup buttermilk and egg. Add wet ingredients to dry ingredients, and stir gently just until dough forms.
4. Transfer dough to center of a jelly-roll pan coated with cooking spray, and, using parchment paper or oiled hands, shape dough into a 7 1/2-inch circle. Slice round into 8 wedges, pulling them apart slightly as you cut.
5. Combine 3 Tbsp. sugar and 1/2 tsp. cinnamon. Brush dough with 1 1/2 Tbsp. buttermilk. Sprinkle with sugar mixture and pecans.
6. Bake in preheated oven until lightly browned, 15 minutes. Serve immediately. Store scones in an airtight container at room temperature for up to 3 days.

Dried Cherry-Pecan Oatmeal

FRUITS & BEVERAGES

Dried Cherry-Pecan Oatmeal

Do your morning bowl of oatmeal one better: Add dried fruit and chopped pecans for a burst of nutrition along with a sweet and satisfying crunch. Using fat-free milk also provides more calcium, vitamin D, and protein.

ACTIVE 10 MIN. - TOTAL 30 MIN.

SERVES 6

- **3 cups water**
- **3 cups fat-free milk**
- **2 cups whole oats (not instant)**
- **1/2 cup dried cherries, coarsely chopped**
- **1/2 tsp. table salt**
- **5 Tbsp. packed brown sugar, divided**
- **1 Tbsp. butter**
- **1/4 tsp. ground cinnamon**
- **1/4 tsp. vanilla extract**
- **2 Tbsp. chopped pecans**

Bring 3 cups water, milk, oats, cherries, and salt to a boil in a saucepan over medium-high; reduce heat, and simmer, stirring occasionally, 20 minutes or until thickened. Remove from heat. Stir in 4 Tbsp. of the brown sugar and next 3 ingredients. Spoon 1 cup oatmeal in each of 6 bowls. Sprinkle with pecans and remaining 1 Tbsp. brown sugar. Serve immediately.

Citrus Salad with Spiced Honey

Use any combination of citrus to compose this vibrant, fresh salad, and present it however you like.

ACTIVE 30 MIN. - TOTAL 1 HOUR, 5 MIN.

SERVES 6-8

- **½ cup honey**
- **1 (3-inch) cinnamon stick**
- **1 bay leaf**
- **1 tsp. black peppercorns**
- **¼ tsp. crushed red pepper**
- **4 whole cloves**
- **½ cup water**
- **3 medium-size oranges**
- **3 mandarin oranges**
- **2 Ruby Red grapefruit**
- **2 limes**
- **6 kumquats (optional)**
- **1 (4.4-oz.) package fresh pomegranate seeds**
- **Toppings: extra-virgin olive oil, fresh mint leaves, sea salt**

1. Bring first 6 ingredients and ½ cup water to a boil over medium-high. Boil, stirring often, 1 minute. Remove from heat, and let stand 30 minutes.
2. Meanwhile, peel oranges, mandarin oranges, next 2 ingredients, and, if desired, kumquats. Cut away bitter white pith. Cut each fruit into thin rounds. Arrange on a serving platter; sprinkle with pomegranate seeds.
3. Pour honey mixture through a fine mesh strainer, discarding solids. Drizzle fruit with desired amount of spiced honey; reserve remaining spiced honey for another use (such as flavoring iced tea). Top with a drizzle of olive oil, a handful of mint leaves, and sea salt.

Note: Pink or red peppercorns may be substituted for black peppercorns.

Honey-Ginger Fruit Salad

The combination of grape juice, honey, and ginger adds pizzazz to whatever fruit you have on hand such as cantaloupe, raspberries, blueberries, kiwifruit, or pineapple. The salad can be served alone or on yogurt.

ACTIVE 20 MIN. - TOTAL 20 MIN.

MAKES 7 CUPS

- **1 cup white grape juice**
- **3 Tbsp. honey**
- **1½ tsp. grated fresh ginger**
- **1 pt. fresh strawberries, halved**
- **3 oranges, sectioned**
- **½ honeydew melon, chopped**
- **1 cup seedless green grapes**

Stir together grape juice, honey, and ginger in a large bowl. Add strawberries, oranges, melon, and grapes, tossing to coat. Serve immediately.

Acai Berry Smoothie Bowl

Acai packs are available at a variety of grocery stores and can also be purchased online. The berries themselves are a rich source of antioxidants and provide a boost of energy to help kick-start your day.

ACTIVE 10 MIN. - TOTAL 10 MIN.

SERVES 1

SMOOTHIE
- **1 frozen unsweetened acai pack (such as Sambazon)**
- **½ frozen banana**
- **½ cup mixed frozen berries (such as strawberries, raspberries, and blueberries)**
- **⅓ cup plain unsweetened almond milk**

TOPPINGS
- **1 Tbsp. granola**
- **½ sliced peeled kiwifruit**
- **½ banana, sliced**
- **2 Tbsp. fresh blueberries**
- **1 Tbsp. unsweetened coconut flakes**

Run the frozen acai pack under warm water for a few seconds before unwrapping. Remove it from its packaging, break it up into chunks, and place it in the blender. Add the frozen banana, mixed berries, and a drizzle of the almond milk, and begin to blend. Slowly drizzle in the remaining almond milk and process until you have reached the desired consistency. Pour the mixture into a bowl, and sprinkle on the toppings.

TRY THIS TWIST!
Goji Berry Smoothie Bowl: Try another exotic berry in your morning bowl by substituting 4 ounces frozen goji berries for the acai in this smoothie.

PB&J Smoothie Bowl

The addition of raspberries gives the bowl a tart punch, which is balanced out nicely by a swirl of Greek yogurt. A sprinkling of granola (use your favorite) adds a toasty crunch. If you're a real sucker for peanut butter, you can drizzle some on top.

ACTIVE 5 MIN. - TOTAL 5 MIN.

SERVES 1

SMOOTHIE
- **½ cup frozen raspberries**
- **½ cup frozen unsweetened strawberries**
- **1 frozen banana**
- **1 Tbsp. creamy peanut butter**
- **¼ cup plain unsweetened almond milk**
- **2 Tbsp. plain fat-free Greek yogurt**

TOPPINGS
- **2 fresh strawberries, sliced**
- **1 Tbsp. granola**

Place the first 5 smoothie ingredients in a blender; process until smooth. Pour the mixture into a bowl, and swirl in the Greek yogurt. Top with the sliced strawberries and granola.

TRY THIS TWIST!
Nut Butter Smoothie Bowl: Match the nut butter and nut milks used in this hearty breakfast bowl—almond butter with almond milk, cashew butter with cashew milk, and so forth.

Creamy Cantaloupe Smoothie

When selecting a cantaloupe, choose one that has a sweet fragrance for the best flavor.

ACTIVE 10 MIN. - TOTAL 10 MIN.
SERVES 2

1/2 cup 1% low-fat milk
2 Tbsp. honey
1/2 tsp. lime zest
1 (5.3-oz.) container vanilla fat-free Greek yogurt
2 1/2 cups (1-inch) cubed cantaloupe, frozen

1. Place the first 4 ingredients in a blender; process until smooth.
2. Remove the center piece of the blender lid; secure the lid on the blender. With the blender on, drop the cantaloupe cubes, 1 at a time, through the center of blender lid; process until smooth. Serve immediately.

Blackberry-Mango Breakfast Smoothie

Sneak silken tofu into a sweet-tart breakfast smoothie. Combined with fiber-rich berries, this is a great way to get extra protein and fiber past pickier palates.

ACTIVE 5 MIN. - TOTAL 5 MIN.
SERVES 4

1 1/2 cups frozen blackberries
1 cup refrigerated mango slices
1 cup reduced-fat soft silken tofu (about 6 1/2 oz.)
1 cup orange juice
3 Tbsp. honey

Place all the ingredients in a blender, and process until smooth. Serve immediately.

TRY THIS TWIST!
Swap the tofu for the same amount of pasteurized liquid egg whites for another protein-packed smoothie option that will keep you satiated until lunchtime.

Blueberry Smoothies

Blueberries are loaded with fiber, vitamin C, and disease-fighting phytonutrients. If you can't get 'em fresh, use frozen ones: They actually yield a brighter color and smoother texture. For a dairy-free version, use vanilla soy milk and soy yogurt.

ACTIVE 5 MIN. - TOTAL 5 MIN.
SERVES 4

2 cups frozen blueberries
1 (6-oz.) container vanilla low-fat yogurt
1 1/2 cups 1% low-fat milk

Process all ingredients in a blender until smooth, stopping to scrape down sides as needed. Serve immediately.

Strawberry-Pineapple Smoothie

Silken tofu and vanilla fro-yo make this smoothie creamy and add protein while keeping calories in check. Garnish the glass with a wedge of pineapple and a strawberry half, if desired.

ACTIVE 10 MIN. - TOTAL 10 MIN.
SERVES 4

2/3 cup soft silken tofu (3 ounces)
1 cup cubed fresh pineapple, frozen
1 cup sliced fresh strawberries, frozen
1/2 cup vanilla low-fat frozen yogurt
1/3 cup fresh orange juice
1 tsp. sugar

Place all the ingredients in a blender; process until smooth. Serve immediately.

Island Sunrise Smoothie

Papayas are full of potassium—just what you need to avoid muscle cramps after a workout. Potassium helps keep your blood pressure on an even keel too.

ACTIVE 10 MIN. - TOTAL 10 MIN.
SERVES 3

2 cups chopped papaya
1/2 cup fresh orange juice
1 Tbsp. honey
2 tsp. fresh lime juice
Pinch of salt
1 cup frozen cubed mango
1 cup frozen strawberries

Place the first 5 ingredients in a blender; process until smooth. Add the mango and strawberries; process until smooth.

Triple Melon Smoothie

The mix of brightly colored melons used in this smoothie gives you a range of disease-fighting antioxidants. Garnish with additional cubed melon, if desired.

ACTIVE 15 MIN. - TOTAL 15 MIN.
SERVES 3

2 1/2 cups chopped seedless watermelon
1/2 cup fresh orange juice
2 tsp. honey
2 1/2 cups (1-inch) cubed cantaloupe, frozen
1 cup (1-inch) cubed honeydew melon, frozen

1. Place the first 3 ingredients in a blender; process until smooth.
2. Remove the center piece of the blender lid; secure the lid on the blender. With the blender on, drop the cantaloupe and honeydew through the center of the lid; process until smooth. Serve immediately.

Triple Melon Smoothie

Green Tea, Kiwi, and Mango Smoothie

Make a colorful and healthy smoothie by pureeing mango, kiwifruit, and spinach with yogurt and honey and spooning into glasses in two layers.

ACTIVE 15 MIN. - TOTAL 15 MIN.
SERVES 4

- **2 1/2 cups frozen cubed mango**
- **3/4 cup vanilla fat-free yogurt, divided**
- **1/4 cup honey, divided**
- **2 Tbsp. water**
- **1/2 tsp. lime zest**
- **3 quartered and peeled kiwifruit**
- **2 cups ice cubes**
- **1/2 cup packed fresh baby spinach**
- **2 Tbsp. bottled green tea**
- **Kiwifruit slices (optional)**

1. Place the mango, 1/2 cup of the yogurt, 2 tablespoons of the honey, 2 tablespoons water, and lime zest in a blender; process until smooth, stirring occasionally. Divide the mango mixture into each of 4 serving glasses; place the glasses in the freezer.
2. Rinse the blender container. Place the remaining 1/4 cup yogurt, 2 tablespoons honey, kiwifruit, and next 3 ingredients in the blender; process until smooth, stirring occasionally. Gently spoon the green tea–kiwifruit mixture onto the mango mixture. Garnish with the kiwifruit slices, and stir to combine flavors, if desired. Serve immediately.

TRY THIS TWIST!
Tropical Jasmine Smoothie: Use 2 tablespoons prepared jasmine tea in place of the green tea in this recipe.

Wake-Up Smoothie

This smoothie will give you a morning boost, incorporating antioxidant-rich coffee into this tasty blend. Coffee has been studied for decades and can claim a number of health benefits, such as reducing the risk of type 2 diabetes and Alzheimer's disease. But don't overdo it. More than 2 or 3 cups daily may increase blood pressure, especially in those individuals whose readings are borderline or high.

ACTIVE 5 MIN. - TOTAL 5 MIN.
SERVES 4

- **1/2 cup chilled strong coffee**
- **1/2 cup coffee low-fat frozen yogurt**
- **1/4 cup ice**
- **1/4 cup unsweetened almond milk**
- **1 Tbsp. ground flaxseed**
- **Pinch of ground cinnamon**

Place all the ingredients in a blender; process until smooth. Serve immediately.

Spiced Chai Frappé

Essentially the chilled version of a chai latte, this frappé is perfect for an afternoon pick-me-up. Top each with a dollop of reduced-calorie whipped topping and a sprinkle of cinnamon, if desired.

ACTIVE 5 MIN. - TOTAL 35 MIN.
SERVES 4

- **1/2 cup boiling water**
- **1/4 cup sugar**
- **4 chai tea bags**
- **2 cups ice**
- **1/2 cup 1% low-fat milk**

1. Combine the first 3 ingredients in a small bowl; cover and steep 5 minutes. Remove and discard the tea bags. Refrigerate 30 minutes or until thoroughly chilled.
2. Place the tea mixture, ice, and milk in a blender; process until smooth. Immediately pour frappé evenly into 2 glasses.

TRY THIS TWIST!
Keto Chai Frappé: Skip the sugar and use 1/2 cup full-fat canned coconut milk. (Be sure to shake the can well before opening to incorporate the cream that has often separated from the milk.)

Blushing Mimosas

The classic mimosa consists of equal parts orange juice and Champagne. In this recipe, pineapple juice and grenadine add a fun twist of flavor and color.

ACTIVE 5 MIN. - TOTAL 5 MIN.
MAKES 6 CUPS

- **2 cups orange juice (not from concentrate), chilled**
- **1 cup pineapple juice, chilled**
- **2 Tbsp. grenadine**
- **1 (750-milliliter) bottle Champagne or sparkling wine, chilled**

Stir together first 3 ingredients. Pour equal parts orange juice mixture and Champagne into Champagne flutes. Serve immediately.

Note: 2 (12-oz.) cans ginger ale or lemon-lime soft drink may be substituted.

Champagne Sparklers

ACTIVE 15 MIN. - TOTAL 8 HOURS, 15 MIN., INCLUDING CHILL TIME
SERVES 10

- **1 (16-oz.) can frozen orange juice concentrate, thawed**
- **1 cup cranberry juice cocktail**
- **1/2 cup granulated sugar**
- **1/2 cup lemon juice**
- **1/2 (375-milliliter) bottle dessert wine**
- **1 (750-milliliter) bottle Champagne or sparkling wine, chilled**
- **Fresh strawberries**

Stir together first 4 ingredients; cover and chill at least 8 hours or up to 2 days. Pour juice mixture into a chilled punch bowl. Stir in dessert wine and Champagne just before serving. Serve with fresh strawberries.

TRY THIS TWIST!
Prosecco Sparklers: Use frozen lemonade concentrate instead and swap the Champagne for Italian Prosecco. Garnish with raspberries.

Bloody Marys by the Pitcher

A great Bloody Mary is a must-have at brunch for some of us. Rather than make several cocktails one by one in glasses, why not stir them up by the pitcher? If your guests cannot agree on an amount of vodka, or perhaps want none at all, omit it from the base recipe and serve it on the side.

ACTIVE 5 MIN. - TOTAL 5 MIN.

MAKES 1 ½ QT.

46 oz. low-sodium vegetable juice, chilled
1 Tbsp. freshly ground black pepper
3 Tbsp. fresh lime juice
1 Tbsp. hot sauce
1 Tbsp. Worcestershire sauce
½ tsp. Old Bay seasoning
½ cup vodka, chilled
Garnish: celery sticks

1. Stir together vegetable juice, pepper, lime juice, hot sauce, Worcestershire, and Old Bay in a large pitcher.
2. Stir in vodka, and serve over ice. Garnish, if desired.

BAKING AT HIGH ALTITUDES

Liquids boil at lower temperatures (below 212°F), and moisture evaporates more quickly at high altitudes. Both of these factors significantly impact the quality of baked goods. Also, leavening gases (air, carbon dioxide, water vapor) expand faster. If you live at 3,000 feet or below, first try a recipe as is. Sometimes few, if any, changes are needed. But the higher you go, the more you'll have to adjust your ingredients and cooking times.

A FEW OVERALL TIPS

- Use shiny new baking pans. This seems to help mixtures rise, especially cake batters.
- Use butter, flour, and parchment paper to prep your baking pans for nonstick cooking. At high altitudes, baked goods tend to stick more to pans.
- Be exact in your measurements (once you've figured out what they should be). This is always important in baking, but especially so when you're up so high. Tiny variations in ingredients make a bigger difference at high altitudes than at sea level.
- Boost flavor. Seasonings and extracts tend to be more muted at higher altitudes, so increase them slightly.
- Have patience. You may have to bake your favorite sea-level recipe a few times, making slight adjustments each time, until it's worked out to suit your particular altitude.

INGREDIENT/TEMPERATURE ADJUSTMENTS

CHANGE	AT 3,000 FEET	AT 5,000 FEET	AT 7,000 FEET
Baking powder or baking soda	• Reduce each tsp. called for by up to ⅛ tsp.	• Reduce each tsp. called for by ⅛ to ¼ tsp.	• Reduce each tsp. called for by ¼ to ½ tsp.
SUGAR	• Reduce each cup called for by up to 1 Tbsp.	• Reduce each cup called for by up to 2 Tbsp.	• Reduce each cup called for by 2 to 3 Tbsp.
LIQUID	• Increase each cup called for by up to 2 Tbsp.	• Increase each cup called for by up to 2 to 4 Tbsp.	• Increase each cup called for by up to 3 to 4 Tbsp.
OVEN TEMPERATURE	• Increase 3° to 5°	• Increase 15°	• Increase 21° to 25°

METRIC EQUIVALENTS

The recipes that appear in this cookbook use the standard United States method for measuring liquid and dry or solid ingredients (teaspoons, tablespoons, and cups). The information on this chart is provided to help cooks outside the U.S. successfully use these recipes. All equivalents are approximate.

METRIC EQUIVALENTS FOR DIFFERENT TYPES OF INGREDIENTS

A standard cup measure of a dry or solid ingredient will vary in weight depending on the type of ingredient. A standard cup of liquid is the same volume for any type of liquid. Use the following chart when converting standard cup measures to grams (weight) or milliliters (volume).

Standard Cup	Fine Powder (ex. flour)	Grain (ex. rice)	Granular (ex. sugar)	Liquid Solids (ex. butter)	Liquid (ex. milk)
1	140 g	150 g	190 g	200 g	240 ml
¾	105 g	113 g	143 g	150 g	180 ml
⅔	93 g	100 g	125 g	133 g	160 ml
½	70 g	75 g	95 g	100 g	120 ml
⅓	47 g	50 g	63 g	67 g	80 ml
¼	35 g	38 g	48 g	50 g	60 ml
⅛	18 g	19 g	24 g	25 g	30 ml

USEFUL EQUIVALENTS FOR DRY INGREDIENTS BY WEIGHT

(To convert ounces to grams, multiply the number of ounces by 30.)

1 oz	=	1/16 lb	=	30 g
4 oz	=	¼ lb	=	120 g
8 oz	=	½ lb	=	240 g
12 oz	=	¾ lb	=	360 g
16 oz	=	1 lb	=	480 g

USEFUL EQUIVALENTS FOR LENGTH

(To convert inches to centimeters, multiply the number of inches by 2.5.)

1 in					=	2.5 cm		
6 in	=	½ ft			=	15 cm		
12 in	=	1 ft			=	30 cm		
36 in	=	3 ft	=	1 yd	=	90 cm		
40 in					=	100 cm	=	1 m

USEFUL EQUIVALENTS FOR LIQUID INGREDIENTS BY VOLUME

¼ tsp							=	1 ml		
½ tsp							=	2 ml		
1 tsp							=	5 ml		
3 tsp	=	1 Tbsp			=	½ fl oz	=	15 ml		
		2 Tbsp	=	⅛ cup	=	1 fl oz	=	30 ml		
		4 Tbsp	=	¼ cup	=	2 fl oz	=	60 ml		
		5⅓ Tbsp	=	⅓ cup	=	3 fl oz	=	80 ml		
		8 Tbsp	=	½ cup	=	4 fl oz	=	120 ml		
		10⅔ Tbsp	=	⅔ cup	=	5 fl oz	=	160 ml		
		12 Tbsp	=	¾ cup	=	6 fl oz	=	180 ml		
		16 Tbsp	=	1 cup	=	8 fl oz	=	240 ml		
		1 pt	=	2 cups	=	16 fl oz	=	480 ml		
		1 qt	=	4 cups	=	32 fl oz	=	960 ml		
						33 fl oz	=	1000 ml	=	1 l

USEFUL EQUIVALENTS FOR COOKING/OVEN TEMPERATURES

	Fahrenheit	Celsius	Gas Mark
Freeze Water	32° F	0° C	
Room Temperature	68° F	20° C	
Boil Water	212° F	100° C	
Bake	325° F	160° C	3
	350° F	180° C	4
	375° F	190° C	5
	400° F	200° C	6
	425° F	220° C	7
	450° F	230° C	8
Broil			Grill

Recipe Title Index

This index alphabetically lists every recipe by exact title.

A

Acai Berry Smoothie Bowl, 343
All-Occasion Cookie Toppers, 303
Almond-Chicken Wrap, 40
Apple, Celery, and Romaine Salad with Pancetta and Blue Cheese, 243
Apple Stack Cake, 226
Apricot-Pecan Cinnamon Rolls, 332
Arroz Verde (Mexican Green Rice), 105
Aunt Grace's Famous Cornbread Dressing, 249

B

Back in the Day Bakery Southern Pumpkin Pie, 261
Bacon-and-Cheddar Corn Muffins, 338
Bacon, Bourbon, and Benne Seed Shortbread Crackers, 285
Bacon, Cheddar, and Chive Scones, 341
Bacon-Hash Brown Quiche, 74
Bacon Mushroom Frittata, 322
Bacon-Spinach-and-Couscous Stuffed Tomatoes, 123
Bacon-Wrapped Chicken Breasts, 74
Baked Rigatoni with Sweet Red Peppers and Fontina, 230
Baked Rigatoni with Zucchini and Mozzarella, 230
Bananas Foster Grilled Pound Cake, 332
Banana-Toffee Coffee Cake Muffins, 340
Basic Buttermilk Biscuits, 338
Basic Pimiento Cheese, 144
Beef Stew, 28
Beef Stew with Cheddar Biscuits, 229
Beer Sauce, 30
Berry Sonker with Dip, 115
Best-Ever Crab Cakes with Green Tomato Slaw, 101
Best-Ever Scones, 341
Best-Ever Succotash, 195
Best White Cake, 303
Big-Batch Bloody Marys, 202
Bite-Size Scones, 341
Black Bean Burgers with Comeback Sauce, 50
Black Beans, 50
Black Bean Tostadas with Mango-Avocado Salsa, 50
Blackberry Butter, 337
Blackberry Jam Cake, 226
Blackberry-Lemon Bread, 336
Blackberry-Mango Breakfast Smoothie, 345
Blackberry Trifles with Pecan Feuilletage and Mascarpone-Cane Syrup Mousse, 155
Black-eyed Pea Ranchero Sauce, 138
Black Pepper-and-Honey Whipped Goat Cheese, 120
Black Pepper-Bacon Biscuits, 338
Bloody Marys by the Pitcher, 347
Blueberry Kolaches, 334
Blueberry-Lemon Crunch Bars, 115
Blueberry Muffins with Lemon-Cream Cheese Glaze, 339
Blueberry-Orange Bread, 336
Blueberry Smoothies, 345
Blushing Mimosas, 346
Boozy Fruitcake Bark, 291
Braised Lamb Shanks with Parmesan-Chive Grits, 45
Breakfast in a Skillet, 322
Brie-and-Veggie Strata, 322
Brined Grilled Chicken with Dipping Sauces, 204
Brisket-and-Black Bean Chili with Cilantro-Lime Crema, 205
Broccoli-Cheese Casserole, 256
Brown Butter-Maple-Pecan Blondies, 209
Brown Sugar-and-Ginger Whipped Cream, 300
Brown Sugar-Pecan Scones, 341
Brussels Sprouts with Bacon and Shallots, 257
Buttermilk and Brown Sugar Waffles, 326
Buttermilk Biscuits with Ham, 69
Buttermilk-Parmesan Ranch, 204
Buttermilk-Pecan Pralines, 291
Butterscotch-Spice Trifle, 263
Buxton Hall Ultimate Apple Pie, 260

C

Cajun Smoked Turkey, 247
Candied Pineapple Wedges, 62
Cantaloupe Soup with Chorizo Relish and Black Pepper-and-Honey Whipped Goat Cheese, 120
Capitol Hill Bean Soup, 32
Caramel Apple Coffee Cake, 331
Caramelized Onion, Spinach, and Pork Strata, 48
Carbonara with Braised Lamb, 45
Champagne Sparklers, 346
Cheddar-Caramelized Onion Bread, 140
Cheddar Shortbread Crackers, 285
Cheesy Potato Casserole, 257
Cherry Flag Pie, 132
Cherry-Nectarine Pandowdy, 115
Cherry Tomato Caprese Salad, 142
Chicken, 47
Chicken Biscuit Sandwiches, 47
Chicken Caesar Salad Sandwiches, 90
Chicken Niçoise Salad, 88
Chicken-Quinoa Salad with Green Goddess Dressing, 90
Chicken Thighs and BBQ Beans, 119
Chipotle Pimiento Cheese, 145
Chive-Radish Compound Butter, 69
Chive Sour Cream, 120
Chocolate-Caramel Cookie Cups, 284
Chocolate-Cherry Scones, 341
Chocolate-Cream Cheese Coffee Cake, 330
Chocolate Mayonnaise Cake, 37
Chocolate-Pear Muffins, 207
Chocolate-Peppermint Swirl Sandwich Cookies, 284
Chocolate Sugar Cookie Dough, 284
Chorizo Relish, 120
Christmas Buttermints, 293
Christmas Tree Bar Cookies, 284
Cilantro-Lime Crema, 205
Cinnamon-Cream Cheese-Banana-Nut Bread, 335
Cinnamon-Raisin Biscuits, 338
Cinnamon Roll Waffles with Bananas Foster Sauce, 327
Citrus Salad with Spiced Honey, 343
Citrus-Salmon Salad, 49
Classic Gingerbread, 300
Classic Hoppin' John, 39
Coconut-Carrot Cake with Coconut Buttercream, 71
Coconut Rice Pudding with Strawberry-Nectarine Compote, 87
Coffee Stout-Braised Beef, 233
Cold Lemon Soufflés with Wine Sauce, 55
Cornmeal Cookie Berry Shortcakes, 133
Cornmeal Crescent Rolls, 287

Corn Pudding, 256
Country Breakfast in a Skillet, 322
Country Captain Chicken, 33
Country Grits-and-Sausage Casserole, 323
Couscous Pilaf, 105
Couscous Pilaf with Roasted Carrots, Chicken, and Feta, 58
Crab-and-Bacon Linguine, 97
Crab Boil with Beer and Old Bay, 97
Crab Pie, 98
Cranberry-Apple Tartlets, 208
Cranberry-Pistachio Scones, 341
Cranberry-Spiced Biscuits, 338
Cream Cheese-and-Caviar Topping, 288
Cream Cheese-Banana-Nut Bread, 335
Cream Cheese-Walnut Stuffed Celery, 252
Cream-Filled Grilled Pound Cake, 332
Creamy Cantaloupe Smoothie, 344
Creamy Cheese Grits, 326
Creamy Feta-and-Herb Dip, 76
Creamy Honey Mustard, 204
Creamy Rice with Scallops, 73
Creole Mayonnaise, 69
Crispy Chicken Cutlets with Blistered Tomatoes, 122
Crispy Potatoes, 141
Crispy Soft-Shell Crab Sandwiches, 101
Croissant French Toast with Fresh Strawberry Syrup, 328
Crunchy Chicken-Peanut Chopped Salad, 157
Cuban Black Bean-and-Yellow Rice Bowls, 57

D

Day-After-Saint Patrick's Day Soup, 79
Deviled Crab Melts, 98
Dried Cherry-Pecan Oatmeal, 342

E

Eggplant-and-Olive Frittata, 322
English Muffin French Toast, 328

F

Farro Bowl with Curry-Roasted Sweet Potatoes and Brussels Sprouts, 36
Festive Dog Cookies, 284
Feta-Oregano Biscuits, 338
Fettuccine Alfredo with Leeks and Peas, 73
Fiery Pickled Carrots, 252
Fiery Sweet Dipping Sauce, 204
Florida Orange Grove Pie, 53
Fontina-Stuffed Pork Chops with Mashed Potatoes, 229
Fourth of July Confetti Roulade, 133
French Onion Puff Pastry Bites, 243
French Onion Soup Casserole, 91
Fresh Salmon Cakes with Buttermilk Dressing, 77
Fried Delacata Catfish, 138
Fruitcake Bark, 290
Fudge Layer Cake with Caramel Buttercream, 264

G

Gingerbread-and-Pear Upside-Down Cake, 301
Gingerbread Cheesecake with Lemon-Ginger Glaze, 300
Gingerbread Fawn Cookies, 303
Gingerbread Roulade and Eggnog Cream, 299
Ginger-Pecan Bourbon Balls, 291
Ginger-Plum Slump, 116
Gnocchi Gratin with Ham and Peas, 229
Goat Cheese-and-Gouda Pimiento Cheese, 145
Goji Berry Smoothie Bowl, 343
Grand Marnier Cakes, 56
Greek Chicken Salad Wedges, 158
Green Bean Casserole with Crispy Leeks, 256
Green Goddess Dressing, 140
Green Tea, Kiwi, and Mango Smoothie, 346
Grillades and Grits, 325
Grilled Eggplant-and-Corn Romesco Napoleons, 154
Grilled Pizza with Summer Veggies and Smoked Chicken, 197
Grilled Pork Meatball Kebabs, 104
Grilled Scallop-and-Mango Salad, 146
Grilled Spice-Rubbed Pork Chops with Scallion-Lime Rice, 108
Grilled Steak Salad with Green Tomato Vinaigrette, 122
Grilled Steak with Blistered Beans and Peppers, 159

H

Halloumi-and-Summer Vegetable Kebabs, 104
Ham-and-Cheese Brioche Casserole, 324
Ham-and-Cheese Croissant Casserole, 324
Ham-and-Swiss Corn Muffins, 339
Ham-and-Swiss Scones, 341
Ham-and-Swiss Sticky Buns, 333
Hard Cider-Braised Pork, 233
Harry Young's Burgoo, 25
Hash Brown Breakfast Casserole, 324
Hasselback Sweet Potato Casserole, 256
Herbed Shrimp-and-Rice Salad, 40
Herb Rub, 108
Herb-Rubbed Smoked Turkey, 247
Home-Style Slow-Cooker Pot Roast, 78
Honey-Ginger Fruit Salad, 343
Horseradish Pimiento Cheese, 145
Hot Chicken-and-Waffle Sandwiches, 327
Hot Fish-and-Waffle Sandwiches, 327
Hot 'n' Spicy Grits-and-Sausage Casseroles, 323
Hummingbird Cake, 61
Hummingbird Cupcakes, 62
Hummingbird Pancakes, 329

I

Iced Cinnamon Rolls, 332
Individual Country Grits-and-Sausage Casseroles, 323
Island Sunrise Smoothie, 345
Italian Brunch Casserole, 325

J

Jambalaya de Covington, 29

K

Kentucky Hot Brown Casserole, 46
Keto Chai Frappé, 346
Kettle Chip-Crusted Fried Green Tomatoes with Tasso Tartar Sauce, 154

L

Lamb Shanks, 45
Lemonade Ice Cubes, 71
Lemon-Almond Tea Bread, 335
Lemon-and-Chocolate Doberge Cake, 227
Lemon-Herb Butter, 337
Lemon-Herb Chicken Kebabs, 103
Lemon-Orange Pound Cake, 54
Lemon-Poppy Seed Zucchini Bread, 336
Lemon Tea Bread, 335
Low-Fat Banana Bread, 335

M

Make-Ahead Croissant Breakfast Casserole, 286
Make-Ahead Gravy, 251
Mashed Potato Bar, 244
Mashed Potatoes, 120
Mexican Hot Chocolate Cookies, 285
Migas Tacos, 326
Mini Cheese Grits Casseroles, 70
Mini Coconut-Key Lime Pies, 93
Mini Mushroom-and-Goat Cheese Pot Pies, 232
Mini Potato Skins, 63
Mini Shrimp Rolls, 147

Mini Tomato Sandwiches with Bacon Mayonnaise, 160
Mini Turkey Pot Pies with Dressing Tops, 244
Mocha-Cream Cheese Latte Cake, 330
Molasses-Soy Glazed Salmon and Vegetables, 35
Morning Glory Muffins, 340

N

New Orleans Beignets, 333
No-Bake Apricot-Coconut-Cashew Bars, 210
No-Bake Cherry-Pistachio Bars, 210
No-Bake Chocolate Chip-Pecan-Sea Salt Bars, 210
No-Bake Granola Bars, 210
No-Bake Peanut Butter-Fudge Ice-Cream Pie, 193
Nut Butter Smoothie Bowl, 343

O

Oatmeal Scones with Pecans, 342
Old-Fashioned Chicken and Dumplings, 26
Old World Hash, 325
Olive Oil Popcorn with Garlic and Rosemary, 211
Ombré Citrus Salad, 286
Orange Rolls, 333
Oven-Fried Chicken Salad with Buttermilk Ranch Dressing, 89
Overnight Blackberry French Toast, 329
Overnight Blueberry French Toast, 329
Oxbow Bakery Pecan Pie, 259

P

Parmesan-and-Black Pepper Topping, 288
Pasta Primavera with Shrimp, 92
Pasta with Shrimp and Tomato Cream Sauce, 122
PB&J Smoothie Bowl, 343
Peach-and-Blackberry Crisp, 141
Peach-Bourbon Upside-Down Bundt Cake, 127
Peach-Raspberry Buckle, 116
Peanut Butter-Banana Muffins, 340
Peanut Butter-Cream Cheese-Banana-Nut Bread, 335
Pecan-and-Thyme Shortbread Crackers, 285
Pecan-Breaded Pork Chops with Beer Sauce, 30
Pecan Cheese Spread, 69
Pecan Crunch Tart, 42
Peppermint Divinity, 290
Permanent Slaw, 143
Pickled Beets, 252
Pickled Shrimp and Vegetables, 126
Pimiento Cheese Biscuits, 338
Pimiento Cheese Scones, 341
Pimiento Cheese Shortbread Crackers, 285
Pitmaster Stew, 229
Pork-and-Farro Bowl with Warm Brussels Sprouts-Fennel Salad, 59
Pork-and-Shaved Vegetable Salad, 48
Pork Chops, 48
Pork Chops with Tomato-Bacon Gravy, 75
Pork Crown Roast, 287
Potato Croquettes, 120
Potato Puffs with Toppings, 288
Praline-Cream Cheese King Cakes, 64
Praline-Pecan French Toast, 328
Prosciutto-Asiago Pimiento Cheese, 145
Prosecco Sparklers, 346
Pumpkin-and-Winter Squash Gratin, 216
Pumpkin Beer-Cheese Soup, 215
Pumpkin-Buttermilk Biscuits with Crispy Ham and Honey Butter, 215
Pumpkin-Coconut Curry, 216
Pumpkin Layer Cake with Caramel-Cream Cheese Frosting, 245
Pumpkin-Pecan Bread, 336
Pumpkin Ravioli with Sage Brown Butter, 218
Pumpkin Spice-Chocolate Marble Loaves, 209
Pumpkin-Spice Magic Cake, 263

Q

Queso-Filled Mini Peppers, 107
Quick Buttermilk Biscuits, 337
Quick Pickled Slaw, 105

R

Red Hot Buttermints, 293
Red Velvet Ice-Cream Cake, 132
Red, White, and Blueberry-Filled Cupcakes, 134
Reunion Pea Casserole, 27
Rich Turkey Broth, 251
Roasted Pumpkin-and-Baby Kale Salad, 215
Roasted Sweet Potato Hummus, 211
Roasted Tomato, Salami, and Mozzarella Pasta, 158
Root Vegetable Fritters, 286
Rosemary, Pear, and Asiago Scones, 341
Rosemary Trees, 304

S

Salmon, 49
Salmon Bagel Sandwiches, 49
Salty-Sweet Nut Brittle, 292
Sausage and Cheese Muffins, 340
Sausage and Kale Pesto Pizza, 35
Sausage Tostadas, 326
Savannah Red Rice, 31
Savory Bacon-and-Cheddar Breakfast Pie, 323
Savory Ham-and-Swiss Breakfast Pie, 323
Savory Sweet Potato Casserole, 287
Scrambled Egg Muffin Sliders, 339
Seared Hanger Steak with Braised Greens and Grapes, 154
Seasoned Flour, 120
Shaker Lemon Pie, 55
Sheet Pan Greek Chicken with Roasted Potatoes, 106
Sheet Pan Nachos with Chorizo and Refried Beans, 204
Sheet Pan Pizza with Corn, Tomatoes, and Sausage, 121
Shepherd's Pie, 45
Shrimp Boil Vegetable Bowls, 156
Shrimp Cobb Salad with Bacon Dressing, 73
Shrimp-Okra-and-Sausage Kebabs, 102
Shrimp, Sausage, and Black Bean Pasta, 51
Skillet Chicken Pot Pie with Leeks and Mushrooms, 47
Skillet Enchiladas Suizas, 212
Skirt Steak and Cauliflower Rice with Red Pepper Sauce, 59
Sliced Pork Chops with Brown Butter-Golden Raisin Relish, 48
Slow-Cooker Bolognese Sauce, 286
Slow-Cooker Chicken Stew with Pumpkin and Wild Rice, 216
Slow-Cooker Cranberry-Pear Butter, 285
Slow-Cooker White Chili with Turkey, 267
Smoked Salmon-and-Chives Topping, 288
Smoky Rub, 108
Smoky Snack Mix, 205
Smoky White Bean Soup, 40
Soba Noodle-and-Shrimp Bowls, 58
Sour Cream-Praline Biscuits, 338
Southwestern Chile-Cheese Corn Muffins, 339
Sparkling Citrus Punch, 71
Spiced Chai Frappé, 346
Spicy Bourbon-Citrus Punch, 285
Spicy Grilled Corn Salad, 143
Spicy Orange-Peach Butter, 69

Spicy Pecans, 205
Spicy Red Curry with Chicken, 47
Spicy Rub, 108
Spicy Tomato Frittata, 322
Stacy and Joyce's Cornbread Dressing, 239
Steak-and-Potato Kebabs, 103
Strawberry-Apricot Hand Pies, 85
Strawberry-Banana Pudding Icebox Cake, 87
Strawberry-Blueberry Cupcakes, 84
Strawberry Butter, 94
Strawberry Fool, 94
Strawberry Frosting, 84
Strawberry Kuchen, 117
Strawberry-Lemon Crêpe Cake, 85
Strawberry-Mango Semifreddo, 86
Strawberry OJ, 94
Strawberry-Pineapple Smoothie, 345
Strawberry-Rhubarb Pretzel Pie, 84
Strawberry-Rhubarb Salad, 71
Strawberry Vinaigrette, 94
Sweet-and-Spicy Sheet Pan Chicken with Cauliflower and Carrots, 34
Sweet Peach Pancakes, 329
Sweet Potato and Edamame Hash, 325
Sweet Potato Coffee Cake, 330

T

Teriyaki Salmon Bowls with Crispy Brussels Sprouts, 49
Thanksgiving Rum Punch, 243
Three-Bean Pasta Salad, 143
Thyme-Scented Blueberry Pie, 109
Toasted Oatmeal Cookies, 209
Toaster Oven Blackberry Cobblers, 198
Tomato-Sausage Frittata, 322
Triple Melon Smoothie, 345
Tropical Chicken Lettuce Wraps, 90
Tropical Jasmine Smoothie, 346
Truffle Oil-and-Rosemary Topping, 288
Turkey and Pimiento Cheese Club Sandwich, 266
Turkey, Apple, and Brie Sandwich, 266
Turkey Breast, 46
Turkey, Caramelized Onion, and Gruyère Grilled Cheese, 266
Turkey, Pesto, and Fresh Mozzarella Sandwich, 266
Turkey with Shallot-Mustard Sauce and Roasted Potatoes, 46
Turnip Green Salad, 140

V

Veggie Frittata, 324

W

Wake-Up Smoothie, 346
Walnut-Honey Butter, 337
Warm Asparagus, Radish, and New Potato Salad with Herb Dressing, 70
Warm Cheese-and-Spicy Pecan Dip, 204
Warm Spinach-Sweet Onion Dip with Country Ham, 205
Watermelon, Cucumber, and Feta Salad, 143
Watermelon Salad, 140
Wedge Salad with Turkey and Blue Cheese-Buttermilk Dressing, 46
West Indies Crab Salad, 101
Whipped Sweet Potato Butter, 141
Whiskey-Apple Cider Punch, 202
White Calzones with Marinara Sauce, 230
Whole-Grain Panzanella, 125
Whole Wheat-Raisin-Nut Bread, 336

Y

Yellow Gazpacho with Herbed Goat Cheese Toasts, 157

Z

Ziti with Mushroom, Fennel, and Tomato Ragu, 36
Zucchini Lasagna, 124

Month-by-Month Index

This index alphabetically lists every food article and accompanying recipes by month.

January

New Year, Same Hoppin' Tradition, 38
Classic Hoppin' John, 39
Old Family Favorites, 24
Beef Stew, 28
Beer Sauce, 30
Capitol Hill Bean Soup, 32
Country Captain Chicken, 33
Harry Young's Burgoo, 25
Jambalaya de Covington, 29
Old-Fashioned Chicken and Dumplings, 26
Pecan-Breaded Pork Chops with Beer Sauce, 30
Reunion Pea Casserole, 27
Savannah Red Rice, 31
***SL* Cooking School, 40**
Almond-Chicken Wrap, 40
Conquer Your Fear of Phyllo Dough, 41
Cook Flawless Fish Fillets, 41
Herbed Shrimp-and-Rice Salad, 40
Pack a Better Brown-Bag Lunch, 40
Pecan Crunch Tart, 42
Smoky White Bean Soup, 40
The Southern Secret to Chocolate Cake, 37
Chocolate Mayonnaise Cake, 37
Weeknights Done Light, 34
Farro Bowl with Curry-Roasted Sweet Potatoes and Brussels Sprouts, 36
Molasses-Soy Glazed Salmon and Vegetables, 35
Sausage and Kale Pesto Pizza, 35
Sweet-and-Spicy Sheet Pan Chicken with Cauliflower and Carrots, 34
Ziti with Mushroom, Fennel, and Tomato Ragu, 36

February

The Beauty of Slow Cooking, 44
Black Bean Burgers with Comeback Sauce, 50
Black Beans, 50
Black Bean Tostadas with Mango-Avocado Salsa, 50
Braised Lamb Shanks with Parmesan-Chive Grits, 45
Caramelized Onion, Spinach, and Pork Strata, 48
Carbonara with Braised Lamb, 45
Chicken, 47
Chicken Biscuit Sandwiches, 47
Citrus-Salmon Salad, 49
Kentucky Hot Brown Casserole, 46
Lamb Shanks, 45
Pork-and-Shaved Vegetable Salad, 48
Pork Chops, 48
Salmon, 49
Salmon Bagel Sandwiches, 49
Shepherd's Pie, 45
Shrimp, Sausage, and Black Bean Pasta, 51
Skillet Chicken Pot Pie with Leeks and Mushrooms, 47
Sliced Pork Chops with Brown Butter-Golden Raisin Relish, 48
Spicy Red Curry with Chicken, 47
Teriyaki Salmon Bowls with Crispy Brussels Sprouts, 49
Turkey Breast, 46
Turkey with Shallot-Mustard Sauce and Roasted Potatoes, 46
Wedge Salad with Turkey and Blue Cheese-Buttermilk Dressing, 46
Game Day Potatoes, 63
Mini Potato Skins, 63
The King of Cakes, 64
Praline-Cream Cheese King Cakes, 64
A League of Their Own, 52
Cold Lemon Soufflés with Wine Sauce, 55
Florida Orange Grove Pie, 53
Grand Marnier Cakes, 56
Lemon-Orange Pound Cake, 54
Shaker Lemon Pie, 55
The Mystery of Hummingbird Cake, 60
Candied Pineapple Wedges, 62
Hummingbird Cake, 61
Hummingbird Cupcakes, 62
***SL* Cooking School, 65**
Choose the Best Model for You, 66
Homemade Stock, Simplified, 65
New Uses for Kitchen Items, 66
Prep Freezer Meals Like a Pro, 65
Super Bowls, 57
Couscous Pilaf with Roasted Carrots, Chicken, and Feta, 58
Cuban Black Bean-and-Yellow Rice Bowls, 57
Pork-and-Farro Bowl with Warm Brussels Sprouts-Fennel Salad, 59
Skirt Steak and Cauliflower Rice with Red Pepper Sauce, 59
Soba Noodle-and-Shrimp Bowls, 58

March

Bacon Makes Everything Better, 72
Bacon-Hash Brown Quiche, 74
Bacon-Wrapped Chicken Breasts, 74
Creamy Rice with Scallops, 73
Fettuccine Alfredo with Leeks and Peas, 73
Pork Chops with Tomato-Bacon Gravy, 75
Shrimp Cobb Salad with Bacon Dressing, 73
A Beautiful Easter Brunch, 68
Buttermilk Biscuits with Ham, 69
Chive-Radish Compound Butter, 69
Coconut-Carrot Cake with Coconut Buttercream, 71
Creole Mayonnaise, 69
Lemonade Ice Cubes, 71
Mini Cheese Grits Casseroles, 70
Pecan Cheese Spread, 69
Sparkling Citrus Punch, 71
Spicy Orange-Peach Butter, 69
Strawberry-Rhubarb Salad, 71
Warm Asparagus, Radish, and New Potato Salad with Herb Dressing, 70
Luck of the Leftovers, 79
Day-After-Saint Patrick's Day Soup, 79
Pot Roast, Please, 78
Home-Style Slow-Cooker Pot Roast, 78
***SL* Cooking School, 80**
Bring Home the Best Bacon, 80
Freeze Leftovers Like a Pro, 80
Vegging Out, 76
Creamy Feta-and-Herb Dip, 76
Wild About Salmon, 77
Fresh Salmon Cakes with Buttermilk Dressing, 77

April

Chicken Salad Gets a Makeover, 88
Chicken Caesar Salad Sandwiches, 90
Chicken Niçoise Salad, 88
Chicken-Quinoa Salad with Green Goddess Dressing, 90
Oven-Fried Chicken Salad with Buttermilk Ranch Dressing, 89
Tropical Chicken Lettuce Wraps, 90
The French Onion Casserole, 91
French Onion Soup Casserole, 91
One-Pot Primavera, 92
Pasta Primavera with Shrimp, 92
***SL* Cooking School, 94**
Chicken Salad Tip, 94
Make the Most of Vidalia Onions, 94
Strawberry Butter, 94
Strawberry Fool, 94
Strawberry OJ, 94
Strawberry Vinaigrette, 94
Strawberry Sidekicks, 82
Coconut Rice Pudding with Strawberry-Nectarine Compote, 87
Strawberry-Apricot Hand Pies, 85
Strawberry-Banana Pudding Icebox Cake, 87
Strawberry-Blueberry Cupcakes, 84
Strawberry Frosting, 84
Strawberry-Lemon Crêpe Cake, 85
Strawberry-Mango Semifreddo, 86
Strawberry-Rhubarb Pretzel Pie, 84
Sweet Tarts, 93
Mini Coconut-Key Lime Pies, 93

May

Gotta Love Crab, 96
Best-Ever Crab Cakes with Green Tomato Slaw, 101
Crab-and-Bacon Linguine, 97
Crab Boil with Beer and Old Bay, 97
Crab Pie, 98
Crispy Soft-Shell Crab Sandwiches, 101
Deviled Crab Melts, 98
West Indies Crab Salad, 101
Modern Mediterranean, 106
Sheet Pan Greek Chicken with Roasted Potatoes, 106
Next-Level Kebabs, 102
Grilled Pork Meatball Kebabs, 104
Halloumi-and-Summer Vegetable Kebabs, 104
Lemon-Herb Chicken Kebabs, 103
Shrimp-Okra-and-Sausage Kebabs, 102
Steak-and-Potato Kebabs, 103
Pick a Pepper, 107
Queso-Filled Mini Peppers, 107
***SL* Cooking School, 110**
Build a Better Kebab, 110
4 Creative Ways to Crimp a Piecrust, 110
The Spice Is Right, 108
Grilled Spice-Rubbed Pork Chops with Scallion-Lime Rice, 108
Superfast Sides, 105
Arroz Verde (Mexican Green Rice), 105
Couscous Pilaf, 105
Quick Pickled Slaw, 105
Thyme for Pie, 109
Thyme-Scented Blueberry Pie, 109

June

Forgotten Fruit Desserts, 112
Berry Sonker with Dip, 115
Blueberry-Lemon Crunch Bars, 115
Cherry-Nectarine Pandowdy, 115
Ginger-Plum Slump, 116
Peach-Raspberry Buckle, 116
Strawberry Kuchen, 117
Lasagna Gets a New Look, 124
Zucchini Lasagna, 124
Let Them Eat Shrimp, 126
Pickled Shrimp and Vegetables, 126
Salad for Supper, 125
Whole-Grain Panzanella, 125
***SL* Cooking School, 128**
The Case for Homemade Croutons, 128
Don't Pick Pink, 128
Reach for the Right Peach, 128
The Soul of a Chef, 118
Black Pepper-and-Honey Whipped Goat Cheese, 120
Cantaloupe Soup with Chorizo Relish and Black Pepper-and-Honey Whipped Goat Cheese, 120
Chicken Thighs and BBQ Beans, 119
Chive Sour Cream, 120
Chorizo Relish, 120
Mashed Potatoes, 120
Potato Croquettes, 120
Seasoned Flour, 120
Twice as Nice, 127
Peach-Bourbon Upside-Down Bundt Cake, 127
You Say Tomato, 121
Bacon-Spinach-and-Couscous Stuffed Tomatoes, 123
Crispy Chicken Cutlets with Blistered Tomatoes, 122
Grilled Steak Salad with Green Tomato Vinaigrette, 122
Pasta with Shrimp and Tomato Cream Sauce, 122
Sheet Pan Pizza with Corn, Tomatoes, and Sausage, 121

July

All-American Desserts, 130
Cherry Flag Pie, 132
Cornmeal Cookie Berry Shortcakes, 133
Fourth of July Confetti Roulade, 133
Red Velvet Ice-Cream Cake, 132
Red, White, and Blueberry-Filled Cupcakes, 134
Fried and True, 135
Black-eyed Pea Ranchero Sauce, 138
Cheddar-Caramelized Onion Bread, 140
Crispy Potatoes, 141
Fried Delacata Catfish, 138
Green Goddess Dressing, 140
Peach-and-Blackberry Crisp, 141
Turnip Green Salad, 140
Watermelon Salad, 140
Whipped Sweet Potato Butter, 141
Pick a Side, 142
Cherry Tomato Caprese Salad, 142
Permanent Slaw, 143
Spicy Grilled Corn Salad, 143
Three-Bean Pasta Salad, 143
Watermelon, Cucumber, and Feta Salad, 143
Ready to Roll, 147
Mini Shrimp Rolls, 147
***SL* Cooking School, 148**
The Best Ways to Baste, 148
Grill Great Corn, 148
3 Tasty Toppings, 148
Stirring Up Controversy, 144
Basic Pimiento Cheese, 144
Chipotle Pimiento Cheese, 145
Goat Cheese-and-Gouda Pimiento Cheese, 145
Horseradish Pimiento Cheese, 145
Prosciutto-Asiago Pimiento Cheese, 145
Summer Scallops, 146
Grilled Scallop-and-Mango Salad, 146

August

Just Chill, 193
No-Bake Peanut Butter-Fudge Ice-Cream Pie, 193
No-Cook Summer Suppers, 156
Crunchy Chicken-Peanut Chopped Salad, 157
Greek Chicken Salad Wedges, 158
Roasted Tomato, Salami, and Mozzarella Pasta, 158
Shrimp Boil Vegetable Bowls, 156

Yellow Gazpacho with Herbed Goat Cheese Toasts, 157
Pizza Night Alfresco, 196
Grilled Pizza with Summer Veggies and Smoked Chicken, 197
Sizzling Skillet Steak, 159
Grilled Steak with Blistered Beans and Peppers, 159
***SL* Cooking School, 198**
The Hottest New Oven, 198
Staples for Stove-Free Suppers, 198
Toaster Oven Blackberry Cobblers, 198
Toaster Treats, 198
Soiree in the Swamp, 150
Blackberry Trifles with Pecan Feuilletage and Mascarpone-Cane Syrup Mousse, 155
Grilled Eggplant-and-Corn Romesco Napoleons, 154
Kettle Chip-Crusted Fried Green Tomatoes with Tasso Tartar Sauce, 154
Seared Hanger Steak with Braised Greens and Grapes, 154
Summer Succotash, 194
Best-Ever Succotash, 195
Tasty Tomato Bites, 160
Mini Tomato Sandwiches with Bacon Mayonnaise, 160

September

Bake Another Batch, 206
Brown Butter-Maple-Pecan Blondies, 209
Chocolate-Pear Muffins, 207
Cranberry-Apple Tartlets, 208
Pumpkin Spice-Chocolate Marble Loaves, 209
Toasted Oatmeal Cookies, 209
Easier Enchiladas, 212
Skillet Enchiladas Suizas, 212
Snack Attack, 210
No-Bake Apricot-Coconut-Cashew Bars, 210
No-Bake Cherry-Pistachio Bars, 210
No-Bake Chocolate Chip-Pecan-Sea Salt Bars, 210
No-Bake Granola Bars, 210
Olive Oil Popcorn with Garlic and Rosemary, 211
Roasted Sweet Potato Hummus, 211
The Southern Living Tailgating Playbook, 200
Away, 205
Brisket-and-Black Bean Chili with Cilantro-Lime Crema, 205
Cilantro-Lime Crema, 205
Smoky Snack Mix, 205
Warm Spinach-Sweet Onion Dip with Country Ham, 205
Home, 204
Brined Grilled Chicken with Dipping Sauces, 204
Buttermilk-Parmesan Ranch, 204
Creamy Honey Mustard, 204
Fiery Sweet Dipping Sauce, 204
Sheet Pan Nachos with Chorizo and Refried Beans, 204
Spicy Pecans, 205
Warm Cheese-and-Spicy Pecan Dip, 204
Spirited Cocktails, 202
Big-Batch Bloody Marys, 202
Whiskey-Apple Cider Punch, 202

October

Fall Layers, 219
Apple Stack Cake, 220, 226
Blackberry Jam Cake, 222, 226
Lemon-and-Chocolate Doberge Cake, 224, 227
Low-and-Slow Pork Supper, 233
Hard Cider-Braised Pork, 233
More Cheese, Please, 228
Baked Rigatoni with Zucchini and Mozzarella, 230
Beef Stew with Cheddar Biscuits, 229
Fontina-Stuffed Pork Chops with Mashed Potatoes, 229
Gnocchi Gratin with Ham and Peas, 229
White Calzones with Marinara Sauce, 230
Muffin Pan Pies, 232
Mini Mushroom-and-Goat Cheese Pot Pies, 232
The Savory Side of Pumpkin, 214
Pumpkin-and-Winter Squash Gratin, 216
Pumpkin Beer-Cheese Soup, 215
Pumpkin-Buttermilk Biscuits with Crispy Ham and Honey Butter, 215
Pumpkin-Coconut Curry, 216
Pumpkin Ravioli with Sage Brown Butter, 218
Roasted Pumpkin-and-Baby Kale Salad, 215
Slow-Cooker Chicken Stew with Pumpkin and Wild Rice, 216
***SL* Cooking School, 234**
Choose the Right Cheese, 234
Pick Me!, 234

November

Chili for a Crowd, 267
Slow-Cooker White Chili with Turkey, 267
Friendsgiving at Joy's, 240
Apple, Celery, and Romaine Salad with Pancetta and Blue Cheese, 243
French Onion Puff Pastry Bites, 243
Mashed Potato Bar, 244
Mini Turkey Pot Pies with Dressing Tops, 244
Pumpkin Layer Cake with Caramel-Cream Cheese Frosting, 245
Thanksgiving Rum Punch, 243
Here Come the Casseroles, 253
Broccoli-Cheese Casserole, 256
Brussels Sprouts with Bacon and Shallots, 257
Cheesy Potato Casserole, 257
Corn Pudding, 256
Green Bean Casserole with Crispy Leeks, 256
Hasselback Sweet Potato Casserole, 256
It's Called Dressing, Not Stuffing, 248
Aunt Grace's Famous Cornbread Dressing, 249
Let's Talk (Smoking) Turkey, 246
Herb-Rubbed Smoked Turkey, 247
"Look What Aunt Lisa Brought!," 262
Butterscotch-Spice Trifle, 263
Fudge Layer Cake with Caramel Buttercream, 264
Pumpkin-Spice Magic Cake, 263
Make the Best Sandwich of the Year, 266
Turkey and Pimiento Cheese Club Sandwich, 266
Turkey, Apple, and Brie Sandwich, 266
Turkey, Caramelized Onion, and Gruyère Grilled Cheese, 266
Turkey, Pesto, and Fresh Mozzarella Sandwich, 266
Old Faithfuls, 258
Back in the Day Bakery Southern Pumpkin Pie, 261
Buxton Hall Ultimate Apple Pie, 260
Oxbow Bakery Pecan Pie, 259
Pass the Gravy, 250
Make-Ahead Gravy, 251
Rich Turkey Broth, 251
Respect the Relish Tray, 252
Cream Cheese-Walnut Stuffed Celery, 252
Fiery Pickled Carrots, 252
Pickled Beets, 252
***SL* Cooking School, 268**
Smart Shortcuts, 268

Thanksgiving at the Farm, 236
Stacy and Joyce's Cornbread Dressing, 239

December

Gingerbread Takes the Cake, 294
Brown Sugar-and-Ginger Whipped Cream, 300
Classic Gingerbread, 300
Gingerbread-and-Pear Upside-Down Cake, 301
Gingerbread Cheesecake with Lemon-Ginger Glaze, 300
Gingerbread Roulade and Eggnog Cream, 299
Merry Christmas, Sugar!, 289
Buttermilk-Pecan Pralines, 291
Christmas Buttermints, 293
Fruitcake Bark, 290
Ginger-Pecan Bourbon Balls, 291
Peppermint Divinity, 290
Salty-Sweet Nut Brittle, 292
Peace of Cake, 302
Best White Cake, 303
Gingerbread Fawn Cookies, 303
The Icing on the Cake, 304
Rosemary Trees, 304
Simply Spectacular, 270
Cheddar Shortbread Crackers, 285
Chocolate-Caramel Cookie Cups, 284
Chocolate-Peppermint Swirl Sandwich Cookies, 284
Chocolate Sugar Cookie Dough, 284
Christmas Tree Bar Cookies, 284
Cornmeal Crescent Rolls, 287
Cream Cheese-and-Caviar Topping, 288
Festive Dog Cookies, 284
Make-Ahead Croissant Breakfast Casserole, 286
Mexican Hot Chocolate Cookies, 285
Ombré Citrus Salad, 286
Parmesan-and-Black Pepper Topping, 288
Pork Crown Roast, 287
Potato Puffs with Toppings, 288
Root Vegetable Fritters, 286
Savory Sweet Potato Casserole, 287
Slow-Cooker Bolognese Sauce, 286
Slow-Cooker Cranberry-Pear Butter, 285
Smoked Salmon-and-Chives Topping, 288
Spicy Bourbon-Citrus Punch, 285
Truffle Oil-and-Rosemary Topping, 288

Our Best Breakfast & Brunch

Cakes & Breads, 330
Apricot-Pecan Cinnamon Rolls, 332
Basic Buttermilk Biscuits, 338
Blackberry Butter, 337
Blueberry Kolaches, 334
Blueberry-Orange Bread, 336
Caramel Apple Coffee Cake, 331
Chocolate-Cream Cheese Coffee Cake, 330
Cinnamon-Raisin Biscuits, 338
Cream Cheese-Banana-Nut Bread, 335
Cream-Filled Grilled Pound Cake, 332
Ham-and-Swiss Sticky Buns, 333
Iced Cinnamon Rolls, 332
Lemon-Herb Butter, 337
Lemon-Poppy Seed Zucchini Bread, 336
Lemon Tea Bread, 335
Low-Fat Banana Bread, 335
New Orleans Beignets, 333
Orange Rolls, 333
Pumpkin-Pecan Bread, 336
Quick Buttermilk Biscuits, 337
Sour Cream-Praline Biscuits, 338
Sweet Potato Coffee Cake, 330
Walnut-Honey Butter, 337
Whole Wheat-Raisin-Nut Bread, 336
Casseroles, 322
Bacon Mushroom Frittata, 322
Breakfast in a Skillet, 322
Brie-and-Veggie Strata, 322
Creamy Cheese Grits, 326
Grillades and Grits, 325
Ham-and-Cheese Croissant Casserole, 324
Hash Brown Breakfast Casserole, 324
Individual Country Grits-and-Sausage Casseroles, 323
Italian Brunch Casserole, 325
Migas Tacos, 326
Sausage Tostadas, 326
Savory Ham-and-Swiss Breakfast Pie, 323
Sweet Potato and Edamame Hash, 325
Veggie Frittata, 324
Fruits & Beverages, 342
Acai Berry Smoothie Bowl, 343
Blackberry-Mango Breakfast Smoothie, 345
Bloody Marys by the Pitcher, 347
Blueberry Smoothies, 345
Blushing Mimosas, 346
Champagne Sparklers, 346
Citrus Salad with Spiced Honey, 343
Creamy Cantaloupe Smoothie, 344
Dried Cherry-Pecan Oatmeal, 342
Green Tea, Kiwi, and Mango Smoothie, 346
Honey-Ginger Fruit Salad, 343
Island Sunrise Smoothie, 345
PB&J Smoothie Bowl, 343
Spiced Chai Frappé, 346
Strawberry-Pineapple Smoothie, 345
Triple Melon Smoothie, 345
Wake-Up Smoothie, 346
Muffins & Scones, 338
Bacon-and-Cheddar Corn Muffins, 338
Banana-Toffee Coffee Cake Muffins, 340
Best-Ever Scones, 341
Blueberry Muffins with Lemon-Cream Cheese Glaze, 339
Morning Glory Muffins, 340
Oatmeal Scones with Pecans, 342
Peanut Butter-Banana Muffins, 340
Sausage and Cheese Muffins, 340
Waffles, French Toast & Pancakes, 326
Buttermilk and Brown Sugar Waffles, 326
Cinnamon Roll Waffles with Bananas Foster Sauce, 327
Croissant French Toast with Fresh Strawberry Syrup, 328
English Muffin French Toast, 328
Hot Chicken-and-Waffle Sandwiches, 327
Hummingbird Pancakes, 329
Overnight Blackberry French Toast, 329
Praline-Pecan French Toast, 328
Sweet Peach Pancakes, 329

General Recipe Index

This index lists every recipe by food category and/or major ingredient.

A

Appetizers
Deviled Crab Melts, 98
Dips
Feta-and-Herb Dip, Creamy, 76
Warm Cheese-and-Spicy Pecan Dip, 204
Warm Spinach-Sweet Onion Dip with Country Ham, 205
Mix, Smoky Snack, 205
Pecans, Spicy, 205
Peppers, Queso-Filled Mini, 107
Potato Skins, Mini, 63
Stuffed Celery, Cream Cheese-Walnut, 252
Apples
Cake, Apple Stack, 226
Coffee Cake, Caramel Apple, 331
Pie, Buxton Hall Ultimate Apple, 260
Salad with Pancetta and Blue Cheese, Apple, Celery, and Romaine, 243
Apricot-Coconut-Cashew Bars, No-Bake, 210
Apricot-Pecan Cinnamon Rolls, 332
Asparagus, Radish, and New Potato Salad with Herb Dressing, Warm, 70

B

Bacon
Biscuits, Black Pepper-Bacon, 338
Corn Muffins, Bacon-and-Cheddar, 338
Crackers, Bacon, Bourbon, and Benne Seed Shortbread, 285
Dressing, Shrimp Cobb Salad with Bacon, 73
Frittata, Bacon Mushroom, 322
Mayonnaise, Mini Tomato Sandwiches with Bacon, 160
Pie, Savory Bacon-and-Cheddar Breakfast, 323
Quiche, Bacon-Hash Brown, 74
Scones, Bacon, Cheddar, and Chive, 341
Stuffed Tomatoes, Bacon-Spinach-and-Couscous, 123
Bananas. *See also* Breads; Muffins
Pound Cake, Bananas Foster Grilled, 332
Sauce, Cinnamon Roll Waffles with Bananas Foster, 327
Beans
BBQ Beans, Chicken Thighs and, 119
Black
Black Beans, start with, 50
Burgers with Comeback Sauce, Black Bean, 50
Cuban Black Bean-and-Yellow Rice Bowls, 57
Tostadas with Mango-Avocado Salsa, Black Bean, 50
Blistered Beans and Peppers, Grilled Steak with, 159
Green Bean Casserole with Crispy Leeks, 256
Salad, Three-Bean Pasta, 143
Soup, Capitol Hill Bean, 32
Succotash, Best-Ever, 195
White Bean Soup, Smoky, 40
Beef. *See also* Beef, Ground
Brisket-and-Black Bean Chili with Cilantro-Lime Crema, 205
Roasts
Braised Beef, Coffee Stout-, 233
Pot Roast, Home-Style Slow-Cooker, 78
Stew, Beef, 28
Soup, Day-After-Saint Patrick's Day, 79
Steaks
Grilled Steak with Blistered Beans and Peppers, 159
Hanger Steak with Braised Greens and Grapes, Seared, 154
Kebabs, Steak-and-Potato, 103
Salad with Green Tomato Vinaigrette, Grilled Steak, 122
Skirt Steak and Cauliflower Rice with Red Pepper Sauce, 59
Beef, Ground
Bolognese Sauce, Slow-Cooker, 286
Burgoo, Harry Young's, 25
Stew with Cheddar Biscuits, Beef, 229
Beets, Pickled, 252
Beverages
Alcoholic
Bloody Marys, Big-Batch, 202
Bloody Marys by the Pitcher, 347
Mimosas, Blushing, 346
Punch, Sparkling Citrus, 71
Punch, Spicy Bourbon-Citrus, 285
Punch, Thanksgiving Rum, 243
Punch, Whiskey-Apple Cider, 202
Sparklers, Champagne, 346
Sparklers, Prosecco, 346
Frappé, Keto Chai, 346
Frappé, Spiced Chai, 346
Ice Cubes, Lemonade, 71
OJ, Strawberry, 94
Smoothies
Blackberry-Mango Breakfast Smoothie, 345
Blueberry Smoothies, 345
Creamy Cantaloupe Smoothie, 344
Green Tea, Kiwi, and Mango Smoothie, 346
Island Sunrise Smoothie, 345
Melon Smoothie, Triple, 345
Strawberry-Pineapple Smoothie, 345
Tropical Jasmine Smoothie, 346
Wake-Up Smoothie, 346
Biscuits
Black Pepper-Bacon Biscuits, 338
Buttermilk Biscuits, Basic, 338
Buttermilk Biscuits, Quick, 337
Buttermilk Biscuits with Ham, 69
Cheddar Biscuits, Beef Stew with, 229
Chicken Biscuit Sandwiches, 47
Cinnamon-Raisin Biscuits, 338
Cranberry-Spiced Biscuits, 338
Feta-Oregano Biscuits, 338
Pimiento Cheese Biscuits, 338
Pumpkin-Buttermilk Biscuits with Crispy Ham and Honey Butter, 215
Sour Cream-Praline Biscuits, 338
Blackberries
Bread, Blackberry-Lemon, 336
Butter, Blackberry, 337
Cake, Blackberry Jam, 226
French Toast, Overnight Blackberry, 329
Trifles with Pecan Feuilletage and Mascarpone-Cane Syrup Mousse, Blackberry, 155
Blueberries
Bars, Blueberry-Lemon Crunch, 115
Bread, Blueberry-Orange, 336
Cupcakes, Red, White, and Blueberry-Filled, 134
French Toast, Overnight Blueberry, 329

Kolaches, Blueberry, 334
Muffins with Lemon-Cream Cheese Glaze, Blueberry, 339
Pie, Thyme-Scented Blueberry, 109
Bowls
Acai Berry Smoothie Bowl, 343
Couscous Pilaf with Roasted Carrots, Chicken, and Feta, 58
Cuban Black Bean-and-Yellow Rice Bowls, 57
Farro Bowl with Curry-Roasted Sweet Potatoes and Brussels Sprouts, 36
Goji Berry Smoothie Bowl, 343
Nut Butter Smoothie Bowl, 343
PB&J Smoothie Bowl, 343
Pork-and-Farro Bowl with Warm Brussels Sprouts-Fennel Salad, 59
Shrimp Boil Vegetable Bowls, 156
Skirt Steak and Cauliflower Rice with Red Pepper Sauce, 59
Soba Noodle-and-Shrimp Bowls, 58
Teriyaki Salmon Bowls with Crispy Brussels Sprouts, 49
Breads. *See also* Biscuits; Crackers; French Toast; Muffins; Pancakes; Rolls and Buns; Scones; Waffles
Banana Bread, Low-Fat, 335
Beignets, New Orleans, 333
Blackberry-Lemon Bread, 336
Blueberry-Orange Bread, 336
Cheddar-Caramelized Onion Bread, 140
Cinnamon-Cream Cheese-Banana-Nut Bread, 335
Cream Cheese-Banana-Nut Bread, 335
King Cakes, Praline-Cream Cheese, 64
Lemon-Almond Tea Bread, 335
Lemon-Poppy Seed Zucchini Bread, 336
Lemon Tea Bread, 335
Peanut Butter-Cream Cheese-Banana-Nut Bread, 335
Pumpkin-Pecan Bread, 336
Pumpkin Spice-Chocolate Marble Loaves, 209
Whole Wheat-Raisin-Nut Bread, 336
Broccoli-Cheese Casserole, 256
Brussels Sprouts
Bacon and Shallots, Brussels Sprouts with, 257
Crispy Brussels Sprouts, Teriyaki Salmon Bowls with, 49
Salad, Pork-and-Farro Bowl with Warm Brussels Sprouts-Fennel, 59
Butter
Blackberry Butter, 337
Chive-Radish Compound Butter, 69
Honey Butter, Pumpkin-Buttermilk Biscuits with Crispy Ham and, 215
Lemon-Herb Butter, 337
Sage Brown Butter, Pumpkin Ravioli with, 218
Slow-Cooker Cranberry-Pear Butter, 285
Spicy Orange-Peach Butter, 69
Strawberry Butter, 94
Walnut-Honey Butter, 337
Whipped Sweet Potato Butter, 141
Butterscotch-Spice Trifle, 263

C

Cakes
Apple Stack Cake, 226
Blackberry Jam Cake, 226
Cheesecake with Lemon-Ginger Glaze, Gingerbread, 300
Chocolate Mayonnaise Cake, 37
Coconut-Carrot Cake with Coconut Buttercream, 71
Coffee Cakes
Caramel Apple Coffee Cake, 331
Chocolate-Cream Cheese Coffee Cake, 330
Mocha-Cream Cheese Latte Cake, 330
Sweet Potato Coffee Cake, 330
Cupcakes
Hummingbird Cupcakes, 62
Red, White, and Blueberry-Filled Cupcakes, 134
Strawberry-Blueberry Cupcakes, 84
Fudge Layer Cake with Caramel Buttercream, 264
Gingerbread-and-Pear Upside-Down Cake, 301
Gingerbread Roulade and Eggnog Cream, 299
Grand Marnier Cakes, 56
Hummingbird Cake, 61
King Cakes, Praline-Cream Cheese, 64
Lemon-and-Chocolate Doberge Cake, 227
Peach-Bourbon Upside-Down Bundt Cake, 127
Peach-Raspberry Buckle, 116
Pound Cake
Bananas Foster Grilled Pound Cake, 332
Cream-Filled Grilled Pound Cake, 332
Lemon-Orange Pound Cake, 54
Pumpkin Layer Cake with Caramel-Cream Cheese Frosting, 245
Pumpkin-Spice Magic Cake, 263
Red Velvet Ice-Cream Cake, 132
Roulade, Fourth of July Confetti, 133
Shortcakes, Cornmeal Cookie Berry, 133
Strawberry-Banana Pudding Icebox Cake, 87
Strawberry Kuchen, 117
Strawberry-Lemon Crêpe Cake, 85
White Cake, Best, 303
Calzones with Marinara Sauce, White, 230
Candies
Bark, Boozy Fruitcake, 291
Bark, Fruitcake, 290
Bourbon Balls, Ginger-Pecan, 291
Brittle, Salty-Sweet Nut, 292
Buttermints, Christmas, 293
Buttermints, Red Hot, 293
Divinity, Peppermint, 290
Pralines, Buttermilk-Pecan, 291
Cantaloupe Soup with Chorizo Relish and Black Pepper-and-Honey Whipped Goat Cheese, 120
Carrots
Cake with Coconut Buttercream, Coconut-Carrot, 71
Pickled Carrots, Fiery, 252
Roasted Carrots, Chicken, and Feta, Couscous Pilaf with, 58
Casseroles. *See also* Gratin; Strata
Breakfast Casserole, Make-Ahead Croissant, 286
Broccoli-Cheese Casserole, 256
Brunch Casserole, Italian, 325
Brussels Sprouts with Bacon and Shallots, 257
Cheese Grits Casseroles, Mini, 70
French Onion Soup Casserole, 91
Green Bean Casserole with Crispy Leeks, 256
Grits-and-Sausage Casserole, Country, 323
Grits-and-Sausage Casseroles, Hot 'n' Spicy, 323
Grits-and-Sausage Casseroles, Individual Country, 323
Ham-and-Cheese Brioche Casserole, 324
Ham-and-Cheese Croissant Casserole, 324
Hash Brown Breakfast Casserole, 324
Kentucky Hot Brown Casserole, 46
Pea Casserole, Reunion, 27
Potato Casserole, Cheesy, 257
Sweet Potato Casserole, Hasselback, 256
Sweet Potato Casserole, Savory, 287
Cauliflower and Carrots, Sweet-and-Spicy Sheet Pan Chicken with, 34

Cauliflower Rice with Red Pepper Sauce, Skirt Steak and, 59
Celery, Cream Cheese-Walnut Stuffed, 252
Cheese. ***See also*** **Appetizers; Breads; Spreads**
Cheesecake with Lemon-Ginger Glaze, Gingerbread, 300
Crackers, Cheddar Shortbread, 285
Crackers, Pimiento Cheese Shortbread, 285
Goat Cheese, Black Pepper-and-Honey Whipped, 120
Grits, Creamy Cheese, 326
Kebabs, Halloumi-and-Summer Vegetable, 104
Peppers, Queso-Filled Mini, 107
Soup, Pumpkin Beer-Cheese, 215
Strata, Brie-and-Veggie, 322
Topping, Cream Cheese-and-Caviar, 288
Topping, Parmesan-and-Black Pepper, 288
Cherries
Bars, No-Bake Cherry-Pistachio, 210
Oatmeal, Dried Cherry-Pecan, 342
Pandowdy, Cherry-Nectarine, 115
Pie, Cherry Flag, 132
Scones, Chocolate-Cherry, 341
Chicken. ***See also*** **Salads and Salad Dressings/Chicken**
Bacon-Wrapped Chicken Breasts, 74
Brined Grilled Chicken with Dipping Sauces, 204
Burgoo, Harry Young's, 25
Chicken, start with, 47
Country Captain Chicken, 33
Couscous Pilaf with Roasted Carrots, Chicken, and Feta, 58
Crispy Chicken Cutlets with Blistered Tomatoes, 122
Curry with Chicken, Spicy Red, 47
Dumplings, Old-Fashioned Chicken and, 26
Enchiladas Suizas, Skillet, 212
Kebabs, Lemon-Herb Chicken, 103
Lettuce Wraps, Tropical Chicken, 90
Pizza with Summer Veggies and Smoked Chicken, Grilled, 197
Pot Pie with Leeks and Mushrooms, Skillet Chicken, 47
Sandwiches, Chicken Biscuit, 47
Sandwiches, Hot Chicken-and-Waffle, 327
Sheet Pan Chicken with Cauliflower and Carrots, Sweet-and-Spicy, 34
Sheet Pan Greek Chicken with Roasted Potatoes, 106
Stew with Pumpkin and Wild Rice, Slow-Cooker Chicken, 216
Thighs and BBQ Beans, Chicken, 119
Wrap, Almond-Chicken, 40
Chili with Cilantro-Lime Crema, Brisket-and-Black Bean, 205
Chili with Turkey, Slow-Cooker White, 267
Coconut-Carrot Cake with Coconut Buttercream, 71
Coconut-Key Lime Pies, Mini, 93
Cookies
Bars and Squares
Apricot-Coconut-Cashew Bars, No-Bake, 210
Blondies, Brown Butter-Maple-Pecan, 209
Blueberry-Lemon Crunch Bars, 115
Cherry-Pistachio Bars, No-Bake, 210
Chocolate Chip-Pecan-Sea Salt Bars, No-Bake, 210
Christmas Tree Bar Cookies, 284
Granola Bars, No-Bake, 210
Chocolate-Caramel Cookie Cups, 284
Chocolate-Peppermint Swirl Sandwich Cookies, 284
Dough, Chocolate Sugar Cookie, 284
Festive Dog Cookies, 284
Gingerbread Fawn Cookies, 303
Mexican Hot Chocolate Cookies, 285
Oatmeal Cookies, Toasted, 209
Corn
Pizza with Corn, Tomatoes, and Sausage, Sheet Pan, 121
Pudding, Corn, 256
Salad, Spicy Grilled Corn, 143
Succotash, Best-Ever, 195
Cornbread Dressing, Aunt Grace's Famous, 249
Cornbread Dressing, Stacy and Joyce's, 239
Couscous Pilaf, 105
Couscous Pilaf with Roasted Carrots, Chicken, and Feta, 58
Crab
Boil with Beer and Old Bay, Crab, 97
Cakes with Green Tomato Slaw, Best-Ever Crab, 101
Deviled Crab Melts, 98
Linguine, Crab-and-Bacon, 97
Pie, Crab, 98
Salad, West Indies Crab, 101
Soft-Shell Crab Sandwiches, Crispy, 101
Crackers
Bacon, Bourbon, and Benne Seed Shortbread Crackers, 285
Cheddar Shortbread Crackers, 285
Pecan-and-Thyme Shortbread Crackers, 285
Pimiento Cheese Shortbread Crackers, 285
Cranberries
Biscuits, Cranberry-Spiced, 338
Butter, Slow-Cooker Cranberry-Pear, 285
Scones, Cranberry-Pistachio, 341
Tartlets, Cranberry-Apple, 208
Curry, Pumpkin-Coconut, 216
Curry with Chicken, Spicy Red, 47

D

Desserts. ***See also*** **Cakes; Candies; Cookies; Pies and Pastries**
Fool, Strawberry, 94
Semifreddo, Strawberry-Mango, 86
Trifle, Butterscotch-Spice, 263
Trifles with Pecan Feuilletage and Mascarpone-Cane Syrup Mousse, Blackberry, 155
Dressings. ***See also*** **Salads and Salad Dressings**
Cornbread Dressing, Aunt Grace's Famous, 249
Cornbread Dressing, Stacy and Joyce's, 239
Tops, Mini Turkey Pot Pies with Dressing, 244
Dumplings, Old-Fashioned Chicken and, 26

E

Edamame Hash, Sweet Potato and, 325
Eggplant-and-Corn Romesco Napoleons, Grilled, 154
Eggplant-and-Olive Frittata, 322
Eggs. ***See also*** **Frittatas**
Breakfast in a Skillet, 322
Breakfast in a Skillet, Country, 322
Casserole, Hash Brown Breakfast, 324
Casserole, Italian Brunch, 325
Casserole, Make-Ahead Croissant Breakfast, 286
Quiche, Bacon-Hash Brown, 74
Sliders, Scrambled Egg Muffin, 339
Tacos, Migas, 326
Tostadas, Sausage, 326
Enchiladas Suizas, Skillet, 212

F

Farro Bowl with Curry-Roasted Sweet Potatoes and Brussels Sprouts, 36
Fish. ***See also*** **Crab; Salmon; Scallop; Shrimp**
Catfish, Fried Delacata, 138
Sandwiches, Hot Fish-and-Waffle, 327

French Toast
Croissant French Toast with Fresh Strawberry Syrup, 328
English Muffin French Toast, 328
Overnight Blackberry French Toast, 329
Overnight Blueberry French Toast, 329
Praline-Pecan French Toast, 328
Frittatas
Bacon Mushroom Frittata, 322
Eggplant-and-Olive Frittata, 322
Tomato Frittata, Spicy, 322
Tomato-Sausage Frittata, 322
Veggie Frittata, 324
Fritters, Root Vegetable, 286
Frosting, Strawberry, 84
Fruit. *See also* specific types and Salads and Salad Dressings
Bark, Boozy Fruitcake, 291
Bark, Fruitcake, 290
Shortcakes, Cornmeal Cookie Berry, 133
Sonker with Dip, Berry, 115

G

Garnishes
All-Occasion Cookie Toppers, 303
Candied Pineapple Wedges, 62
Rosemary Trees, 304
Gingerbread
Cheesecake with Lemon-Ginger Glaze, Gingerbread, 300
Classic Gingerbread, 300
Cookies, Gingerbread Fawn, 303
Roulade and Eggnog Cream, Gingerbread, 299
Upside-Down Cake, Gingerbread-and-Pear, 301
Gnocchi Gratin with Ham and Peas, 229
Goji Berry Smoothie Bowl, 343
Granola Bars, No-Bake, 210
Gratin, Pumpkin-and-Winter Squash, 216
Gratin with Ham and Peas, Gnocchi, 229
Gravy, Make-Ahead, 251
Gravy, Pork Chops with Tomato-Bacon, 75
Greens and Grapes, Seared Hanger Steak with Braised, 154
Grits. *See also* Casseroles
Cheese Grits, Creamy, 326
Grillades and Grits, 325
Parmesan-Chive Grits, Braised Lamb Shanks with, 45

H

Ham. *See also* Casseroles
Biscuits with Ham, Buttermilk, 69
Corn Muffins, Ham-and-Swiss, 339
Hash, Old World, 325
Jambalaya de Covington, 29
Pie, Savory Ham-and-Swiss Breakfast, 323
Prosciutto-Asiago Pimiento Cheese, 145
Scones, Ham-and-Swiss, 341
Sticky Buns, Ham-and-Swiss, 333
Hash, Old World, 325
Hash, Sweet Potato and Edamame, 325
Hoppin' John, Classic, 39
Hummus, Roasted Sweet Potato, 211

J

Jambalaya de Covington, 29

K

Kebabs
Halloumi-and-Summer Vegetable Kebabs, 104
Lemon-Herb Chicken Kebabs, 103
Pork Meatball Kebabs, Grilled, 104
Shrimp-Okra-and-Sausage Kebabs, 102
Steak-and-Potato Kebabs, 103

L

Lamb
Carbonara with Braised Lamb, 45
Shanks, Lamb, 45
Shanks with Parmesan-Chive Grits, Braised Lamb, 45
Shepherd's Pie, 45
Lasagna, Zucchini, 124
Linguine, Crab-and-Bacon, 97

M

Mango-Avocado Salsa, Black Bean Tostadas with, 50
Mayonnaise, Creole, 69
Mayonnaise, Mini Tomato Sandwiches with Bacon, 160
Muffins
Bacon-and-Cheddar Corn Muffins, 338
Banana-Toffee Coffee Cake Muffins, 340
Blueberry Muffins with Lemon-Cream Cheese Glaze, 339
Chocolate-Pear Muffins, 207
Ham-and-Swiss Corn Muffins, 339
Morning Glory Muffins, 340
Peanut Butter-Banana Muffins, 340
Sausage and Cheese Muffins, 340
Sliders, Scrambled Egg Muffin, 339
Southwestern Chile-Cheese Corn Muffins, 339
Mushrooms
Frittata, Bacon Mushroom, 322
Pot Pies, Mini Mushroom-and-Goat Cheese, 232
Ragu, Ziti with Mushroom, Fennel, and Tomato, 36

N

Nachos with Chorizo and Refried Beans, Sheet Pan, 204
Napoleons, Grilled Eggplant-and-Corn Romesco, 154
Noodle-and-Shrimp Bowls, Soba, 58

O

Oatmeal
Cookies, Toasted Oatmeal, 209
Dried Cherry-Pecan Oatmeal, 342
Scones with Pecans, Oatmeal, 342
Orange
Butter, Spicy Orange-Peach, 69
Cakes, Grand Marnier, 56
Pie, Florida Orange Grove, 53
Rolls, Orange, 333

P

Pancakes, Hummingbird, 329
Pancakes, Sweet Peach, 329
Pasta. *See also* Lasagna; Linguine; Ravioli
Bolognese Sauce, Slow-Cooker, 286
Carbonara with Braised Lamb, 45
Fettuccine Alfredo with Leeks and Peas, 73
Primavera with Shrimp, Pasta, 92
Rigatoni with Sweet Red Peppers and Fontina, Baked, 230
Rigatoni with Zucchini and Mozzarella, Baked, 230
Roasted Tomato, Salami, and Mozzarella Pasta, 158
Salad, Three-Bean Pasta, 143
Shrimp and Tomato Cream Sauce, Pasta with, 122
Shrimp, Sausage, and Black Bean Pasta, 51
Ziti with Mushroom, Fennel, and Tomato Ragu, 36
Peaches
Buckle, Peach-Raspberry, 116
Cake, Peach-Bourbon Upside-Down Bundt, 127
Crisp, Peach-and-Blackberry, 141
Pancakes, Sweet Peach, 329
Peanut
Bread, Peanut Butter-Cream Cheese-Banana-Nut, 335

Brittle, Salty-Sweet Nut, 292
Ice-Cream Pie, No-Bake Peanut Butter-Fudge, 193
Muffins, Peanut Butter-Banana, 340
Smoothie Bowl, PB&J, 343
Pear, and Asiago Scones, Rosemary, 341
Peas, Black-eyed
Casserole, Reunion Pea, 27
Hoppin' John, Classic, 39
Sauce, Black-eyed Pea Ranchero, 138
Pecans
Biscuits, Sour Cream-Praline, 338
Blondies, Brown Butter-Maple-Pecan, 209
Bourbon Balls, Ginger-Pecan, 291
Crackers, Pecan-and-Thyme Shortbread, 285
Feuilletage and Mascarpone-Cane Syrup Mousse, Blackberry Trifles with Pecan, 155
French Toast, Praline-Pecan, 328
King Cakes, Praline-Cream Cheese, 64
Muffins, Morning Glory, 340
Pie, Oxbow Bakery Pecan, 259
Pork Chops with Beer Sauce, Pecan-Breaded, 30
Pralines, Buttermilk-Pecan, 291
Scones, Brown Sugar-Pecan, 341
Scones with Pecans, Oatmeal, 342
Spicy Pecans, 205
Spread, Pecan Cheese, 69
Tart, Pecan Crunch, 42
Peppers
Blistered Beans and Peppers, Grilled Steak with, 159
Chipotle Pimiento Cheese, 145
Gazpacho with Herbed Goat Cheese Toasts, Yellow, 157
Mini Peppers, Queso-Filled, 107
Red Pepper Sauce, Skirt Steak and Cauliflower Rice with, 59
Sweet Red Peppers and Fontina, Baked Rigatoni with, 230
Pies and Pastries
Apple Pie, Buxton Hall Ultimate, 260
Blueberry Pie, Thyme-Scented, 109
Cherry Flag Pie, 132
Coconut-Key Lime Pies, Mini, 93
Crisp, Peach-and-Blackberry, 141
Lemon Pie, Shaker, 55
Main Dish
Bacon-and-Cheddar Breakfast Pie, Savory, 323
Chicken Pot Pie with Leeks and Mushrooms, Skillet, 47
Crab Pie, 98
Ham-and-Swiss Breakfast Pie, Savory, 323
Mushroom-and-Goat Cheese Pot Pies, Mini, 232
Shepherd's Pie, 45
Turkey Pot Pies with Dressing Tops, Mini, 244
Orange Grove Pie, Florida, 53
Pandowdy, Cherry-Nectarine, 115
Peanut Butter-Fudge Ice-Cream Pie, No-Bake, 193
Pecan Pie, Oxbow Bakery, 259
Pumpkin Pie, Back in the Day Bakery Southern, 261
Slump, Ginger-Plum, 116
Sonker with Dip, Berry, 115
Strawberry-Apricot Hand Pies, 85
Strawberry-Rhubarb Pretzel Pie, 84
Tartlets, Cranberry-Apple, 208
Tart, Pecan Crunch, 42
Pineapple Wedges, Candied, 62
Pizza
Grilled Pizza with Summer Veggies and Smoked Chicken, 197
Sausage and Kale Pesto Pizza, 35
Sheet Pan Pizza with Corn, Tomatoes, and Sausage, 121
Plum Slump, Ginger-, 116
Popcorn with Garlic and Rosemary, Olive Oil, 211
Pork. *See also* Bacon; Ham; Sausage
Bowl with Warm Brussels Sprouts-Fennel Salad, Pork-and-Farro, 59
Braised Pork, Hard Cider-, 233
Burgoo, Harry Young's, 25
Chops
Grilled Spice-Rubbed Pork Chops with Scallion-Lime Rice, 108
Pecan-Breaded Pork Chops with Beer Sauce, 30
Pork Chops, start with, 48
Salad, Pork-and-Shaved Vegetable, 48
Sliced Pork Chops with Brown Butter-Golden Raisin Relish, 48
Strata, Caramelized Onion, Spinach, and Pork, 48
Stuffed Pork Chops with Mashed Potatoes, Fontina-, 229
Tomato-Bacon Gravy, Pork Chops with, 75
Crown Roast, Pork, 287
Grillades and Grits, 325
Meatball Kebabs, Grilled Pork, 104
Stew, Pitmaster, 229
Potatoes. *See also* Sweet Potatoes
Casserole, Cheesy Potato, 257
Crispy Potatoes, 141
Croquettes, Potato, 120
Hash Brown Breakfast Casserole, 324
Hash Brown Quiche, Bacon-, 74
Hash, Old World, 325
Kebabs, Steak-and-Potato, 103
Mashed
Bar, Mashed Potato, 244
Mashed Potatoes, 120
Pork Chops with Mashed Potatoes, Fontina-Stuffed, 229
Shepherd's Pie, 45
Puffs with Toppings, Potato, 288
Roasted Potatoes, Sheet Pan Greek Chicken with, 106
Roasted Potatoes, Turkey with Shallot-Mustard Sauce and, 46
Skins, Mini Potato, 63
Soup, Capitol Hill Bean, 32
Pudding, Corn, 256
Pudding with Strawberry-Nectarine Compote, Coconut Rice, 87
Pumpkin
Biscuits with Crispy Ham and Honey Butter, Pumpkin-Buttermilk, 215
Bread, Pumpkin-Pecan, 336
Cake, Pumpkin-Spice Magic, 263
Cake with Caramel-Cream Cheese Frosting, Pumpkin Layer, 245
Curry, Pumpkin-Coconut, 216
Gratin, Pumpkin-and-Winter Squash, 216
Loaves, Pumpkin Spice-Chocolate Marble, 209
Pie, Back in the Day Bakery Southern Pumpkin, 261
Ravioli with Sage Brown Butter, Pumpkin, 218
Salad, Roasted Pumpkin-and-Baby Kale, 215
Soup, Pumpkin Beer-Cheese, 215
Stew with Pumpkin and Wild Rice, Slow-Cooker Chicken, 216

Q

Quiche, Bacon-Hash Brown, 74

R

Radish Compound Butter, Chive-, 69
Ragu, Ziti with Mushroom, Fennel, and Tomato, 36
Ravioli with Sage Brown Butter, Pumpkin, 218
Relish, Chorizo, 120
Relish, Sliced Pork Chops with Brown Butter-Golden Raisin, 48
Rice
Arroz Verde (Mexican Green Rice), 105
Hoppin' John, Classic, 39
Pudding with Strawberry-Nectarine Compote, Coconut Rice, 87
Red Rice, Savannah, 31

Scallion-Lime Rice, Grilled Spice-Rubbed Pork Chops with, 108
Scallops, Creamy Rice with, 73
Yellow Rice Bowls, Cuban Black Bean-and-, 57
Rolls and Buns
Cinnamon Rolls, Apricot-Pecan, 332
Sticky Buns, Ham-and-Swiss, 333
Yeast
Blueberry Kolaches, 334
Cinnamon Rolls, Iced, 332
Cornmeal Crescent Rolls, 287
Orange Rolls, 333

S

Salads and Salad Dressings
Apple, Celery, and Romaine Salad with Pancetta and Blue Cheese, 243
Asparagus, Radish, and New Potato Salad with Herb Dressing, Warm, 70
Brussels Sprouts-Fennel Salad, Pork-and-Farro Bowl with Warm, 59
Caprese Salad, Cherry Tomato, 142
Chicken
Caesar Salad Sandwiches, Chicken, 90
Crunchy Chicken-Peanut Chopped Salad, 157
Greek Chicken Salad Wedges, 158
Niçoise Salad, Chicken, 88
Oven-Fried Chicken Salad with Buttermilk Ranch Dressing, 89
Quinoa Salad with Green Goddess Dressing, Chicken-, 90
Citrus Salad, Ombré, 286
Citrus Salad with Spiced Honey, 343
Citrus-Salmon Salad, 49
Corn Salad, Spicy Grilled, 143
Crab Salad, West Indies, 101
Fruit Salad, Honey-Ginger, 343
Green Goddess Dressing, 140
Panzanella, Whole-Grain, 125
Pork-and-Shaved Vegetable Salad, 48
Pumpkin-and-Baby Kale Salad, Roasted, 215
Salmon Cakes with Buttermilk Dressing, Fresh, 77
Scallop-and-Mango Salad, Grilled, 146
Shrimp-and-Rice Salad, Herbed, 40
Shrimp Cobb Salad with Bacon Dressing, 73
Slaws
Green Tomato Slaw, Best-Ever Crab Cakes with, 101
Permanent Slaw, 143
Quick Pickled Slaw, 105
Steak Salad with Green Tomato Vinaigrette, Grilled, 122
Strawberry-Rhubarb Salad, 71
Strawberry Vinaigrette, 94
Three-Bean Pasta Salad, 143
Turnip Green Salad, 140
Watermelon, Cucumber, and Feta Salad, 143
Watermelon Salad, 140
Wedge Salad with Turkey and Blue Cheese-Buttermilk Dressing, 46
Salmon
Bowls with Crispy Brussels Sprouts, Teriyaki Salmon, 49
Cakes with Buttermilk Dressing, Fresh Salmon, 77
Molasses-Soy Glazed Salmon and Vegetables, 35
Salad, Citrus-Salmon, 49
Salmon, start with, 49
Sandwiches, Salmon Bagel, 49
Smoked Salmon-and-Chives Topping, 288
Salsa, Black Bean Tostadas with Mango-Avocado, 50
Sandwiches
Burgers with Comeback Sauce, Black Bean, 50
Calzones with Marinara Sauce, White, 230
Chicken Biscuit Sandwiches, 47
Chicken Caesar Salad Sandwiches, 90
Hot Chicken-and-Waffle Sandwiches, 327
Hot Fish-and-Waffle Sandwiches, 327
Rolls, Mini Shrimp, 147
Salmon Bagel Sandwiches, 49
Sliders, Scrambled Egg Muffin, 339
Soft-Shell Crab Sandwiches, Crispy, 101
Tomato Sandwiches with Bacon Mayonnaise, Mini, 160
Turkey
Apple, and Brie Sandwich, Turkey, 266
Club Sandwich, Turkey and Pimiento Cheese, 266
Grilled Cheese, Turkey, Caramelized Onion, and Gruyère, 266
Pesto, and Fresh Mozzarella Sandwich, Turkey, 266
Wrap, Almond-Chicken, 40
Wraps, Tropical Chicken Lettuce, 90
Sauces. *See also* Gravy; Salsa; Toppings
Bananas Foster Sauce, Cinnamon Roll Waffles with, 327
Beer Sauce, 30
Black-eyed Pea Ranchero Sauce, 138
Bolognese Sauce, Slow-Cooker, 286
Buttermilk-Parmesan Ranch, 204
Chive Sour Cream, 120
Cilantro-Lime Crema, 205
Comeback Sauce, Black Bean Burgers with, 50
Creamy Honey Mustard, 204
Fiery Sweet Dipping Sauce, 204
Marinara Sauce, White Calzones with, 230
Red Pepper Sauce, Skirt Steak and Cauliflower Rice with, 59
Shallot-Mustard Sauce and Roasted Potatoes, Turkey with, 46
Tasso Tartar Sauce, Kettle Chip-Crusted Fried Green Tomatoes with, 154
Tomato Cream Sauce, Pasta with Shrimp and, 122
Sausage. *See also* Casseroles
Bolognese Sauce, Slow-Cooker, 286
Breakfast in a Skillet, 322
Breakfast in a Skillet, Country, 322
Chorizo and Refried Beans, Sheet Pan Nachos with, 204
Chorizo Relish, 120
Frittata, Tomato-Sausage, 322
Jambalaya de Covington, 29
Muffins, Sausage and Cheese, 340
Pizza, Sausage and Kale Pesto, 35
Pizza with Corn, Tomatoes, and Sausage, Sheet Pan, 121
Tostadas, Sausage, 326
Scallop-and-Mango Salad, Grilled, 146
Scallops, Creamy Rice with, 73
Scones
Bacon, Cheddar, and Chive Scones, 341
Best-Ever Scones, 341
Bite-Size Scones, 341
Brown Sugar-Pecan Scones, 341
Chocolate-Cherry Scones, 341
Cranberry-Pistachio Scones, 341
Ham-and-Swiss Scones, 341
Oatmeal Scones with Pecans, 342
Pimiento Cheese Scones, 341
Rosemary, Pear, and Asiago Scones, 341
Seasonings
Herb Rub, 108
Seasoned Flour, 120
Smoky Rub, 108
Spicy Rub, 108
Shrimp
Bowls, Shrimp Boil Vegetable, 156
Bowls, Soba Noodle-and-Shrimp, 58
Kebabs, Shrimp-Okra-and-Sausage, 102

Pasta Primavera with Shrimp, 92
Pasta, Shrimp, Sausage, and Black Bean, 51
Pasta with Shrimp and Tomato Cream Sauce, 122
Pickled Shrimp and Vegetables, 126
Rolls, Mini Shrimp, 147
Salad, Herbed Shrimp-and-Rice, 40
Salad with Bacon Dressing, Shrimp Cobb, 73

_SL_ Cooking School
Almond-Chicken Wrap, 40
Bacon, Bring Home the Best, 80
Baste, The Best Ways to, 148
cake layers, smoothing tops of, 234
Cheese, Choose the Right, 234
Choose the Best Model for You (slow cooker), 66
fast turkey and dumplings, 268
Great Debate 128
The Case for Homemade Croutons, 128
Deb Wise: All About the Oven, 128
Karen Rankin: Swears by Stove-Top, 128
Herbed Shrimp-and-Rice Salad, 40
In Season
Don't Pick Pink, 128
Make the Most of Vidalia Onions, 94
Pick Me!, 234
Reach for the Right Peach, 128
Know-How
Build a Better Kebab, 110
Chicken Salad Tip, 94
Freeze Leftovers Like a Pro, 80
Grill Great Corn, 148
Homemade Stock, Simplified, 65
Toaster Treats, 198
New Uses for Kitchen Items, 66
New Year's Resolutions
Conquer Your Fear of Phyllo Dough, 41
Cook Flawless Fish Fillets, 41
Pack a Better Brown-Bag Lunch, 40
Oven, The Hottest New, 198
Pecan Crunch Tart, 42
Piecrust, 4 Creative Ways to Crimp a, 110
Prep Freezer Meals Like a Pro, 65
removing fat from a braising liquid or sauce, 66
Shortcuts, Smart, for store-bought products, 268
Staples for Stove-Free Suppers, 198
Strawberries, 4 Ways To Use Past-Their-Prime, 94
Smoky White Bean Soup, 40
Toppings, 3 Tasty, 148

Slow Cooker
Butter, Slow-Cooker Cranberry-Pear, 285
Main Dishes
Beef, Coffee Stout-Braised, 233
Bolognese Sauce, Slow-Cooker, 286
Chili with Turkey, Slow-Cooker White, 267
Pork, Hard Cider-Braised, 233
Pot Roast, Home-Style Slow-Cooker, 78
Stew with Pumpkin and Wild Rice, Slow-Cooker Chicken, 216

Smoothies. _See_ Beverages/Smoothies
Snack Mix, Smoky, 205
Soufflés with Wine Sauce, Cold Lemon, 55
Soups. _See also_ Chili; Stews
Bean Soup, Capitol Hill, 32
Broth, Rich Turkey, 251
Cantaloupe Soup with Chorizo Relish and Black Pepper-and-Honey Whipped Goat Cheese, 120
Day-After-Saint Patrick's Day Soup, 79
Gazpacho with Herbed Goat Cheese Toasts, Yellow, 157
Pumpkin Beer-Cheese Soup, 215
White Bean Soup, Smoky, 40
Spinach-Sweet Onion Dip with Country Ham, Warm, 205
Spreads. _See also_ Butter; Mayonnaise
Pecan Cheese Spread, 69
Pimiento Cheese, Basic, 144
Pimiento Cheese, Chipotle, 145
Pimiento Cheese, Goat Cheese-and-Gouda, 145
Pimiento Cheese, Horseradish, 145
Pimiento Cheese, Prosciutto-Asiago, 145
Squash
Gratin, Pumpkin-and-Winter Squash, 216
Zucchini
Bread, Lemon-Poppy Seed Zucchini, 336
Lasagna, Zucchini, 124
Rigatoni with Zucchini and Mozzarella, Baked, 230
Stews. _See also_ Chili; Curry; Hash; Jambalaya; Ragu; Soups
Beef Stew, 28
Beef Stew with Cheddar Biscuits, 229
Burgoo, Harry Young's, 25
Chicken Stew with Pumpkin and Wild Rice, Slow-Cooker, 216
Pitmaster Stew, 229
Strata, Brie-and-Veggie, 322
Strata, Caramelized Onion, Spinach, and Pork, 48
Strawberries. _See also_ Cakes
Butter, Strawberry, 94
Compote, Coconut Rice Pudding with Strawberry-Nectarine, 87
Fool, Strawberry, 94
Frosting, Strawberry, 84
Pies, Strawberry-Apricot Hand, 85
Pie, Strawberry-Rhubarb Pretzel, 84
Salad, Strawberry-Rhubarb, 71
Semifreddo, Strawberry-Mango, 86
Syrup, Croissant French Toast with Fresh Strawberry, 328
Vinaigrette, Strawberry, 94
Succotash, Best-Ever, 195
Sweet Potatoes. _See also_ Casseroles
Butter, Whipped Sweet Potato, 141
Coffee Cake, Sweet Potato, 330
Crispy Potatoes, 141
Curry-Roasted Sweet Potatoes and Brussels Sprouts, Farro Bowl with, 36
Hash, Sweet Potato and Edamame, 325
Hummus, Roasted Sweet Potato, 211
Syrup, Croissant French Toast with Fresh Strawberry, 328

T

Tacos, Migas, 326
Toasts, Yellow Gazpacho with Herbed Goat Cheese, 157
Tomatoes. _See also_ Salads and Salad Dressings
Blistered Tomatoes, Crispy Chicken Cutlets with, 122
Fried Green Tomatoes with Tasso Tartar Sauce, Kettle Chip-Crusted, 154
Frittata, Spicy Tomato, 322
Frittata, Tomato-Sausage, 322
Gazpacho with Herbed Goat Cheese Toasts, Yellow, 157
Gravy, Pork Chops with Tomato-Bacon, 75
Roasted Tomato, Salami, and Mozzarella Pasta, 158
Sandwiches with Bacon Mayonnaise, Mini Tomato, 160
Sauce, Pasta with Shrimp and Tomato Cream, 122
Stuffed Tomatoes, Bacon-Spinach-and-Couscous, 123
Vinaigrette, Grilled Steak Salad with Green Tomato, 122
Toppings
Savory
Cream Cheese-and-Caviar Topping, 288

Parmesan-and-Black Pepper Topping, 288
Smoked Salmon-and-Chives Topping, 288
Truffle Oil-and-Rosemary Topping, 288
Sweet
Brown Sugar-and-Ginger Whipped Cream, 300
Eggnog Cream, Gingerbread Roulade and, 299
Tostadas, Sausage, 326
Tostadas with Mango-Avocado Salsa, Black Bean, 50
Turkey. *See also* Sandwiches/Turkey
Breast, Turkey, 46
Broth, Rich Turkey, 251
Cajun Smoked Turkey, 247
Casserole, Kentucky Hot Brown, 46
Chili with Turkey, Slow-Cooker White, 267
Herb-Rubbed Smoked Turkey, 247
Jambalaya de Covington, 29
Pot Pies with Dressing Tops, Mini Turkey, 244
Salad with Turkey and Blue Cheese-Buttermilk Dressing, Wedge, 46
Shallot-Mustard Sauce and Roasted Potatoes, Turkey with, 46

V

Vegetables. *See also* specific types
Frittata, Veggie, 324
Fritters, Root Vegetable, 286
Kebabs, Halloumi-and-Summer Vegetable, 104
Pickled Shrimp and Vegetables, 126
Salmon and Vegetables, Molasses-Soy Glazed, 35
Soup, Day-After-Saint Patrick's Day, 79
Strata, Brie-and-Veggie, 322

W

Waffles
Buttermilk and Brown Sugar Waffles, 326
Cinnamon Roll Waffles with Bananas Foster Sauce, 327
Sandwiches, Hot Chicken-and-Waffle, 327
Sandwiches, Hot Fish-and-Waffle, 327
Watermelon, Cucumber, and Feta Salad, 143
Watermelon Salad, 140

Published by Oxmoor House, an imprint of Time Inc. Books
225 Liberty Street, New York, NY 10281

Executive Editor: Katherine Cobbs
Project Editor: Lacie Pinyan
Editorial Assistant: Lauren Moriarty
Design Director: Melissa Clark
Photo Director: Paden Reich
Designer: AnnaMaria Jacob
Recipe Developers and Testers: Time Inc. Food Studios
Production Manager: Greg A. Amason
Copy Editor: Donna Baldone
Proofreader: Norma McKittrick
Indexer: Mary Ann Laurens

ISBN-13: 978-0-8487-5760-1
ISSN: 0272-2003

First Edition 2018

Printed in the United States of America

10 9 8 7 6 5 4 3 2 1

We welcome your comments and suggestions about Time Inc. Books.
Time Inc. Books
Attention: Book Editors
P.O. Box 62310
Tampa, Florida 33662-2310
(800) 765-6400

Time Inc. Books products may be purchased for business or promotional use. For information on bulk purchases, please contact Christi Crowley in the Special Sales Department at (845) 895-9858.

Cover: Best White Cake, page 303
Photography by Victor Protasio; Food Styling by Torie Cox

Page 1 (from top): Buxton Hall Ultimate Apple Pie, page 260; Oxbow Bakery Pecan Pie, page 259; Back in the Day Bakery Southern Pumpkin Pie, page 261

Favorite Recipes Journal

Jot down your family's and your favorite recipes for quick and handy reference. And don't forget to include the dishes that drew rave reviews when company came for dinner.

Recipe	Source/Page	Remarks

Recipe	Source/Page	Remarks